Scott Mitchell

M000033968

ASP.NET Data Web Controls Kick Start

SΛMS

201 West 103rd Street, Indianapolis, Indiana 46290

ASP.NET Data Web Controls Kick Start

International Standard Book Number: 0-672-32501-2

Library of Congress Catalog Card Number: 2002112960

Printed in the United States of America

First Printing: February 2003

06   05   04   03   4   3   2

Trademarks

Warning and Disclaimer

Associate Publisher
Michael Stephens

Acquisitions Editor
Neil Rowe

Development Editor
Rebecca Riordan

Managing Editor
Charlotte Clapp

Production Editor
Seth Kerney

Indexers
Chris Barrick
Mandie Frank

Proofreader
Suzanne Thomas

Technical Editor
Alex Lowe

Team Coordinator
Cindy Teeters

Multimedia Developer
Dan Scherf

Interior Designer
Gary Adair

Cover Designer
Gary Adair

Contents at a Glance

Table of Contents

Foreword

It is almost impossible to build a Web application today that does not interact in some way with live data—whether by presenting data in a report, editing data within a database, or simply displaying dynamic information within a page. It is through this rich presentation and interaction of data that Web applications often add their unique value and power to users.

Unfortunately for Web developers, though, building data-driven Web applications is often not as easy as they would like. It is extremely challenging to build rich data pages that operate in the confines of HTML and a stateless Web browser world. Adding richer data features like paging, sorting, row editing, and data validation makes the task even more daunting.

To help with this, we built in a suite of powerful server controls with ASP.NET that help developers more easily interact with data. These controls automatically manage a variety of common scenarios, and can literally save a Web developer days of effort when used correctly. Best of all, they are designed to emit only standard HTML down to clients—ensuring that they work great with all desktop browsers.

Scott Mitchell has done an excellent job providing a concise and precise guide on how to use the ASP.NET Data Controls for both the most simple and the most advanced tasks. The content within these chapters will help ASP.NET developers save valuable time and effort—and ensure that the Web solutions they build are rich and robust. The book is an invaluable resource for the ASP.NET development community.

Scott Guthrie
ASP.NET Development Team
Redmond, Washington

About the Author

As editor and main contributor to 4GuysFromRolla.com, a popular ASP/ASP.NET resource Web site, Scott Mitchell has authored hundreds of articles on Microsoft Web Technologies since 1998. In addition to his vast collection of online article, Scott has written three previous books on ASP/ASP.NET: *Sams Teach Yourself Active Server Pages 3.0 in 21 Days* (Sams); *Designing Active Server Pages* (O'Reilly); and *ASP.NET: Tips, Tutorials, and Code* (Sams). Scott has also written a number of magazine articles, including articles for Microsoft's *MSDN Magazine* and *asp.netPRO*.

Scott's non-writing accomplishments include speaking at numerous ASP/ASP.NET user groups across the country and at ASP.NET conferences. Scott has also taught three ASP.NET classes at the University of California—San Diego University Extension. Additionally, he created WebForums.NET, which was purchased by Microsoft and transformed into the ASP.NET Forums (with numerous enhancements added by Rob Howard and his team). The ASP.NET Forums can be visited online at `http://www.asp.net/Forums/`. Currently, Scott is wrapping up his master's degree in computer science at the University of California—San Diego.

Scott can be reached at `mitchell@4guysfromrolla.com`.

♥Dedication♥

This book, and the many months of long hours that went into it, is dedicated to Jisun, my beautiful, charming, loving, intelligent, hilarious girlfriend.

Jisun, these past two years have been the happiest of my life, for I have at long last met my soul mate. I never imagined that there could exist another human being with whom I could feel so much love, and who could love me so strongly in return. One whose happiness and well-being can mean so much to me. One whose presence feels natural and peaceful, and whose absence feels foreign.

Jisun, I love you with my entire being and want to spend the rest of my life with you. I want to take care of you. I want to raise a family with you. I want to marry you. Jisun, will you marry me?

Acknowledgments

This book would not have been possible without the neverending support and unconditional love from my wonderful family that I have received for the past 24 years. I am fortunate to have such a caring and warm family.

Thanks also to Neil Rowe, my acquisitions editor at Sams Publishing. He allowed me the freedom to craft this book as I saw fit, and was a great editorial and technical editor to boot! Also, I'd like to thank Alex Lowe, who served as the technical editor. His knowledge on .NET and ASP.NET is impressive. Be sure to check out the many articles Alex has written at http://www.aspalliance.com/aldotnet/.

We Want to Hear from You!

As the reader of this book, *you* are our most important critic and commentator. We value your opinion and want to know what we're doing right, what we could do better, what areas you'd like to see us publish in, and any other words of wisdom you're willing to pass our way.

As an associate publisher for Sams Publishing, I welcome your comments. You can email or write me directly to let me know what you did or didn't like about this book—as well as what we can do to make our books better.

Please note that I cannot help you with technical problems related to the *topic* of this book. We do have a User Services group, however, where I will forward specific technical questions related to the book.

When you write, please be sure to include this book's title and author as well as your name, email address, and phone number. I will carefully review your comments and share them with the author and editors who worked on the book.

Email: feedback@samspublishing.com

Mail: Michael Stephens
         Associate Publisher
         Sams Publishing
         201 West 103rd Street
         Indianapolis, IN 46290 USA

For more information about this book or another Sams title, visit our Web site at www.samspublishing.com. Type the ISBN (excluding hyphens) or the title of a book in the Search field to find the page you're looking for.

Introduction

ASP.NET contains a plethora of Web controls, from TextBoxes to Calendars, but the most powerful ones are the data Web controls, which are used to display data, such as the DataGrid, DataList, and Repeater. As an ASP.NET developer, you'll find yourself using these three controls extensively. The good news is that these controls allow developers to quickly display data on their Web site in much less time than would be required using a script-based Web programming technology. There are so many features in each of these controls, however, that at times the data Web controls can seem overwhelming.

If you visit Microsoft's ASP.NET Forums at http://www.asp.net/forums, you'll notice that the forum for the DataGrid, DataList, and Repeater controls has thousands of messages, averaging nearly 40 questions per day. The Microsoft.public.dotnet. framework.aspnet.datagridcontrol newsgroup, designed specifically for questions about the DataGrid Web control, has received at the time of this writing over 1,500 questions. As editor and primary author of articles on 4GuysFromRolla.com, a popular ASP/ASP.NET resource Web site, I can attest to several emails from visitors each day asking questions about these Web controls. These numbers don't lie, and are a testament to both the usefulness and difficulty arising from the data Web controls.

This book will help demystify these robust controls, and have you using these powerful controls like a pro. We begin with an introductory examination of the DataGrid, DataList, and Repeater, but quickly cover more advanced topics with solutions for real-world scenarios.

For example, in Chapter 3, "Customizing the HTML Output," we'll see how to alter the appearance of the data Web controls, such as formatting the data contained within the controls, or displaying certain rows or columns using a certain style. In Chapter 5, "Adding Command Buttons to the Data Web Controls," we'll examine how to include buttons that activate specific actions. In Chapter 7, "Sorting the DataGrid's Data," we'll look at how to allow the user to sort the data displayed in a DataGrid Web control.

This book was written for the ASP.NET developer who wants to become proficient in using the DataGrid, DataList, and Repeater Web controls. Each of this book's twelve chapters examines these three controls in great detail. If you are looking for solid, concise information with many examples illustrating how to accomplish common tasks with these controls, your search is over.

Happy Programming!

Scott Mitchell

mitchell@4guysfromrolla.com

PART I

The material in Part I is geared toward the developer who is relatively new to the DataGrid, DataList, and Repeater controls. Perhaps you have used the DataGrid before, but aren't familiar with the DataList or Repeater. Or perhaps your experience with these controls has been to just cut and paste examples from the Web. In either case, the material in this first part will serve as a good start and should be closely read before moving on to Part II.

On the other hand, if you've used the DataGrid, DataList, and Repeater controls many times, you might only need to quickly browse over the material in Part I, although I'd encourage readers of all levels to fully understand the concepts presented in Chapter 2.

Specifically, Part I serves as an introduction to these three useful Web controls. Part I is comprised of three chapters. The first chapter, "An Introduction to the DataGrid, DataList, and Repeater," discusses for the uses of these controls, the similarities and differences among them, and when you could expect to use these controls in real-world scenarios.

The second chapter, "Binding Data to the Data Controls," examines how one binds data to the control, and what kind of data can be bound to a data Web control. Finally, the third chapter, "Customizing the HTML Output," looks at how to tweak the HTML output by these controls to customize the appearance of the control in the user's browser.

By the end of this part, you will have mastered the fundamental concepts of the data Web controls and be comfortable using these controls to display data in an aesthetically pleasing manner.

1

An Introduction to the DataGrid, DataList, and Repeater

The DataGrid, DataList, and Repeater are three Web controls provided by ASP.NET, each of which can be used to display data on an ASP.NET Web page. At first glance, these three controls might seem very similar. After all, they are all useful for displaying data in a structured manner, as we'll briefly touch upon in this chapter, but that is about where the similarities end. Their differences, which we'll also be examining in this chapter, are subtler.

Along with the similarities and differences among these controls, each control carries with it a set of advantages and disadvantages. For example, the DataGrid Web control provides built-in capabilities for paging and sorting the data, while the Repeater does not. However, the DataGrid is always rendered as an HTML table, whereas the Repeater allows for much more flexibility, allowing the developer to specify exactly the HTML that should appear in the rendered output.

When using these controls in a real-world project, one must examine the subtle differences between them, along with their associated advantages and disadvantages, when deciding which control to use for a given situation. This chapter concludes with a discussion of what controls are appropriate in what circumstances, along with some real-world examples and what controls one might want to use.

What Are Data Web Controls?

ASP.NET provides a number of controls to accomplish a plethora of potential tasks. One very common task Web developers face is displaying data from some data store, usually a database, on a Web page. ASP.NET contains three controls designed specifically for displaying data on a Web page: the DataGrid, the DataList, and the Repeater. Throughout the rest of this book I will refer to these three controls as the data Web controls.

NOTE

There are ASP.NET Web controls other than the DataGrid, DataList, and Repeater that support data binding, such as the RadioButtonList, CheckBoxList, DropDownList, and ListBox Web controls. However, I will not be referring to these controls as data Web controls. Instead, when discussing these controls, I will refer to the control's name explicitly.

To use the data Web controls, simply add the appropriate control to an ASP.NET Web page and set its properties. If you are using an editor like Visual Studio .NET or the Matrix Web Project, this can be as simple as dragging the control from the toolbar onto the ASP.NET Web page.

Each of the data Web controls contains a DataSource property, which should be set to the data that you wish to have displayed in the data Web control. Realize that the data to be displayed can be data from a database, an XML file, a collection, and other sources. We'll delve into the specifics of the DataSource property and what types of objects can and cannot be used as a DataSource in the next chapter; for now, we'll just demonstrate setting the DataSource to the results of a database query.

After you've set the DataSource property, it's simply a matter of calling the control's DataBind() method. This method call will render the control, turning the dynamic data specified by the DataSource into HTML that can be rendered on the user's browser. Listing 1.1 contains a very simple ASP.NET Web page that illustrates the use of a DataGrid Web control.

LISTING 1.1   Displaying Data with a Data Web Control Is Simple!

```
 1: <%@ import Namespace="System.Data" %>
 2: <%@ import Namespace="System.Data.SqlClient" %>
 3: <script runat="server">
 4:     Sub Page_Load(sender as Object, e as EventArgs)
 5:        '1. Create a connection
 6:        Const strConnString as String = _
 7:              "server=localhost;uid=sa;pwd=;database=pubs"
 8:        Dim objConn as New SqlConnection(strConnString)
 9:
10:        '2. Create a command object for the query
11:        Const strSQL as String = "SELECT * FROM authors"
12:        Dim objCmd as New SqlCommand(strSQL, objConn)
13:
```

LISTING 1.1   Continued

```
14:        '3. Create the DataAdapter
15:        Dim objDA as New SqlDataAdapter()
16:        objDA.SelectCommand = objCmd
17:
18:        '4. Populate the DataSet and close the connection
19:        Dim objDS as New DataSet()
20:        objDA.Fill(objDS)
21:        objConn.Close()
22:
23:        'Finally, specify the DataSource and call DataBind()
24:        dgAuthors.DataSource = objDS
25:        dgAuthors.DataBind()
26:     End Sub
27: </script>
28:
29: <asp:datagrid id="dgAuthors" runat="server" />
```

The SqlConnection object on line 8, objConn, makes a connection to the pubs database. Line 11 specifies a SQL query that grabs all the rows and columns from the authors table. On line 20 the DataSet object objDS is filled with the results from the SQL query, and on line 24 the DataGrid's DataSource property is set to the DataSet objDS.

When the DataGrid's DataBind() method is called (line 25), the DataGrid is rendered. A DataGrid converts each item in the DataSource to a row in an HTML table (via the tr tag); for each field in the current DataSource row, a column in the HTML table is added (via the td tag). If you view the ASP.NET page from Listing 1.1 in a browser, you will note that the HTML emitted by the page is a simple HTML table, as shown in Listing 1.2. A screenshot of what the end user will see in his browser is shown in Figure 1.1.

LISTING 1.2   The DataGrid Renders into an HTML table

```
1: <table cellspacing="0" rules="all" border="1" id="dgAuthors" style=
➥"border-collapse:collapse;">
2:     <tr>
3:        <td>au_id</td><td>au_lname</td><td>au_fname</td><td>phone</td><td>
➥address</td><td>city</td><td>state</td><td>zip</td><td>contract</td>
4:     </tr><tr>
5:        <td>172-32-1176</td><td>White</td><td>Johnson</td><td>408 496-7223
➥</td><td>10932 Bigge Rd.</td><td>Menlo Park</td><td>CA</td><td>94025
➥</td><td>True</td>
```

LISTING 1.2   Continued

```
 6:     </tr><tr>
 7:            <td>213-46-8915</td><td>Green</td><td>Marjorie</td><td>415 986-7020
➡</td><td>309 63rd St. #411</td><td>Oakland</td><td>CA</td><td>94618
➡</td><td>True</td>
 8:     </tr><tr>
 9:            <td>238-95-7766</td><td>Carson</td><td>Cheryl</td><td>415 548-7723
➡</td><td>589 Darwin Ln.</td><td>Berkeley</td><td>CA</td><td>94705</td>
➡<td>True</td>
10:     </tr><tr>
11:            <td>267-41-2394</td><td>O'Leary</td><td>Michael</td><td>408 286-2428
➡</td><td>22 Cleveland Av. #14</td><td>San Jose</td><td>CA</td><td>95128
➡</td><td>True</td>
12:     </tr><tr>
13:            ... some rows omitted for brevity ...
14: </table>
```

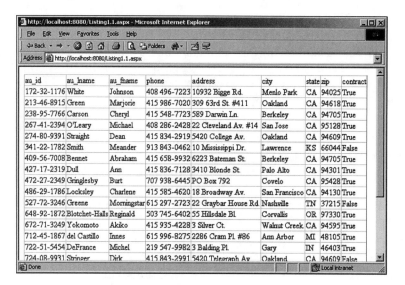

FIGURE 1.1   The DataGrid is rendered as a vanilla HTML `table`.

A Note About the Code Examples

Most of the code examples in this book use data from a Microsoft SQL Server 2000 database. Hence, the code uses the `SqlClient` data provider, meaning that I will be using classes like `SqlConnection`, `SqlCommand`, `SqlDataAdapter`, `SqlDataReader`, and so on.

If you are not using Microsoft SQL Server 7.0 or later, you will need to use the `OleDb` data provider. The code in Listing 1.1 would need to be marginally edited to use the `OleDb` provider. Specifically, line 2 would need to be changed to

```
<%@ import Namespace="System.Data.OleDb" %>
```

Furthermore, all objects beginning with the prefix `Sql` would need to be changed to have the prefix `OleDb`. For example, line 8 in Listing 1.1 would be changed to

```
Dim objConn as New OleDbConnection(strConnString)
```

The majority of the code examples use the `pubs` database, which is a standard sample database that has long been shipped with Microsoft SQL Server.

NOTE

If you do not have access to a copy of Microsoft SQL Server, you might want to consider using Microsoft's MSDE. MSDE is a free, scaled-down version of SQL Server, and includes the pubs database. You can download MSDE from `http://asp.net/msde/default.aspx`. More information regarding MSDE can be found in the "On the Web" section at the end of this chapter.

Expect to see code examples primarily in Visual Basic .NET. There are some C# code examples as well, though. Personally, I prefer C# over Visual Basic .NET, but it is my estimation that the majority of ASP.NET developers use Visual Basic .NET instead of C#. Furthermore, most developers who know C# likely have had some exposure to Visual Basic at some point in their career, and will find translating from Visual Basic .NET to C# to be relatively painless. For some assistance in converting between the two languages, be sure to read "From VB .NET to C# and Back Again" at `http://www.4GuysFromRolla.com/webtech/012702-1.shtml`.

Finally, my examples use server-side script blocks as opposed to code-behind pages. Although I like the separation of code and content that code-behind pages provide, I find that code examples are easier to follow if both the code and HTML content can be shown in the same listing. Furthermore, using code-behind Web pages is a pain if you're using any editor other than Visual Studio .NET. Although I own a copy of Visual Studio .NET, I am using the ASP.NET team's fine Web Matrix Editor, which can be downloaded for free at `http://www.asp.net/WebMatrix/`. In any event, for those using code-behind, converting the code samples from the server-side script model to code-behind is trivial—simply place the functions and event handlers in the server-side script block into the code-behind class, and make sure any `import` directives (such as `<%@ import Namespace="Some.Namespace" %>`) appear as Implements *Some.Namespace* (Visual Basic .NET) or using *Some.Namespace* (C#) in your code-behind file.

Why Do We Need Data Web Controls?

Take a moment to look over Listing 1.1, the resulting HTML in Listing 1.2, and the output in Figure 1.1. Notice that we got quite a bit of HTML markup for just a few lines of code. Although Listing 1.1 might feel like it has a lot of source code, realize that the vast majority of it is the code to make a connection to the database and populate a DataSet. The code needed to actually declare the DataGrid, tie the DataSet to the DataGrid, and then to render the DataGrid comprised an entire three lines of code (lines 24, 25, and 29).

Before ASP.NET broke onto the scene in 2002, Microsoft Web developers were using ASP, henceforth referred to as classic ASP. Classic ASP is still in use today, and is still supported on Microsoft's IIS Web server software; in fact, both classic ASP and ASP.NET Web pages can be served from the same Web server. If you've developed data-driven Web sites using classic ASP, you're no doubt painfully familiar with the script code shown in Listing 1.3.

LISTING 1.3   Displaying Database Data Using Classic ASP and VBScript

```
 1: <%@ LANGUAGE="VBSCRIPT" %>
 2: <%
 3:    Option Explicit
 4:
 5:    '1. Create a connection
 6:    Const strConnString = "Provider=SQLOLEDB;Data Source=(local);Initial
➥Catalog=pubs;User ID=sa;Password=;"
 7:    Dim objConn, objRS
 8:    Set objConn = Server.CreateObject("ADODB.Connection")
 9:    objConn.Open(strConnString)
10:
11:    '2. Populate the Recordset with the SQL query
12:    Const strSQL = "SELECT * FROM authors"
13:    Set objRS = Server.CreateObject("ADODB.Recordset")
14:    objRS.Open strSQL, objConn
15:
16:    'Display a table
17:    Response.Write("<table cellspacing=""0"" border=""1"">")
18:
19:    Dim objColumn
20:    Response.Write("<tr>")
21:    For Each objColumn in objRS.Fields
22:      Response.Write("<td>" & objColumn.Name & "</td>")
23:    Next
24:    Response.Write("</tr>")
25:
```

LISTING 1.3 Continued

```
26:    Do While Not objRS.EOF
27:      Response.Write("<tr>")
28:      For Each objColumn in objRS.Fields
29:        Response.Write("<td>" & objColumn.Value & "</td>")
30:      Next
31:      Response.Write("</tr>")
32:
33:      objRS.MoveNext
34:    Loop
35:    Response.Write("</table>")
36:
37:    objRS.Close()
38:    Set objRS = Nothing
39:
40:    objConn.Close()
41:    Set objRS = Nothing
42: %>
```

The output of the code from Listing 1.3 is identical to that of Listing 1.1, which can be seen in Figure 1.1. A quick comparison of the two listings reveals two important facts:

1. The classic ASP code (Listing 1.3) requires much more code to render the HTML table than the ASP.NET code using the DataGrid. Compare the 3 lines required in Listing 1.1 to the 15 or so lines needed in Listing 1.3 (lines 20–35).

2. The classic ASP code tightly intermingles the source code and the HTML markup. For example, on lines 27–31 the Response.Write statements output both HTML markup and data. Compare this to the separation of code and HTML style in Listing 1.1.

Both of these facts illustrate the importance of the data Web controls. The benefits derived from Fact 1 are fairly obvious: less code means less time spent programming. Less time spent programming means fewer opportunities for mistakes, which means fewer bugs in your application. Additionally, the fewer lines of code in an ASP.NET Web page, the easier it is to understand what it is the page is supposed to do. Such code readability is vitally important when debugging!

To understand the importance of Fact 2, which deals with the separation of code and content, imagine for a moment that you are presented with the classic ASP code in Listing 1.3. If you want to change the appearance of the resulting HTML table, you would need to pick through the source code finding the appropriate Response.Write statements. Now, imagine that your company's graphic designer is faced with this challenge!

Making such changes with the DataGrid example in Listing 1.1 is exponentially simpler and less error-prone because of the separation of code and content provided by ASP.NET's Web controls. Notice that the code associated with the DataGrid—setting the `DataSource` and calling `DataBind()` method—occurs in the server-side script block. (For further separation of code and content, this could be placed in a code-behind file.) The HTML specifications for the DataGrid occur in the HTML section (line 29 in Listing 1.1). Although we have not specified any HTML stylistic properties on line 29, we could easily add some. For example, if we want to set each row's background color to #EEEEEE (a light gray), we can replace line 29 in Listing 1.1 with

```
<asp:datagrid id="dgAuthors" runat="server" BackColor="#EEEEEE" />
```

To make this same change in the classic ASP code in Listing 1.3, we'd have to either add a `bgcolor` attribute to each `td` tag, (meaning we'd have to alter the `Response.Write` statements in lines 22 and 29), or add a `background-color` style attribute to the `table` tag or the `td` tags. Clearly, making these changes, which would require picking through source code, is not as easy or as clean as the changes needed with ASP.NET data control.

Now that we've examined *why* the data Web controls are important, let's look at each of the data Web controls in more detail.

The DataGrid Web Control

The DataGrid Web control was designed to render data into an HTML `table` tag, as was shown in Listing 1.2 and Figure 1.1. That is, for each row in the DataGrid's `DataSource`, an HTML table row (`tr`) is added, and for each column in each row a table column cell is added (`td`).

The DataGrid declaration shown in line 29 of Listing 1.1 was the DataGrid in its simplest form: simply displaying all the rows and columns in the `DataSource` using the default formatting options. What Listing 1.1 does not show is the DataGrid's rich set of capabilities, which include the following:

- Custom formatting of the columns from the `DataSource`.
- Customizing the appearance of the DataGrid.
- Allowing the user to sort the results of the DataGrid.
- Providing pagination support, so that the user can page through the DataGrid's results.
- A means to edit the data within the DataGrid.

Many of the features listed here and more will be covered later in the book. In this section, the only feature we'll examine in any detail is the first one. We will also discuss some of the features of the DataGrid that are not present in the DataList or Repeater.

Specifying the Columns to Display

As you may have noted in Listing 1.1, the DataGrid will display *all* fields in the DataSource in the order they appear by default. However, there might be times when you only want to display a subset of the fields in the DataSource, or you want them to appear in a different left-to-right ordering. The AutoGenerateColumns property of the DataGrid class indicates whether all the DataSource's fields will be automatically added to the DataGrid; by default this property is set to True.

If you want to specify what fields should appear in the DataGrid Web control, you should first make sure that the AutoGenerateColumns property is set to False (as shown in Listing 1.4), and then add a Columns tag that explicitly lists the fields that you want to appear.

> **NOTE**
>
> If you forget to set the AutoGenerateColumns property to False, but still supply a Columns tag, all of the DataSource's fields will be displayed in the DataGrid, along with whatever fields you specify in the Columns tag.

You can use the BoundColumn control to explicitly add a column to the Columns tag. The vital property of the BoundColumn control is the DataField property, which specifies the column name in the DataSource that you want to display. If this is not quite clear, hopefully an example will help!

Listing 1.4 contains the same source code from Listing 1.1—the only change is in the DataGrid declaration. Rather than having the DataGrid automatically create its columns from the DataSource, we set the AutoGenerateColumns property to False, and then explicitly list the fields we'd like to have present in our DataGrid in the Columns section using BoundColumn controls.

LISTING 1.4   You Can Specify the Columns that Should Appear in a DataGrid

```
1: <%@ import Namespace="System.Data" %>
2: <%@ import Namespace="System.Data.SqlClient" %>
3: <script runat="server">
4:
5:     Sub Page_Load(sender as Object, e as EventArgs)
6:        '1. Create a connection
```

LISTING 1.4   Continued

```
 7:        Const strConnString as String = "server=localhost;uid=sa;pwd=;
➥database=pubs"
 8:        Dim objConn as New SqlConnection(strConnString)
 9:
10:        '2. Create a command object for the query
11:        Const strSQL as String = "SELECT * FROM authors"
12:        Dim objCmd as New SqlCommand(strSQL, objConn)
13:
14:        '3. Create the DataAdapter
15:        Dim objDA as New SqlDataAdapter()
16:        objDA.SelectCommand = objCmd
17:
18:        '4. Populate the DataSet and close the connection
19:        Dim objDS as New DataSet()
20:        objDA.Fill(objDS)
21:        objConn.Close()
22:
23:        'Finally, specify the DataSource and call DataBind()
24:        dgAuthors.DataSource = objDS
25:        dgAuthors.DataBind()
26:     End Sub
27:
28: </script>
29:
30: <asp:datagrid id="dgAuthors" runat="server"
31:         AutoGenerateColumns="False">
32:    <Columns>
33:     <asp:BoundColumn DataField="au_fname" HeaderText="First " />
34:     <asp:BoundColumn DataField="au_lname" HeaderText="Last " />
35:     <asp:BoundColumn DataField="phone" HeaderText="Phone #" />
36:    </Columns>
37: </asp:datagrid>
```

The output of the above ASP.NET page, when viewed through a browser, can be seen in Figure 1.2. Note that on line 31 we set the DataGrid's AutoGenerateColumns property to False; next, on lines 32–36 we specify the columns that should appear in the DataGrid using BoundColumn controls. Using the BoundColumn controls, the DataField property specifies the name of the column in the DataSource that should be displayed, while the HeaderText property indicates what text should appear in the column's heading. The BoundColumn controls contain a number of other properties to aid in specifying the stylistic properties for the particular column. We'll be examining these properties in detail in Chapter 3, "Customizing the HTML Output."

NOTE

If you omit the `HeaderText` property in the BoundColumn control, the name of the column—au_fname, au_lname, and phone, in Listing 1.4—will be displayed instead.

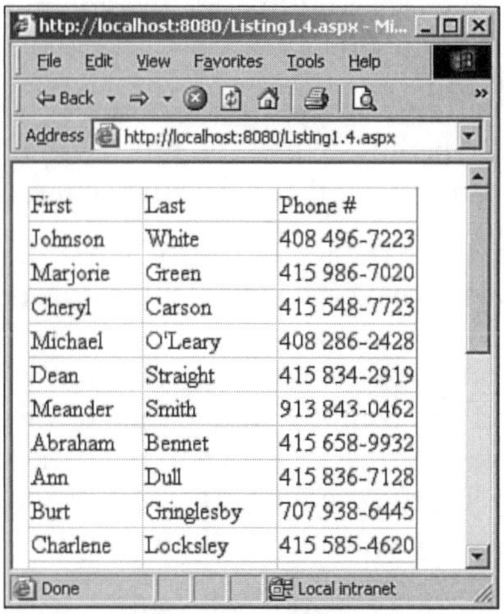

FIGURE 1.2   Only the specified columns appear in the DataGrid.

The `Columns` section of the DataGrid Web control can contain more than just BoundColumns. As we'll see in Chapter 4, "Adding Buttons and Hyperlinks to the DataGrid Web Control," you can add ButtonColumn and HyperLinkColumn controls to associate a button or hyperlink with each row. The HyperLinkColumn control is useful for providing navigation related to each row: perhaps a link to a View More Details page on each row of a DataGrid that displays product information. The ButtonColumn control is useful for assigning some sort of action for a particular row. For example, you might use a DataGrid to display the items in a customer's shopping cart; a ButtonColumn could be used to provide a Remove Item from Cart button that would remove the specified item.

The Columns section can also contain an EditColumn control, which provides an Edit button for each row for times when you want to allow the user to edit the data within a DataGrid. We'll look at how to provide such functionality for the DataGrid in Chapter 9, "Editing the DataGrid Web Control."

Lastly, the Columns section can also include a TemplateColumn, which allows the developer to specify templates. Templates are a mix of HTML markup and content from the `DataSource`. Templates are used extensively with the DataList and Repeater controls, which we'll be examining shortly. Furthermore, in Chapter 3 we will look at using templates in the DataGrid in more detail.

DataGrid Features Not Found in the Other Data Web Controls

Next we'll turn to a brief examination of the DataList and Repeater Web controls, but before we do, let's take note of some of the more interesting features of the DataGrid that are not present in these other data Web controls. The two most prominent features present in the DataGrid that are missing in the other data Web controls are sorting and pagination support.

By enabling the DataGrid's sorting feature, the title of each column in the DataGrid Web control becomes a hyperlink. When the link for a column is clicked, the DataGrid's contents are ordered by that particular column.

The pagination features of the DataGrid control allow for only a portion of the rows in the DataSource to be displayed at a time, with navigation to allow the user to page through the results. For example, if the DataSource is comprised of, say, 500 rows, presenting all 500 rows to the end user on one Web page would make the information hard to read and comprehend. Rather, using the DataGrid's pagination support, you could display 15 rows at a time to the user. The user could then specify what page of data she'd like to view next. The sorting and paging capabilities of the DataGrid Web control are presented in detail in Chapters 7 and 8, respectively.

Now that we've looked at the DataGrid Web control, let's turn our attention next to the DataList.

The DataList Web Control

Like the DataGrid, the DataList is rendered into an HTML table, creating a table row for each row in the DataSource. However, unlike the DataGrid, with its AutoGenerateColumn property, the DataList does not support any kind of automatic column generation. When using the DataList, the developer must specify a template, which can contain both HTML markup and content from the DataSource. When the DataList's DataBind() method is called a new table row is added for each row in the DataSource, with the contents of the template being placed inside the table row.

Using the same source code from our previous listings (Listing 1.1 and 1.4), Listing 1.5 displays the last and first names of the authors using a DataList. Note how the DataList's template (ItemTemplate) specifies *both* HTML markup (the bold tag and a comma) as well as content from the DataSource (via the DataBinder.Eval calls).

LISTING 1.5   The DataList Renders Templates into an HTML table

```
1: <%@ import Namespace="System.Data" %>
2: <%@ import Namespace="System.Data.SqlClient" %>
3: <script runat="server">
4:
```

LISTING 1.5   Continued

```
 5:    Sub Page_Load(sender as Object, e as EventArgs)
 6:
 7:    ... Code the same from previous listings. Omitted for brevity ...
 8:
 9:       'Finally, specify the DataSource and call DataBind()
10:       dlAuthors.DataSource = objDS
11:       dlAuthors.DataBind()
12:    End Sub
13:
14: </script>
15:
16: <asp:datalist id="dlAuthors" runat="server">
17:   <ItemTemplate>
18:     <b><%# DataBinder.Eval(Container.DataItem, "au_lname") %>,
19:     <%# DataBinder.Eval(Container.DataItem, "au_fname") %></b>
20:   </ItemTemplate>
21: </asp:datalist>
```

The HTML output of Listing 1.5, when viewed through a browser, can be seen in Listing 1.6. A screenshot can be seen in Figure 1.3.

LISTING 1.6   An HTML table Has Been Rendered

```
 1: <table id="dlAuthors" cellspacing="0" border="0" style="border-collapse:
➡collapse;">
 2:    <tr><td>
 3:      <b>White,
 4:      Johnson</b>
 5:    </td>
 6:    </tr><tr>
 7:    <td>
 8:      <b>Green,
 9:      Marjorie</b>
10:    </td>
11:    </tr><tr>
12:    <td>
13:      <b>Carson,
14:      Cheryl</b>
15:    </td>
16:    </tr>
17:    ... some lines removed for brevity ...
18: </table>
```

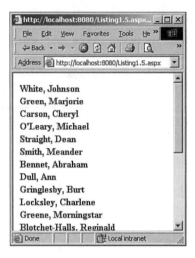

FIGURE 1.3   The list of authors is presented in an HTML `table`.

The templates in a DataList allow for both HTML markup and values from the `DataSource`. Adding HTML markup is a matter of simply adding the HTML tag(s) in the template. For example, in Listing 1.5, a bold HTML tag is used on lines 18 and 19. Furthermore, a comma is placed between the author's last name and first name.

To display a value from the `DataSource`, data-binding syntax is employed. This syntax has the form

```
<%# ... %>
```

To grab a value from the `DataSource`, we use the `DataBinder.Eval()` method, which takes two parameters: an object and a string. In our examples, we'll be using `Container.DataItem` as the object, which is, in essence, the current row of the `DataSource` that's being enumerated. For the string parameter, specify the name of the column you want to have displayed. Hence, in order to output the value of the `au_fname` column using data-binding syntax in a template, one would use

```
<%# DataBinder.Eval(Container.DataItem, "au_fname") %>
```

We will discuss the use of templates and the `DataBinder.Eval` method in much greater detail in both the next chapter and Chapter 3. For now, realize that the ItemTemplate is only one kind of template. As we will see when discussing the Repeater control, there are other types of templates, including the following:

- AlternatingItemTemplate
- EditItemTemplate

- FooterTemplate
- HeaderTemplate
- SelectedItemTemplate
- SeparatorTemplate

These are the templates that can be used by the DataList. The Repeater, however, can use only a subset of these templates; likewise, the DataGrid, with its TemplateColumn control, can only use a subset of these templates.

Before moving onto the Repeater control, let's take a moment to note some of the DataList's features. Although the DataList does not have the DataGrid's built-in paging and sorting support, it does allow for editing of the data.

One especially cool feature of the DataList is in its RepeatColumns property. By tweaking this property, you can give the DataList a grid-like effect, where you can specify how many columns wide the grid should be. For example, Listing 1.7 shows an altered DataList declaration, with its RepeatColumns property set to 4 (line 2). (All other code from Listing 1.5 has remained unchanged.)

LISTING 1.7   The RepeatColumns Property "Stretches" the DataList

```
1: <asp:datalist id="dlAuthors" runat="server"
2:       RepeatColumns="4">
3:   <ItemTemplate>
4:     <b><%# DataBinder.Eval(Container.DataItem, "au_lname") %>,
5:     <%# DataBinder.Eval(Container.DataItem, "au_fname") %></b>
6:   </ItemTemplate>
7: </asp:datalist>
```

Notice how the screenshot of Listing 1.7 (shown in Figure 1.4) depicts an HTML table with four columns per row, as opposed to one column per row (as in Figure 1.3)—specifically, the HTML table in Figure 1.4 has four td tags per tr.

We'll be examining some of the DataList's other features in future chapters. For now, though, let's turn our attention to the last of the three data Web controls: the Repeater control.

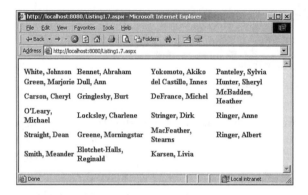

FIGURE 1.4   The `RepeatColumns` specifies the number of columns per row in the HTML table.

The Repeater Control

As we have seen, the DataGrid and DataList, when viewed through a browser, are rendered as HTML `table` tags. The DataGrid imposes a grid, with one row for each row in the `DataSource`, and one column for each field in the `DataSource`. The DataList, on the other hand, provides a more flexible structure, allowing the developer to specify the HTML markup and data from the `DataSource` that should appear in each `table` row.

The Repeater control contains templates like the DataList, but does not place the templates in an HTML `table`. Absolutely no additional HTML markup is added when using the Repeater. If you want your data to exist in a `table`, you need to explicitly provide the opening and closing HTML `table` tags, as well as the other associated table tags (`tr`, `td`, `th`, and so on). An example should clear up any confusion.

First, let's look at mimicking the behavior of the DataList using a Repeater. Recall that the DataList automatically adds a `table` tag, and then a `tr` and a specified number of `td` tags for each row in the `DataSource`. Using the Repeater control, our ItemTemplate will be identical to the one in Listings 1.5 and 1.7. However, we must also supply a HeaderTemplate and FooterTemplate template, which will be used to emit the `table`, `tr`, and `td` tags. Listing 1.8 demonstrates the use of the Repeater.

LISTING 1.8   Using a Repeater to Mimic the Output of a DataList

```
1: <%@ import Namespace="System.Data" %>
2: <%@ import Namespace="System.Data.SqlClient" %>
3: <script runat="server">
4:
```

LISTING 1.8 Continued

```
 5:    Sub Page_Load(sender as Object, e as EventArgs)
 6:
 7:    ... Code the same from previous listings. Omitted for brevity ...
 8:
 9:        'Finally, specify the DataSource and call DataBind()
10:        rptAuthors.DataSource = objDS
11:        rptAuthors.DataBind()
12:    End Sub
13:
14: </script>
15:
16: <asp:repeater id="rptAuthors" runat="server">
17:    <HeaderTemplate>
18:      <table id="dlAuthors" cellspacing="0" border="0" style="border-collapse:
➥collapse;">
19:    </HeaderTemplate>
20:
21:    <ItemTemplate>
22:      <tr>
23:        <td>
24:          <b><%# DataBinder.Eval(Container.DataItem, "au_lname") %>,
25:          <%# DataBinder.Eval(Container.DataItem, "au_fname") %></b>
26:        </td>
27:      </tr>
28:    </ItemTemplate>
29:
30:    <FooterTemplate>
31:      </table>
32:    </FooterTemplate>
33: </asp:repeater>
```

The HTML output of Listing 1.8 is identical to that of the DataList example in Listing 1.5, and can be seen in Listing 1.6; to view a screenshot of the this code, refer to Figure 1.3.

Notice that Listing 1.8 contains the entire HTML markup that was produced for us automatically by the DataList. The HeaderTemplate, which is rendered once when the data binding begins, simply emits the HTML table tag. The ItemTemplate, which is rendered for each row in the DataSource, emits an HTML table row with a single column, and with the last and first name of the current author. Finally, the FooterTemplate, which is rendered once at the end of the data binding process, emits the closing table tag.

Using the Repeater control to display data in an HTML `table` is pretty silly, because there are already two fine data Web controls that do just that. You will more often use the Repeater to list data in ways that do not involve HTML `tables`, such as in an ordered list, perhaps. Listing 1.9 provides an alternative Repeater declaration that lists the authors in an ordered list. A screenshot of Listing 1.9 can be seen in Figure 1.5.

LISTING 1.9   Repeaters Can Be Used to Produce Ordered Lists

```
 1: <asp:repeater id="rptAuthors" runat="server">
 2:   <HeaderTemplate>
 3:     <ol>
 4:   </HeaderTemplate>
 5:
 6:   <ItemTemplate>
 7:     <li><b><%# DataBinder.Eval(Container.DataItem, "au_lname") %>,
 8:     <%# DataBinder.Eval(Container.DataItem, "au_fname") %></b></li>
 9:   </ItemTemplate>
10:
11:   <FooterTemplate>
12:     </ol>
13:   </FooterTemplate>
14: </asp:repeater>
```

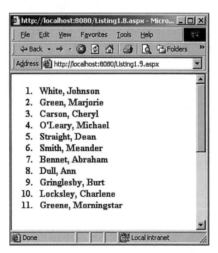

FIGURE 1.5   A list of authors is presented as an ordered list.

Although the Repeater allows the most flexibility in the emitted HTML, it also has the fewest bells and whistles. The Repeater control lacks inherent support for pagination, sorting, and editing, features the DataGrid and DataList have. Of course, this extra functionality can be added to an ASP.NET page that uses a Repeater control, but requires much additional coding.

Now that we've taken a quick look at the three data Web controls, let's take a moment to examine some real-world applications and determine which of the data Web controls would be the best fit.

Determining What Data Web Control to Use

Once you are familiar with the differences between the data Web controls, choosing which control to use in a given situation should be relatively straightforward. Let's examine a few real-world scenarios and discuss which control (or controls) we might want to choose. Don't worry if you are having difficulty deciding what control would be best for each given situation—as your experience with these controls increases, you'll be able to quickly determine which control would be best for a given situation.

For these real-world scenarios, imagine that you are employed by a company that has an online store. The various scenarios listed here are actual tasks an employee of an e-commerce company might face.

An Online Shopping Cart

One task required for every online store is creating a shopping cart, which records what items your customer has currently "checked out." The customer should be able to view a list of items in her cart, remove any items, and view more details about any item.

Assume that we have already completed the business logic necessary to populate the shopping cart, provide detailed information about each order, remove an item from the cart, and so on, and only need to decide what data Web control to use to display the data in the shopping cart. The design team has decided that the shopping cart data should be displayed in an HTML `table`, with each row of the `table` corresponding to an item in the user's cart. For each row, there will be multiple columns, such as the product name, price, and buttons to remove an item from the cart and to retrieve more information about a particular item in the cart.

As with most real-world scenarios, any of the three data Web controls *could* be used, but which one(s) would be the best fit, requiring the least amount of additional work? The Repeater is clearly not the best choice—while you could add buttons to the ItemTemplate, it seems like a lot of unnecessary work; furthermore, you would need to emit the code to produce an HTML `table`, something the DataList and DataGrid can do for us free of charge.

In my opinion, the best bet would be the DataGrid. To provide the More Details and Remove from Cart buttons, you could simply add a ButtonColumn control for each. Because you would not likely need to use templates (you could just use a BoundColumn control for each field in the shopping cart `DataSource`), I find it hard to justify using the DataList, where you would need to use the template syntax. (Although the template syntax provides a high degree of layout and presentation customization, you'll hopefully agree that its mix of HTML markup and data binding syntax is messier than using column controls via the DataGrid.)

A Small 2×2 Grid Containing Pictures of the Store's Current Specials

You want to display a 2×2 grid with small pictures of the day's current specials on the front page of your company's Web site. Under each picture you want to have a short description of the product, the price, and a hyperlink that will take the customer to the order page for that particular item. Assume that the product specials are stored in a database table with columns like `ProductName`, `ProductPrice`, `ProductID`, `PictureURL`, and so on, with one row for each of the special items.

Using the DataGrid for such an assignment would be difficult at best. Because the DataGrid emits one HTML table row per row in the `DataSource`, it would be quite difficult to tweak the DataGrid to emit a 2×2 HTML table. Although the Repeater control could be used, it would require some tricky template syntax to get the 2×2 grid to appear correctly.

The optimal choice here is the DataList, which is a natural candidate because of its `RepeatColumns` property. As we saw in Listing 1.7 and Figure 1.4, by setting the `RepeatColumns` property to a value of *n*, one can easily transform the DataList into an *n*×*m* grid, where *m* is the number of rows in the `DataSource` divided by *n*.

As we'll see in Chapter 3, one can easily convert the `ProductURL` field into an `img` tag to display the product on the Web page by using some relatively straightforward template markup. Additionally, a hyperlink can be easily added that takes the user to a product information page for the particular item by passing the item's `ProductID` to the product information Web page via the QueryString.

Listing the Features for a Particular Product

Each item sold in your company's online store has a number of features. For example, a computer system for sale might have features specifying the processor speed, the amount of RAM, the video card manufacturer, what peripherals are included, and so on. This data is stored in a database table called `ProductFeatures`, which has a `ProductID` as a foreign key. So, to see the features of Product 1001, one could simply issue a query for all rows in the `ProductFeatures` table whose foreign key value equals 1001.

You have been asked to display this information on the Product Details Web page. Specifically, this information is to be displayed as a bulleted list. What control would be the best fit here?

As with our first example, any of the controls could fit the bill. For example, you could use a DataGrid or DataList by simply specifying that the contents for each row begin with an li tag. The user could then surround the actual control with a ul tag, as shown in Listing 1.10.

LISTING 1.10   Using a DataList to Display a Bulleted List

```
1: <ul>
2: <asp:DataList id="dlProductDetails" runat="server">
3:   <ItemTemplate>
4:     <li><%# DataBinder.Eval(Container.DataItem, "Feature") %></li>
5:   </ItemTemplate>
6: </asp:DataList>
7: </ul>
```

Using a DataGrid would be similar, except you would use a TemplateColumn in the Columns tag, an exercise we're saving to examine until Chapter 3. Although the code in Listing 1.10 will produce the desired effect, it needlessly encapsulates the list of features within an HTML table (recall that the DataGrid and DataList render as HTML tables).

CAUTION

Although most browsers will render the HTML produced by Listing 1.10 as a bulleted list, realize that the HTML would be invalid by HTML 3.2 standard specifications. The HTML produced by Listing 1.10 places a table tag within a ul tag, which is not allowed according to the W3C's HTML 3.2 standards.

A better option, in my opinion, would be to use a Repeater control. In the HeaderTemplate, you could add an opening ul tag; the ItemTemplate would be identical to the ItemTemplate in Listing 1.10 (lines 3–5); and the FooterTemplate would contain a closing ul tag. Essentially, the code for the Repeater control would be identical to that in Listing 1.9, replacing the ol tags in lines 3 and 12 with ul tags.

Summary

In this chapter, we briefly examined the three data Web controls: the DataGrid, DataList, and Repeater. We looked at how each one is used, their feature-sets, and their advantages and disadvantages. We wrapped up this chapter by looking at some real-world problems, and discussing what data Web control might be the best fit for each scenario.

Over the remainder of the book, we will delve into the functionality of these three controls. This chapter has just scratched the surface of the true power of these controls. In the next chapter, we'll look at the `DataSource` property and `DataBind()` method for these controls in finer detail. In Chapter 3, we'll wrap up the first part of the book by examining how to customize the visual features of the controls through styles, properties, templates, and HTML markup.

On the Web

At the end of each chapter, you will find an "On the Web" section. This section contains hyperlinks to specific online articles that contain additional information about the material presented in the chapter. You are encouraged to explore these resources, as they will likely further your knowledge on the material covered in the chapter.

- Download MSDE—`http://asp.net/msde/default.aspx`

- "What Is MSDE?"—
  `http://www.sqlmag.com/Articles/Index.cfm?ArticleID=7840`

- "An Extensive Examination of the DataGrid Web Control: Part 1"—
  `http://aspnet.4guysfromrolla.com/articles/040502-1.aspx`

- "Accessing Data with ASP.NET"—`http://msdn.microsoft.com/library/en-us/cpguide/html/cpconaccessingdatawithaspnet.asp`

- "DataList vs. DataGrid in ASP.NET"—
  `http://msdn.microsoft.com/msdnmag/issues/01/12/asp/asp0112.asp`

- "The DataGrid Web Server Control"—`http://www.aspalliance.com/aspxtreme/webforms/controls/datagrid.aspx`

- "The DataList Web Server Control"—`http://www.aspalliance.com/aspxtreme/webforms/controls/datalist.aspx`

- "The Repeater Web Server Control"—`http://www.aspalliance.com/aspxtreme/webforms/controls/repeater.aspx`

Please note that the URLs in the "On the Web" sections were verified as of December 2002. We apologize if any of the hyperlinks here are no longer working at the time you attempt to access them.

2

Binding Data to the Data Controls

In the previous chapter we examined the three data Web controls at a very high level. We looked at the distinctions among the controls, their various advantages and disadvantages, and studied simple code examples for each control. The purpose of the data Web controls is to display data on an ASP.NET Web page, while attempting to keep the source code and HTML presentation markup as separate as possible.

The standard way of rendering one of these controls is to first grab some data from a data store. An example would be filling a DataSet with the results of a SQL query against a Microsoft Access database. As we saw in the previous chapter, once the data has been populated in a DataSet, or in another appropriate object, we bound the data to the control by assigning the DataSet to the control's DataSource property. The last step involved was to call the control's DataBind() method.

Up to this point, we've only set the DataSource property to a DataSet object. However, other types of objects can be assigned to the DataSource, and hence rendered in a data Web control. We'll examine the criteria an object must fit for it to be assignable to the DataSource property. In this chapter we'll also take a closer look at the DataBind() method, and what's happening behind the scenes when this method is called.

Specifying a DataSource

When first examining the data Web controls, one might (incorrectly) assume that these controls can only render data from a traditional database, such as Oracle, Microsoft

SQL Server, Microsoft Access, and so on. As we've seen thus far, the `DataSource` can be assigned to a DataSet object, which can not only be populated from traditional data stores, but also from well-formed XML files or strings (see the "On the Web" section at the end of this chapter for further references on binding to an XML file or string), or can be constructed by hand.

There are other objects that qualify to be assigned to a control's `DataSource`. Specifically, the object must implement the `IEnumerable` interface.

NOTE

An *interface* is essentially a list of empty methods. It contains no code for the methods, just the methods' declaration. An interface can be thought of as a contract: When a class implements an interface, it is guaranteeing to the world that those methods will be defined in the interface.

The `IEnumerable` interface defines only one method, `GetEnumerator()`, which returns an object that implements the `IEnumerator` interface. The `IEnumerator` interface contains one property, `Current`, and two methods: `MoveNext()` and `Reset()`. A class that implements the `IEnumerable` interface is essentially announcing that it provides a standard means for stepping through some collection of items.

Hence, any object you want to assign to a data Web control's `DataSource` property must implement, either directly or indirectly, the `IEnumerable` interface. For example, when the DataSet is bound to a data Web control, the first item in the DataSet's `Tables` collection is grabbed and its `DefaultView` property is referenced. The `DefaultView` property returns a `DataView` instance, and the `DataView` class implements the `IEnumerable` interface.

If you are thoroughly confused at this point, don't worry. For now, just rest assured that the DataSet can be assigned to the `DataSource` because it can be enumerated. Similarly, DataReaders (`OleDbDataReader` and `SqlDataReader`) can be assigned to a data Web control's `DataSource` property, as it directly implements the `IEnumerable` interface.

In fact, nearly all the collection classes in the `System.Collections` namespace implement the `IEnumerable` interface, meaning you can assign objects like `ArrayLists`, `Hashtables`, `SortedLists`, `Stacks`, and `Queues` to the `DataSource` property. Similarly, the `Array` class in the `System` namespace implements `IEnumerable`, meaning standard arrays can also be used.

To summarize, the following types of objects can be assigned to the `DataSource` property:

- DataSet

- DataReader objects (`OleDbDataReader`, `SqlDataReader`, and so on)

- Arrays

- The collection classes (ArrayList, Queue, Hashtable, and so on)

Of course, you can write your own classes that implement IEnumerable, or implement an interface that implements IEnumerable. In fact, we'll examine a code sample where we do just that in a bit, but first, let's look at two quick examples using a DataReader, an array, and a Hashtable.

Binding a SqlDataReader to a DataGrid

Listing 2.1 has the same output as Listing 1.1, and the DataGrid declaration is the same. The only difference is that we're populating the database data via a SqlDataReader, as opposed to using a DataSet.

LISTING 2.1   Displaying Data from a SqlDataReader

```
 1: <%@ import Namespace="System.Data" %>
 2: <%@ import Namespace="System.Data.SqlClient" %>
 3: <script runat="server">
 4:     Sub Page_Load(sender as Object, e as EventArgs)
 5:        '1. Create a connection
 6:         Const strConnString as String = "server=localhost;uid=sa;pwd=;
➥database=pubs"
 7:         Dim objConn as New SqlConnection(strConnString)
 8:
 9:        '2. Create a command object for the query
10:        Const strSQL as String = "SELECT * FROM authors"
11:        Dim objCmd as New SqlCommand(strSQL, objConn)
12:
13:        objConn.Open()    'Open the connection
14:
15:        'Finally, specify the DataSource and call DataBind()
16:        dgAuthors.DataSource = objCmd.ExecuteReader
➥(CommandBehavior.CloseConnection)
17:        dgAuthors.DataBind()
18:
19:        objConn.Close()    'Close the connection
20:     End Sub
21: </script>
22:
23: <asp:datagrid id="dgAuthors" runat="server" />
```

The HTML output of the code in Listing 2.1 is identical to that in Listing 1.2. Furthermore, a screenshot of the output of Listing 2.1 can be seen back in Figure 1.1.

Binding an Array to a DataList

Recall that an array can be assigned to a data Web control's `DataSource` property, because the `Array` class implements the `IEnumerable` interface. This fact is quite useful, because there are many scenarios where you might have an array of information that you want to display on a Web page. In classic ASP, you would have to iterate through the array, emitting the array's contents and some HTML markup. However, with ASP.NET, you can simply bind the contents of an array to an appropriate data Web control.

Listing 2.2 illustrates the binding of a DataList to the contents of an array. Specifically, the files in a directory are displayed on an ASP.NET Web page via the `Directory.GetFiles(directoryPath)` method. This method returns a string array of file names from the directory *directoryPath*.

LISTING 2.2   You Can Bind an Array to a DataList

```
 1: <%@ import Namespace="System.IO" %>
 2: <script runat="server">
 3:
 4:     Sub Page_Load(sender as Object, e as EventArgs)
 5:       'Set the DataSource to a String array of file names
 6:       dgFiles.DataSource = Directory.GetFiles("C:\Inetpub\wwwroot\")
 7:       dgFiles.DataBind()
 8:     End Sub
 9:
10: </script>
11:
12: <asp:datalist id="dgFiles" runat="server"
13:       RepeatColumns="2" CellSpacing="5">
14:   <ItemTemplate>
15:     <%# Container.DataItem %>
16:   </ItemTemplate>
17: </asp:datalist>
```

Note that on line 15, where we perform our data-binding syntax in the ItemTemplate, we simply refer to `Container.DataItem`, rather than using the `DataBinder.Eval()` method. We'll examine why in more detail later on in this chapter. For now, just take notice of how an array can be assigned to the `DataSource` property. A screenshot of Listing 2.2, when viewed through a browser, can be seen in Figure 2.1.

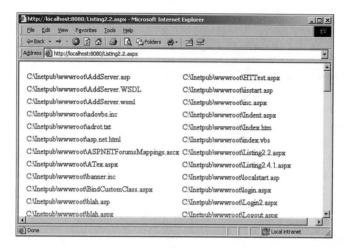

FIGURE 2.1   A list of the files in the `C:\Inetpub\wwwroot` directory is listed in a two-column grid.

Binding a `Hashtable` to a Repeater

Collections in the `Systems.Collections` namespace implement the `IEnumerable` interface, and are therefore candidates for binding to a data Web control. In Listing 2.3, we examine the binding of a `Hashtable` class. Hash tables are data structures that are like arrays, but indexed by a string key rather than by a numeric index. (For this reason, hash tables are also referred to as associative arrays.)

In Listing 2.3, we create our own `Hashtable` object to store point values for the various cards in a card game called Crazy Eights. (See `http://www.pagat.com/eights/crazy8s.html` for the rules of Crazy Eights.) We'd like our `Hashtable` object, `cardValues`, to be indexed by the name of the card whose point value we're interested in. Therefore, if we wanted to see how many points a Jack was worth, we'd simply check `cardValues["Jack"]` (C# syntax), which would return the value 10. (We'd use `cardValues("Jack")` if we were using Visual Basic .NET.)

Listing 2.3 simply creates the `cardValues` Hashtable object (line 6) and then adds an item to the `Hashtable` for each card type. Finally, the `Hashtable` is bound to a Repeater control, which lists the cards and their associated values in a bulleted list.

LISTING 2.3   A `Hashtable`, or any Collection that Implements `IEnumerable`, Can Be Bound to a Data Web Control

```
1: <script runat="server" language="C#">
2:
3:    void Page_Load(Object sender, EventArgs e)
```

LISTING 2.3   Continued

```
 4:    {
 5:      // create a Hashtable
 6:      Hashtable cardValues = new Hashtable();
 7:
 8:      // populate the Hashtable with some values
 9:      cardValues.Add("Two", 20);
10:      cardValues.Add("Three", 3);
11:      cardValues.Add("Four", 4);
12:      ... some lines removed for brevity ...
13:      cardValues.Add("King", 10);
14:      cardValues.Add("Ace", 10);
15:
16:      // bind the Hashtable to the repeater
17:      rptCardValues.DataSource = cardValues;
18:      rptCardValues.DataBind();
19:    }
20:
21: </script>
22:
23: <p>
24: Card values for Crazy Eights!
25: <asp:repeater id="rptCardValues" runat="server">
26:    <HeaderTemplate>
27:      <ul>
28:    </HeaderTemplate>
29:    <ItemTemplate>
30:      <li><%# DataBinder.Eval(Container.DataItem, "Key") %> -
31:      <%# DataBinder.Eval(Container.DataItem, "Value") %></li>
32:    </ItemTemplate>
33:    <FooterTemplate>
34:      </ul>
35:    </FooterTemplate>
36: </asp:repeater>
37: </p>
```

As with Listing 2.2, in Listing 2.3 we have some potentially confusing data binding syntax in the ItemTemplate (lines 30 and 31). Here we use the `DataBinder.Eval` method, and in the second parameter, we have "Key" and "Value" (lines 30 and 31, respectively). Don't worry if this doesn't make sense; we'll discuss this matter thoroughly soon. Instead, focus on the fact that we could bind a `Hashtable` to a `Repeater`.

Figure 2.2 shows a screenshot of Listing 2.3 when viewed through a browser. One interesting thing to note is that the cards and their associated values in the screenshot are not in the same order as they were added to the `Hashtable` in the code (lines 9 through 14). This is because of the internal storage semantics of the `Hashtable` class—the items are not necessarily stored in the order in which they were entered. Consult the .NET Framework documentation on the `Hashtable` class for more information about the algorithms used to store items in a `Hashtable`. (There's also a direct link to the online documentation for the `Hashtable` class in the "On the Web" section at the end of this chapter.)

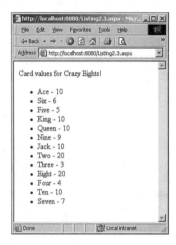

FIGURE 2.2   A bulleted list of the cards and their associated values.

At this point, we've looked at assigning four different types of objects to the `DataSource` property: a DataSet, a `SqlDataRepeater`, an array, and a `Hashtable`. Essentially, we can assign any object that implements the `IEnumerable` interface to the `DataSource` property. In fact, in a later section in this chapter, "Building a Class That Implements `IEnumerable`," we'll examine how to construct our own class that can be assigned to a data Web control's `DataSource` property.

Before we do that, though, let's turn our attention to the `DataBind()` method and examine what's happening behind the scenes. This next section examines why, among other things, why the data-binding syntax was the way it was for the ItemTemplates in Listings 2.2 and 2.3 (refer back to line 15 and lines 30 and 31 in Listings 2.2 and 2.3, respectively). Personally, I think the next section is important and worth reading for a deeper understanding of the low-level details of the data Web controls; however, a thorough understanding is not necessary. If you need to skip the next section, or don't fully understand it or its concepts, don't worry! You can continue working through the rest of the book.

The Ins and Outs of the `DataBind()` Method

The `DataBind()` method is a method defined in the `System.Web.UIControl` class. All ASP.NET Web and HTML controls (including the data Web controls) are derived from this base class, so all controls support a `DataBind()` method. However, this method is *virtual*, meaning it contains no defined body, and it's up to the derived classes that want to use the functionality to override the method name, associating some action with the method call.

Most controls do not override the default `DataBind()` method, so calling `DataBind()` on most controls, such as the TextBox control, has no effect. The important controls that have overridden the `DataBind()` method are the `Page` class, the list Web controls (`DropDownList`, `ListBox`, `RadioButtonList`, and `CheckBoxList`), and the data Web controls.

> **NOTE**
>
> Every ASP.NET Web page, when first visited, is converted into a class that is derived from the `Page` class. If you use code-behind pages, you are likely aware that the code-behind class inherits the `Page` class.
>
> Essentially, the `Page` class contains properties, methods, and events that abstractly define an ASP.NET Web page. In the HTML section of an ASP.NET Web page you can use data-binding syntax referencing a variable, expression, or method call. For example, you could use data binding to emit the current date and time like this:
>
> ```
> <%# DateTime.Now %>
> ```
>
> To have the data-binding syntax dynamically rendered, you'd need to ensure that you call `Page.DataBind()` somewhere in your code section.
>
> Although data binding at the page level is worth investigating, this book is neither the time nor the place for such a study. Instead, we will focus on data binding at the data Web control level. For more information on data binding at the page level, refer to the resources in the "On the Web" section.

It's important to note that when a control's `DataBind()` method is called, the call is cascaded through the control's child controls. That is, if you call the DataList's `DataBind()` method, the `DataBind()` method is also called on the HeaderTemplate, FooterTemplate, ItemTemplate, and whatever other templates might be defined for the DataList.

The First Steps of the `DataBind()` Method Call

When the `DataBind()` method is called, the following sequence of events occur (note that some of the finer details have been omitted, focusing instead on the germane details):

First, the object specified by the DataSource property is enumerated. Recall that the DataSource must implement the IEnumerable interface, so we know with certainty that we'll be able to enumerate over whatever object has been assigned to the DataSource property.

At each step in the enumeration, an appropriate Item object is created. If the data Web control being used is a DataGrid, a DataGridItem object is created; for the DataList, a DataListItem is created; and for the Repeater, a RepeaterItem is created. Each of these objects has an ItemType property that indicates whether the row being added is a standard Item, an AlternatingItem (every even row), the SelectedItem (the item that has been selected), an EditItem (the item currently being edited), a Header, a Footer, and so on. (We'll be discussing these item types in future chapters.)

> **NOTE**
>
> The DataGridItem, DataListItem, and RepeaterItem are classes in the System.Web.UI.WebControls namespace that abstractly define an item in the DataGrid, DataList, and Repeater Web controls, respectively.

At this point, the paths of the various data Web controls diverge a bit. Therefore, let us examine the path each data Web control takes separately.

Completing the DataBind() Method Call for the DataGrid

The DataGridItem class is derived from the TableRow class. This isn't surprising, because for each row in the DataSource, an HTML table row is rendered.

Let's focus specifically on the DataGrid for a moment. For each column in the current item of the DataSource, a TableCell object is created. If the AutoGenerateColumns property is set to True, the Text property of the TableCell is set equal to the value of the associated column in the current item of the DataSource. If AutoGenerateColumns is set to False, a different action is taken, depending on the control specified in the Columns tag. If a BoundColumn is used, then, as with AutoGenerateColumns set to True, the value of the column is placed in the Text property. If a HyperLinkColumn is used, a HyperLink Web control is added as a child of the TableCell object.

Completing the DataBind() Method Call for the DataList

Turning our attention to the DataList, we find that the DataListItem is derived from the WebControl class. At first, one might assume that the DataListItem would be derived from the TableRow, just like the DataGridItem. However, recall that each "row" in the DataSource does not necessarily correspond to an HTML table row. In fact, this is only the case when the RepeatColumns property equals 1 (the default).

When `RepeatColumns` is set to a value of *n* (*n* greater than 1), then there are *n* "rows" from the `DataSource` per HTML table row.

Recall that the DataList's rendering is determined by the templates it specifies, and that the DataList can support a multitude of template types, such as the ItemTemplate, AlternatingItemTemplate, EditItemTemplate, and so on. These templates are defined as properties of the DataList class, which includes classes that implement the `ITemplate` interface. A class implementing the `ITemplate` interface need only have one method: `InstantiateIn(container)`, where *container* is an object of type `Control`. Essentially, the `InstantiateIn()` method turns the template into a series of child controls, whose parent control is the control specified by *container*.

You'll remember that at this point the DataList's `DataSource` is being enumerated through, and for each item in the `DataSource`, a `DataListItem` object is created. Next, the appropriate template's `InstantiateIn()` method is called, passing in the `DataListItem` object as the parameter to the `InstantiateIn()` call. This has the effect of implementing the contents of the template as child controls of the `DataListItem` object. (If you're wondering what the "appropriate template" in the second sentence refers to, remember that what template we use depends on the `ItemType` of the `DataListItem`. That is, if the current `DataListItem` is an `AlternatingItem`, we want to use the AlternatingItemTemplate, if it exists.)

At this point, the current item of the `DataSource` being enumerated over is assigned to the `DataItem` property of the `DataListItem`. (Note that both the `DataGridItem` and `RepeaterItem` have a `DataItem` property as well.) The `DataBind()` method of the `DataListItem` is then called. This has the effect of resolving any data binding syntax that might have appeared in the template that was attached to the `DataListItem`.

This concludes the steps needed to be taken to display a particular field from the DataSource in the data Web control. Of course, this process must be repeated for each item in the `DataSource`.

Recall that Listings 2.2 and 2.3 had some data-binding syntax in the ItemTemplates that we had not seen before. Take a moment to look back at these code listings, paying attention to the ItemTemplates in both examples. In Listing 2.2, the `DataSource` was set to an array of strings. This means that when the `DataSource` is being enumerated over, each item is of type `string`. Hence, in our ItemTemplate for Listing 2.2 (line 15) we simply have

```
<%# Container.DataItem %>.
```

Why does `Container.DataItem` render the file name? Recall that the `DataListItem` has a property named `DataItem`, which was assigned the value of the current `DataSource` item. The reason we have to predicate it with `Container` is because the data-binding syntax appears in the template, which is instantiated as a child control of the DataListItem. Hence, we are not referring to the template object, but to its container, the DataListItem object.

Because the DataSource in Listing 2.2 is a string array, each DataItem is a string. Therefore, our data-binding syntax is complete with just Container.DataItem.

NOTE

The type returned by data-binding syntax (<%# ... %>) depends on the context with which the data-binding syntax is used. For now, we'll just concentrate on having the data-binding syntax return string values. This is an appropriate return type for the types of data binding we've been using thus far; we're simply using data binding to emit a dynamic string into an HTML table cell.

As we will see in the next chapter, we can use data binding to return a plethora of different types, thereby allowing us to dynamically assign values to various properties via data-binding syntax.

In Listing 2.3, our data-binding syntax was a bit more hairy. Recall that here the DataSource was specified as a Hashtable. The ItemTemplate (lines 30 and 31) contains the following HTML markup and data-binding syntax:

```
<li><%# DataBinder.Eval(Container.DataItem, "Key") %> -
<%# DataBinder.Eval(Container.DataItem, "Value") %></li>
```

When a Hashtable is enumerated over, each item returned is a DictionaryEntry structure. The DictionaryEntry structure contains two properties: Key and Value, which correspond to the key and value of the particular Hashtable entry. Because the DataSource in Listing 2.3 is a Hashtable, each DataItem is a DictionaryEntry. Because our data-binding syntax must return a type of string, if we just use <%# Container.DataItem %> as we did in Listing 2.2, the output will be the result of the ToString() method call of the DictionaryEntry structure, resulting in an output of

```
"System.Collections.DictionaryEntry."
```

Because we want to display the key and value, we need to return those properties from the DataItem object. One might think this would be as easy as using <%# Container.DataItem.Key%> and <%# Container.DataItem.Value %>. However, this will not work, because the DataItem property is defined as an instance of the Object class, which has no properties, and only a handful of very generic methods (Equals(*object*), GetType(), ToString(), and so on). That is, DataItem has no way of knowing that it is actually a DictionaryEntry object.

To circumvent this problem, we must use the DataBinder.Eval method. The DataBinder.Eval() can accept either two or three parameters. In the two-parameter version, it takes an *object* and a *string* as input. It then determines, via reflection, whether `object.string` is a legal call; if it is, it performs it. Hence, to grab the value of the `Key` property from the current `DictionaryEntry` object, we use

```
<%# DataBinder.Eval(Container.DataItem, "Key") %>
```

and to obtain the value of the `Value` property from the current `DictionaryEntry` object, we use

```
<%# DataBinder.Eval(Container.DataItem, "Value") %>
```

Note that

```
DataBinder.Eval(Container.DataItem, "Key")
```

and

```
DataBinder.Eval(Container, "DataItem.Key")
```

are equivalent, because in the end both resolve down to checking whether `Container.DataItem.Key` is a valid call.

> **NOTE**
>
> When programming with .NET, all objects contain metadata that describe the object, its type, its properties, events, methods, and so on. *Reflection* is the process of inspecting this metadata to determine such high-level information about an object at run-time. For more information on reflection, check out the `System.Reflection` namespace, or view the suggested link in the "On the Web" section at the end of this chapter.

Applying Style Information for the DataGrid and DataList

Realize that both the DataGrid and DataList Web controls contain a number of properties to specify stylistic information. These properties include those that apply to the entire control, like `BackColor`, `ForeColor`, and `Font`, and those that apply specifically to each item or alternating item, such as `ItemStyle` and `AlternatingItemStyle`.

We'll examine these various properties and how to use them to make your DataGrid and DataList's output more aesthetically pleasing in Chapter 3, "Customizing the HTML Output." For now, though, understand that these styles are applied at different times during the `DataBind()` call. For example, the styles that apply to an HTML table row, such as the `ItemStyle`, are applied to the `DataGridItem` and `DataListItem` controls.

Note that the Repeater control does not support any style properties. With the Repeater, such style information must be explicitly coded into the HTML markup in the various templates.

Completing the DataBind() Method Call for the Repeater

To complete our examination of the DataBind() method call, we must examine what occurs with the Repeater control once the DataSource is being enumerated. Not surprisingly, the series of steps the Repeater takes is nearly identical to that taken by the DataList. But there are some subtle differences: rather than DataListItems being created, RepeaterItems are created instead. Regarding the Repeater's templates, the same series of steps are taken as with the DataList.

Now that we've examined what happens to the various data Web controls when the DataBind() method is called, let's return to a topic we touched upon earlier in this chapter: creating our own class that implements the IEnumerable interface and using it as the DataSource for a data Web control.

Building a Class that Implements IEnumerable

Recall from the earlier section "Specifying a DataSource" that any object that implemented the IEnumerable interface can be assigned as a DataSource. To prove this point, let's take a moment to create our own class that implements IEnumerable, and then use this class as a DataSource for one of the data Web controls.

Because we want to create a class that can be enumerated, we need some way to store the data that can be enumerated. For example, imagine that we're working on the postal service's Web site, and we want a collection of shipping options. Although we could implement this as a simple collection (perhaps as an ArrayList), we might also want to implement it as its own class (perhaps it also has to have a variety of methods and events). Clearly, we would need to use some sort of private variable to store the various shipping options.

Creating the Enumerable Class

For this exercise, let's just use an array. Specifically, we will use an array of integers that will hold the first 20 Fibonacci numbers.

NOTE

The Fibonacci sequence is a series of numbers defined as follows: the first two numbers are both 1. The ith Fibonacci number is defined as the sum of the $i - 1$ and $i - 2$ Fibonacci numbers. Therefore, the sequence is 1, 1, 2 (which is 1+1), 3 (2+1), 5 (3+2), 8 (5+3), and so on.

The code for the class can be found in Listing 2.4. Because this class implements IEnumerable (line 4), it must have a GetEnumerator method that returns an object that implements IEnumerator. Because we are storing the Fibonacci series in an array, we can simply return the array's enumerator via the Array class's GetEnumerator method (lines 24 through 28). (The reason the Array class has a GetEnumerator method is because it implements the IEnumerable interface—that's the reason why we opted to store the Fibonacci numbers in an array, to make our task easier!)

LISTING 2.4   The FibSeries Class Implements the IEnumerable Interface

```
 1: using System;
 2: using System.Collections;
 3:
 4: public class FibSeries : IEnumerable
 5: {
 6:   // we must have something to enumerate over,
 7:   // let's just use an integer array
 8:   int [] data;
 9:
10:   public FibSeries(int size)
11:   {
12:     // create the array
13:     data = new int[size];
14:
15:     // populate the array
16:     data[0] = 1;
17:     data[1] = 1;
18:
19:     for (int i = 2; i < size; i++)
20:       data[i] = data[i-1] + data[i-2];
21:   }
22:
23:   // since we implement IEnumerable we must provide a GetEnumerator method
24:   public IEnumerator GetEnumerator()
25:   {
26:     // simply return the array's enumerator
27:     return data.GetEnumerator();
28:   }
29: }
```

As can be seen in Listing 2.4, the FibSeries class has a private integer array, data, defined on line 8. This array will hold a number of Fibonacci numbers. The constructor (lines 10 through 21) requires an input parameter of type integer, which consists of the amount of Fibonacci numbers the user wants. There should definitely be some bounds-checking going on here, ensuring that size isn't negative or less than 2. I leave this as an exercise to the reader.

On lines 16 and 17, the first two Fibonacci numbers are added to the data array. Then, a loop populates the remainder of the array values.

Compiling the Class and Deploying the Assembly

Once we've written this class, we'll need to compile it into an assembly (a DLL). If you are using Visual Studio .NET, you'll want to create a C# class. Simply compile the project, and the assembly is ready. If you do not have Visual Studio .NET, you will have to use the command line compiler. Start by creating a text file named FibSeries.cs, and copy in the text from Listing 2.4. Drop to the command prompt, navigate to the directory where FibSeries.cs is located, and type

```
csc /t:library FibSeries.cs
```

This will create an assembly named FibSeries.dll. Regardless of whether you use Visual Studio .NET or if you compile the assembly via the command line, you'll need to copy the DLL to our ASP.NET project's /bin folder. Once the DLL is there, we can use the class in our ASP.NET Web page.

Using the Class as a DataSource

Listing 2.5 illustrates the use of the FibSeries class as a DataSource for the DataList Web control.

LISTING 2.5   The FibSeries Class Can Be Used As a DataSource

```
 1: <script runat="server" language="C#">
 2:
 3:     void Page_Load(Object sender, EventArgs e)
 4:     {
 5:       FibSeries fibTest = new FibSeries(25);
 6:
 7:       Fib.DataSource = fibTest;
 8:       Fib.DataBind();
 9:     }
10:
11: </script>
12:
13: <asp:DataList runat="server" id="Fib" RepeatColumns="5"
```

LISTING 2.5   Continued

```
14:     CellPadding="5" ItemStyle-HorizontalAlign="Right"
15:     ItemStyle-BorderStyle="Solid" RepeatDirection="Horizontal">
16:   <ItemTemplate>
17:     <%# String.Format("{0:#,###}", Container.DataItem) %>
18:   </ItemTemplate>
19: </asp:DataList>
```

Because the `FibSeries.DLL` file has been copied into our ASP.NET Web site's `/bin` directory, we can start using the `FibSeries` class. On line 5, we create a new instance of the `FibSeries` class, specifying that we'd like the first 25 Fibonacci numbers. On line 7, the `FibSeries` instance `fibTest` is assigned to the DataList's `DataSource`, and on line 8, the `DataBind()` method is called.

In lines 13–19, the DataList is declared. We create a 5×5 grid with the `RepeatColumns` property. The `RepeatDirection` property indicates that the items should repeat horizontally as opposed to vertically in the rendered HTML `table`. The `ItemStyle-HorizontalAlign` property setting on line 14 dictates that the cells of the DataList should be right-aligned, while the `ItemStyle-BorderStyle` property setting on line 15 indicates that a border should be displayed. (We'll cover these two aesthetic properties and more in the next chapter.)

Finally, in the ItemTemplate, we use a more complicated data-binding expression than we have seen thus far. Because our `DataSource` returns integers during each iteration (recall that we are enumerating over an integer array), we *could* just use `<%# Container.DataItem %>` for our data-binding syntax. However, we can make the numbers easier to read by having commas inserted every three decimal places. To accomplish this, we use the `String.Format` method to apply formatting to the `Container.DataItem` value. Don't concern yourself with the details of the `String.Format` method just yet; we'll get to that in Chapter 3. For now, just note that we can use the result of a method call in our data-binding syntax (we'll discuss this, as well, in the next chapter).

A screenshot of Listing 2.5 when viewed through a browser can be seen in Figure 2.3. Note that there is a border around each table cell and that the cells are right-aligned. Furthermore, notice that those numbers longer than three digits have commas every three digits (courtesy of the `String.Format` call).

FIGURE 2.3   The first 25 Fibonacci numbers are shown using a DataList.

Summary

In this chapter, we examined what types of objects could be used as a DataSource. This includes DataSets, DataReaders, arrays, and collections. More generally, any class that implements the IEnumerable interface is a candidate for being a DataSource. This fact was demonstrated when we built a custom class that implemented the IEnumerable interface, and then used this class as the DataSource for the DataList control.

We also took an intimate look at what happens with each of the data Web controls when the DataBind() method is called. By examining the way templates are handled in the DataBind() call, we arrived at a better understanding of the data-binding syntax than we've seen thus far in Repeater and DataList templates.

Up to this point, the HTML output of our data Web controls has been anything but exciting. However, the DataGrid and DataList contain numerous properties geared solely toward improving the aesthetic appearance. We'll delve into these properties in the next chapter. We'll also examine more powerful ways in which templates can be used to produce a higher degree of customized output!

On the Web

For more information on the topics discussed in this chapter, consider perusing the following online resources:

- "The Hashtable Class Documentation"—
  http://msdn.microsoft.com/library/default.asp?url=/library/en-us/cpref/html/frlrfSystemCollectionsHashtableClassTopic.asp

- "The IEnumerable Interface Documentation"—
  http://msdn.microsoft.com/library/default.asp?url=/library/en-
  us/cpref/html/frlrfsystemcollectionsienumerableclasstopic.asp

- "Binding an XML File to a DataGrid"—
  http://aspnet.4guysfromrolla.com/articles/052902-1.aspx

- Binding an XML String to a DataGrid—
  http://aspnet.4guysfromrolla.com/articles/071702-1.aspx

- "Databinding Overview and Syntax"—http://samples.gotdotnet.com/quick-
  start/aspplus/doc/webdatabinding.aspx

- "C# Reflection and Dynamic Method Invocation"—
  http://my.execpc.com/~gopalan/dotnet/reflection.html

- "Generate and Execute Dynamic Script with .NET Using Reflection"—
  http://www.devx.com/dotnet/articles/rh062502/rh062502-1.asp

3

Customizing the HTML Output

W e have used the data Web controls a number of times in code examples in the past two chapters. However, the appearance of the output has left a lot to be desired. Fortunately, making the DataGrid and DataList output more visually pleasing is quite simple, even for artistically challenged developers like myself!

As we will see in this chapter, both the DataGrid and DataList expose a number of properties that make specifying these details a breeze. Additionally, we'll look at how editors like Visual Studio .NET and the Web Matrix Project make specifying the appearance of the DataGrid and DataList as easy clicking a few buttons. (Note that the Repeater control does not contain any sort of stylistic properties; the developer is responsible for specifying any aesthetic properties directly in the HTML markup of the Repeater's templates.)

In this chapter we will also look at how to use built-in methods and custom functions to alter the output of data binding expressions in templates. For example, in Chapter 2's Listing 2.5, the `String.Format()` method is used within the data-binding expression of an ItemTemplate to have the number returned by `Container.DataItem` formatted with commas every three digits (line 17). (That is, 17711 [the 22nd Fibonacci number] is displayed as 17,711.) We'll examine how to use this approach to further customize the HTML emitted by data-bound values in a template.

By the end of this chapter, you will be able to generate professional-looking DataGrids and DataLists with just the setting of a few properties, or if you're using Visual Studio .NET or the Web Matrix Project, with simply the click of the mouse.

Specifying Display Properties in the DataGrid and DataList

Although the code examples we've studied thus far have been very useful in their structured display of data, they have been far from eye-pleasing. When viewing the screenshots of the code examples, did you ever think, "I wonder how I can change the font?" or "Wouldn't it look nicer if the cells in the DataGrid header were center-aligned?" If you did, you'll be pleased to learn that specifying such stylistic properties for the DataGrid and DataList is quite simple, as we will see in this section.

Recall that the DataGrid and DataList controls render into HTML `table` tags. When you think of a table, there are three levels to which stylistic formatting can be applied.

First, formatting can be applied to the entire table. This might include setting the font for the entire table to Verdana, or specifying the CellPadding or CellSpacing for the table.

> **NOTE**
>
> CellPadding and CellSpacing are two stylistic properties of an HTML table. The CellPadding specifies the number of pixels between the cell's border and the cell's textual content. The CellSpacing specifies, in pixels, the spacing between neighboring table cells.

Second, formatting can be applied at the table row level. This row-level formatting can be specified for all rows in the table; for example, you might want all the rows to have a certain background color. Of course, setting this property for all the rows is synonymous with setting the property for the entire table.

You can also specify row-level formatting for just a subset of the rows. For example, you might opt for the rows' background to alternate between two colors. (That is, each even row might have a white background, and each odd row might have a light gray background.) Additionally, you can use row-level formatting to specify formatting for a single row. With the DataGrid and DataList, you can select a row and edit its data. You might want to use an alternative font for the row that is being edited. (We'll look at how to edit data in Chapter 9, "Editing the DataGrid Web Control.") In a similar vein, you might want to have a different style for the header and footer rows of the table.

The third level of stylistic formatting can be applied to the column level. Recall that the DataGrid has a `Columns` tag in which you can explicitly specify what columns should appear in the DataGrid control. Not surprisingly, you can apply stylistic settings to these columns. For example, you might want to have certain columns center- or right-aligned.

In this section, we will look at each of these levels of formatting separately and how to apply them programmatically. After this, we will look at specifying this formatting information using Visual Studio .NET and the Web Matrix Project. As we will see, specifying this property information with these tools is quite simple, requiring just a few clicks of the mouse.

Specifying Table-Level Display Properties

The DataGrid and DataList contain a number of table-level properties. Table 3.1 lists some of the more useful ones, along with a short description of each.

TABLE 3.1 Common Table-Level Properties for DataGrid and DataList

Property	Description
BackColor	The background color of the table.
BorderColor	The color of the table border.
BorderStyle	The border style. Must be set to a member of the BorderStyle enumeration.
BorderWidth	The width of the border.
CellPadding	The cellpadding attribute of the table tag.
CellSpacing	The cellspacing attribute of the table tag.
CssClass	A cascading stylesheet class for the table that specifies style information.
Font	Font information for the table. Specifies the font's name, size, and style options (bolded, italicized, underlined, and so on).
ForeColor	The foreground color of the table.
Height	The height of the table, in either pixels or percentages.
HorizontalAlign	The horizontal alignment of the table (Left, Right, or Center).
Width	The width of the table, in either pixels or percentages.

These stylistic properties can be assigned programmatically, in the ASP.NET Web page's server-side script block or code-behind page, or declaratively, in the control's definition in the HTML section of the ASP.NET Web page.

Listing 3.1 illustrates the setting of a DataGrid's stylistic properties both programmatically and declaratively. Note that the majority of the contents of Listing 3.1 are identical to the code in Listing 2.1. The only differences are the DataGrid declaration on lines 30 and 31 and lines 23–25, where two display properties of the DataGrid are set programmatically.

LISTING 3.1 A DataGrid's Display Properties Are Set Declaratively and Programmatically

```
1: <%@ import Namespace="System.Data" %>
2: <%@ import Namespace="System.Data.SqlClient" %>
3: <script runat="server" language="VB">
4:
5:   Sub Page_Load(sender as Object, e as EventArgs)
6:     '1. Create a connection
```

LISTING 3.1   Continued

```
 7:    Const strConnString as String = "server=localhost;uid=sa;pwd=;
➥database=pubs"
 8:    Dim objConn as New SqlConnection(strConnString)
 9:
10:    '2. Create a command object for the query
11:    Const strSQL as String = "SELECT * FROM authors"
12:    Dim objCmd as New SqlCommand(strSQL, objConn)
13:
14:    objConn.Open()   'Open the connection
15:
16:    'Finally, specify the DataSource and call DataBind()
17:    dgAuthors.DataSource = objCmd.ExecuteReader(CommandBehavior.
➥CloseConnection)
18:    dgAuthors.DataBind()
19:
20:    objConn.Close()   'Close the connection
21:
22:
23:    ' Set some DataGrid display properties programmatically
24:    dgAuthors.HorizontalAlign = HorizontalAlign.Center
25:    dgAuthors.Font.Bold = True
26:   End Sub
27:
28: </script>
29:
30: <asp:datagrid id="dgAuthors" runat="server" Font-Name="Verdana"
31:    Width="50%" />
```

Note that the DataGrid in Listing 3.1 has its display properties specified both programmatically (lines 24 and 25) and declaratively (lines 30 and 31). In the declarative section, we specify that the Verdana font should be used, and that the table should have a width of 50%. And in the Page_Load event handler, we specify that the table should be center-aligned and have a bold font.

One thing to note is the syntax used when specifying the font name. The Font property of the DataGrid (and DataList) is an instance of the System.Web.UI. WebControls.FontInfo class, which contains a number of properties, such as Name, Bold, Italic, Size, and so on. Therefore, we don't want to assign "Verdana" to the Font property, but instead to the Font.Name property. However, this dot notation, which we use when specifying a property programmatically (see line 25), does not work when setting a property declaratively. Rather, we have to replace all dots with dashes. Hence, instead of saying `Font.Name = "Verdana"` we do `Font-Name="Verdana"` (line 30).

On lines 24 and 25 we set two properties declaratively. The first is the `HorizontalAlign` property, which specifies that the table should be center-aligned. Note that the `HorizontalAlign` property needs to be assigned a value from the `HorizontalAlign` enumeration, so we assign it to `HorizontalAlign.Center` (line 24). If we were setting this property declaratively, however, we could omit the enumeration name, and just use `HorizontalAlign="Center"`. On line 25 we specify that the contents of the table should be displayed in bold.

NOTE

Had we used a DataList instead of a DataGrid in Listing 3.1, neither the programmatic nor declarative property settings would need to be changed in any way.

Figure 3.1 depicts a screenshot of Listing 3.1 when viewed through a browser.

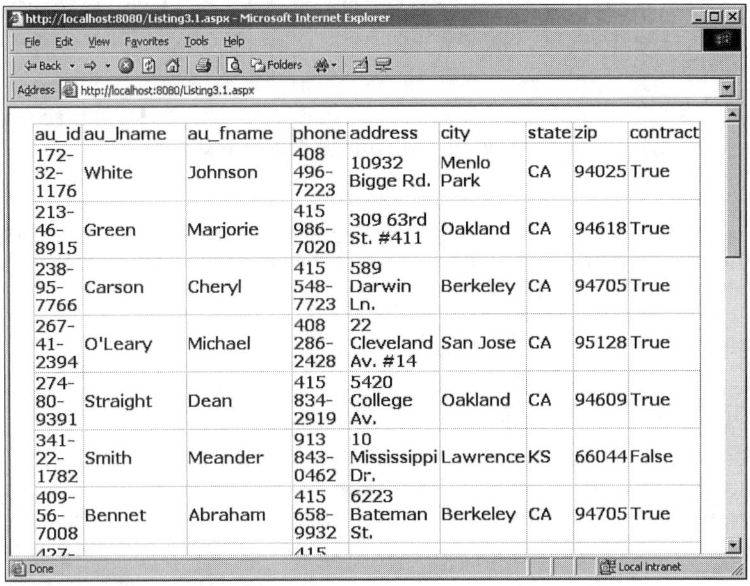

au_id	au_lname	au_fname	phone	address	city	state	zip	contract
172-32-1176	White	Johnson	408 496-7223	10932 Bigge Rd.	Menlo Park	CA	94025	True
213-46-8915	Green	Marjorie	415 986-7020	309 63rd St. #411	Oakland	CA	94618	True
238-95-7766	Carson	Cheryl	415 548-7723	589 Darwin Ln.	Berkeley	CA	94705	True
267-41-2394	O'Leary	Michael	408 286-2428	22 Cleveland Av. #14	San Jose	CA	95128	True
274-80-9391	Straight	Dean	415 834-2919	5420 College Av.	Oakland	CA	94609	True
341-22-1782	Smith	Meander	913 843-0462	10 Mississippi Dr.	Lawrence	KS	66044	False
409-56-7008	Bennet	Abraham	415 658-9932	6223 Bateman St.	Berkeley	CA	94705	True

FIGURE 3.1 A centered table displayed in bold with a width of 50% is rendered.

Specifying Row-Level Display Properties

In the previous section, we noted a number of display properties that apply to the entire table rendered by the DataGrid or DataList. Most of these properties can also be applied at the row level, as we will see shortly.

To enable the developer to set row-level properties, the DataList and DataGrid provide a number of "ItemStyle" properties. These properties are called "ItemStyle" properties because they specify style information for the `DataGridItem` and `DataListItem` controls, which, as you'll recall from the previous chapter, are rendered as rows in the resulting table. The "ItemStyle" properties include the following:

- `ItemStyle`
- `AlternatingItemStyle`
- `EditItemStyle`
- `SelectedItemStyle`
- `HeaderStyle`
- `FooterStyle`

The last four "ItemStyle" properties—`EditItemStyle`, `SelectedItemStyle`, `HeaderItemStyle`, and `FooterItemStyle`—specify row-level styles for exactly one row. For example, the `HeaderItemStyle` specifies style information for the header row.

On the other hand, the `ItemStyle` and `AlternatingItemStyle` properties specify style settings for multiple rows. If the `AlternatingItemStyle` style is specified, it is applied to each alternating row in the table. If it is not specified, the `ItemStyle` is applied to all rows in the table.

Each of these "ItemStyle" properties is defined as a `TableItemStyle` instance. Table 3.2 shows the germane display properties of the `TableItemStyle` class.

TABLE 3.2   Common `TableItemStyle` Display Properties, Which Can Be Used to Specify Row-Level Display Properties

Property	Description
BackColor	The background color of the table row.
BorderColor	The color of the table row's border.
BorderStyle	The border style. Must be set to a member of the `BorderStyle` enumeration.
BorderWidth	The width of the border.
CssClass	A cascading stylesheet class for the table that specifies style information.
Font	Font information for the table row. Specifies the font's name, size, and style options (bolded, italicized, underlined, and so on).
ForeColor	The foreground color of the table row.
Height	The height of the table row, in either pixels or percentages.
HorizontalAlign	The horizontal alignment of the table row (Left, Right, or Center).
VerticalAlign	The vertical alignment of the table row (Top, Middle, or Bottom).
Width	The width of the table row, in either pixels or percentages.
Wrap	Specifies whether the contents in the cell should wrap—defaults to True.

Comparing Table 3.2 to Table 3.1, you can see that Table 3.2 does not include properties like CellPadding and CellSpacing, which are clearly table-level display settings. Furthermore, Table 3.1 does not contain the obvious row-level display settings, such as VerticalAlign and Wrap. The overlapping display properties, though, are common to both Tables 3.1 and 3.2.

As with the table-level display properties, the row-level display properties can be set both declaratively and programmatically. In addition to being set declaratively, the "ItemStyle" properties can also be set using embedded tags inside the DataGrid or DataList tag, as shown in Listing 3.2 on lines 9 and 10. The remaining source code has been omitted from Listing 3.2; essentially it is identical to the source code in Listing 3.1, with lines 22–25 from Listing 3.1 omitted. Figure 3.2 shows a screenshot of Listing 3.2 when viewed through a browser.

LISTING 3.2 A DataList Is Used to Display Mailing Labels for the Various Authors

```
 1: <asp:datalist id="dlAuthorMailLabels" runat="server" Font-Name="Verdana"
 2:    HorizontalAlign="Center"
 3:    CellSpacing="10"
 4:
 5:    ItemStyle-Font-Size="8"
 6:
 7:    AlternatingItemStyle-BackColor="#dddddd">
 8:
 9:    <HeaderStyle HorizontalAlign="Center" Font-Bold="True"
10:          BackColor="Blue" ForeColor="White" />
11:
12:    <HeaderTemplate>
13:     Mailing Labels
14:    </HeaderTemplate>
15:
16:    <ItemTemplate>
17:     <%# DataBinder.Eval(Container.DataItem, "au_fname") %>
18:     <%# DataBinder.Eval(Container.DataItem, "au_lname") %>
19:     <br />
20:     <%# DataBinder.Eval(Container.DataItem, "address") %>
21:     <br />
22:     <%# DataBinder.Eval(Container.DataItem, "city") %>,
23:     <%# DataBinder.Eval(Container.DataItem, "state") %>
24:          
25:     <%# DataBinder.Eval(Container.DataItem, "zip") %>
26:    </ItemTemplate>
27: </asp:datalist>
```

FIGURE 3.2　The authors' contact information is presented as a list of mailing labels.

As mentioned earlier, one of the "ItemStyles" is the HeaderStyle, which specifies the display properties for the header. With the DataGrid, the header is automatically generated, containing the name of the columns. With the DataList, we have to supply our own header using the HeaderTemplate. In Listing 3.2, we simply give a title to our table in the HeaderTemplate (lines 12–14).

> **NOTE**
>
> The *header* is the first row displayed in a data Web control, and typically contains a title for each column of data.

On lines 9 and 10, the HeaderStyle properties are set. Note that with the "ItemStyle" properties, we can use an alternative form of declaratively defining the properties. Simply put, we use a tag within the DataList (or DataGrid) tag. The tag name is the name of the "ItemStyle" property that we want to work with. We can then set the properties of that "ItemStyle" property by specifying them as attributes in the tag. For example, on line 10, we set the BackColor and ForeColor of the HeaderStyle to Blue and White, respectively.

On line 5 we set the ItemStyle's Font property's Size object to 8 point. On line 7 we set the AlternatingItemStyle's BackColor property to #dddddd, which is a light gray.

This has the effect of alternating the background color between white and light gray for each alternating row in the DataList.

The ItemTemplate in Listing 3.2 (lines 17–25) is fairly straightforward, and is intended to display a list that can be used for mailing labels. First, the author's first and last names are shown, then a break (<br />), then the author's address, then another break, and finally the author's city, state, and zip code. Note that the   is HTML markup to display nonbreaking whitespace. The five instances of   (line 24) set the zip code five spaces from the end of the state in the city, state, and zip code line.

The code in Listing 3.2 does not demonstrate how to set "ItemStyle" properties programmatically. However, it is likely that your intuition can tell you the syntax. For example, to set the HeaderStyle's HorizontalAlign property to center, we could use

```
dlAuthorMailLabels.HeaderStyle.HorizontalAlign = HorizontalAlign.Center
```

To set the ItemStyle's Font's Size to 8 point, we could use

```
dlAuthorMailLabels.ItemStyle.Font.Size = FontUnit.Point(8)
```

A bit more care must be taken when setting the property of a data Web control programmatically versus setting it declaratively. When setting the font size declaratively, we simply use

```
<asp:DataList Font-Size="8pt" ... />
```

Notice that we essentially set the DataList's Font.Size property to the string "8pt". When setting the property programmatically, however, we just assign the Font.Size property to a string. That is, if we tried to set the DataList's Font.Size property to "8pt" using

```
dlAuthorMailLabels.ItemStyle.Font.Size = "8pt"
```

we'd get a compile-time error because of the mismatched types. That is, the Size property of the DataList's Font property expects a value of type System.Web.UI. WebControls.FontUnit, not of type string. That is why, in our earlier example, we set the DataList's Font.Size property to the FontUnit instance returned by the FontUnit.Point method:

```
dlAuthorMailLabels.ItemStyle.Font.Size = FontUnit.Point(8)
```

You might be wondering how I knew that the DataList's Font property's Size property was expecting a value of type FontUnit and not string. If you are given an expression like

```
dlAuthorMailLabels.ItemStyle.Font.Size
```

and you need to determine the type of that expression, simply start with the leftmost object and work your way to the right end. That is, the leftmost object, dlAuthorMailLabels, is a DataList object. It has an ItemStyle property, which is the second leftmost object. This ItemStyle property is of type TableItemStyle, as we discussed eariler. The TableItemStyle class has a property Font, which is of type FontInfo. The FontInfo class has a property Size, which is of type FontUnit. Hence, the type of the entire expression

```
dlAuthorMailLabels.ItemStyle.Font.Size
```

is FontUnit, meaning we must assign a value of type FontUnit to this expression.

NOTE

Given this information, you might now be wondering why the Font.Size property can be assigned a string in the declarative form. That is, given what we just discussed, why doesn't

```
<asp:DataList Font-Size="8pt" ... />
```

generate a type mismatch compile-time error? The reason is because, behind the scenes, the string "8pt." is being automatically converted into an appropriate FontUnit instance.

Specifying Column-Level Display Properties

As we've seen in previous chapters, the DataGrid control, by default, creates an HTML table with as many rows and columns as there are in the DataSource. However, by setting the AutoGenerateColumns property to False, you can explicitly specify what fields from the DataSource should be included in the DataGrid. Recall that to add a column to the DataGrid you must add an appropriate control in the DataGrid's Columns tag. That is, using our authors example, a DataGrid that had columns for the author's first and last name might look like this:

```
<asp:DataGrid runat="server" id="dgAuthorsNames">
 <Columns>
  <asp:BoundColumn DataField="au_fname" HeaderText="First Name" />
  <asp:BoundColumn DataField="au_lname" HeaderText="Last Name" />
 </Columns>
</asp:DataGrid>
```

Recall that the following controls can be used within the Columns tag:

- BoundColumn

- TemplateColumn

- EditColumn

- ButtonColumn

- HyperLinkColumn

Not surprisingly, you can specify various display properties for each of these column controls. In this chapter, we'll look at customizing the stylistic properties for the BoundColumn and TemplateColumn controls. For now we'll omit examination of EditColumn, ButtonColumn, and HyperLinkColumn, because we'll be seeing much more of these controls in later chapters.

Specifying Display Properties for the BoundColumn Control

The BoundColumn control contains three "ItemStyle" properties: `ItemStyle`, `HeaderStyle`, and `FooterStyle`. These "ItemStyle" properties indicate style information for the particular column. They contain the same set of display properties as the "ItemStyle" properties examined in the previous section.

In addition to these "ItemStyle" properties, the BoundColumn control contains a few other display properties. One we've seen in past examples is the `HeaderText` property, which specifies the text that should appear in the header of the column. This is useful if your `DataSource` has obscure field names (such as au_lname). A `FooterText` property is also included. The BoundColumn control also contains a `HeaderImageUrl` property, which, if specified, will place an `img` tag in the header.

The final display property for the BoundColumn control is the `DataFormatString` property. This string property specifies how the data in the column should be formatted. The syntax for the format string is a bit strange at first glance: `{0:formatString}`. This is the same syntax used for the `String.Format()` method, which we saw in a code example at the end of Chapter 2.

The `String.Format()` method accepts a string as its first parameter, and then accepts a variable number of parameters of type `Object`. The string parameter is a format string, which can contain a mix of normal text and format placeholders. The objects are the variables whose values we want to have plugged into the formatting placeholders.

For example, imagine that we have two variables of type `float` in C#, or of type `Single` in Visual Basic .NET, called `basePrice` and `salesTax`. The `basePrice` variable contains the sum of the prices for the products ordered by our customer, whereas the `salesTax` price is the sales tax on the customer's purchase; hence the total price due is the sum of these two variables.

Now, it would be nice to display a message indicating the customer's total, and how it was derived. We might want to have an output like: "Your total comes to $6.50. The base price was $5.75 and the sales tax was $0.75." To accomplish this, we could use the `String.Format` method like so:

```
String s = String.Empty;
String strFormat = "Your total comes to {0:c}. The base price was {1:c} " +
        "and the sales tax was {2:c}.";
s = String.Format(strFormat, basePrice+salesTax, basePrice, salesTax)
```

Note that the formatting placeholders ({0:c}, {1:c}, and {2:c}) indicate two things: the ordinal ranking of the variable whose value should be used when applying the formatting information, and the formatting to use. That is, {0:c} will apply a currency formatting to the 0th parameter (basePrice+salesTax)—note that c represents a currency formatting. {1:c} will apply a currency formatting to the 1st parameter, basePrice (really the 2nd one, because we start counting at 0). Finally, {2:c} will apply a currency formatting to the 2nd parameter, salesTax.

The DataStringFormat property of the BoundColumn control works in a similar fashion: Here you must specify the formatting placeholder. Keep in mind that the value that is inserted into the cell from the DataSource is the 0th parameter. Hence, if you have a field that stores, say, the price of each product, you can have it displayed as a currency by setting the BoundColumn control's DataFormatString to {0:c}. That is, the DataGrid might look like this:

```
<asp:DataGrid runat="server" id="dgAuthorsNames">
 <Columns>
  <asp:BoundColumn DataField="Name" HeaderText="Product Name" />
  <asp:BoundColumn DataField="Price" HeaderText="Price"
          DataFormatString="{0:c}" />
 </Columns>
</asp:DataGrid>
```

Clearly the c format string formats the specified variable value as a currency, but what other format strings are available? Table 3.3 lists a few of the more common ones, but there are far too many possibilities to list here. Instead, check out Microsoft's Formatting Overview page at http://msdn.microsoft.com/library/default.asp?url=/library/en-us/cpguide/html/cpconformattingoverview.asp.

TABLE 3.3   Common Formatting Strings

Formatting String	Effect
c	Displays numeric values in currency format
d	Displays numeric values in decimal format and date/time variables in a short date pattern
x	Displays numeric values in hexadecimal format

Listing 3.3 illustrates setting a number of display properties for the BoundColumn controls. The source code is omitted from the listing, but it is the same as the source code from Listing 3.1, except that the SQL query on line 11 has been changed from SELECT * FROM authors to SELECT * FROM titles. Hence, the code in Listing 3.3 presents information about the various books in the database.

LISTING 3.3   Column-Level Display Properties Can Be Set via the BoundColumn Control

```
 1: <asp:datagrid id="dgTitles" runat="server"
 2:    AutoGenerateColumns="False"
 3:    Font-Name="Verdana" Width="50%"
 4:    HorizontalAlign="Center" ItemStyle-Font-Size="9">
 5:
 6: <HeaderStyle BackColor="Navy" ForeColor="White"
 7:    HorizontalAlign="Center" Font-Bold="True" />
 8:
 9: <AlternatingItemStyle BackColor="#dddddd" />
10:
11: <Columns>
12:   <asp:BoundColumn DataField="title" HeaderText="Title"
13:           ItemStyle-Width="70%" />
14:
15:   <asp:BoundColumn DataField="price" HeaderText="Price"
16:           DataFormatString="{0:c}"
17:           ItemStyle-HorizontalAlign="Right"
18:           ItemStyle-Width="15%" />
19:
20:   <asp:BoundColumn DataField="ytd_sales" HeaderText="Sales"
21:           DataFormatString="{0:#,###}"
22:           ItemStyle-HorizontalAlign="Right"
23:           ItemStyle-Width="15%" />
24: </Columns>
25: </asp:datagrid>
```

In Listing 3.3, there are three BoundColumns presenting key information from the titles table in the pubs database. The first BoundColumn (lines 12 and 13) simply shows the book's title. On line 13, the Width of the column is set to 70% via the ItemStyle property. Because we are working with column-level display properties, this width setting is relative to the table width, meaning the first column will be 70% of the total width of the table. Note that in line 3 we specified that the table should have a Width of 50% (this is relative to the Web page).

The second BoundColumn (lines 15–18) displays the price of the book. Line 16 sets the `DataFormatString` so that the value will be formatted as a currency. On line 17, the column values are specified to be right-aligned, and on line 18, the `Width` of the column is set to 15% (of the total width of the table).

The last BoundColumn (lines 20–23) displays the year-to-date sales. The `DataFormatString` on line 21 indicates that there should be a comma separating each of the three digits. The `HorizontalAlign` and `Width` properties on lines 22 and 23 mirror those on lines 17 and 18.

Figure 3.3 shows a screenshot of Listing 3.3 when viewed through a browser.

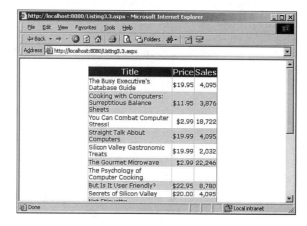

FIGURE 3.3   Each column has specific stylistic properties set, such as formatting and alignment.

Specifying Display Properties for the TemplateColumn

Recall that the DataGrid can employ templates through the use of the TemplateColumn control. This control applies a template to a specific column in the DataGrid, as shown in the following code snippet:

```
<asp:DataGrid runat="server" id="dgTemplateColumnExample">
 <Columns>
  <asp:TemplateColumn>
   <ItemTemplate>
    <%# DataBinder.Eval(Container.DataItem, "SomeColumnName") %>
   </ItemTemplate>
  </asp:TemplateColumn>
 </Columns>
<asp:DataGrid>
```

The display properties of the TemplateColumn are a subset of those of the
BoundColumn. Specifically, the TemplateColumn's display properties include the
following:

- `HeaderText`
- `HeaderImageUrl`
- `FooterText`
- `ItemStyle`
- `HeaderStyle`
- `FooterStyle`

With the TemplateColumn, you have more control over the display in the header
and footer through the use of the HeaderTemplate and FooterTemplate.

Let's look at some code. Listing 3.4 contains a DataGrid that uses the same source
code as Listing 3.3—it populates a `SqlDataReader` with the query `SELECT * FROM
titles` and binds it to the DataGrid `dgTitles`. As with Listing 3.3, the source code
has been removed from Listing 3.4 for brevity.

In Listing 3.4, a DataGrid with a BoundColumn control and a TemplateColumn
control is created. The BoundColumn control displays the title of the book, and the
TemplateColumn control displays information on the book's sales performance—
essentially a simple sentence noting how many copies have been sold at what price.
Three of the TemplateColumn control's display properties—`HeaderText` (line 15), and
two `ItemStyle` properties (`HorizontalAlign` and `Wrap` on lines 16 and 17, respectively)—have been set declaratively.

LISTING 3.4   The TemplateColumn Control Contains Display Properties Nearly Identical
to That of the BoundColumn Control

```
1: <asp:datagrid id="dgTitles" runat="server"
2:    AutoGenerateColumns="False"
3:    Font-Name="Verdana" Width="50%"
4:    HorizontalAlign="Center" ItemStyle-Font-Size="9">
5:
6: <HeaderStyle BackColor="Navy" ForeColor="White"
7:    HorizontalAlign="Center" Font-Bold="True" />
8:
9: <AlternatingItemStyle BackColor="#dddddd" />
10:
11: <Columns>
12:  <asp:BoundColumn DataField="title" HeaderText="Title"
```

LISTING 3.4   Continued

```
13:                ItemStyle-Width="70%" />
14:
15:    <asp:TemplateColumn HeaderText="Sales Performance"
16:        ItemStyle-HorizontalAlign="Right"
17:        ItemStyle-Wrap="False">
18:      <ItemTemplate>
19:        <b><%# DataBinder.Eval(Container.DataItem, "ytd_sales", "{0:#,###}")
➥%></b>
20:        copies sold at
21:        <b><%# DataBinder.Eval(Container.DataItem, "price", "{0:c}") %></b>
22:      </ItemTemplate>
23:    </asp:TemplateColumn>
24:  </Columns>
25: </asp:datagrid>
```

Notice that we set the `ItemStyle.Wrap` property to `False` on line 17. This means that the text in this column will not wrap. Because the overall table width is defined to be 50% of the page (see the `Width` property on line 3), if we shrink the browser or lower the monitor resolution, the second column's text will remain all on one line, and the Title column's text will start wrapping.

Also notice that the `DataBinder.Eval()` method call on lines 19 and 21 uses *three* parameters instead of the two we've seen thus far. The third parameter specifies a format string (which follows the same guidelines and rules as the format string in the `String.Format()` method or the BoundColumn control's `DataFormatString` property. Hence, on lines 19 and 21 the value of the `ytd_sales` and `price` fields are formatted as currency (recall that the c applies a currency format).

Figure 3.4 shows a screenshot of the code in Listing 3.4 when viewed through a browser. Note that the rows that have NULLs for `price` and `ytd_sales` (*The Psychology of Computer Cooking* and *Net Etiquette*) are missing the numeric values for the sales number and sales price, but still have the string "copies sold at" present. Ideally, we don't want this string to display fields that have NULL values for these two database fields; perhaps we'd like to have a message like "Currently no copies of this book have been sold" appear instead. We'll see how to accomplish this later in this chapter, in the section "Customizing Data-Binding Output in Templates."

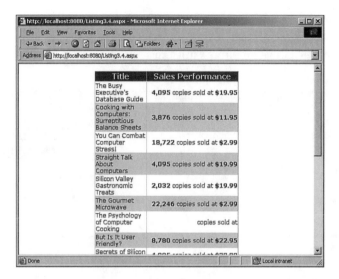

FIGURE 3.4   A TemplateColumn is used to display the sales and price for each book.

Using Developer Tools to Specify Display Properties

Hopefully you've found that specifying display properties for the DataGrid and DataList controls is relatively easy. Unfortunately, for people like myself who are anything but artistic, getting an aesthetically pleasing DataGrid or DataList can still pose a bit of a challenge. I find that while setting the display properties might be easy enough, knowing what colors go well together and what fonts and font settings to use to create eye-pleasing output can be quite a challenge.

If your artistic skills are at all like mine, you'll find developer tools like Visual Studio .NET and the Web Matrix Project to be indispensable.

When creating ASP.NET Web pages with either of these tools, you can enter what is called the Design view, which presents a WYSIWYG view of the ASP.NET Web page called the Designer. From this Design view, you'll be able to drag and drop Web controls that are shown in the toolbox on the left.

After you drag a control onto the Designer you can click on the control, and a list of its properties should appear in the bottom right-hand corner. Figure 3.5 shows a screenshot of an ASP.NET Web page in the Web Matrix Project after a DataGrid has been dragged onto the Designer. You can specify various display properties from the properties window in the bottom right-hand corner.

NOTE

Although the following screenshots show the Web Matrix Project in use, Visual Studio .NET provides an identical user experience when it comes to working with the Designer.

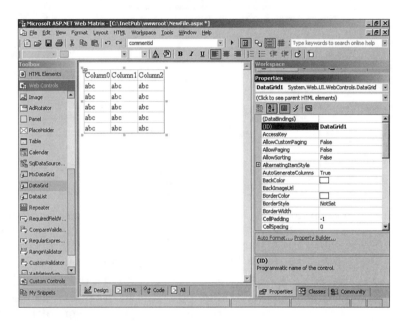

FIGURE 3.5   You can set the DataGrid's display properties through the Properties window.

Although the Properties window is a nice way to quickly set display properties, a real gem for artistically challenged individuals is hidden in the Auto Format link at the bottom of the Properties window. After clicking on the Auto Format link, a dialog box appears with a listing of various style schemes and a preview of the style scheme (see Figure 3.6).

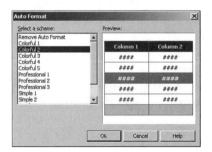

FIGURE 3.6   The Auto Format dialog box allows you to quickly choose a style scheme for your DataGrid or DataList control.

After you have selected a style scheme and clicked the OK button, the Designer is updated to show the new look and feel of the style scheme you have chosen (see Figure 3.7). This also has the effect of updating the DataGrid (or DataList) control, automatically specifying the style properties. For example, Listing 3.5 contains the control markup automatically added to the ASP.NET Web page by simply dragging a DataGrid onto the Designer and opting for the Colorful 5 style scheme.

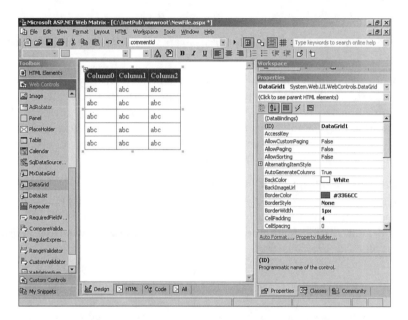

FIGURE 3.7 The DataGrid's style has been updated with the format chosen in Figure 3.6.

LISTING 3.5 The Auto Format Dialog Box Can Automatically Set Display Properties for Your DataGrid

```
1: <asp:DataGrid id="DataGrid1" runat="server" GridLines="None" BorderWidth="1px"
➥BorderColor="Tan" BackColor="LightGoldenrodYellow" CellPadding="2"
➥ForeColor="Black">
2:    <FooterStyle backcolor="Tan"></FooterStyle>
3:    <HeaderStyle font-bold="True" backcolor="Tan"></HeaderStyle>
4:    <PagerStyle horizontalalign="Center" forecolor="DarkSlateBlue"
➥backcolor="PaleGoldenrod"></PagerStyle>
5:    <SelectedItemStyle forecolor="GhostWhite" backcolor="DarkSlateBlue">
➥</SelectedItemStyle>
6:    <AlternatingItemStyle backcolor="PaleGoldenrod"></AlternatingItemStyle>
7: </asp:DataGrid>
```

> **NOTE**
>
> Line 4 in Listing 3.5 contains a `PagerStyle` tag, which sets properties for the `PagerStyle` property of the DataGrid. The `PagerStyle` property, which we've yet to discuss, is an "ItemStyle" property of the DataGrid. It is useful for specifying paging styles for DataGrids that support pagination. We'll be examining this property in more detail in Chapter 8, "Providing DataGrid Pagination."

A Note on How the Display Properties Are Rendered in the Browser

One of the nice things about ASP.NET Web controls is that they are adaptive to the user's browser. By that I mean the HTML markup emitted by an ASP.NET Web page's Web controls is dependent upon the browser being used to view the page. For example, the ASP.NET validation Web controls will emit client-side validation code if the user's browser is deemed to be an *uplevel* browser; if the browser is deemed to be a *downlevel* browser, then no such client-side code is emitted.

An uplevel browser is one that can support client-side JavaScript, HTML version 4.0, the Microsoft Document Object Model, and cascading stylesheets (CSS). You can define what constitutes an uplevel and a downlevel browser in the `machine.config` file; by default, Microsoft Internet Explorer 4.0 and later are considered uplevel, whereas all other browsers are considered downlevel.

> **NOTE**
>
> Uplevel and downlevel status is only based upon the browser being used. That is, a user with Internet Explorer 6.0 would be detected as having an uplevel browser, even if the user has disabled JavaScript support in his browser.

The display properties for the DataGrid and DataList are rendered differently depending upon whether the user visiting the page is using an uplevel or a downlevel browser. If an uplevel browser is being used, the display properties are emitted as CSS. For example, in Listing 3.4, the header's style properties are set on lines 6 and 7. Specifically, the `BackGround` is set to Navy, and the `ForeGround` to White; the text is centered and made bold. When visiting with an uplevel browser, the header for the HTML `table` is rendered as the following:

```
<tr align="Center" style="color:White;background-color:Navy;font-weight:bold;">
    <td>Title</td><td>Sales Performance</td>
</tr>
```

Note that the properties are all set in a `style` attribute of the `tr` tag.

However, if we visit this page with a downlevel browser (*any* browser other than Internet Explorer 4.0 or later), the following HTML is emitted:

```
<tr align="Center" bgcolor="Navy">
    <td><font face="Verdana" color="White"><b>Title</b></font></td>
        <td><font face="Verdana" color="White"><b>Sales Performance</b></font></td>
</tr>
```

Here the display properties are set using HTML instead of CSS.

If you are curious about the rendering differences between an uplevel and downlevel browser, you can do one of two things: view the same page with an uplevel browser (such as Internet Explorer 6.0) and a downlevel browser (such as Opera), comparing the HTML output that each browser receives; or programmatically specify how the controls on the page should be rendered by using the `ClientTarget` attribute in the `@Page` directive.

Using the `ClientTarget` attribute, you can have the controls on an ASP.NET Web page render as if the page were being visited by an uplevel or downlevel browser, independent of the actual browser being used. To specify that the controls should render as if being visited by an uplevel browser, use the following:

```
<%@ Page ClientTarget="uplevel" %>
```

Similarly, to force the controls to render as if they were being visited by a downlevel browser, use this:

```
<%@ Page ClientTarget="downlevel" %>
```

What About the Repeater Control?

The Repeater control does not have any display properties. Rather, to customize the HTML output of the Repeater, you must explicitly specify the HTML markup to use in the Repeater's templates. That is, if you want to have the Repeater output bold text, you have to specifically surround the text with the `bold` tag, or surround the text with a `span` tag whose `style` attribute contains a CSS rule to set the `font-weight` accordingly. (Realize that the DataList and DataGrid's templates can also be customized in this fashion.)

Of course, any time you encapsulate the appearance in HTML markup in a template, you are mixing code and content. Ideally, these two should be kept separate. By setting the appearance of the DataGrid and DataList via the display properties, it is much easier to make changes to the control or template markup later.

For example, imagine that you are using a DataGrid with a couple of TemplateColumns and you want the text in the TemplateColumn to be bold. Although you could simply add

```
<span style="font-weight:bold;">
 Template Markup
</span>
```

it would be cleaner to set the TemplateColumn's `ItemStyle-Font-Bold` property to `True`. If you later needed to change the TemplateColumn's output to italic instead of bold, changing the display property would be simpler than picking through the template markup. (Although it might not be much simpler in this trivial example, imagine that you have a large number of display properties set, and you want to change just one of them. Clearly, making such a change would be simpler using the display properties than if you use a large number of HTML tags to specify the style settings.)

Another advantage of using the display properties is that the HTML emitted is adaptive to the user's browser. If you had used the CSS markup shown previously to make the template's contents bold, a visitor using an older browser that does not support CSS would miss out on the intended visual experience. By using display properties, the correct markup is automatically chosen and sent to the user based upon her browser.

Customizing Data-Binding Output in Templates

Until now, the majority of the examples we've examined that have used data-binding syntax within templates have simply output a particular value from the current item from the `DataSource`. The syntax for this has looked like either

```
<%# Container.DataItem %>
```

or

```
<%# DataBinder.Eval(Container.DataItem, "SomePropertyOrValue") %>
```

depending on the `DataSource`. The former example would be used if the `DataSource` is a string array, and the latter example might be used if the `DataSource` is a DataSet, DataReader, or some other complex object.

If we limit ourselves to such simple data binding, templates are only useful for customizing the look and feel of the data Web control's output, and little else. That is, because data-binding syntax is used only within templates, if the data binding is limited only to re-emitting the `DataSource` values as is, then why would one need to use a template, other than to specify the placement of HTML markup and data?

In this section, we will examine how to customize the values output by data-binding expressions. Before we look at ways to accomplish this, though, it is important that you have a thorough understanding of the type and value of data-binding expressions.

The Type and Value of a Data-Binding Expression

Every expression in any programming language has a type and a value. For example, the expression 4+5 is of type integer and has a value of 9. One of the things a compiler does is determine the type of expressions to ensure type safety. For example, a function that accepts an integer parameter could be called as

```
MyFunction(4+5)
```

because the expression 4+5 has the type integer.

Not surprisingly, data-binding expressions have a type and a value associated with them as well. In Listing 3.2, line 17, the data-binding expression

```
<%# DataBinder.Eval(Container.DataItem, "au_fname") %>
```

has a type of string, because the field au_fname in the authors table is a varchar(20). The value of the data binding expression depends on the value of Container.DataItem, which is constantly changing as the DataSource is being enumerated over. Hence, for the first row produced, the data-binding expression has a value of Johnson; the next row has a value of Marjorie; and so on. (See Figure 3.2 for a screenshot of Listing 3.2.)

When the Type of an Expression Is Known: Compile-Time Versus Runtime

The type of an expression is most commonly known at compile-time. If you have a type error, such as trying to assign a string to an integer, you will get a compile-time error. Being able to detect errors at compile-time has its advantages when it comes to debugging—it's much easier to fix a problem you find when trying to compile the program than it is to fix a problem you can't find until you actually run the program.

Data binding expressions, however, have their type determined at runtime. This is because it would be impossible to determine the type at compile-time, because there's no way the compiler can determine the type structure of the DataSource, let alone the type that the DataBinder.Eval() method will return.

What Type Should Be Returned by a Data-Binding Expression?

Just like other expressions, the type that should be returned by the data-binding syntax depends upon where the data-binding expression is used. If it is used in a template to emit HTML, then a string type should be returned. Because all types support the ToString() method, literally any type can be accepted by a data-binding syntax that is to emit HTML in a template.

NOTE

There are data-binding situations that we've yet to examine in which the data-binding expression needs to be a complex data type.

Determining the Type of a Data-Binding Expression

Determining the type of a data-binding expression is fairly straightforward. Recall that the Container.DataItem has the type of whatever object the DataSource is enumerating over. Hence, if the DataSource is an integer array, the integers are being enumerated over, so the type of Container.DataItem is integer.

For complex objects like the DataSet and DataReader, determining what type of object being enumerated over can be a bit more work. The simplest way, in my opinion, is to just create a simple ASP.NET Web page that uses a DataList with an ItemTemplate. Inside the ItemTemplate, simply place <%# Container.DataItem %> (see Listing 3.6, line 27). When emitted as HTML, the Container.DataItem's ToString() method will be called, which will have the effect of displaying the Container.DataItem's namespace and class name. Listing 3.6 shows a simple DataGrid example that illustrates this point.

LISTING 3.6　To Determine the Type of Container.DataItem, Simply Add <%# Container.DataItem %> to the ItemTemplate

```
 1: <%@ import Namespace="System.Data" %>
 2: <%@ import Namespace="System.Data.SqlClient" %>
 3: <script runat="server" language="VB">
 4:
 5:   Sub Page_Load(sender as Object, e as EventArgs)
 6:     '1. Create a connection
 7:     Const strConnString as String = "server=localhost;uid=sa;pwd=;
➥database=pubs"
 8:     Dim objConn as New SqlConnection(strConnString)
 9:
10:     '2. Create a command object for the query
11:     Const strSQL as String = "SELECT * FROM authors"
12:     Dim objCmd as New SqlCommand(strSQL, objConn)
13:
14:     objConn.Open()   'Open the connection
15:
16:     'Finally, specify the DataSource and call DataBind()
```

LISTING 3.6   Continued

```
17:     dlDataItemTypeTest.DataSource = objCmd.ExecuteReader(CommandBehavior.
➥CloseConnection)
18:     dlDataItemTypeTest.DataBind()
19:
20:     objConn.Close()   'Close the connection
21:   End Sub
22:
23: </script>
24:
25: <asp:datalist id="dlDataItemTypeTest" runat="server">
26:   <ItemTemplate>
27:    <%# Container.DataItem %>
28:   </ItemTemplate>
29: </asp:datalist>
```

Figure 3.8 shows the output of Listing 3.6 when viewed through a browser. Note that the type is `System.Data.Common.DbDataRecord`.

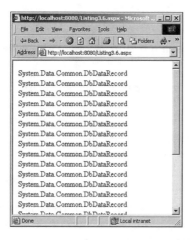

FIGURE 3.8   The type of `Container.DataItem` is displayed on the page.

Building on the type of `Container.DataItem`, we can determine the type returned by `DataBinder.Eval()`. For example, if line 27 in Listing 3.6 was changed to

```
<%# DataBinder.Eval(Container.DataItem, "au_fname") %>
```

the type returned by the data binding expression would be the type of the `au_fname` field represented by the current `DbDataRecord` object. Because `au_fname` is of type varchar(20), the type of `<%# DataBinder.Eval(Container.DataItem, "au_fname") %>` is string.

Using Built-In Methods and Custom Functions in Data-Binding Syntax

At this point, we've examined the type issues involving data-binding syntax, and how to determine the type of a data-binding expression. Furthermore, we discussed what the type of a data-binding expression should be when it is in a template for the purpose of emitting HTML (type string).

Now that you have a solid understanding of typing and the data-binding syntax, we can look at using both built-in methods and custom functions to further enhance the output generated by data-binding expressions.

NOTE

By *built-in methods* I am referring to methods available in the .NET Framework classes, such as `String.Format()` or `Regex.Replace()`; recall that in Chapter 2's Listing 2.5 we saw an example of using the `String.Format()` method call in a data-binding syntax setting (line 17). By *custom functions*, I am referring to functions that you write and include in your ASP.NET page's server-side script block or code-behind class.

A built-in method or custom function can be used in a data-binding expression like so:

```
<%# FunctionName(argument1, argument2, ..., argumentN) %>
```

More likely than not, the argument(s) to the function will involve the `Container.DataItem` object, most likely in a `DataBinder.Eval()` method call. The function *FunctionName* should return a string (the HTML to be emitted) and accept parameters of the appropriate type.

To help clarify things, let's look at a simple example. Imagine that we are displaying sales information about the various books in the pubs database, as we did in Listing 3.4. As you'll recall, Listing 3.4 displayed a list of each book along with the book's year-to-date sales and price. Perhaps we'd like to customize our output so that books that have sold more than 10,000 copies have their sales data highlighted. Listing 3.7 contains the code for an ASP.NET Web page that provides such functionality.

Before you delve into the code in any great detail, first take a look at the screenshot of Listing 3.7, shown in Figure 3.9. Note that those books that have sold more than 10,000 copies have their sales figure highlighted.

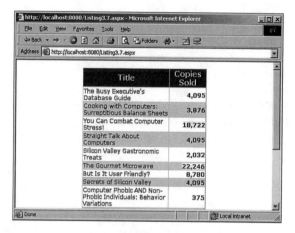

FIGURE 3.9   Books with more than 10,000 sales have their sales figure highlighted.

LISTING 3.7   Books with Sales Greater Than 10,000 Copies Are Highlighted

```
1: <%@ import Namespace="System.Data" %>
2: <%@ import Namespace="System.Data.SqlClient" %>
3: <script runat="server" language="C#">
4:
5:   void Page_Load(Object sender, EventArgs e)
6:   {
7:     // 1. Create a connection
8:     const string strConnString = "server=localhost;uid=sa;pwd=;database=pubs";
9:     SqlConnection objConn = new SqlConnection(strConnString);
10:
11:    // 2. Create a command object for the query
12:    const string strSQL = "SELECT * FROM titles WHERE NOT ytd_sales IS NULL";
13:    SqlCommand objCmd = new SqlCommand(strSQL, objConn);
14:
15:    objConn.Open();  // Open the connection
16:
17:    //F inally, specify the DataSource and call DataBind()
18:    dgTitles.DataSource = objCmd.ExecuteReader(CommandBehavior.
➥CloseConnection);
19:    dgTitles.DataBind();
20:
21:    objConn.Close();  // Close the connection
22:   }
23:
```

LISTING 3.7   Continued

```
24:   string Highlight(int ytdSales)
25:   {
26:    if (ytdSales > 10000)
27:    {
28:     return "<span style=\"background-color:yellow;\">" +
29:         String.Format("{0:#,###}", ytdSales) + "</span>";
30:    }
31:    else
32:     return String.Format("{0:#,###}", ytdSales);
33:   }
34:
35: </script>
36: <asp:datagrid id="dgTitles" runat="server"
37:    AutoGenerateColumns="False"
38:    Font-Name="Verdana" Width="50%"
39:    HorizontalAlign="Center" ItemStyle-Font-Size="9">
40:
41:  <HeaderStyle BackColor="Navy" ForeColor="White"
42:     HorizontalAlign="Center" Font-Bold="True" />
43:
44:  <AlternatingItemStyle BackColor="#dddddd" />
45:
46:  <Columns>
47:   <asp:BoundColumn DataField="title" HeaderText="Title"
48:          ItemStyle-Width="70%" />
49:
50:   <asp:TemplateColumn HeaderText="Copies Sold"
51:      ItemStyle-HorizontalAlign="Right"
52:      ItemStyle-Wrap="False">
53:    <ItemTemplate>
54:     <b><%# Highlight((int) DataBinder.Eval(Container.DataItem,
➥"ytd_sales")) %></b>
55:    </ItemTemplate>
56:   </asp:TemplateColumn>
57:  </Columns>
58: </asp:datagrid>
```

In examining the code in Listing 3.7, first note that the SQL string (line 12) has a WHERE clause that retrieves only books whose ytd_sales field is not NULL. The titles database table is set up so that the ytd_sales field allows NULL, representing a book with no sales. Because accepting NULLs slightly complicates our custom function, I've decided to omit books whose ytd_sales field contains NULLs—we'll look at how to handle NULLs shortly.

Next, take a look at the Highlight() function (lines 24—33). The function is rather simple, taking in a single parameter (an int) and returning a string. The function simply checks whether the input parameter, ytdSales, is greater than 10,000—if it is, a string is returned that contains a span HTML tag with its background-color style attribute set to yellow; the value of ytdSales, formatted using String.Format() to include commas every three digits; and a closing span tag (lines 28 and 29). If ytdSales is not greater than 10,000, the value of ytdSales is returned, formatted to contain commas every three digits (line 22).

Finally, check out the ItemTemplate (line 54) in the TemplateColumn control. Here we call the Highlight() function, passing in a single argument: DataBinder. Eval(Container.DataItem, "ytd_sales"). At first glance, you might think that the type returned by DataBinder.Eval() here is type integer, because ytd_sales is an integer field in the pubs database. This is only half-correct. While the DataBinder. Eval() call is returning an integer, the compiler is expecting a return value of type Object. (Realize that all types are derived from the base Object type.) Because C# is type-strict, we must cast the return value of the DataBinder.Eval() method to an int, which is the data type expected by the Highlight() function. (Note that if you are using Visual Basic .NET, you do not need to provide such casting unless you specify strict casting via the Strict="True" attribute in the @Page directive; for more information on type strictness, see the resources in the "On the Web" section.)

Handling NULL Database Values
The custom function in Listing 3.7 accepts an integer as its input parameter. If the database field being passed into the custom function can return a NULL (type DBNull), then a runtime error can result when a NULL value is attempted to be cast into an int.

NOTE

NULL values in database systems represent unknown data. For example, imagine that you had a database table of employees, and one of the table fields was BirthDate, which stored the employee's date of birth. If for some reason you did not have the date of birth information for a particular employee, you could store the value NULL for that employee's BirthDate field. It is important to note that NULL values should not be used to represent zero, since any expression involving a NULL field results in a NULL value.

To handle NULLs, we'll adjust the Highlight() function to accept inputs of type Object, thus allowing *any* class to be passed in (because all classes are derived, directly or indirectly, from the Object class). Then, in the Highlight() function we'll check to see whether the passed-in value is indeed a NULL. If it is, we can output some message like, "No sales yet reported." If it is not NULL, we'll simply cast it to an int and use the code we already have to determine whether it should be highlighted. Listing 3.8 contains the changes needed for Listing 3.7 to accept NULLs:

LISTING 3.8   The Highlight Function Has Been Adjusted to Accept NULLs

```
 1: <%@ Page Language="c#" %>
 2: <%@ import Namespace="System.Data" %>
 3: <%@ import Namespace="System.Data.SqlClient" %>
 4: <script runat="server">
 5:
 6:   void Page_Load(Object sender, EventArgs e)
 7:   {
 8:     // 1. Create a connection
 9:     const string strConnString = "server=localhost;uid=sa;pwd=;database=pubs";
10:     SqlConnection objConn = new SqlConnection(strConnString);
11:
12:     // 2. Create a command object for the query
13:     const string strSQL = "SELECT * FROM titles";
14:     SqlCommand objCmd = new SqlCommand(strSQL, objConn);
15:
16:     objConn.Open();  // Open the connection
17:
18:     //F inally, specify the DataSource and call DataBind()
19:     dgTitles.DataSource = objCmd.ExecuteReader(CommandBehavior.
➥CloseConnection);
20:     dgTitles.DataBind();
21:
22:     objConn.Close();  // Close the connection
23:   }
24:
25:   string Highlight(object ytdSales)
26:   {
27:     if (ytdSales.Equals(DBNull.Value))
28:     {
29:       return "<i>No sales yet reported...</i>";
30:     }
31:     else
32:     {
33:       if (((int) ytdSales) > 10000)
34:       {
35:         return "<span style=\"background-color:yellow;\">" +
```

LISTING 3.8   Continued

```
36:            String.Format("{0:#,###}", ytdSales) + "</span>";
37:       }
38:     else
39:     {
40:       return String.Format("{0:#,###}", ytdSales);
41:       }
42:     }
43:   }
44:
45: </script>
46:
47: <asp:datagrid id="dgTitles" runat="server"
48:
49:   ... some DataGrid markup removed for brevity ...
50:
51:   <asp:TemplateColumn HeaderText="Copies Sold"
52:     ItemStyle-HorizontalAlign="Right"
53:     ItemStyle-Wrap="False">
54:    <ItemTemplate>
55:     <b><%# Highlight(DataBinder.Eval(Container.DataItem, "ytd_sales")) %></b>
56:    </ItemTemplate>
57:   </asp:TemplateColumn>
58:  </Columns>
59: </asp:datagrid>
```

Listing 3.8 contains a few changes. The two subtle changes occur on lines 13 and 55. On line 13, the SQL query is altered so that *all* rows from the titles table are returned, not just those that are not NULL. On line 55, the cast to int was removed, because the DataBinder.Eval() function might return NULLs as well as integers.

The more dramatic change occurs in the Highlight function (lines 25–43). In Listing 3.8, Highlight() accepts an input parameter of type Object; this allows for any type to be passed into the function (of course, we only expect types of integers or DBNull to be passed in). On line 27, a check is made to determine whether the ytdSales parameter is of type DBNull (the DBNull.Value property is a static property of the DBNull class that returns an instance of the DBNull class—the Equals method determines whether two objects are equal). If ytdSales represents a NULL database value, the string "No sales yet reported" is returned on line 29. Otherwise, ytdSales is cast to an int and checked to see whether it is greater than 10,000. The remaining lines of Highlight() are identical to the code from Highlight in Listing 3.7.

Figure 3.10 shows a screenshot from the code in Listing 3.8. Note that those rows that have NULL values for their ytd_sales field have No sales yet reported... listed under the Copies Sold column.

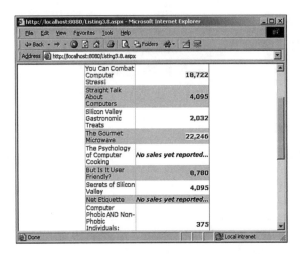

FIGURE 3.10   Database columns that have a NULL value have a helpful message displayed.

A Closing Word on Using Custom Functions in Templates

As we have seen, using customized functions in a data-binding setting allows for the data-bound output to be altered based upon the value of the data itself. For example, if you were displaying profit and loss information in a data Web control, you might opt to use such custom functions to have negative profits appear in red.

The last two examples showed the use of simple custom functions that accept one parameter. Of course, there is no reason why you couldn't pass in more than one parameter. Perhaps you want to pass in two database field values and then output something based on the two values.

Another neat thing you can do with these custom functions is add information to your data Web controls that might not exist in the database. For example, from the titles table, we have both a ytd_sales field and a price field. Imagine that we want to display the book's total revenues—this would be simply the sales multiplied by the price.

Listing 3.9 shows a quick example of how to accomplish this. Essentially, all we have to do is pass both the ytd_sales and price fields to our custom function, multiply them, and then return the value.

LISTING 3.9   Custom Functions Can Include Multiple Input Parameters

```
 1: <%@ import Namespace="System.Data" %>
 2: <%@ import Namespace="System.Data.SqlClient" %>
 3: <script runat="server" language="VB">
 4:
 5:    Sub Page_Load(sender as Object, e as EventArgs)
 6:      '1. Create a connection
 7:      Const strConnString as String = "server=localhost;uid=sa;pwd=;
➥database=pubs"
 8:      Dim objConn as New SqlConnection(strConnString)
 9:
10:      '2. Create a command object for the query
11:      Const strSQL as String = "SELECT * FROM titles WHERE NOT ytd_sales IS NULL"
12:      Dim objCmd as New SqlCommand(strSQL, objConn)
13:
14:      objConn.Open()  'Open the connection
15:
16:      'Finally, specify the DataSource and call DataBind()
17:      dgTitles.DataSource = objCmd.ExecuteReader(CommandBehavior.CloseConnection)
18:      dgTitles.DataBind()
19:
20:      objConn.Close()   'Close the connection
21:    End Sub
22:
23:
24:    Function CalcRevenues(sales as Integer, price as Single)
25:      Return String.Format("{0:c}", sales * price)
26:    End Function
27:
28: </script>
29: <asp:datagrid id="dgTitles" runat="server"
30:
31:  ... some DataGrid markup removed for brevity ...
32:
33:    <asp:TemplateColumn HeaderText="Revenues"
34:       ItemStyle-HorizontalAlign="Right"
35:       ItemStyle-Wrap="False">
36:     <ItemTemplate>
37:        <b><%# CalcRevenues(DataBinder.Eval(Container.DataItem, "ytd_sales"),
➥DataBinder.Eval(Container.DataItem, "price")) %></b>
38:     </ItemTemplate>
39:    </asp:TemplateColumn>
40:   </Columns>
41: </asp:datagrid>
```

Note that here, as with Listing 3.7, our SQL query only grabs those rows whose ytd_sales field is not NULL (line 11). My motivation behind this was to keep the CalcRevenues() custom function as clean as possible; you are encouraged to adjust the code in Listing 3.9 to allow for NULLs.

The custom function, CalcRevenues(), calculates the total revenues for each book. It accepts two input parameters (sales and price, an integer and single, respectively), and then multiplies them, using the String.Format() method to format the result into a currency. The string returned by the String.Format() method is then returned as the data-binding expression's value and is emitted as HTML.

Line 37 contains the call to CalcRevenues() in the data-binding syntax. Note that two database values are passed into CalcRevenues()—the ytd_sales field value and the price field value.

Figure 3.11 contains a screenshot of the code in Listing 3.9 when viewed through a browser.

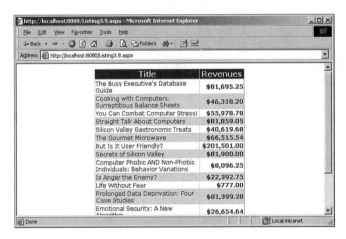

FIGURE 3.11   The total revenue for each book is shown.

In closing, realize that the amount of customization you can do using the data-binding syntax is virtually limitless.

Summary

In this chapter, we examined how to improve the appearance of the DataGrid and DataList Web controls though the use of display properties. These properties can be applied at the table level, the row level, and the column level, allowing developers to create aesthetically pleasing DataGrids and DataLists without requiring extensive HTML and CSS markup.

Additionally, we saw how tools like Visual Studio .NET and the Web Matrix Project can be used to automatically provide style schemes. For those of us who are artistically challenged, the Auto Formatting features are a godsend.

This chapter concluded with an examination of customizing the data-binding output in templates. We saw how to supply dynamic data as parameters to built-in and custom functions, which could then tweak the data and produce customized output. The capability to provide custom functions to alter the data-bound output at runtime is a powerful technique that we will take advantage of many times throughout the remainder of this book.

This chapter concludes Part I. By this point, you should be comfortable using the data Web controls, binding a variety of types of data to the controls, and making the controls visually appealing. In Part II, we'll examine how to associate actions with the data Web controls!

On the Web

For more information on the topics discussed in this chapter, consider perusing the following online resources:

- Formatting Overview—`http://msdn.microsoft.com/library/ default.asp?url=/library/en-us/cpguide/html/ cpconformattingoverview.asp`

- The `<clientTarget>` Element (used for determining uplevel and downlevel browsers)—`http://msdn.microsoft.com/library/ default.asp?url=/library/en-us/cpgenref/html/ gngrfclienttargetelement.asp`

- "Formatting the DataGrid with the ASP.NET Web Matrix Project"— `http://www.asp.net/webmatrix/tour/section4/formatdatagrid.aspx`

- "Highlighting Search Keywords in a DataGrid"—`http://aspnet.4guysfrom- rolla.com/articles/072402-1.aspx`

- "Strict Typing in VB.NET"—`http://msdn.microsoft.com/vstudio/ techinfo/articles/developerproductivity/language.asp#type`

PART II

In Part I we examined the basics of the data Web controls. Specifically, we began with a high-level introduction to the data Web controls, followed by a thorough examination of binding data to these controls. Part I concluded with an examination of how to customize the HTML output of the data Web controls to achieve a more aesthetically pleasing result.

Part I showed how the data Web controls could be used to easily and quickly display structured data. Although the data Web controls do an outstanding job displaying data, they are capable of much more, as we will see in the remainder of this book!

In Part II, we will look at how to associate actions with a data Web control. In Chapter 4, "Adding Buttons and HyperLinks to the DataGrid Web Control," we'll look at how to add Button and HyperLink columns— two Column types mentioned in the first chapter—to the DataGrid. The generic Button column is useful for associating some kind of action with each row in a DataGrid. The HyperLink column can be used to provide a simple data-bound hyperlink for each row. For example, you could use a DataGrid to display a list of products your company sells, with each row in the DataGrid having a link that takes the user to a "Details" page featuring extensive information about a particular product.

In Chapter 5, "Adding Command Buttons to the Data Web Controls," we'll cover how to create special types of controls in templates that trigger a specific event when clicked. With these controls you can provide, among other things, simple update and delete capabilities. Specifically, we'll examine how to provide such functionality in a DataList control.

In Chapter 6, "Using External Web Controls to Achieve Effects on the Web Control," we'll examine how Web controls not directly associated with the data Web control have an effect on the data Web control. For example, you might have a DataList that displays all of your company's products, but you would like to allow the user to filter the results so that she only sees products of a certain category. To accomplish this, you can present the user with a RadioButtonList containing one radio button for each product category. When the user selects a specific category from the list, the page is posted back and the DataList only shows those products that have the specified category.

By the end of Part II you should be comfortable associating simple actions with the data Web controls. This understanding is essential for Part III, in which we'll examine a number of the advanced features of the DataGrid control, including sorting, paging, and editing.

4

Adding Buttons and Hyperlinks to the DataGrid Web Control

By this point, you should be comfortable using the data Web controls to display data from various sources. If you still feel a bit lost when it comes to displaying data through a data Web control, I'd strongly encourage you to reread the first three chapters and to take the time to read the resources in the "On the Web" sections accompanying each chapter. A great place to start online is the "An Extensive Examination of the DataGrid Web Control" article series, which can be found at http://aspnet. 4guysfromrolla.com/articles/040502-1.aspx.

Now that you're comfortable using the data Web controls for displaying data, we'll spend the next few chapters examining how to change the data Web controls in response to a user's actions. For example, in this chapter we'll see how to add buttons to a DataGrid that fire some server-side code.

As this and the next few chapters will show, the data Web controls can do much more than simply display data. As we look at various ways to make the data Web controls more interactive, note how little code is needed. If you have ever had to provide similar functionality in a classic ASP page, you will be amazed at the overall reduction of code and the much improved separation of code and content that the ASP.NET data Web controls provide.

A Quick Review of the DataGrid Column Controls

As we saw in Chapter 1, there are two ways to specify the columns that should appear in the DataGrid:

1. Implicitly, by setting the AutoGenerateColumns property to True (the default). This will create a DataGrid with a column for each field in the DataSource.

2. Explicitly, by setting the AutoGenerateColumns property to False and specifying the columns that should appear under the Columns tag.

Although the first method is clearly a much easier and quicker way to display data in a DataGrid, the second method allows for much more flexibility, because you can specify the ordering of the columns and formatting information like horizontal alignment, font settings, and colors (as we saw in Chapter 3, "Customizing the HTML Output").

Recall that when explicitly specifying the columns that should be displayed in the DataGrid Web control, we used the BoundColumn control to indicate that the column should display the value of a particular field in the DataSource. There are other types of columns that can be added to the DataGrid, though. For example, the ButtonColumn, which we'll be examining shortly, displays a button in each row. The five built-in DataGrid column types can be seen in Table 4.1.

TABLE 4.1   There Are Five Different Built-in DataGrid Column Types

Column Type	Description
BoundColumn	Displays a column bound to a field in the DataSource.
ButtonColumn	Displays a button for each row in the column.
EditCommandColumn	Displays a column that contains Edit, Update, and Cancel buttons useful for editing.
HyperLinkColumn	Displays a hyperlink in each row of the column. The URL and/or text of the hyperlink can be bound to fields in the DataSource.
TemplateColumn	Displays the cell's contents as specified by a provided template.

In Chapter 3 we examined the use of the TemplateColumn column control. In this chapter we will look at ButtonColumn and HyperLinkColumn controls in detail. We will not be discussing the EditCommandColumn control until Chapter 9, "Editing the DataGrid Web Control."

If none of the built-in column controls meet the functionality you need, you can always write your own DataGrid column control. We'll examine how to do this in Chapter 12, "Creating Custom Column Controls for the DataGrid."

Before we delve into using the ButtonColumn control, let's take a quick moment to review the syntax for explicitly specifying columns in a DataGrid Web control.

Listing 4.1 contains the DataGrid declaration section from Listing 3.4. Note that to explicitly specify the DataGrid's column layout, you need to do two things: first, ensure that the AutoGenerateColumns property is set to False (if you forget to do this, *all* the DataSource's fields will be displayed along with the columns you explicitly indicate to be displayed); second, using the Columns tag, explicitly specify those columns that should appear in the DataGrid.

When specifying the columns to be displayed, you can choose from any of the column types listed in Table 4.1. Listing 4.1 shows a BoundColumn being used to display the title database field (lines 12 and 13), and a TemplateColumn used to display the ytd_sales and price fields (lines 19 and 21, respectively).

LISTING 4.1   A DataGrid's Column Layout Can Be Specified Explicitly

```
 1: <asp:datagrid id="dgTitles" runat="server"
 2:    AutoGenerateColumns="False"
 3:    Font-Name="Verdana" Width="50%"
 4:    HorizontalAlign="Center" ItemStyle-Font-Size="9">
 5:
 6:  <HeaderStyle BackColor="Navy" ForeColor="White"
 7:     HorizontalAlign="Center" Font-Bold="True" />
 8:
 9:  <AlternatingItemStyle BackColor="#dddddd" />
10:
11:  <Columns>
12:   <asp:BoundColumn DataField="title" HeaderText="Title"
13:          ItemStyle-Width="70%" />
14:
15:   <asp:TemplateColumn HeaderText="Sales Performance"
16:      ItemStyle-HorizontalAlign="Right"
17:      ItemStyle-Wrap="False">
18:    <ItemTemplate>
19:     <b><%# DataBinder.Eval(Container.DataItem, "ytd_sales", "{0:#,###}
➥") %></b>
20:      copies sold at
21:     <b><%# DataBinder.Eval(Container.DataItem, "price", "{0:c}") %></b>
22:    </ItemTemplate>
23:   </asp:TemplateColumn>
24:  </Columns>
25: </asp:datagrid>
```

Along with specifying the DataGrid columns that should appear, the code in Listing 4.1 also includes a number of stylistic settings, such as the AlternatingItemStyle setting (line 9), as well as various DataGrid display properties (lines 3 and 4). For more information on these display properties, refer back to Chapter 3. Figure 4.1 shows a screenshot of Listing 4.1 when viewed through a browser.

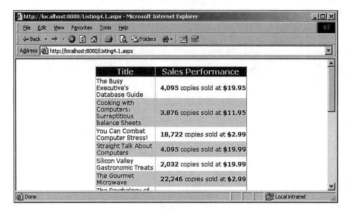

FIGURE 4.1   The columns displayed in the DataGrid are those that have been explicitly specified.

Adding Button Columns to the DataGrid Web Control

The ButtonColumn class, as its name implies, adds a column to the DataGrid that contains a button in each row. To add a ButtonColumn to a DataGrid, simply add an `<asp:ButtonColumn ... />` tag to the Columns tag in the DataGrid.

For example, imagine that we want to use a DataGrid to list the various books in the `titles` database table. We'd like to present a button along with each book that adds the specified book to the user's shopping cart. To accomplish this, the first thing we need to do is add a ButtonColumn to our DataGrid. Listing 4.2 shows a DataGrid that contains a BoundColumn for the title of the book (line 39), and a ButtonColumn titled "Add to Cart" (line 38).

LISTING 4.2   Adding a ButtonColumn Includes a Button on Each Row in the DataGrid

```
1: <%@ import Namespace="System.Data" %>
2: <%@ import Namespace="System.Data.SqlClient" %>
3: <script runat="server" language="VB">
4:
5:   Sub Page_Load(sender as Object, e as EventArgs)
6:     If Not Page.IsPostBack then
7:       '1. Create a connection
```

LISTING 4.2   Continued

```
 8:     Const strConnString as String = "server=localhost;uid=sa;pwd=;
➥database=pubs"
 9:     Dim objConn as New SqlConnection(strConnString)
10:
11:     '2. Create a command object for the query
12:     Const strSQL as String = "SELECT * FROM titles"
13:     Dim objCmd as New SqlCommand(strSQL, objConn)
14:
15:     objConn.Open()   'Open the connection
16:
17:     'Finally, specify the DataSource and call DataBind()
18:     dgTitles.DataSource = objCmd.ExecuteReader(CommandBehavior.
➥CloseConnection)
19:     dgTitles.DataBind()
20:
21:     objConn.Close()   'Close the connection
22:    End If
23:   End Sub
24:
25: </script>
26: <form runat="server">
27:  <asp:datagrid id="dgTitles" runat="server"
28:    AutoGenerateColumns="False"
29:    Font-Name="Verdana" Width="50%"
30:    HorizontalAlign="Center" ItemStyle-Font-Size="9">
31:
32:   <HeaderStyle BackColor="Navy" ForeColor="White"
33:      HorizontalAlign="Center" Font-Bold="True" />
34:
35:   <AlternatingItemStyle BackColor="#dddddd" />
36:
37:   <Columns>
38:    <asp:ButtonColumn Text="Add to Cart" />
39:    <asp:BoundColumn DataField="title" HeaderText="Title" />
40:   </Columns>
41:  </asp:datagrid>
42: </form>
```

Before we examine the code in detail, first take a moment to examine Figure 4.2, which is a screenshot of Listing 4.2 when viewed through a browser.

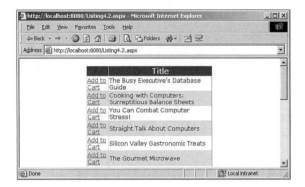

FIGURE 4.2   The ButtonColumn adds a button to each row.

Note that each button is rendered as a hyperlink (see Figure 4.2). This is the default behavior, but you can specify that the ButtonColumn control render its buttons as actual HTML push buttons by setting the ButtonType property of the ButtonColumn control to PushButton. That is, you could alter line 38 as follows:

```
<asp:ButtonColumn Text="Add to Cart" ButtonType="PushButton" />
```

Realize that the ButtonType property is purely an aesthetic property—regardless of whether you set ButtonType to LinkButton (the default) or PushButton, the semantics of the ButtonColumn will be the same.

Did you notice the Web form in use in Listing 4.2, starting on line 26 with the <form runat="server"> and ending on line 42 with </form>? When using a ButtonColumn within a DataGrid, you must have the DataGrid inside a Web form (also referred to as a "server-side form"). If you fail to do this, your ASP.NET Web page will generate an error when viewed through a browser.

Finally, note that the code in the Page_Load event that retrieves the database information and binds it to the DataGrid is inside an If statement, and is only executed if the page is not being posted back (lines 6 through 22).

Realize that the Web form that surrounds the DataGrid (lines 26–42) is rendered as a standard HTML form whose action parameter is set to the current page's URL. Such a form is called a *postback* form, because when the form is submitted it posts back to the current page, as opposed to some other Web page.

When the button or hyperlink generated by one of the ButtonColumns is clicked, the Web form is submitted, thereby causing a postback to occur. However, because the Page_Load event handler contains an If statement checking to see whether a postback has occurred (line 6), the DataGrid's DataSource will not be set and the DataBind() method will not be called on the postback.

Initially you might think that this approach would cause the DataGrid to "disappear" upon postback, because on a postback the DataGrid's DataSource is not set and its DataBind() method is not called. However, this is an incorrect assumption. By placing the DataGrid inside of a Web form the contents of the DataGrid are saved to the ASP.NET page's ViewState.

NOTE

The ViewState is a property that all ASP.NET controls have; it is an accumulation of the all the control's property values, and is used to maintain state across postbacks. For more information on the life cycle of ASP.NET Web controls and how information is persisted to the ViewState, be sure to peruse the links in the "On the Web" section at the end of this chapter.

Because the contents of the DataGrid were saved in the ViewState, when the Web page is posted back the contents of the DataGrid can be automatically reconstructed without needing to set the DataSource and call the DataBind() method. This approach has both advantages and disadvantages.

The main disadvantage is that the data in your DataGrid can become stale. Because the DataBind() method is only being called on the first visit to the page and *not* on subsequent postbacks, if the user makes a number of postbacks, he'll still be viewing the data from when he first visited the page no matter how many times he submits the page. For example, imagine that you have a DataGrid that lists a number of stocks and their current details. These details might include the current bid and ask prices, the stock's daily volume, and so on. Now, imagine that there is a ButtonColumn that has a "Buy This Stock" button next to each stock and its details that causes a postback, running some code that automatically buys the stock for the user and then redisplaying the list of stocks and their details. If you set the DataSource and call the DataBind() method for the DataGrid only on the first visit to the page, the stock details the user will see upon subsequent postbacks will be the stock's details when he first visited the page. Instead, if you reset the DataSource and recall the DataBind method every time the page is posted back, the stock details will be updated to reflect the current information with each purchase.

Although this disadvantage might seem paramount, it is really only a concern for sites working with rapidly changing data. Using a DataGrid to display such data might not be suitable for these sites. Fortunately, the majority of data-driven Web sites use data that changes rather infrequently.

Where the data is relatively stable, there is a performance advantage to not resetting the DataSource and not recalling the DataGrid's DataBind() method on every postback. Chances are the code needed to populate the DataSource, which usually involves database calls or reading XML files, is the slowest component of your ASP.NET Web page. By omitting these calls on each postback, you can expect a small performance gain. (Of course, the gain you'll see depends on how expensive your call is to populate your DataSource.)

The biggest advantage to using the ViewState to store the DataGrid's contents as opposed to simply resetting the DataSource and recalling the DataBind() method is that the state of the DataGrid is maintained. We've yet to explore any examples where the DataGrid's state has come into play, but there are plenty of examples that we'll be investigating in future chapters. For example, in Chapter 8, "Paging the DataGrid Results," we'll see how to add pagination support to the DataGrid. When the user steps from one page to the next, the Web form is posted back. The DataGrid's state, in this scenario, includes what "page" of data is currently being displayed. If the DataSource is reset and the DataBind() method recalled on every postback, this state is lost between postbacks.

Because of these advantages, especially the latter one, it will be increasingly important to place the code that sets the DataGrid's DataSource property and calls its DataBind() method inside an If Not Page.IsPostBack then ... End If block. In fact, in future code examples (starting with Listing 4.3), we will be moving the code that performs these tasks from the Page_Load event handler into a separate function, BindData. This function will then be called from the Page_Load event handler only on the first visit to the page. That is, our code will look like this:

```
Sub Page_Load(sender as Object, e as EventArgs)
 If Not Page.IsPostBack then
  'Call the Sub to handle our DataGrid's data binding
  BindData()
 End If
End Sub

Sub BindData()
 ' Populate a DataSet or DataReader...
 ' Set the DataGrid's DataSource property accordingly...
 ' Call the DataGrid's DataBind() method...
End Sub
```

Using a separate function to handle the DataGrid data binding will prove to be especially useful when we reach Part III, "Advanced Features of the DataGrid Web Control," in which we'll be examining how to page, sort, and edit the DataGrid's data.

You might be wondering when to reset the DataGrid's DataSource property and recall its DataBind() method on postbacks and when *not* to do this. A general rule of thumb is that if the DataGrid is in a Web form and you have any controls on the page that will be posting back (such as ButtonColumns in the DataGrid or generic

Buttons somewhere within the Web form), you should only set the `DataSource` property and call the `DataBind()` method on the first page load, and not on the postbacks.

Responding to a User Clicking a ButtonColumn

Recall that when a button or hyperlink generated by a ButtonColumn control is clicked, the Web form is submitted, causing a postback to the ASP.NET Web page. When the postback occurs, the DataGrid control's `ItemCommand` event is fired. Hence, to have server-side code execute when a ButtonColumn is clicked, you simply need to add an event handler for the DataGrid's `ItemCommand` event.

The event handler for the DataGrid's `ItemCommand` event must have the following definition:

```
' In VB.NET
Public Sub EventHandlerName(sender as Object, e as DataGridCommandEventArgs)

// In C#
public void EventHandlerName(object sender, DataGridCommandEventArgs e)
```

In addition to providing an event handler, you must specify that the DataGrid's `ItemCommand` should be handled by your event handler. To accomplish this, simply add `OnItemCommand="EventHandlerName"` to the DataGrid declaration, as seen in Listing 4.3.

CAUTION

Imagine that you have set up your DataGrid with a ButtonColumn button and have written an `ItemCommand` event handler that performs some action. In testing the ASP.NET page, you first load it into your browser with no errors reported. Next, you click on one of the buttons—the page is posted back, but the action you expected when the ButtonColumn button was clicked fails to happen. Argh!

You might find yourself in this situation, banging your head against the wall for hours trying to figure out what's wrong. Be sure to take a moment to ensure that the `ItemCommand` event handler is wired up to the DataGrid's `ItemCommand` event! If you leave out `OnItemCommand="EventHandlerName"` from the DataGrid's declaration, the `ItemCommand` event handler won't fire, so your ButtonColumn buttons or hyperlinks will seem lifeless, never performing the actions you expect.

Let's take a moment to create a simple event handler, wiring it up to the DataGrid's `ItemCommand` event. Building on the code from Listing 4.2, we simply need to add an event handler in the server-side script block (or add it to the code-behind class, if you're using the code-behind technique) and specify in the DataGrid declaration that when the ItemCommand event is fired, the appropriate event handler should be called. Listing 4.3 contains these needed additions.

LISTING 4.3   The DataGrid's ItemCommand Event Fires When the User Clicks the ButtonColumn

```
 1: <%@ import Namespace="System.Data" %>
 2: <%@ import Namespace="System.Data.SqlClient" %>
 3: <script runat="server">
 4:
 5:   Sub Page_Load(sender as Object, e as EventArgs)
 6:     If Not Page.IsPostBack then
 7:       BindData()
 8:     End If
 9:   End Sub
10:
11:
12:   Sub BindData()
13:     '1. Create a connection
14:     Const strConnString as String = "server=localhost;uid=sa;pwd=;
➥database=pubs"
15:     Dim objConn as New SqlConnection(strConnString)
16:
17:     '2. Create a command object for the query
18:     Const strSQL as String = "SELECT * FROM titles"
19:     Dim objCmd as New SqlCommand(strSQL, objConn)
20:
21:     objConn.Open()  'Open the connection
22:
23:     'Finally, specify the DataSource and call DataBind()
24:     dgTitles.DataSource = objCmd.ExecuteReader(CommandBehavior.CloseConnection)
25:     dgTitles.DataBind()
26:
27:     objConn.Close()  'Close the connection
28:   End Sub
29:
30:
31:   Sub dgTitles_ItemCommand(sender as Object, e as DataGridCommandEventArgs)
32:     Response.Write("A ButtonColumn has been clicked!")
33:   End Sub
34:
```

LISTING 4.3   Continued

```
35: </script>
36:
37: <form runat="server">
38:  <asp:datagrid id="dgTitles" runat="server"
39:    AutoGenerateColumns="False"
40:    Font-Name="Verdana" Width="50%"
41:    HorizontalAlign="Center" ItemStyle-Font-Size="9"
42:    OnItemCommand="dgTitles_ItemCommand">
43:
44:    <HeaderStyle BackColor="Navy" ForeColor="White"
45:      HorizontalAlign="Center" Font-Bold="True" />
46:
47:    <AlternatingItemStyle BackColor="#dddddd" />
48:
49:    <Columns>
50:     <asp:ButtonColumn Text="Add to Cart" />
51:     <asp:BoundColumn DataField="title" HeaderText="Title" />
52:    </Columns>
53:  </asp:datagrid>
54: </form>
```

First note that we moved the code that sets the DataGrid's DataSource property and calls its DataBind() method from the Page_Load event handler (lines 5 through 9) into a separate function, BindData() (lines 12 through 28). Future code examples will use this style to separate the DataGrid data binding from the Page_Load event handler.

Next take a moment to examine the dgTitles_ItemCommand event handler spanning lines 31 to 33. This very simple event handler merely uses the Response.Write method to output "A ButtonColumn has been clicked!" On line 42 we tie this event handler to the DataGrid's ItemCommand event by simply adding OnItemCommand="dgTitles_ItemCommand" to the DataGrid's declaration. With these two additions—the event handler and wiring up the event handler to the DataGrid's ItemCommand event handler—we now have an action occur when a ButtonColumn is clicked. Figure 4.3 depicts a screenshot after one of the ButtonColumn hyperlinks has been clicked.

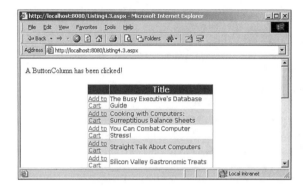

FIGURE 4.3   The message "A ButtonColumn has been clicked!" is displayed.

Determining What ButtonColumn Row Has Been Clicked

Because a ButtonColumn adds a hyperlink or button to each row in the DataGrid, it is natural to associate the ButtonColumn in a particular row with the data displayed in the same row. For example, in Figure 4.3 the user is presented with a list of books with a "Add to Cart" hyperlink next to each title. Clearly, the user will assume that clicking the Add to Cart hyperlink next to the *The Busy Executive's Database Guide* title will add that book to their shopping cart.

Recall that when *any* ButtonColumn button or hyperlink is clicked, the DataGrid's ItemCommand event is fired. Of course, we will have as many ButtonColumn buttons or hyperlinks as there are rows in the DataGrid, so it's important to be able to determine which of the ButtonColumns was indeed clicked.

As we saw in Chapter 2, "Binding Data to the Data Controls," each row of the DataGrid is represented by a DataGridItem instance. When a ButtonColumn button or hyperlink is clicked, the DataGridItem that contains the clicked button or hyperlink is passed to the ItemCommand event handler as the Item property of the DataGridCommandEventArgs parameter.

The following is the DataGrid's ItemCommand event handler from Listing 4.3 (lines 31–33):

```
Sub dgTitles_ItemCommand(sender as Object, e as DataGridCommandEventArgs)
  Response.Write("A ButtonColumn has been clicked!")
End Sub
```

Note that the second parameter to the event handler is of type DataGridCommandEventArgs, and has been named e. Hence, we can programmatically access the DataGridItem that contains the ButtonColumn that was clicked by using e.Item.

The `DataGridItem` class contains a number of properties that describe the contents and appearance of the row in the DataGrid. There are a number of display properties, such as `BackColor`, `BorderColor`, `HorizontalAlign`, `VerticalAlign`, and `Width`. The property you'll find yourself using most often is the `Cells` property, which is a collection of `TableCell` objects. Each `TableCell` object represents a column in the particular row represented by the `DataGridItem`.

Returning to our book example from Listing 4.3, we can amend our event handler (`dgTitles_ItemCommand`) to emit the title of the book whose ButtonColumn hyperlink was clicked, changing the event handler in Listing 4.3 to the event handler shown in Listing 4.4:

LISTING 4.4   The Event Handler Now Displays the Title of the Book Whose ButtonColumn Hyperlink Was Clicked

```
1: Sub dgTitles_ItemCommand(sender as Object, e as DataGridCommandEventArgs)
2:  Dim strTitle as String
3:  strTitle = e.Item.Cells(1).Text
4:  Response.Write("Adding <i>" & strTitle & "</i> to your shopping cart")
5: End Sub
```

To determine the book's title, we referenced the second item in the `Cells` collection, which represents the second column in the DataGrid (line 3). (Because all collections in .NET are zero-based, `Cells(1)` returns the second `TableCell`, not the first.) The reason we accessed the second DataGrid column as opposed to the first is because the first column is the ButtonColumn—it's the second column where the title of the book is displayed.

After getting the second `TableCell` (`e.Item.Cells(1)`), we access the `Text` property of the `TableCell`, which returns the title of the book (line 3). Finally, on line 4 we emit a short message using `Response.Write`, informing the user of the title he added to his shopping cart. You'll notice that the actual code to add an item to the user's shopping cart is missing. Because this topic is far beyond the scope of this book, I'll just mention that such logic would appear after line 4 and leave it at that.

Determining Which ButtonColumn Column Has Been Clicked

As we have seen in previous DataGrid examples, a DataGrid can contain multiple BoundColumn controls. It should come as no surprise, then, that a DataGrid can also contain multiple ButtonColumn controls. Let's look at an example that includes a DataGrid with more than one ButtonColumn, paying attention to the issues that arise when using multiple ButtonColumns.

Imagine that we have a shopping cart that lists the name and price of the products that the user has currently placed in the cart. Alongside each item are two buttons:

a Remove button that removes the selected item from the cart, and a Details button that displays details about the particular item. For this example, let's keep it simple: the "Details" will simply be a textual description.

For this example we'll assume that there is some function called ItemsInCart(), which returns an object that implements an IEnumerable that has a row for each item in the shopping cart and exposes the following fields for the particular product: the ProductID, the name, and the price. (Recall from Chapter 2 that the DataSource can be any object that implements IEnumerable. It might help to just think that the ItemsInCart() method returns either a DataSet or DataReader of some kind.) The ProductID is an integer value that uniquely identifies each product available in our online store. Furthermore, let's assume that there's also a function called GetProductDescription(ID), which returns the description for the product specified by the input parameter ID. Finally, there will need to be a RemoveItemFromCart(ID) function that removes a selected product from the user's shopping cart.

Listing 4.5 contains our first attempt at this example. Note that Listing 4.5 does not contain the ItemsInCart(), GetProductDescription(ID), or RemoveItemFromCart(ID) functions. This is for three reasons: first, their details are irrelevant; second, they have been removed for brevity; and lastly, in a real-world project they would likely be methods in a .NET component, meaning that these functions would not appear in the ASP.NET Web page.

LISTING 4.5   A DataGrid Is Used to Represent a Shopping Cart

```
 1: <%@ import Namespace="System.Data" %>
 2: <%@ import Namespace="System.Data.SqlClient" %>
 3: <script runat="server" language="C#">
 4:   void Page_Load(object sender, EventArgs e)
 5:   {
 6:    if (!Page.IsPostBack)
 7:      BindData();
 8:   }
 9:
10:
11:   void BindData()
12:   {
13:    dgCart.DataSource = ItemsInCart();
14:    dgCart.DataBind();
15:   }
16:
17:
18:   void dgCart_ItemCommand(object sender, DataGridCommandEventArgs e)
19:   {
```

LISTING 4.5   Continued

```
20:    Response.Write("A button was clicked...");
21:  }
22: </script>
23:
24: <form runat="server">
25:  <asp:DataGrid runat="server" id="dgCart"
26:     AutoGenerateColumns="False"
27:     Font-Name="Verdana"
28:     Font-Size="8pt"
29:     OnItemCommand="dgCart_ItemCommand">
30:
31:   <HeaderStyle HorizontalAlign="Center" Font-Bold="True"
32:     Font-Size="11pt" BackColor="Navy" ForeColor="White" />
33:
34:   <Columns>
35:    <asp:ButtonColumn Text="Remove" ButtonType="PushButton"
36:        HeaderText="Remove" />
37:    <asp:ButtonColumn Text="Details" ButtonType="PushButton"
38:        HeaderText="Details" />
39:
40:    <asp:BoundColumn DataField="Name" HeaderText="Product Name" />
41:    <asp:BoundColumn DataField="Price" HeaderText="Price"
42:        ItemStyle-HorizontalAlign="right"
43:        DataFormatString="{0:c}" />
44:   </Columns>
45:  </asp:DataGrid>
46: </form>
```

A screenshot of Listing 4.5 can be seen in Figure 4.4. With the ButtonColumns on lines 35 through 38, we've set the ButtonType property to PushButton, which renders the ButtonColumn as a traditional HTML button (see Figure 4.4). Note that we've also added an event handler for the DataGrid's ItemCommand event (dgCart_ItemCommand, lines 18–21).

Take a moment to inspect the code and try to ascertain whether Listing 4.5 will work. Hopefully you were able to identify the following fault: the DataGrid has only one ItemCommand event, which is raised when *any* ButtonColumn button or hyperlink is clicked. For instance, suppose that the Remove button for Item 1 is clicked. Although we can determine the precise row that had a button clicked (via e.Item in the dgCart_ItemCommand event handler), we cannot programmatically determine whether it was the Remove button or the Details button that was clicked. This is because both ButtonColumn buttons (Remove and Details) both raise the same DataGrid event, `ItemCommand`.

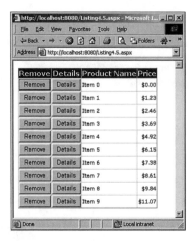

FIGURE 4.4   Each item in the shopping cart has two buttons.

To handle this, the ButtonColumn class contains a string property called `CommandName`. This property can be used to uniquely identify each ButtonColumn in the DataGrid control. For example, in Listing 4.5 we could give each ButtonColumn a `CommandName` by changing lines 35 through 38 to the following:

```
<asp:ButtonColumn Text="Remove" ButtonType="PushButton"
    HeaderText="Remove" CommandName="RemoveButton" />
<asp:ButtonColumn Text="Details" ButtonType="PushButton"
    HeaderText="Details" CommandName="DetailsButton" />
```

From the `ItemCommand` event handler, we can determine what ButtonColumn was clicked by checking the `e.CommandName` property (where e is the `DataGridCommandEventArgs` parameter of the `ItemCommand` event handler). Given this, our `dgCart_ItemCommand` event handler would be changed to the following:

```
void dgCart_ItemCommand(object sender, DataGridCommandEventArgs e)
{
 if (e.CommandName == "RemoveButton")
 {
  // the Remove button has been clicked...
 }
 if (e.CommandName == "DetailsButton")
 {
```

```
// the Details button has been clicked...
  }
}
```

All that remains now is to write the code to remove an item from the shopping cart and provide details about a particular item from the shopping cart. At first glance, this might seem quite trivial—after all, we have the `GetProductDescription(ID)` and `RemoveItemFromCart(ID)` functions to aid us. Realize however that these two functions require a `ProductID` as the input parameter. Hence, we need some way to determine the `ProductID` of the item whose Remove or Details button was clicked.

There are two ways to accomplish this:

1. Use a hidden BoundColumn in the DataGrid, and then reference the `Text` property of the `TableCell` representing this BoundColumn in the `dgCart_ItemCommand` event handler.

2. Set the `DataKeyField` property of the DataGrid control to `ProductID` and use the `DataKeys` collection in the `dgCart_ItemCommand` event handler.

Essentially these are two different ways to pass on a primary key for a row in the DataGrid to the event handler, a task that we'll find ourselves doing quite frequently in Part III. In the next two sections we'll examine how to use these two approaches. Be sure to carefully read over these next two sections, as we'll be using the techniques learned here extensively throughout the remainder of this book.

Using a Hidden BoundColumn to Pass Along a Primary Key Field
To use the first method, we need to add a BoundColumn to the DataGrid for the `ProductID` field from our `DataSource`. Because we don't want to show the `ProductID` BoundColumn in our shopping cart, we set the `Visible` property of the BoundColumn to `False`. The code following shows the DataGrid declaration with the added BoundColumn (some of the DataGrid's stylistic properties have been omitted for brevity):

```
<asp:DataGrid runat="server" id="dgCart"
   AutoGenerateColumns="False"
   OnItemCommand="dgCart_ItemCommand"
   ... >

 <Columns>
  <asp:ButtonColumn Text="Remove" ButtonType="PushButton"
     HeaderText="Remove" CommandName="RemoveButton" />
  <asp:ButtonColumn Text="Details" ButtonType="PushButton"
     HeaderText="Details" CommandName="DetailsButton" />
```

```
    <asp:BoundColumn DataField="ProductID" Visible="False" />
    <asp:BoundColumn DataField="Name" HeaderText="Product Name" />
    <asp:BoundColumn DataField="Price" HeaderText="Price"
        ItemStyle-HorizontalAlign="right"
        DataFormatString="{0:c}" />
  </Columns>
 </asp:DataGrid>
```

The preceding DataGrid will be rendered the same as the DataGrid in Figure 4.4. However, now we can reference the ProductID as the third Cell in the DataGridItem whose ButtonColumn button was clicked in the dgCart_ItemCommand event handler. That is, we can use the following code in the dgCart_ItemCommand event handler to get the ProductID of the product whose associated ButtonColumn button was clicked:

```
int selectedProductID = Convert.ToInt32(e.Item.Cells[2].Text);
```

Note that we are grabbing the third Cell from the selected DataGridItem using e.Item.Cells[2]—remember that the Cells collection is zero-based, so Cells[2] is retrieving the *third* entry. This returns a TableCell, whose Text property we then read. This gives us the ProductID as a string, but we need it as an integer; hence, the Convert.ToInt32 method is used to convert the string into an integer.

Listing 4.6 contains the complete code for our shopping cart example using the hidden BoundColumn to pass along the primary key. Figure 4.5 shows a screenshot of the code in Listing 4.6 after the user has clicked on the Details button for a particular item.

LISTING 4.6   A Hidden BoundColumn Is Used to Pass Along the Primary Key

```
 1: <%@ import Namespace="System.Data" %>
 2: <%@ import Namespace="System.Data.SqlClient" %>
 3: <script runat="server" language="C#">
 4:   void Page_Load(object sender, EventArgs e)
 5:   {
 6:    if (!Page.IsPostBack)
 7:     BindData();
 8:   }
 9:
10:
11:   void BindData()
12:   {
13:    dgCart.DataSource = ItemsInCart();
14:    dgCart.DataBind();
15:   }
```

LISTING 4.6   Continued

```
16:
17:
18:    void dgCart_ItemCommand(object sender, DataGridCommandEventArgs e)
19:    {
20:      // Get the ProductID of the selected row.
21:      int selectedProductID = Convert.ToInt32(e.Item.Cells[2].Text);
22:
23:      if (e.CommandName == "RemoveButton")
24:      {
25:        // Remove the Product from the Cart and rebind the DataGrid
26:        RemoveItemFromCart(selectedProductID);
27:        BindData();
28:      }
29:      if (e.CommandName == "DetailsButton")
30:      {
31:        // Display the Product Details
32:        lblProductDetails.Text = GetProductDescription(selectedProductID);
33:      }
34:    }
35:  </script>
36:  <form runat="server">
37:    <p>
38:    <asp:label runat="server" id="lblProductDetails"
39:        Font-Name="Verdana" Font-Size="11pt" />
40:    </p>
41:
42:    <asp:DataGrid runat="server" id="dgCart"
43:        AutoGenerateColumns="False"
44:        Font-Name="Verdana" Font-Size="8pt"
45:        OnItemCommand="dgCart_ItemCommand">
46:
47:    <HeaderStyle HorizontalAlign="Center" Font-Bold="True"
48:        Font-Size="11pt" BackColor="Navy" ForeColor="White" />
49:
50:    <Columns>
51:      <asp:ButtonColumn Text="Remove" ButtonType="PushButton"
52:          HeaderText="Remove" CommandName="RemoveButton" />
53:      <asp:ButtonColumn Text="Details" ButtonType="PushButton"
54:          HeaderText="Details" CommandName="DetailsButton" />
55:
56:      <asp:BoundColumn DataField="ProductID" Visible="False" />
57:      <asp:BoundColumn DataField="Name" HeaderText="Product Name" />
```

LISTING 4.6   Continued

```
58:    <asp:BoundColumn DataField="Price" HeaderText="Price"
59:        ItemStyle-HorizontalAlign="right"
60:        DataFormatString="{0:c}" />
61:    </Columns>
62:    </asp:DataGrid>
63: </form>
```

The first thing to note in Listing 4.6 is the addition of a Label control, lblProductDetails (lines 38 and 39). When the Details button is clicked, this Label control is used to display the information about the particular product.

Next, take a moment to examine the dgCart_ItemCommand event handler. On line 21 the selectedProductID variable is set to the Text of the hidden ProductID BoundColumn. Lines 25 through 27 are executed if the Remove button was clicked. On line 26 the RemoveItemFromCart(ID) function is called, passing in the selectedProductID. Following that, on line 27 the BindData() function is called, repopulating the DataSource and rebinding the DataGrid. If line 27 is omitted, and the call to BindData() is *not* made, then upon postback the DataGrid would contain the same rows it contained prior to the user clicking the Remove button.

If the user clicked the Details button for a particular item, lines 31 and 32 are executed. On line 32 the lblProductDetails Label control's Text property is set to the string value returned by the GetProductDescription(ID) function. Again, we pass in the selectedProductID.

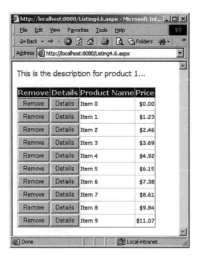

FIGURE 4.5   The details are displayed for a particular product.

Using the `DataKeyField` **Property and the** `DataKeys` **Collection to Pass Along a Primary Key Field**

Another, more natural way to pass along primary key field information through a DataGrid is to use the `DataKeyField` property. The `DataKeyField` property is a string property of the DataGrid class. Simply set this property equal to the name of the primary key field in the `DataSource`. Returning to our example from Listing 4.5, to use the `DataKeyField` property approach, the DataGrid declaration would be changed to

```
<asp:DataGrid runat="server" id="dgCart"
    AutoGenerateColumns="False"
    Font-Name="Verdana"
    Font-Size="8pt"
    OnItemCommand="dgCart_ItemCommand"
    DataKeyField="ProductID">

  <Columns>
    ...
  </Columns>
</asp:DataGrid>
```

By setting the `DataKeyField` property, we can now access the DataGrid's `DataKeys` property. This property is a collection and contains an entry for each row in the `DataSource`. The value of each entry is the value of the specified `DataKeyField`. That is, the first (0th) element in the `DataKeys` collection is equal to the value of the `ProductID` for the first row in the DataGrid, the second (1st) element in the `DataKeys` collection is equal to the value of the `ProductID` for the second row in the DataGrid, and so on.

Given this fact, all we need to do to set the `selectedProductID` variable in our `dgCart_ItemCommand` event handler is set it to the proper item of the `DataKeys` collection. The proper `DataKeys` item has the same index as the DataGrid row whose ButtonColumn was clicked. Fortunately, the `DataGridItem` class contains an `ItemIndex` property that returns the row's index in the DataGrid (again, like .NET collections, this is zero-based). Hence, the following code will successfully return the `ProductID` of the shopping cart item whose ButtonColumn button was clicked, assigning the result to the `selectedProductID` variable:

```
int selectedProductID = (int) dgCart.DataKeys[e.Item.ItemIndex];
```

Listing 4.7 contains source code to use the `DataKeyField` and `DataKeys` properties to pass along primary key field information. Note that aesthetically and semantically the output from Listing 4.7 is identical to that of Listing 4.6; therefore, to see a screenshot of the code in Listing 4.6, simply refer back to Figure 4.5.

LISTING 4.7   The DataKeyField and DataKeys Properties Are Used to Pass Along Primary Key Information

```
 1: <%@ import Namespace="System.Data" %>
 2: <%@ import Namespace="System.Data.SqlClient" %>
 3: <script runat="server">
 4:   void Page_Load(object sender, EventArgs e)
 5:   {
 6:    if (!Page.IsPostBack)
 7:     BindData();
 8:   }
 9:
10:
11:   void BindData()
12:   {
13:    dgCart.DataSource = ItemsInCart();
14:    dgCart.DataBind();
15:   }
16:
17:
18:   void dgCart_ItemCommand(object sender, DataGridCommandEventArgs e)
19:   {
20:    // Get the ProductID of the selected row.
21:    int selectedProductID = (int) dgCart.DataKeys[e.Item.ItemIndex];
22:
23:    if (e.CommandName == "RemoveButton")
24:    {
25:     // Remove the Product from the Cart and rebind the DataGrid
26:     RemoveItemFromCart(selectedProductID);
27:     BindData();
28:    }
29:    if (e.CommandName == "DetailsButton")
30:    {
31:     // Display the Product Details
32:     lblProductDetails.Text = GetProductDescription(selectedProductID);
33:    }
34:   }
35: </script>
36: <form runat="server">
37:  <p>
38:  <asp:label runat="server" id="lblProductDetails"
39:     Font-Name="Verdana" Font-Size="11pt" />
40:  </p>
41:
```

LISTING 4.7 Continued

```
42:  <asp:DataGrid runat="server" id="dgCart"
43:    AutoGenerateColumns="False"
44:    Font-Name="Verdana" Font-Size="8pt"
45:    OnItemCommand="dgCart_ItemCommand"
46:    DataKeyField="ProductID">
47:
48:  <HeaderStyle HorizontalAlign="Center" Font-Bold="True"
49:    Font-Size="11pt" BackColor="Navy" ForeColor="White" />
50:
51:  <Columns>
52:   <asp:ButtonColumn Text="Remove" ButtonType="PushButton"
53:       HeaderText="Remove" CommandName="RemoveButton" />
54:   <asp:ButtonColumn Text="Details" ButtonType="PushButton"
55:       HeaderText="Details" CommandName="DetailsButton" />
56:
57:   <asp:BoundColumn DataField="Name" HeaderText="Product Name" />
58:   <asp:BoundColumn DataField="Price" HeaderText="Price"
59:       ItemStyle-HorizontalAlign="right"
60:       DataFormatString="{0:c}" />
61:  </Columns>
62:  </asp:DataGrid>
63: </form>
```

The key pieces to Listing 4.7 include setting the DataKeyField property to the primary key field (ProductID, line 46), and then determining the ProductID of the row whose ButtonColumn button was clicked via the DataKeys collection (line 21). Other than line 21, the dgCart_ItemCommand event handler in Listing 4.7 is identical to the event handler in Listing 4.6.

What Method Is Best for Passing Along Primary Key Information?
In comparing the two methods for passing along primary key information, you'll probably agree with me that the latter approach using the DataKeyField and DataKeys properties is more straightforward than using hidden BoundColumns. The shortcoming with the DataKeyField/DataKeys approach is that it can only work with data that has *one* primary key column. If you are displaying data in a DataGrid that has a composite primary key (that is, a primary key that is composed of two or more fields), and you need to reference the rows by the composite primary key in some fashion, then you will have no choice but to use multiple hidden BoundColumns.

Hence, I recommend using the DataKeyField and DataKeys properties for simple primary key fields, and only resorting to hidden BoundColumns for more complex scenarios.

NOTE

As we'll see in the next chapter, the DataList also supports the `DataKeyField` and `DataKeys` properties. This is yet another reason to become comfortable using this approach in passing along primary key information.

Common Uses for ButtonColumns

As we saw with the examples in the past few sections, ButtonColumns have a number of real-world purposes in a DataGrid. ButtonColumns are excellent candidates when you need to enable the user to modify the state of a DataGrid in some way. As we saw in Listings 4.5, 4.6, and 4.7, a ButtonColumn was used for a Remove button, which updated the state of the DataGrid by removing an item from the DataGrid's `DataSource` and then rebinding the DataGrid.

ButtonColumns are also great for having some action occur on the same page that the DataGrid exists on. Imagine that you have a list of stocks in a DataGrid and alongside each stock you have a Current Quote button. As we already know, when clicked this button would cause a postback to the ASP.NET Web page, firing the DataGrid's `ItemCommand` event. In our event handler, we could make a call to our data store, obtaining the current quote information for the selected stock. This information could then be displayed in a Label control on the same page as the DataGrid that lists the various stocks. For an example of this technique, be sure to read "An Extensive Examination of the DataGrid Web Control: Part 3," which is listed in the "On the Web" section at the end of this chapter.

ButtonColumns can also be used as simple redirects. For example, you might have a page that displays a list of products, and next to each product you want a link that will lead the user to a separate ASP.NET Web page, passing along the product's unique ID in the QueryString. This separate ASP.NET page would read in the product's unique ID from the QueryString and display the details about the specified item.

To accomplish this functionality, we could use a ButtonColumn hyperlink, and simply issue a `Response.Redirect` to the product details page in the `ItemCommand` event handler, passing along the `ProductID` in the QueryString. However, as we'll see in the next section, such functionality can probably be added by using the HyperLinkColumn, one of the other built-in DataGrid column types. Unfortunately the HyperLinkColumn has its limitations, as we'll see shortly, and for certain situations it might be ideal to use the ButtonColumn for a redirect.

Adding HyperLinkColumns to the DataGrid Web Control

In the previous section we saw how to use the ButtonColumn control to add a button or hyperlink to each row in a DataGrid. Recall that the semantics of the ButtonColumn were as follows: When a user clicks a button or hyperlink generated by the ButtonColumn, the ASP.NET Web page is posted back and the DataGrid's `ItemCommand` event is fired. To have server-side code execute in response to the clicking of a ButtonColumn button or hyperlink, we simply needed to provide a suitable event handler and wire up the event handler to the DataGrid's `ItemCommand` event, which can be done in the DataGrid's declaration.

There are times, though, when this series of events is much more complex than necessary. For example, with many Web site search engines, when the user searches on a particular query, she is shown a listing of links of articles that match the search query. The first few sentences of the article might even be included in the search result. To view the full details of the article, though, the user must click on a link to an article, whereby she'll be taken directly to the complete article.

The DataGrid provides a special built-in column type to handle situations just like this one: the HyperLinkColumn. In its simplest form, the HyperLinkColumn need only supply two properties:

- `Text`—The text for the hyperlink

- `NavigateUrl`—The URL for the hyperlink

For example, Listing 4.8 illustrates this simplified usage of the HyperLinkColumn. The HyperLinkColumn (line 27) specifies only the `Text` and `NavigateUrl` properties.

LISTING 4.8   The HyperLinkColumn Displays a Hyperlink in Each Row of the DataGrid

```
 1: <%@ import Namespace="System.Data" %>
 2: <%@ import Namespace="System.Data.SqlClient" %>
 3: <script runat="server" language="VB">
 4:   Sub Page_Load(sender as Object, e as EventArgs)
 5:    If Not Page.IsPostBack then
 6:     BindData()
 7:    End If
 8:   End Sub
 9:
10:
11:   Sub BindData()
12:    '... Code removed for brevity, same as Listing 4.4 ...
13:   End Sub
14: </script>
15:
```

LISTING 4.8   Continued

```
16: <asp:datagrid id="dgTitles" runat="server"
17:    AutoGenerateColumns="False"
18:    Font-Name="Verdana" Width="50%"
19:    HorizontalAlign="Center" ItemStyle-Font-Size="9pt">
20:
21: <HeaderStyle BackColor="Navy" ForeColor="White"
22:    HorizontalAlign="Center" Font-Bold="True" />
23:
24: <AlternatingItemStyle BackColor="#dddddd" />
25:
26: <Columns>
27:   <asp:HyperLinkColumn Text="View Details" NavigateUrl="details.aspx" />
28:   <asp:BoundColumn DataField="title" HeaderText="Title"
29:            ItemStyle-Width="70%" />
30: </Columns>
31: </asp:datagrid>
```

As you can see from the screenshot in Figure 4.6, the value of the Text property is the value of the hyperlink's text when rendered to the browser. What's a bit harder to see from the screenshot is that each of these hyperlinks goes to the URL specified by NavigateUrl. That is, each and every one of the hyperlinks in the HyperLinkColumn in Figure 4.6 will take the user to details.aspx.

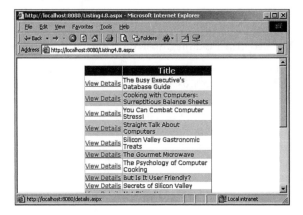

FIGURE 4.6   The HyperLinkColumn isn't very useful when using the Text and NavigateUrl properties.

Clearly, we'd like to be able to have the URL of each hyperlink generated by the HyperLinkColumn to be distinct. For example, rather than having all hyperlinks link

to details.aspx, we might want each hyperlink to link to
details.aspx?id=*title_id*, where *title_id* is the primary key, uniquely identifying
each book.

To accomplish this with the HyperLinkColumn, we need to use the
DataNavigateUrlField and DataNavigateUrlFormatString properties instead of the
NavigateUrl property. The DataNavigateUrlField is a string property that should be
set to the DataSource field that you want to have vary for each hyperlink generated
by the HyperLinkColumn. If we want to have the hyperlinks navigate the user to
details..aspx?id=*title_id*, we'd set the DataNavigateUrlField to title_id, the
primary key field of the title database table.

The DataNavigateUrlFormatString property specifies the URL to which the hyperlink should direct the user. In this URL string, you can specify where you want the
value of the DataNavigateurlField property to appear by using {0}. Given our
earlier example, we'd set the DataNavigateUrlFormatString property to
details.aspx?id={0}.

Similarly, we can specify dynamic text for the hyperlinks by using the DataTextField
and DataTextFormatString properties, which work in the same fashion as the
DataNavigateUrlField and DataNavigateUrlFormatString properties.

Listing 4.9 is a slight update from Listing 4.8; instead of having a static hyperlink
text and URL, though, Listing 4.9 uses the DataTextField, DataTextFormatString,
DataNavigateUrlField, and DataNavigateUrlFormatString properties to have the
text and URLs customized for each DataGrid row. Listing 4.9 contains only the
DataGrid declaration—the server-side script block for Listing 4.9 has been omitted,
because it is identical to that of Listing 4.8.

LISTING 4.9   The Text and URLs of the Hyperlinks Are Now Customized for Each
DataGrid Row

```
 1: <asp:datagrid id="dgTitles" runat="server"
 2:     AutoGenerateColumns="False"
 3:     Font-Name="Verdana" Width="50%"
 4:     HorizontalAlign="Center" ItemStyle-Font-Size="9pt">
 5:
 6: <HeaderStyle BackColor="Navy" ForeColor="White"
 7:     HorizontalAlign="Center" Font-Bold="True" />
 8:
 9: <AlternatingItemStyle BackColor="#dddddd" />
10:
11: <Columns>
12:  <asp:HyperLinkColumn DataTextField="title"
13:       DataTextFormatString="View Details for {0}"
```

LISTING 4.9   Continued

```
14:        DataNavigateUrlField="title_id"
15:        DataNavigateUrlFormatString="/details.aspx?id={0}" />
16:  <asp:BoundColumn DataField="title" HeaderText="Title"
17:        ItemStyle-Width="70%" />
18:  </Columns>
19: </asp:datagrid>
```

Figure 4.7 contains a screenshot of the DataGrid in Listing 4.9 when viewed through a browser. Note that the text of the hyperlinks in the HyperLinkColumn contains the title of the book. Also, the URLs that the hyperlinks navigate to differ for each row. For example, the link for *The Busy Executive's Database Guide* points to details.aspx?id=BU1032, while the link for *Cooking with Computers* points to details.aspx?id=PC8888.

> **NOTE**
>
> Recall that when using a ButtonColumn in a DataGrid, we needed to place the DataGrid within a server-side Web form because when the button is clicked, the ASP.NET Web page is posted back. HyperLinkColumns, however, are rendered as hyperlinks and do not cause a postback. Therefore, when using a HyperLinkColumn, you do not need to place the DataGrid within a Web form.

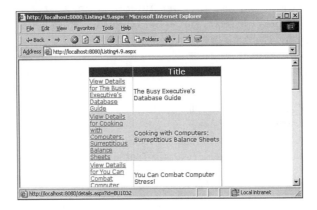

FIGURE 4.7   The text and URLs of the hyperlink are different for each DataGrid row.

Using Two or More DataSource Fields in the Text and NavigateUrl Properties

Although the DataTextField, DataTextFormatString, DataNavigateUrlField, and DataNavigateUrlFormatString properties are quite useful for generating dynamic text and URLs for the hyperlinks created by the HyperLinkColumn, they are limited in that they can only add one DataSource field to the Text or NavigateUrl properties. That is, you can't use the DataNavigateUrlField and DataNavigateUrlFormatString properties to build a hyperlink with the form

```
details.aspx?id=title_id&title=bookTitle
```

where *title_id* and bookTitle are the ID and title of the book, fields provided in the DataSource. Similarly, if you wanted the hyperlink's text to incorporate more than one DataSource field, you would be out of luck if you tried to use the DataTextField and DataTextFormatString properties.

There are three workaround options to this shortcoming:

1. Use a ButtonColumn instead of a HyperLinkColumn (you can have the ButtonColumn rendered as a hyperlink if you like, to maintain a visual similarity between the ButtonColumn and HyperLinkColumn). In the DataGrid's ItemCommand event handler, you can build up a URL with the proper DataSource fields and then use Response.Redirect() to send the user to the desired page.

2. Use actual HTML markup code within a TemplateColumn, using data-binding syntax to populate the hyperlink's text and URL portions with the proper DataSource fields.

3. Programmatically set the HyperLinkColumn's Text and NavigateUrl properties through the DataGrid's ItemDataBound event.

Option 1 was discussed briefly at the end of the ButtonColumn section in this chapter. The two main downsides with this approach are that the Text of the ButtonColumn is static, unless you use a method similar to option 3, and the user will have to endure two Web page requests as opposed to one to get to the desired page—one for the postback, and then a second one for the Response.Redirect() to the appropriate page.

Options 2 and 3 deserve a bit more attention. We'll examine these two approaches in the next two sections.

Using a TemplateColumn to Create the Hyperlink
As we saw in Chapter 3, DataGrids can include a TemplateColumn. This TemplateColumn contains, at minimum, an ItemTemplate, which specifies both HTML markup and data that is to be included dynamically from the DataSource. Using a TemplateColumn to generate the hyperlink offers the most flexibility. Listing 4.10 contains the DataGrid declaration for a DataGrid that utilizes option 2.

LISTING 4.10   A Hyperlink Can Be Created in a TemplateColumn

```
 1: <asp:datagrid id="dgTitles" runat="server"
 2:    AutoGenerateColumns="False"
 3:    Font-Name="Verdana" Width="50%"
 4:    HorizontalAlign="Center" ItemStyle-Font-Size="9pt">
 5:
 6: <HeaderStyle BackColor="Navy" ForeColor="White"
 7:      HorizontalAlign="Center" Font-Bold="True" />
 8:
 9: <AlternatingItemStyle BackColor="#dddddd" />
10:
11: <Columns>
12:   <asp:TemplateColumn>
13:    <ItemTemplate>
14:     <a href="details.aspx?id=<%# Server.UrlEncode(DataBinder.Eval
➥(Container.DataItem, "title_id")) %>&title=<%# Server.UrlEncode
➥(DataBinder.Eval(Container.DataItem, "title")) %>">
15:       Details for <%# DataBinder.Eval(Container.DataItem, "title") %>
16:     </a>
17:    </ItemTemplate>
18:   </asp:TemplateColumn>
19:   <asp:BoundColumn DataField="title" HeaderText="Title"
20:           ItemStyle-Width="70%" />
21: </Columns>
22: </asp:datagrid>
```

Listing 4.10 creates an actual HTML `href` tag. The URL for the `href` tag contains two dynamic fields: `id` and `title`. Note that the dynamic values are "inserted" by simply placing the proper data-binding syntax precisely where the dynamic text should be inserted. This method of creating data-driven Web pages will be all too familiar with the classic ASP developer.

NOTE

Notice that the presence of the call to `Server.UrlEncode` inside each of the data-binding calls in the URL portion of the `href` tag. `Server.UrlEncode` transforms characters that are illegal URL characters into legal ones. For example, each space is converted into +, each apostrophe into a %22, and so on.

The HTML generated by the preceding TemplateColumn will, of course, differ per DataGrid row. For example, for the book *You Can Combat Computer Stress*, the following HTML is generated:

```
<a href="details.aspx?title=BU2075&price=You+Can+Combat+Computer+Stress!">
  Details for You Can Combat Computer Stress!
</a>
```

Whereas for the book *The Busy Executive's Database Guide*, the following HTML is generated:

```
<a
href="details.aspx?id=BU1032&title=The+Busy+Executive's+Database+Guide">
  Details for The Busy Executive's Database Guide
</a>
```

When viewing the DataGrid in Listing 4.10 through a browser, the user will see the same output as shown in Figure 4.7.

Using the `ItemDataBound` Event to Programmatically Set the HyperLinkColumn's `Text` and `NavigateUrl` Properties

Although the TemplateColumn approach affords the most customizability, it clearly mixes the source code (the data-binding syntax) with the HTML content. Ideally, we'd like to keep these two things separate, which is possible with option 3: using the DataGrid's `ItemDataBound` event to programmatically set the `Text` and `NavigateUrl` properties of the HyperLinkColumn.

Recall from Chapter 2 that each of the three data Web controls performs data binding in *roughly* the same manner. The `DataSource` is enumerated over one record at a time, and for each record, something is added to the data Web control. For the DataGrid, each `DataSource` record corresponds to a `DataGridItem`; for the DataList, a `DataListItem`; and for the Repeater, a `RepeaterItem`.

At each iteration through the `DataSource`, two events are raised: The first one is the `ItemCreated` event, which is raised when the `DataGridItem`, `DataListItem`, or `RepeaterItem` is created, but before it is data-bound; the second event is the `ItemDataBound` event, which is raised after the current `DataSource` item has been data-bound to the `DataGridItem`, `DataListItem`, or `RepeaterItem`, but before the `DataGridItem`, `DataListItem`, or `RepeaterItem` has been rendered.

We can provide an event handler for the DataGrid's `ItemDataBound` event using the following definition:

```
Sub EventHandlerName(sender As Object, e As DataGridItemEventArgs)
```

Like the `ItemCommand` event handler, we need to wire up the DataGrid's `ItemDataBound` event to the event handler we create. This is accomplished by adding

```
OnItemDataBound="EventHandlerName"
```

to the DataGrid's declaration.

In the event handler, we need to programmatically reference the HyperLinkColumn column. After we've done this, we can set the HyperLinkColumn's `Text` and `NavigateUrl` properties in whatever manner we see fit. Listing 4.11 illustrates how to accomplish this with code.

LISTING 4.11   The DataGrid's `ItemDataBound` Method Can Be Used to Set the HyperLinkColumn's `Text` and `NavigateUrl` Properties

```
 1: <%@ import Namespace="System.Data" %>
 2: <%@ import Namespace="System.Data.SqlClient" %>
 3: <script runat="server" language="VB">
 4:    ... Page_Load and BindData omitted for brevity ...
 5:         ... Consult Listing 4.4 ...
 6:
 7:    Sub SetHyperLinkColumnProps(sender as Object, e as DataGridItemEventArgs)
 8:      If e.Item.ItemType <> ListItemType.Header and _
 9:         e.Item.ItemType <> ListItemType.Footer then
10:      Dim hl as HyperLink = e.Item.Cells(0).Controls(0)
11:      hl.Text = "Details for " & _
12:          DataBinder.Eval(e.Item.DataItem, "title")
13:
14:      Dim navUrl as String
15:      navUrl = "details.aspx?id=" & _
16:          Server.UrlEncode(DataBinder.Eval(e.Item.DataItem, "title_id")) & _
17:          "&title=" & _
18:          Server.UrlEncode(DataBinder.Eval(e.Item.DataItem, "title"))
19:      hl.NavigateUrl = navUrl
20:      End If
21:    End Sub
22: </script>
23: <asp:datagrid id="dgTitles" runat="server"
24:    AutoGenerateColumns="False"
25:    Font-Name="Verdana" Width="50%"
26:    HorizontalAlign="Center" ItemStyle-Font-Size="9pt"
27:    OnItemDataBound="SetHyperLinkColumnProps">
28:
29:  <HeaderStyle BackColor="Navy" ForeColor="White"
30:      HorizontalAlign="Center" Font-Bold="True" />
31:
32:  <AlternatingItemStyle BackColor="#dddddd" />
33:
34:  <Columns>
35:   <asp:HyperLinkColumn />
```

LISTING 4.11   Continued

```
36:     <asp:BoundColumn DataField="title" HeaderText="Title"
37:              ItemStyle-Width="70%" />
38:   </Columns>
39: </asp:datagrid>
```

Notice that the HyperLinkColumn in Listing 4.11 (line 35) does not contain any properties. The reason we don't set any is because we are setting them programmatically in the `ItemDataBound` event handler (lines 7 through 21). Had we set the properties in the HyperLinkColumn declaration on line 35, the values would just be written over in the event handler.

Spanning lines 7–21 you'll find the `ItemDataBound` event handler, `SetHyperLinkColumnProps`. Realize that the HyperLinkColumn we added to our DataGrid on line 35 is turned into a HyperLink Web control prior to `ItemDataBound` being fired. Hence, our event handler needs to find the HyperLink control and set its `Text` and `NavigateUrl` properties accordingly.

The `ItemDataBound` event is fired for every row in the DataGrid, even the header and footer rows; however, these header and footer rows do not contain a HyperLink control. Instead, they contain only a textual label. Therefore, in our `SetHyperLinkColumnProps` event handler, we want to look for a HyperLink control only if we are dealing with a row other than a header or footer. On line 8 and 9, we check the `DataGridItem`'s `ItemType` property. Recall from Chapter 2 that the `ItemType` property indicates the type of the row, and can have values like `Header`, `Footer`, `Item`, `AlternatingItem`, and so on.

We reach line 10 only if we are not working with a header or footer row. At this point, we want to grab the HyperLink control from the `DataGridItem`. Because the HyperLinkColumn is the first (0th) column in the DataGrid, we reference `Cells(0)`, which gets us back the proper `TableCell` object. Next, we grab the first (0th) control from the `TableCell`'s `Controls` collection.

NOTE

Each ASP.NET control contains a `Controls` collection, which stores the child controls (if any) for a control. For example, when using a Web form (server-side form), all the controls that appear within the Web form are children of the Web form and appear in the Web form's `Controls` collection. On line 10, we are simply grabbing the first control out of the first `TableCell`, which happens to be the HyperLink control we're after.

After we have the HyperLink control, we store it in the variable `hl`. Next, on lines 11 and 12, the `Text` property of the HyperLink control is set. Notice that we are using the DataBinder.Eval() function like we would in data-binding syntax in a template. The only difference is that instead of referring to Container.DataItem, we refer to e.Item.DataItem, which is referencing the current item being enumerated through in the DataSource. The reason this code needs to appear in the DataGrid's ItemDataBound event handler as opposed to its ItemCreated event handler is because we need to access the data that is being bound to the DataGridItem from the DataSource. (That data being the title field of the DataSource.) This information is not present when the ItemCreated event fires.

On lines 15 through 18 we build up a string for the NavigateUrl property that will have the title_id and title values for the record in the QueryString portion of the URL. As with our TemplateColumn example, on lines 16 and 18 we use Server.UrlEncode to ensure that we encode any illegal URL characters that might appear in the title_id or title fields.

Finally, note that we wire up the SetHyperLinkColumnProps event handler to the DataGrid's ItemDataBound event on line 27. The output and semantics for Listing 4.11 are identical to those in Listing 4.10. A screenshot can be seen back in Figure 4.7.

> **NOTE**
>
> We will be discussing the ItemDataBound and ItemCreated events for the data Web controls in much greater detail in Chapter 11, "Altering the Data Before It's Rendered."

Summary

In this chapter we started by examining how to add ButtonColumns to the DataGrid Web control. We noted that these ButtonColumns can be rendered as hyperlinks or traditional HTML buttons. When a ButtonColumn button or hyperlink is clicked, the DataGrid's ItemCommand event is fired; to have some action associated with the clicking of a ButtonColumn, we need to provide an event handler for the ItemCommand event.

We also looked at using HyperLinkColumns to generate a hyperlink in each row of the DataGrid that ushers the user immediately to a specified Web page. We saw how the DataTextField, DataTextFormatString, DataNavigateUrlField, and DataNavigateUrlFormatString properties can be used to have the text and URL portions of the resulting hyperlink contain data from the particular DataGrid row on which they appeared.

Unfortunately, these properties are somewhat limiting in that they only allow for one DataSource field to be tied to the text and URL portions of the hyperlink. To overcome this limitation, we examined three different methods: using a

ButtonColumn, using a TemplateColumn, and programmatically altering the `Text` and `NavigateUrl` properties of the HyperLinkColumn in the DataGrid's `ItemDataBound` event handler.

The main difference between ButtonColumns and HyperLinkColumns is that ButtonColumns, when clicked, result in a postback to the ASP.NET Web page as well as the firing of the DataGrid's `ItemCommand` event; HyperLinkColumns, on the other hand, immediately direct the user to the specified Web page, without performing a postback.

In the next chapter we'll look at how to use the standard ASP.NET Button and LinkButton controls within templates. When these buttons are clicked by the user, the data Web control's `ItemCommand` event is fired, which can be caught and handled by a server-side event handler. This approach not only allows both DataLists and Repeaters to utilize buttons, but also provides more flexibility than the DataGrid's ButtonColumn class.

On the Web

For more information on the topics discussed in this chapter, consider perusing the following online resources:

- "An Extensive Examination of the DataGrid Web Control, Part 3"— `http://aspnet.4guysfromrolla.com/articles/042402-1.aspx`

- "Control Execution Lifecycle"—`http://msdn.microsoft.com/ library/default.asp?url=/library/en-us/cpguide/html/ cpconcontrolexecutionlifecycle.asp`

- "Web Forms State Management"—`http://msdn.microsoft.com/library/ default.asp?url=/library/en-us/vbcon/html/vbconwebformstate.asp`

- "Taking a Bite Out of ASP.NET ViewState"—`http://msdn.microsoft.com/ library/en-us/dnaspnet/html/asp11222001.asp`

- "Server-Side Data Access"—`http://samples.gotdotnet.com/quickstart/ aspplus/doc/webdataaccess.aspx`

- "The DataGrid's ItemDataBound Event"—`http://msdn.microsoft.com/ library/default.asp?url=/library/en-us/cpref/html/ frlrfsystemwebuiwebcontrolsdatagridclassitemdataboundtopic.asp`

5

Adding Command Buttons to the Data Web Controls

IN THIS CHAPTER

- Adding a Command Button to a Template
- Command Buttons That Trigger Events Other Than ItemCommand
- Creating Select Command Buttons
- On the Web

In the last chapter we examined how to extend the functionality of the DataGrid Web control by adding ButtonColumn and HyperLinkColumn columns. The ButtonColumn, as you'll recall, adds either a standard HTML button or hyperlink to each row in the DataGrid; when this button or hyperlink is clicked, the ASP.NET Web page is posted back, and the DataGrid's ItemCommand event is fired. With the HyperLinkColumn, a standard hyperlink is added to each row in the DataGrid; when clicked, the user is automatically taken to the specified URL.

Unfortunately, the ButtonColumn and HyperLinkColumn can only be used with the DataGrid Web control, and not with the DataList or Repeater. The reason these column controls are absent is because the DataList and Repeater do not support the notion of columns like the DataGrid does. Rather, the DataList and Repeater are built from templates.

The good news is that the data Web controls can have standard ASP.NET Button and LinkButton controls added to their templates. When these Button and LinkButton controls are clicked, the data Web control's ItemCommand event is fired, just like it is for the DataGrid's ButtonColumn control.

In this chapter, we'll examine how to add command buttons—ASP.NET's Button, LinkButton, and ImageButton controls—to data Web control templates. Specifically, we'll be looking at using these controls in the templates for the DataList and Repeater, as well as in the TemplateColumns of the DataGrid.

Adding a Command Button to a Template

As we have seen in past code examples in both Chapters 1 and 3, the ASP.NET data
Web controls all provide template support. Recall that a template includes both
HTML markup and data from the DataSource—to emit data from the DataSource in
the template we use the data-binding syntax, which takes the form <%# ... %>.

Typically, inside the <%# ... %> tags we call the DataBinder.Eval() method, passing
in Container.DataItem as the first parameter, and the name of the field we want to
have returned as the second column. That is, if our DataSource was, for instance, a
SqlDataReader that contained a field named ProductID, we could emit the
ProductID in the template by using the following data-binding syntax:

```
<%# DataBinder.Eval(Container.DataItem, "ProductID") %>
```

In addition to HTML markup and data-binding syntax, templates can contain
ASP.NET Web controls. For example, Listing 5.1 shows a DataList whose
ItemTemplate contains an ASP.NET Button control, as well as some HTML markup
and data-binding syntax.

LISTING 5.1   An ASP.NET Button Control Is Contained Within a DataList's ItemTemplate

```
 1: <%@ import Namespace="System.Data" %>
 2: <%@ import Namespace="System.Data.SqlClient" %>
 3: <script runat="server" language="VB">
 4:   Sub Page_Load(sender as Object, e as EventArgs)
 5:    If Not Page.IsPostBack then
 6:      BindData()
 7:    End If
 8:   End Sub
 9:
10:
11:   Sub BindData()
12:    '1. Create a connection
13:    Const strConnString as String = "server=localhost;uid=sa;pwd=;
➥database=pubs"
14:    Dim objConn as New SqlConnection(strConnString)
15:
16:    '2. Create a command object for the query
17:    Const strSQL as String = "SELECT * FROM titles"
18:    Dim objCmd as New SqlCommand(strSQL, objConn)
19:
20:    objConn.Open()  'Open the connection
21:
```

LISTING 5.1   Continued

```
22:    'Finally, specify the DataSource and call DataBind()
23:    dlTitles.DataSource = objCmd.ExecuteReader(CommandBehavior.CloseConnection)
24:    dlTitles.DataBind()
25:
26:    objConn.Close()  'Close the connection
27:  End Sub
28: </script>
29:
30: <form runat="server">
31:  <asp:DataList runat="server" id="dlTitles">
32:   <ItemTemplate>
33:    <b>Title:</b> <%# DataBinder.Eval(Container.DataItem, "title") %>
34:    <br />
35:    <asp:Button runat="server" id="btnDetails"
36:      Text="View Book Details" />
37:   </ItemTemplate>
38:
39:   <SeparatorTemplate>
40:    <hr>
41:   </SeparatorTemplate>
42:  </asp:DataList>
43: </form>
```

As with the ButtonColumn control that we examined in the previous chapter, when using a Button control within a data Web control's template, you must place the data Web control inside a Web form (see lines 30 and 43). This is because when the user clicks one of the Button controls, a postback is performed.

NOTE

Recall from Chapter 4, "Adding Buttons and Hyperlinks to the DataGrid Web Control," that a *postback* is when a form whose action parameter is set to the current page URL is submitted. It's referred to as a postback because the Web pages posts its data back to itself, as opposed to some other page. Because we want some server-side code to execute when the user clicks a DataGrid button, it is vital that the button click triggers a postback. Therefore, when using Button controls within a DataGrid, the DataGrid needs to be enclosed by a Web form.

Currently the code in Listing 5.1 does nothing but display a list of titles from the titles table (line 33). Underneath each book title is a View Book Details button (lines 35 and 36).

The SeparatorTemplate is a template that both the DataList and Repeater Web controls have at their disposal. This particular template dictates the content that should be placed between each ItemTemplate. In Listing 5.1, the SeparatorTemplate consists of a horizontal rule tag (<hr>) (line 40).

Figure 5.1 depicts a screenshot of Listing 5.1 when viewed through a browser.

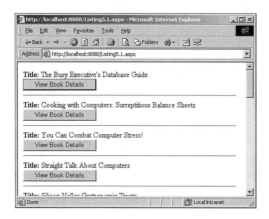

FIGURE 5.1   An ASP.NET Button control is included in each row in the DataList.

Recall that the DataGrid's ButtonColumn has a `ButtonType` property, which determines whether the ButtonColumn is rendered as a hyperlink or traditional HTML button. Unfortunately, the ASP.NET Button control does not contain such a property—it *always* renders as a standard HTML button. If you want to create a hyperlink that has the same semantic behavior as the Button control, use the ASP.NET LinkButton control.

Figure 5.2 shows what the user would see if we were to change lines 35 and 36 from Listing 5.1 to

```
<asp:LinkButton runat="server" id="btnDetails"
        Text="View Book Details" />
```

Furthermore, ASP.NET ImageButtons can be used in place of the standard Button or LinkButton controls by changing lines 35 and 36 from Listing 5.1 to

```
<asp:ImageButton runat="server" id="btnDetails"
   AlternateText="View Book Details" ImageUrl="details.gif" />
```

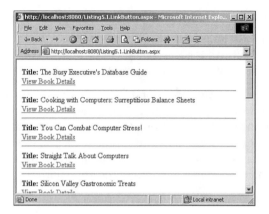

FIGURE 5.2   The LinkButton is rendered as a hyperlink.

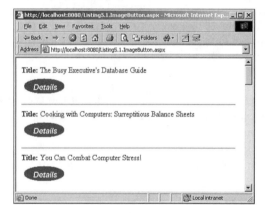

FIGURE 5.3   The ImageButton is rendered as an image tag.

Again, the semantics of the DataList in Figures 5.2 and 5.3 is identical to that in Figure 5.1. The only difference is an aesthetic one: Figure 5.1 uses a Button control, which renders HTML buttons; Figure 5.2 uses a LinkButton control, which renders a hyperlink; and Figure 5.3 uses an ImageButton control, which renders an image tag. These three controls—the Button, LinkButton, and ImageButton—are referred to as command buttons.

NOTE

Listing 5.1 illustrates the use of a Button control inside the ItemTemplate of a DataList. However, we could have just as easily used a Repeater or DataGrid. Recall that to use templates within a DataGrid, you must use a TemplateColumn column type in the Columns tag. (Refer back to Listing 3.4 in Chapter 3, "Customizing the HTML Output," for an example of using TemplateColumns in a DataGrid.)

Responding to the Clicking of a Command Button

When a command button placed inside of a template is clicked, a postback occurs and the data Web control's ItemCommand event is fired. This scenario is identical to that of the DataGrid's ButtonColumn control.

The similarities between using command buttons in templates and the DataGrid's ButtonColumn control do not end here. The command buttons contain a number of properties similar to that of the ButtonColumn control. For example, recall that if multiple ButtonColumns were used, the CommandName property could be set to uniquely identify each ButtonColumn. The command buttons contain a CommandName property as well, which serves the same purpose.

> **NOTE**
>
> Given the similarities between the DataGrid's ButtonColumn and the use of the ASP.NET Button and LinkButton controls in templates, you might not be surprised to learn that the DataGrid's ButtonColumn is actually rendered as an actual Button or DataGridLinkButton control, depending on the ButtonColumn's ButtonType property. (The DataGridLinkButton control extends the LinkButton control, hence it contains the same base properties and methods as the LinkButton.)

Let's extend Listing 5.1, adding an event handler for the ItemCommand event and giving the View Book Details button a CommandName. Listing 5.2 contains these extensions.

LISTING 5.2   When a Command Button Is Clicked, the Data Web Control's
ItemCommand Event Is Raised

```
 1: <%@ import Namespace="System.Data" %>
 2: <%@ import Namespace="System.Data.SqlClient" %>
 3: <script runat="server" language="VB">
 4: ' ... Page_Load and BindData have been removed for brevity ...
 5: ' ... Consult Listing 5.1 for their details ...
 6:
 7:   Sub dlTitles_ItemCommand(sender as Object, e as DataListCommandEventArgs)
 8:     If e.CommandName = "Details" then
 9:       ' The Details button has been clicked.
10:     End If
11:   End Sub
12: </script>
13:
14: <form runat="server">
```

LISTING 5.2   Continued

```
15:  <asp:DataList runat="server" id="dlTitles"
16:      OnItemCommand="dlTitles_ItemCommand">
17:   <ItemTemplate>
18:    <b>Title:</b> <%# DataBinder.Eval(Container.DataItem, "title") %>
19:    <br />
20:    [<asp:LinkButton runat="server" id="btnDetails"
21:       Text="View Book Details" CommandName="Details" />]
22:   </ItemTemplate>
23:
24:   <SeparatorTemplate> <hr> </SeparatorTemplate>
25:  </asp:DataList>
26: </form>
```

As with the DataGrid's ButtonColumn class, to handle an event, we must first create an event handler. Lines 7–10 contain a suitable event handler named dlTitles_ItemCommand. Note its definition:

```
Sub EventHandlerName(sender as Object, e as DataListCommandEventArgs)
```

This is identical to the event handler we used for the DataGrid's ItemCommand event handler, save one important detail. With the DataList, the second parameter to the event handler is of type DataListCommandEventArgs, whereas with the DataGrid was of type DataGridCommandEventArgs. Not surprisingly, when writing an ItemCommand event handler for the Repeater control, the second parameter must be of type RepeaterCommandEventArgs.

In the dlTitles_ItemCommand event handler, we simply check whether the item triggering the event is our View Book Details LinkButton control. Notice that we check the CommandName property of the DataListCommandEventArgs parameter (e) on line 8, and that on line 21 we specify that the LinkButton's CommandName property is Details. If the event was indeed triggered by the details button, we begin executing on line 9. (In the next code listing, we'll come back and insert some code starting at line 9, but for now let's just concentrate on the code needed to set up and handle the LinkButton's click.)

The last step is an important one: wiring up the DataList's ItemCommand event to the dlTitles_ItemCommand event handler. As with the DataGrid, this is accomplished using OnItemCommand="EventHandlerName" in the DataList's declaration. (This is also the technique used when wiring up a Repeater's ItemCommand event to a suitable event handler.)

Passing Along Primary Key Information

In our example Listing 5.2, we need to be able to obtain the primary key field (title_id) of the book whose View Book Details button was clicked to retrieve the book's details. As we saw in Chapter 4, when dealing with the DataGrid and ButtonColumns, there are two ways to retrieve the clicked row's primary key field: using a hidden BoundColumn that contains the primary key information, or using the DataKeyField and DataKeys properties.

When using the DataList and templates, the same two options for passing along primary key information exist—you can store the primary key information in a hidden Web control in the template and then programmatically access its value in the ItemCommand event handler; or you can use the DataList's DataKeyField and DataKeys properties. Unfortunately, the Repeater control does not have the DataKeyField and DataKeys properties; therefore, if you're using the Repeater and need to pass along primary key information, you'll need to resort to hiding the information in hidden Web controls in the template.

In addition to these two techniques, a third option exists. The command buttons contain a property called CommandArgument. This property is similar to the CommandName property in that it is also an optional string property. The two properties differ in that the CommandName is typically used to differentiate which command button was clicked in a given row, whereas the CommandArgument is typically used to differentiate which row of the data Web control had its command button clicked. This, understandably, might sound a bit confusing, but when we examine a code example utilizing the CommandName and CommandArgument properties, this confusion will hopefully clear up.

As we've already examined how to use the DataKeyField and DataKeys properties (see the section "Using the DataKeyField Property and the DataKeys Collection to Pass Along a Primary Key Field" in Chapter 4), let's focus our attention on the other two approaches. In the next two sections, we'll look at how to use hidden Web controls in a template to pass primary key field information along, and then how to use the CommandArgument property to achieve the same ends.

Storing Primary Key Field Information in a Hidden Web Control

In this section we'll be examining how to determine the primary key field of a data Web control row that had a command button clicked. Specifically, we'll be looking at how to retrieve and display the selected book's details.

For this example, let's use a Repeater control, because we've yet to show an example using these techniques for this control. First, we need to add a hidden Web control to the template that contains the primary key field from the Repeater's DataSource. To accomplish this, we'll use a Label Web control with its Visible property set to False. We'll then dynamically set the Label control's Text property to the primary key field using data-binding syntax. The following code snippet presents the Repeater declaration needed to hide the primary key field in a hidden Web control:

```
<asp:Repeater runat="server" id="prtTitles"
  OnItemCommand="rptTitles_ItemCommand">
 <ItemTemplate>
  ... markup and data binding syntax ...

  <asp:label id="lblTitleID" Visible="False" runat="Server"
    Text='<%# DataBinder.Eval(Container.DataItem, "title_id") %>' />
 </ItemTemplate>
</asp:Repeater>
```

Note that the Label control's Visible property is set to False, meaning that it won't be rendered into HTML like the other ItemTemplate contents. However, it is still programmatically accessible. The value of the Text property is set using data-binding syntax; specifically, it is assigned the value of the primary key field (title_id).

NOTE

When setting an ASP.NET Web control's property using data binding, you must delimit the data-binding expression with a single apostrophe ('), as opposed to the standard double apostrophe (").

All that remains now is to write the code for the Repeater's ItemCommand event handler, such that when it is fired we can determine the value of the primary key field of the row whose command button was clicked. Listing 5.3 shows how to accomplish this feat.

LISTING 5.3   The Hidden Web Control Can Be Programmatically Accessed in the ItemCommand Event Handler

```
 1: <%@ import Namespace="System.Data" %>
 2: <%@ import Namespace="System.Data.SqlClient" %>
 3: <script runat="server" language="VB">
 4:   ' ... Page_Load and BindData have been removed for brevity ...
 5:     ' ... Consult Listing 5.1 for their details ...
 6:
 7:   Sub rptTitles_ItemCommand(sender As Object, e As RepeaterCommandEventArgs)
 8:    If e.CommandName = "Details" then
 9:     ' The details button has been clicked, find out the PK field value
10:     ' First, create a variable to hold the appropriate Label control
11:     Dim lc as Label = e.Item.FindControl("lblTitleID")
12:
```

LISTING 5.3   Continued

```
13:    'Next, read the value of the Label control
14:    Dim strTitleID as String = lc.Text
15:
16:    ' ... code to retrieve / display the book details goes here ...
17:    End If
18:    End Sub
19: </script>
20:
21: <form runat="server">
22:  <asp:Repeater runat="server" id="rptTitles"
23:      OnItemCommand=rptTitles_ItemCommand">
24:   <ItemTemplate>
25:    <b>Title:</b> <%# DataBinder.Eval(Container.DataItem, "title") %>
26:    <br />
27:    [<asp:LinkButton runat="server" id="btnDetails"
28:       Text="View Book Details" CommandName="Details" />]
29:
30:    <asp:label id="lblTitleID" Visible="False" runat="Server"
31:       Text='<%# DataBinder.Eval(Container.DataItem, "title_id") %>' />
32:   </ItemTemplate>
33:
34:   <SeparatorTemplate> <hr> </SeparatorTemplate>
35:  </asp:Repeater>
36: </form>
```

Lines 11 through 14 of Listing 5.3 illustrates how to programmatically access the hidden Label control that is added to the template on lines 30 and 31. Our dlTitles_ItemCommand event handler begins by checking to see whether it was the View Book Details LinkButton that triggered the ItemCommand event (line 8). If that is the case, line 11 is reached next, which accesses the Label control. Here we simply create a local variable named lc of type Label. We then set it equal to the control returned by the FindControl method of the RepeaterItem returned by e.Item. Note that we pass the name of the control we want to retrieve into the FindControl method—lblTitleID is the name of the hidden Label that stores the primary key field value (see line 30).

After we have a reference to the Label control (lc), we can read its Text property (line 14) and store it in a variable (strTitleID). At this point, we will need to write the code to access the details information for a particular book and then display that information. We'll examine how to do this shortly, but for now, make sure that you understand how the value of the hidden Label control is programmatically accessed in the ItemCommand event handler.

Finally, be sure to take note that the Repeater's `ItemCommand` event handler's second parameter is of type `RepeaterCommandEventArgs`. Recall that each data Web control has a unique signature for its `ItemCommand` event handler.

NOTE

The `FindControl` method is a method defined in the `Control` base class, meaning that every ASP.NET control has this method at its disposal. When using `SomeControl.FindControl(ID)`, the children controls of `SomeControl` are searched for a child control whose `ID` property matches the supplied `ID` input parameter. The `RepeaterItem`, which represents a "row" in the Repeater control, contains as children controls all the controls that appear in the template that was used to generate the row. For more information on the `FindControl` method, consult the resources in the "On the Web" section at the end of this chapter.

Now that we have looked at how to programmatically retrieve the value of the hidden Label control, let's finish off this example by completing the `ItemCommand` event handler so that the book whose LinkButton was clicked has its details displayed. To accomplish this, we'll need to add a new function, `GetBookDetails(TitleID)`, which returns a `SqlDataReader` with the details for a particular book. The code for the completed example is shown in Listing 5.4, while a screenshot can be seen in Figure 5.4.

LISTING 5.4   Clicking the Show Book Details Link Displays the Book's Details in a DataGrid

```
 1: <%@ import Namespace="System.Data" %>
 2: <%@ import Namespace="System.Data.SqlClient" %>
 3: <script runat="server" language="VB">
 4:   ' ... Page_Load and BindData have been removed for brevity ...
 5:     ' ... Consult Listing 5.1 for their details ...
 6:
 7:
 8:   Function GetBookDetails(TitleID as String) as SqlDataReader
 9:     '1. Create a connection
10:     Const strConnString as String = "server=localhost;uid=sa;pwd=;
➥database=pubs"
11:     Dim objConn as New SqlConnection(strConnString)
12:
13:     '2. Create a command object for the query
14:     Dim strSQL as String
15:     strSQL = "SELECT title, type, pubdate, notes FROM titles " & _
16:         "WHERE title_id = @TitleID"
17:     Dim objCmd as New SqlCommand(strSQL, objConn)
18:
```

LISTING 5.4   Continued

```
19:    '3. Create a parameter for the TitleID param
20:    Dim paramTitleID as SqlParameter
21:    paramTitleID = New SqlParameter("@TitleID", SqlDbType.VarChar, 10)
22:    paramTitleID.Value = TitleID
23:    objCmd.Parameters.Add(paramTitleID)
24:
25:    objConn.Open()   'Open the connection
26:
27:    'Finally, return the SqlDataReader
28:    Return objCmd.ExecuteReader(CommandBehavior.CloseConnection)
29:  End Function
30:
31:
32:  Sub rptTitles_ItemCommand(sender As Object, e As RepeaterCommandEventArgs)
33:   If e.CommandName = "Details" then
34:    ' The details button has been clicked, find out the PK field value
35:    ' First, create a variable to hold the appropriate Label control
36:    Dim lc as Label = e.Item.FindControl("lblTitleID")
37:
38:    'Next, read the value of the Label control
39:    Dim strTitleID as String = lc.Text
40:
41:    ' Display the book's details
42:    dgBookDetails.DataSource = GetBookDetails(strTitleID)
43:    dgBookDetails.DataBind()
44:
45:    ' Make sure the dgBookDetails DataGrid is Visible
46:    dgBookDetails.Visible = True
47:   End If
48:  End Sub
49: </script>
50:
51: <form runat="server">
52:  <%-- The dgBookDetails DataGrid displays the details
53:       for the selected book... --%>
54:  <asp:DataGrid runat="server" id="dgBookDetails"
55:    Font-Name="Verdana" HorizontalAlign="Center"
56:    Visible="False" Width="85%">
57:   <HeaderStyle BackColor="Navy" ForeColor="White"
58:     Font-Size="11pt" HorizontalAlign="Center" />
59:
```

LISTING 5.4   Continued

```
60:    <ItemStyle BackColor="#eeeeee" Font-Size="9pt" />
61:    </asp:DataGrid>
62:    <p> </p>
63:
64:    <%-- The rptTitles Repeater displays all of the books --%>
65:    <asp:Repeater runat="server" id="rptTitles"
66:       OnItemCommand="rptTitles_ItemCommand">
67:     <ItemTemplate>
68:      <b>Title:</b> <%# DataBinder.Eval(Container.DataItem, "title") %>
69:      <br />
70:      [<asp:LinkButton runat="server" id="btnDetails"
71:        Text="View Book Details" CommandName="Details" />]
72:
73:      <asp:label id="lblTitleID" Visible="False" runat="Server"
74:         Text='<%# DataBinder.Eval(Container.DataItem, "title_id") %>' />
75:     </ItemTemplate>
76:
77:     <SeparatorTemplate> <hr> </SeparatorTemplate>
78:    </asp:Repeater>
79:  </form>
```

Whew! Listing 5.4 is a lengthy code sample (and I even omitted the code for the Page_Load event handler and BindData function!). Before we delve into what's new with the Listing 5.4, let's take a look at what's the same from Listing 5.3. First, the Repeater code (lines 65 through 78) has not changed one iota from Listing 5.3; furthermore, the rptTitles_ItemCommand event handler's first few lines (lines 32 through 39) are the same as they were in Listing 5.3 (lines 7–14).

In the HTML section, a DataGrid control (lines 54–61) has been added. This DataGrid control (dgBookDetails) will be used to display the details about a particular book. Its declaration sets some display properties—the Font, Width, HorizontalAlign, HeaderStyle, and ItemStyle properties—as well as its Visible property, which is set to False (line 56). Because the Visible property is initially set to False, the dgBookDetails DataGrid won't be shown on the user's first visit to the page.

The rptTitles_ItemCommand event handler has had a few lines added. Recall that in Listing 5.3, we had coded the rptTitles_ItemCommand event handler only up until the point where we retrieved the book's title_id from the hidden Label Web control. In Listing 5.4 (lines 41 through 46), we complete the code for this event handler by passing the retrieved title_id to the GetBookDetails(*TitleID*) function (lines 8–29). The GetBookDetails(*TitleID*) function returns a SqlDataReader that contains the title, type, pubdate, and notes fields from the titles table for the particular book. This returned SqlDataReader is specified as the dgBookDetails DataSource (line 42). The DataBind() method is then called, and the DataGrid's Visible property is set to True, so that the book details' DataGrid is displayed.

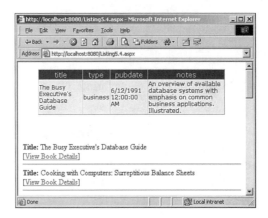

FIGURE 5.4   The details for the selected book are displayed in a DataGrid.

Storing Primary Key Field Information in the CommandArgument Property

Now that we have examined how to pass along primary key field information through hidden Web controls, let's look at a more elegant solution: using the CommandArgument property. To store primary key field information in this property, we simply need to set the command button's CommandArgument property equal to the primary key field of the DataSource. We can accomplish this by using the same data-binding syntax used in Listing 5.4 (line 74), where we set the Text property of the hidden Label control to the title_id field of the DataSource.

To apply the CommandArgument technique to our book details example, we'd start by specifying the CommandArgument of our command button like so:

```
<ItemTemplate>
  <b>Title:</b> <%# DataBinder.Eval(Container.DataItem, "title") %>
  <br />
  [<asp:LinkButton runat="server" id="btnDetails"
   Text="View Book Details" CommandName="Details"
   CommandArgument='<%# DataBinder.Eval(Container.DataItem, "title_id") %>' />]
</ItemTemplate>
```

Then, in our ItemCommand event handler, we can reference this primary key field value by simply accessing the CommandArgument parameter of the second parameter to the event handler (which is either of type DataGridCommandEventHandler, DataListCommandEventHandler, or RepeaterCommandEventHandler, depending on what data Web control is being used).

Listing 5.5 illustrates how to pass along and read the primary key field information using the LinkButton's `CommandArgument` property. In this example, we use a DataGrid's TemplateColumn to display the list of books, as opposed to using a Repeater or DataList.

LISTING 5.5   The LinkButton's `CommandArgument` Property Is Used to Pass on the Primary Key Field Information

```
 1: <%@ import Namespace="System.Data" %>
 2: <%@ import Namespace="System.Data.SqlClient" %>
 3: <script runat="server" language="VB">
 4:   ' ... Page_Load and BindData have been removed for brevity ...
 5:    ' ... Consult Listing 5.1 for their details ...
 6:
 7:   ' ... For the GetBookDetails function, see Listing 5.4 ...
 8:
 9:
10:   Sub dgTitles_ItemCommand(sender As Object, e As DataGridCommandEventArgs)
11:     If e.CommandName = "Details" then
12:      ' The details button has been clicked, find out the PK field value
13:      Dim strTitleID as String = e.CommandArgument
14:
15:       ' Display the book's details
16:       dgBookDetails.DataSource = GetBookDetails(strTitleID)
17:       dgBookDetails.DataBind()
18:
19:       ' Make sure the dgBookDetails DataGrid is Visible
20:       dgBookDetails.Visible = True
21:     End If
22:   End Sub
23: </script>
24:
25: <form runat="server">
26: <%-- The dgBookDetails DataGrid displays the details
27:        for the selected book... --%>
28: <asp:DataGrid runat="server" id="dgBookDetails"
29:     Font-Name="Verdana" HorizontalAlign="Center"
30:     Visible="False" Width="85%">
31:   <HeaderStyle BackColor="Navy" ForeColor="White"
32:     Font-Size="11pt" HorizontalAlign="Center" />
33:
34:   <ItemStyle BackColor="#eeeeee" Font-Size="9pt" />
35: </asp:DataGrid>
36: <p> </p>
37:
```

LISTING 5.5   Continued

```
38:  <%-- The dgTitles DataGrid displays all of the books --%>
39:  <asp:DataGrid runat="server" id="dgTitles"
40:    OnItemCommand="dgTitles_ItemCommand"
41:    AutoGenerateColumns="False" ShowHeader="False">
42:   <Columns>
43:    <asp:TemplateColumn>
44:     <ItemTemplate>
45:      <b>Title:</b>
46:      <%# DataBinder.Eval(Container.DataItem, "title") %>
47:      <br />
48:      [<asp:LinkButton runat="server" id="btnDetails"
49:       Text="View Book Details" CommandName="Details"
50:       CommandArgument='<%# DataBinder.Eval(Container.DataItem, "title_id")
➡ %>' />]
51:     </ItemTemplate>
52:    </asp:TemplateColumn>
53:   </Columns>
54:  </asp:DataGrid>
55: </form>
```

The key lines in Listing 5.5 are the setting of the LinkButton's `CommandArgument` property on line 50 and the use of the `CommandArgument` property of the `DataGridCommandEventArg` variable e in the `dgTitles_ItemCommand` event handler on line 13. Figure 5.5 shows a screenshot of Listing 5.5 when viewed through a browser.

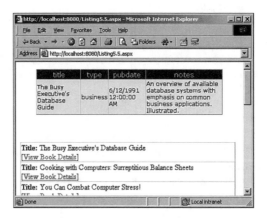

FIGURE 5.5   The `CommandArgument` property can be used to pass along primary key field information.

Deciding Which Method to Use to Pass Primary Key Field Information

Recall that by placing command buttons in templates, there are three ways to pass primary key field information:

1. Using hidden Web controls.

2. Using the `CommandArgument` property.

3. Using the `DataKeyField` and `DataKeys` properties (only applicable for the DataGrid and DataList Web controls).

Which method is the best? Personally, I find the `DataKeyField` and `DataKeys` approach to be the most natural option. Of course, this is only an option if you are using the DataGrid or DataList controls; even then, as you'll recall from Chapter 4, the `DataKeyField` and `DataKeys` approach only works with simple, single-field primary keys. Similarly, the `CommandArgument` approach does not naturally work for composite primary keys. Although you could programmatically set the `CommandArgument` property to contain multiple primary key fields in an `ItemDataBound` event handler, it would require some complicated programming. The hidden Web controls approach grants you the most flexibility in passing along data, but is clearly the most complicated and non-natural approach. Ideally, try to use the `DataKeyField` and `DataKeys` properties, if possible.

Command Buttons That Trigger Events Other Than `ItemCommand`

As we have seen thus far, when any command button in a template is clicked, the `ItemCommand` event of the data Web control that contains the command button is fired. However, the DataGrid and DataList contain a bevy of other events that can be triggered in addition to the `ItemCommand` event. Tables 5.1 and 5.2 list the additional events for the DataGrid and DataList, respectively.

TABLE 5.1 Additional Command Button-Triggered Events for the DataGrid

Event	Description
CancelCommand	Occurs when a command button with a Cancel CommandName is clicked.
DeleteCommand	Occurs when a command button with a Delete CommandName is clicked.
EditCommand	Occurs when a command button with a Edit CommandName is clicked.
SortCommand	Occurs when a command button with a Sort CommandName is clicked.
UpdateCommand	Occurs when a command button with a Update CommandName is clicked.

TABLE 5.2   Additional Command Button-Triggered Events for the DataList

Event	Description
CancelCommand	Occurs when a command button with a Cancel CommandName is clicked.
DeleteCommand	Occurs when a command button with a Delete CommandName is clicked.
EditCommand	Occurs when a command button with a Edit CommandName is clicked.
UpdateCommand	Occurs when a command button with a Update CommandName is clicked.

The only difference between the DataGrid and DataList control is that the DataList does not contain a SortCommand event.

NOTE

The only command button event for the Repeater control is the ItemCommand event.

When a command button contains as its CommandName property one of the reserved command names—Cancel, Delete, Edit, Sort, or Update—when the command button is clicked, *both* the ItemCommand event is fired along with the appropriate additional event. That is, if you add a command button to a DataList with the CommandName Update, when the command button is clicked, the ASP.NET page will be posted back and the DataList's ItemCommand event *and* UpdateCommand events will be fired.

The Purpose of the Additional Events

As we've seen in this chapter, the command buttons enable developers to associate server-side event handlers with the user's click of a command button. The examples we've worked on in this chapter use these command buttons to provide a Details button that displays detailed information about a particular record in a separate Web control. Although command buttons can certainly be used for this purpose, the Microsoft developers who designed the data Web controls reasoned that one of the more common uses of these command buttons would be for sorting, deleting, and editing data.

With this assumption in mind, the developers created the additional events listed in the Tables 5.1 and 5.2 to make adding such functionality to the DataGrid and DataList much simpler. If you're wondering how these events make adding such functionality to your DataGrid or DataList simpler, imagine for a moment that those events listed in Tables 5.1 and 5.2 don't exist. If we want to add a button to the DataList that deletes the associated record, what would we need to do?

As we've seen in our examples in this chapter, we would start by creating a command button of some kind with an appropriately named CommandName (such as Delete). Next, we would probably want to use the DataKeyField/DataKeys properties to track the primary key; therefore, we would specify the `DataSource`'s primary key field in the `DataKeyField` property. Following that, we are ready to add the `ItemCommand` event handler. In this event handler, we would check to see whether the `CommandName` equals `Delete`. If it does, we would retrieve the primary key field value of the item being deleted, and then make the appropriate database call to delete the record. Finally, we would repopulate the `DataSource` (because we now have one fewer record) and rebind it to the DataList.

At this point, I probably haven't convinced you that the additional events make adding such functionality easier. But imagine for a moment that we want to add an Edit command button. We haven't yet looked at how to edit data in a data Web control (we will, though, in Chapter 9, "Editing the DataGrid Web Control"), but it involves supplying an EditItemTemplate and programmatically setting the data Web control's `EditItemIndex` property to the row that we want to edit. Again, all this functionality can be encapsulated in the `ItemCommand` event handler, and the same applies to the Update and Cancel buttons that we would want to add to the EditItemTemplate.

The point is, as we add more and more command buttons, the `ItemCommand` event handler becomes more and more unwieldy. For example, with all the buttons listed in the preceding, the `ItemCommand` event handler would start to look like

```
Sub dlTitles_ItemCommand(sender as Object, e as DataListCommandEventArgs)
  If e.CommandName = "Delete" then
    ' handle the delete case
  End If

  If e.CommandName = "Edit" then
    ' handle the edit case
  End If

  If e.CommandName = "Update" then
    ' handle the update case
  End If

  If e.CommandName = "Cancel" then
    ' handle the cancel case
  End If
End Sub
```

and so on—one `If` statement for each command button type. Because the code to handle each command button can be quite long, the `ItemCommand` event handler can very quickly balloon in size! By breaking these common command button cases into separate events, it allows for a much more readable program, which would instead look like this:

```
Sub DeleteCommandEventHandler(sender as Object, e as DataListCommandEventArgs)
 ' handle the delete case
End Sub

Sub EditCommandEventHandler(sender as Object, e as DataListCommandEventArgs)
 ' handle the edit case
End Sub

Sub UpdateCommandEventHandler(sender as Object, e as DataListCommandEventArgs)
 ' handle the update case
End Sub

Sub CancelCommandEventHandler(sender as Object, e as DataListCommandEventArgs)
 ' handle the cancel case
End Sub
```

We will not be looking at how to add edit, delete, and sorting capabilities to the data Web controls in this chapter. Instead there are future chapters reserved for the discussion of such functionality. These chapters fall in Part III, "Advanced Features of the DataGrid Web Control":

- Chapter 7—"Sorting the DataGrid's Data"
- Chapter 9—"Editing the DataGrid Web Control"
- Chapter 10—"Putting It All Together—A Real-World Example"

If you're anxious to get to this exciting material, don't worry. The next chapter is the last chapter in Part II—after that, we'll dive headfirst into sorting, paging, and editing the DataGrid control!

Creating Select Command Buttons

All the examples we've looked at in this and the previous chapter have had one underlying theme in common: the user is presented with a command button of some kind on each row in the data Web control that performs some sort of action based upon the row whose command button was clicked. In our running example in this chapter, we've been looking at how to add a Details button to each row that displays more in-depth information about the particular row.

On an aesthetic level, it would be nice to let users know what row they have clicked through the use of visual cues. Perhaps the row whose command button was clicked will have its text displayed in bold or a different color background than the other rows. To facilitate this, the DataGrid and DataList controls contain a `SelectedIndex` property that can be used to designate which row of the DataGrid or DataList is the "selected" row. In addition to this, both controls contain a display property called `SelectedItemStyle`, through which style information for the selected row can be specified.

There are two ways to designate what row is the selected row:

1. Explicitly, by programmatically setting the `SelectedIndex` property.

2. Implicitly, by setting the command button's `CommandName` property to Select.

To explicitly indicate that a row is the selected row, you first need to create a command button that makes the row the selected row. In our Details example, this would simply be the Details button. In the `ItemCommand` event handler, you would test to see whether the Details button is the button that triggered the `ItemCommand` event; if it is, you want to then set the DataGrid or DataList's `SelectedIndex` property equal to the `ItemIndex` property of the DataGrid's `DataGridItem` or DataList's `DataListItem` that was clicked. That is, if we were using a DataList, you would declare your DataList like so:

```
<asp:DataList runat="server" id="dlTitles"
   OnItemCommand="dlTitles_ItemCommand" ...>
 <ItemTemplate>
  <asp:Button runat="server" Text="Details" CommandName="Details" />
  ...
 </ItemTemplate>
</asp:DataList>
```

Then, in the `dlTitles_ItemCommand` event handler, you would set the `SelectedIndex` property with

```
Sub dlTitles_ItemCommand(sender as Object, e as DataListCommandEventArgs)
 ' Make sure it was the "Details" command button that was clicked...
 If e.CommandName = "Details" then
  ' Now, programmatically set the SelectedIndex property
  dlTitles.SelectedIndex = e.Item.ItemIndex
 End If
End Sub
```

Although explicitly setting the `SelectedIndex` property is not terribly difficult, the DataGrid and DataList will automatically set the `SelectedIndex` property accordingly when a command button with its `CommandName` property set to "Select" is clicked. Listing 5.6, which we'll examine shortly, illustrates using a command button with its `CommandName` set to "Select".

Altering the Display Properties of the Selected Row

The DataGrid and DataList contain a `SelectedItemStyle` display property that is applied to the selected item. Recall from Chapter 3 that style properties are actually full-blown classes themselves and incorporate a number of properties, such as `Font`, `HorizontalAlign`, `BackColor`, `ForeColor`, and so on. Listing 5.6 contains a DataGrid declaration that specifies a `SelectedItemStyle`—the server-side script block has been omitted, for it simply contains the `Page_Load` event handler and the `BindData` function that has already been presented in previous code listings in this chapter.

LISTING 5.6   The `SelectedItemStyle` Property Specifies the Aesthetic Settings for the Selected Item

```
 1: <form runat="server">
 2:  <asp:DataGrid AutoGenerateColumns="False"
 3:     runat="server" id="dgTitles"
 4:     Font-Name="Verdana" Font-Size="9pt">
 5:
 6:   <SelectedItemStyle BackColor="#dddddd" Font-Italic="True"
 7:      Font-Size="15pt" />
 8:
 9:   <HeaderStyle BackColor="Navy" ForeColor="White"
10:      Font-Bold="True" HorizontalAlign="Center"
11:      Font-Size="11pt" />
12:
13:   <Columns>
14:    <asp:ButtonColumn Text="Details" CommandName="Select"
15:        HeaderText="View Details" ItemStyle-HorizontalAlign="Center" />
16:    <asp:BoundColumn DataField="Title" HeaderText="Title" />
17:   </Columns>
18:  </asp:DataGrid>
19: </form>
```

When the ASP.NET Web page on which the DataGrid from Listing 5.6 resides on is first visited, each row of the DataGrid will look the same, with its Verdana 9 pt. font. Each row will also contain a Details hyperlink created by the ButtonColumn control (line 14). Note that the CommandName is set to "Select", which will cause the SelectedIndex to be updated to the index of the row whose Details button was clicked. (Note that the initial value of the SelectedIndex is -1.)

When a row's Details button is clicked, the ASP.NET page posts back and the DataGrid's SelectedIndex property is automatically updated. In addition, the DataGrid's SelectedIndexChanged event is fired. This event is fired whenever the DataGrid's SelectedIndex property changes between postbacks. We'll examine

some potential uses for this event in a bit, but for now realize that the
SelectedIndex property is updated for you automatically when you use a command
button with its CommandName property set to "Select".

When a Details button is clicked and the SelectedIndex property is set accordingly,
the SelectedItemStyle property's attributes are applied to the selected row. Figure
5.6 illustrates this—note that after a particular row has been clicked, the ASP.NET
page is posted back and the row that was clicked is then displayed with a different
color background, in italics, and with a larger font.

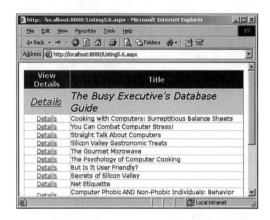

FIGURE 5.6   The row whose Details button was clicked is clearly marked.

Figure 5.6 shows that when a row is selected, it takes on a different appearance from
the other rows in the DataGrid. However, the details for the selected row are not
shown. In Listing 5.5, we saw how to display such details in a separate DataGrid
Web control when setting each row's primary key field information to the command
button's CommandArgument property.

In Listing 5.6, however, we're using a ButtonColumn control, which doesn't contain
a CommandArgument property. At this point, we have two options. The first is to
convert the ButtonColumn into a TemplateColumn, which would then include a
command button in the ItemTemplate. This command button would have its
CommandName property set to "Select" and its CommandArgument property set to the
primary key field via data-binding syntax. That is, lines 14 and 15 in Listing 5.6
would become

```
<asp:TemplateColumn>
 <ItemTemplate>
  <asp:LinkButton runat="server" CommandName="Select" Text="Details"
       CommandArgument='<%# DataBinder.Eval(Container.DataItem, "title_id") %>' />
 </ItemTemplate>
</asp:TemplateColumn>
```

This primary key field information could then be extracted in the `ItemCommand` event handler, which would look like

```
Sub dgTitles_ItemCommand(sender As Object, e As DataGridCommandEventArgs)
  If e.CommandName = "Select" then
    ' The details button has been clicked, find out the PK field value
    Dim strTitleID as String = e.CommandArgument

    ' Display the book's details
    dgBookDetails.DataSource = GetBookDetails(strTitleID)
    dgBookDetails.DataBind()

    ' Make sure the dgBookDetails DataGrid is Visible
    dgBookDetails.Visible = True
  End If
End Sub
```

Note that the `If` statement on the second line checks to see whether the `CommandName` equals "Select", because that is the name of our LinkButton control in the DataGrid's TemplateColumn. This is the technique we discussed earlier in this chapter in the "Storing Primary Key Field Information in the `CommandArgument` Property" section.

The other option involves leaving the ButtonColumn control untouched and moving the logic to the DataGrid's `SelectedItemChanged` event handler. Recall that the `SelectedItemChanged` event handler is fired whenever the DataGrid's `SelectedIndex` property's value changes between postbacks. Hence, when the code in the `SelectedItemChanged` event handler is being executed, we know that the user has selected a new row. Therefore, we can move the logic to populate the dgBookDetails DataGrid with the particular book's details into this event handler. This means that the `SelectedItemChanged` event handler will have to call the `GetBookDetails(TitleID)` function, but to do this, we need to know the primary key field value of the selected row. Because we're using the ButtonColumn control and not a command button in a template, we can't use the `CommandArgument` approach. Instead, we'll fall back on the preferred technique: using the `DataKeyField` and `DataKeys` properties.

Listing 5.7 enhances Listing 5.6 so as to actually display the book's details when the user selects a particular row. Note that the semantics of Listing 5.7 are identical to that of Listing 5.5; the only differences are visual ones. For example, using the `SelectedItemStyle` and a command button with a `CommandName` of "Select", Listing 5.7 has the selected row visually different from the other rows.

LISTING 5.7   The Book Whose Details Are Being Displayed Is Visually Different from the Other Books in the DataGrid

```
 1: <%@ import Namespace="System.Data" %>
 2: <%@ import Namespace="System.Data.SqlClient" %>
 3: <script runat="server" language="C#">
 4:   ' ... the Page_Load event handler, and the BindData and
 5:   '   GetBookDetails functions have been omitted for brevity ...
 6:
 7:   void ShowDetails(object sender, EventArgs e)
 8:   {
 9:     // Get the TitleID
10:     string strTitleID = dgTitles.DataKeys[dgTitles.SelectedIndex].ToString();
11:
12:     // Display the book's details
13:     dgBookDetails.DataSource = GetBookDetails(strTitleID);
14:     dgBookDetails.DataBind();
15:
16:     // Make sure the dgBookDetails DataGrid is Visible
17:     dgBookDetails.Visible = true;
18:   }
19: </script>
20:
21: <form runat="server">
22:   <%-- The dgBookDetails DataGrid displays the details
23:          for the selected book... --%>
24:   <asp:DataGrid runat="server" id="dgBookDetails"
25:     Font-Name="Verdana" HorizontalAlign="Center"
26:     Visible="False" Width="85%">
27:     <HeaderStyle BackColor="Navy" ForeColor="White"
28:       Font-Size="11pt" HorizontalAlign="Center" />
29:
30:     <ItemStyle BackColor="#eeeeee" Font-Size="9pt" />
31:   </asp:DataGrid>
32:   <p> </p>
33:
34:   <%-- The dgTitles DataGrid displays all of the books --%>
35:   <asp:DataGrid AutoGenerateColumns="False"
36:     runat="server" id="dgTitles"
37:     OnSelectedIndexChanged="ShowDetails"
38:     DataKeyField="title_id"
39:     Font-Name="Verdana" Font-Size="9pt">
40:
```

LISTING 5.7   Continued

```
41:    <SelectedItemStyle BackColor="#dddddd" Font-Italic="True"
42:       Font-Size="15pt" />
43:
44:    <HeaderStyle BackColor="Navy" ForeColor="White"
45:       Font-Bold="True" HorizontalAlign="Center"
46:       Font-Size="11pt" />
47:
48:    <Columns>
49:     <asp:ButtonColumn Text="Details" CommandName="Select"
50:       HeaderText="View Details" ItemStyle-HorizontalAlign="Center" />
51:     <asp:BoundColumn DataField="Title" HeaderText="Title" />
52:    </Columns>
53:   </asp:DataGrid>
54: </form>
```

The major difference between Listing 5.7 and Listing 5.5 is that Listing 5.7 has removed the ItemCommand event handler entirely. Instead, it has been replaced by the SelectedIndexChanged event handler, ShowDetails (lines 7–18). ShowDetails is executed whenever the user clicks on a "Select" command button that is not in the currently selected row.

The first thing we do in ShowDetails is determine the primary key field of the selected row; this is accomplished by consulting the DataKeys collection (line 10) and grabbing the item whose index matches that of the DataGrid's SelectedIndex property. Note that the signature for the SelectedIndexChanged event handler has as its second parameter a variable of type EventArgs, as opposed to the DataGridCommandEventArgs type that was used for the DataGrid's ItemCommand event. This limits us in that we cannot reference the CommandName or CommandArgument that corresponds to the command button that caused the SelectedIndex to change; nor can we access the DataGridItem that corresponds to the DataGrid row that contains the command button that caused the SelectedIndex to change. Fortunately, we can use the DataGrid's SelectedIndex property to correctly index the DataKeys field to get the appropriate primary key field value.

Figure 5.7 contains a screenshot of Listing 5.7 when viewed through a browser. Note that the output generated by Listing 5.5 (Figure 5.5) and Listing 5.7 differs only in visual aspects.

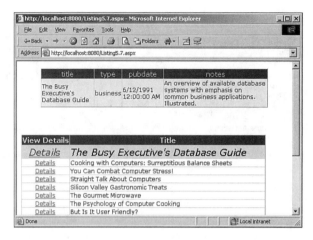

FIGURE 5.7   The book's details are displayed in a separate DataGrid.

Altering the Content of the Selected Row

In the previous section, we looked at how to alter the display properties of the selected item via the `SelectedItemStyle`. We also examined how to use a command button that automatically updates the DataGrid's `SelectedIndex` property. Although our examples in the prior section used a DataGrid Web control, realize that the DataList also supports this same functionality.

In fact, the DataList includes some additional functionality that's missing in the DataGrid. Specifically, when using the DataList, you can specify a SelectedItemTemplate. This template is used instead of the ItemTemplate when rendering the row whose index is equal to the `SelectedIndex` property.

In our previous examples, we displayed the details of the book by populating a separate DataGrid (`dgBookDetails`) with the results of a SQL query that returned the details for the particular book. Using the DataList's SelectedItemTemplate, we can have the details shown in row itself. That is, when the user clicks the Details button, the `SelectedIndex` property will be set to the row clicked and the DataList will be rebound to the `DataSource`; when the DataList is rendered, the row whose index is equal to the `SelectedIndex` will be rendered using the SelectedItemTemplate. Hence, the row whose Details button was clicked will have the details for that row displayed in place.

To understand what we're after, take a moment to examine Figure 5.8, which shows a screenshot of the code in Listing 5.8. In Figure 5.8, the user has already clicked on a book's Details button, thus causing a postback and the rebinding of the DataList.

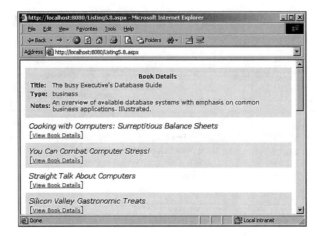

FIGURE 5.8   The book's details are shown in place.

Now to write the code to produce the output shown in Figure 5.8! Listing 5.8 contains the source code needed to produce a DataList that uses a SelectedItemTemplate to display a book's details in place.

LISTING 5.8   The SelectedItemTemplate Allows for Different Content for the Selected Row

```
1: <%@ import Namespace="System.Data" %>
2: <%@ import Namespace="System.Data.SqlClient" %>
3: <script runat="server" language="C#">
4:   void Page_Load(object sender, EventArgs e)
5:   {
6:     if (!Page.IsPostBack)
7:       BindData();
8:   }
9:
10:
11:   void BindData()
12:   {
13:     // 1. Create a connection
14:     const string strConnString = "server=localhost;uid=sa;pwd=;database=pubs";
15:     SqlConnection objConn = new SqlConnection(strConnString);
16:
17:     // 2. Create a command object for the query
18:     const string strSQL = "SELECT * FROM titles";
19:     SqlCommand objCmd = new SqlCommand(strSQL, objConn);
20:
```

LISTING 5.8   Continued

```
21:    objConn.Open();  // Open the connection
22:
23:    //Finally, specify the DataSource and call DataBind()
24:    dlTitles.DataSource = objCmd.ExecuteReader
➥(CommandBehavior.CloseConnection);
25:    dlTitles.DataBind();
26:
27:    objConn.Close();  // Close the connection
28:    }
29:
30:
31:    void DisplayBookDetails(object sender, EventArgs e)
32:    {
33:    // simply rebind the DataList
34:    BindData();
35:    }
36: </script>
37: <form runat="server">
38:  <asp:DataList runat="server" id="dlTitles"
39:    OnSelectedIndexChanged="DisplayBookDetails"
40:    Font-Name="Verdana" Font-Size="11pt"
41:    ItemStyle-BackColor="#eeeeee"
42:    AlternatingItemStyle-BackColor="White"
43:    HorizontalAlign="Center" CellPadding="8">
44:
45:    <ItemTemplate>
46:    <i><%# DataBinder.Eval(Container.DataItem, "title") %></i>
47:    <br />
48:    [<asp:LinkButton runat="server" CommandName="Select"
49:      Font-Size="8pt" Text="View Book Details" />]
50:    </ItemTemplate>
51:
52:    <SelectedItemTemplate>
53:    <table border="0" style="font-size:9pt;">
54:     <tr><th colspan="2">Book Details</th></tr>
55:     <tr>
56:      <td><b>Title:</b></td>
57:      <td><%# DataBinder.Eval(Container.DataItem, "title") %></td>
58:     </tr>
59:     <tr>
60:      <td><b>Type:</b></td>
```

LISTING 5.8   Continued

```
61:        <td><%# DataBinder.Eval(Container.DataItem, "type") %></td>
62:      </tr>
63:      <tr>
64:       <td><b>Notes:</b></td>
65:       <td><%# DataBinder.Eval(Container.DataItem, "notes") %></td>
66:      </tr>
67:     </table>
68:    </SelectedItemTemplate>
69:   </asp:DataList>
70: </form>
```

The DataList in Listing 5.8 contains two templates—the ItemTemplate (lines 45–50) and the SelectedItemTemplate (lines 52–68). The ItemTemplate is used to render each non-selected row, whereas the SelectedItemTemplate is used to render the row whose index equals the DataList's SelectedIndex property.

In the ItemTemplate, a command button is added (lines 48 and 49). Because this command button's CommandName property has been set to "Select", when it is clicked, the row that contained the clicked button will become the selected row. When this happens, the SelectedIndexChanged event will fire. On line 39, we specify that when the SelectedIndexChanged event fires, the DisplayBookDetails event handler should be executed. This event handler, defined on lines 31–35, simply calls the BindData() function, which rebuilds the DataSource and rebinds the DataList (line 34).

If you omit the call to the BindData() method in the DisplayBookDetails event handler, the selected row of the DataList will appear to be delayed. That is, if you click the Details link for *The Busy Executive's Database Guide*, the ASP.NET page will be posted back, and it will appear as though nothing has happened. If you then click the Details button for *But Is It User Friendly?*, the details will appear for *The Busy Executive's Database Guide*. This is because the view state for the DataList is loaded before the SelectedIndex is changed by the DataList. Therefore, the DataList will be rendered using the prior view state representation of the DataList. To get around this dilemma, we simply force the DataList to rebind itself in the SelectedIndexChanged event handler.

NOTE

Although the code in Listing 5.8 does not set any SelectedItemStyle properties, rest assured that the DataList does indeed contain a SelectedItemStyle that can be used to customize the appearance of the selected row, exactly as we saw in the previous section with the DataGrid control. The SelectedItemTemplate, however, is unique to the DataList.

Summary

In this chapter, we examined how to use command buttons in the templates of the data Web controls. Recall that the command buttons include the ASP.NET Button, LinkButton, and ImageButton controls. When placed in a template, the command button causes a postback to the ASP.NET page, raising the `ItemCommand` event for the data Web control. By providing an event handler for this event, you can associate server-side code with the user's action of clicking a command button.

We also briefly looked at the additional command button events provided by the DataGrid and DataList, which include: `SortCommand`, `EditCommand`, `UpdateCommand`, `CancelCommand`, and `DeleteCommand`. These events have been added to make programming for sorting, editing, and deleting functionality easier and the end code more readable.

Finally, we examined how to use command buttons to mark a row as "selected." To specify that a row is the selected one, you can either explicitly set the `SelectedIndex` property programmatically, or simply set the `CommandName` property to "Select" for the command button that is responsible for designating a row as being selected. With both the DataGrid and DataList controls, a selected row can have its display properties specified by the `SelectedItemStyle` property. The DataList, however, can also customize the actual content of the selected row via the SelectedItemTemplate.

In this and the previous chapter we studied how to add command buttons to the various data Web controls and how to have the data Web controls respond to the user clicking the command buttons. In the next chapter, we'll look at how to have the events raised by controls external to the data Web controls affect the data Web controls.

On the Web

For more information on the topics discussed in this chapter, consider perusing the following online resources:

- "Technical Documentation for the `Control.FindControl` Method"—
  `http://msdn.microsoft.com/library/default.asp?url=/library/en-us/cpref/html/frlrfsystemwebuicontrolclassfindcontroltopic.asp`

- "Working with Command Button Controls"—
  `http://www.aspalliance.com/aspxtreme/webforms/controls/buttons.aspx`

- "Working with the DataList"—
  `http://samples.gotdotnet.com/quickstart/aspplus/samples/webforms/ctrl ref/webctrl/datalist/doc_datalist.aspx`

- "Working with the DataGrid"—
  http://samples.gotdotnet.com/quickstart/aspplus/samples/webforms/ctrl
  ref/webctrl/datagrid/doc_datagrid.aspx

- "Data Access and Customization"—http://samples.gotdotnet.com/quick-
  start/aspplus/doc/webdatalist.aspx

- "Selecting Items with the DataList and DataGrid Controls"—
  http://www.dotnetjunkies.com/tutorials.aspx?tutorialid=51

6

Using External Web Controls to Achieve Effects on the Web Control

In the past two chapters, we examined how to add command buttons to the data Web controls. When adding a command button to a data Web control, the command button is placed in each row of the data Web control. This is useful if you want to associate some action with a particular row in the data Web control. For example, in the last chapter, we saw how to use a command button to add a Details button to each row in a DataGrid, DataList, or Repeater. When a particular row's Details button was clicked, the ASP.NET page would be posted back, and the details for the clicked row would be displayed.

There are situations, however, where we might not want one button for every row, but rather one button that affects the entire data Web control. For example, imagine that you have a DataGrid that displays a list of employees from your company's database. For each employee, there might be information like name, hire date, contact information, and department (such as sales, IT, executive, and so on). If your company has hundreds or thousands of employees, it would be difficult to find a particular employee if you simply list all the employees. To make using the list easier, you could provide a series of filtering buttons external to the DataGrid control. For example, there might be a Show All Employees in Sales button that shows only the sales employees.

In this chapter, we'll look at a couple of real-world scenarios in which external Web controls can be used to enhance the functionality and usability of a data Web control.

Creating Filtering Buttons

When displaying data, it is often the case that there is so much that attempting to display it all on one Web page would make the information difficult to read and comprehend. Imagine for a moment how well you could analyze a company's financial data if you were shown weekly revenue numbers for the past 10 years all on one page! Clearly, to make data consumable, it is vital that it be presented in smaller chunks.

One way to space out data on a Web page is to paginate the data and enable the user to page through the information. Search engines are a classic example of pagination—a search on Google for "ASP.NET" yields more than 1.2 million hits, but fortunately I am only shown 10 results at a time. In Chapter 8, "Providing DataGrid Pagination," we'll examine how to provide pagination support for the DataGrid Web control.

Another more user-proactive approach to reducing the sheer amount of data is to provide filter buttons. Filter buttons are simple ASP.NET command button controls (Buttons, LinkButtons, or ImageButtons) that enable the user to filter the results of a data Web control.

In the past couple of chapters, we have been looking at code examples that have involved the `titles` database table. One of the fields in the `titles` table is `type`. Let's look at an example that provides a series of filter buttons to display the various types of books in the `titles` table.

Before we concern ourselves with creating filter buttons, though, let's create an ASP.NET Web page that uses a DataGrid to display *all* the rows in the `titles` table. After this, we'll add our filter buttons and examine the code changes needed to support filtering. Listing 6.1 contains the complete code and HTML markup for an ASP.NET Web page that displays the entire contents of the `titles` table.

LISTING 6.1   The Contents of the `titles` Table Are Displayed

```
1: <%@ import Namespace="System.Data" %>
2: <%@ import Namespace="System.Data.SqlClient" %>
3: <script runat="server" language="VB">
4:   Sub Page_Load(sender as Object, e as EventArgs)
5:     If Not Page.IsPostBack then
6:       BindData()
7:     End If
```

LISTING 6.1   Continued

```
 8:    End Sub
 9:
10:
11:    Sub BindData()
12:      '1. Create a connection
13:      Const strConnString as String = "server=localhost;uid=sa;pwd=;
➥database=pubs"
14:      Dim objConn as New SqlConnection(strConnString)
15:
16:      '2. Create a command object for the query
17:      Const strSQL as String = "SELECT * FROM titles"
18:      Dim objCmd as New SqlCommand(strSQL, objConn)
19:
20:      objConn.Open()   'Open the connection
21:
22:      'Finally, specify the DataSource and call DataBind()
23:      dgTitles.DataSource = objCmd.ExecuteReader(CommandBehavior.CloseConnection)
24:      dgTitles.DataBind()
25:
26:      objConn.Close()   'Close the connection
27:    End Sub
28: </script>
29:
30: <form runat="server">
31:  <asp:DataGrid runat="server" id="dgTitles"
32:    AutoGenerateColumns="False" CellPadding="5"
33:    Font-Name="Verdana" Font-Size="9pt"
34:    AlternatingItemStyle-BackColor="#dddddd">
35:
36:    <HeaderStyle BackColor="Navy" ForeColor="White" Font-Size="13pt"
37:        Font-Bold="True" HorizontalAlign="Center" />
38:
39:    <Columns>
40:    <asp:BoundColumn DataField="title_id" HeaderText="Title ID"
41:        ItemStyle-HorizontalAlign="Center" />
42:    <asp:BoundColumn DataField="title" HeaderText="Title" />
43:    <asp:BoundColumn DataField="type" HeaderText="Type" />
44:    </Columns>
45:  </asp:DataGrid>
46: </form>
```

You should be comfortable with the code in Listing 6.1. It simply calls the BindData() function on the first page load (when Page.IsPostBack is False, lines 5–7) and binds the results of the SQL query SELECT * FROM titles to the DataGrid dgTitles (lines 18–24). The DataGrid control (lines 31–45) displays three of the titles table's fields—title_id, title, and type (lines 40–43)—and specifies some stylistic and display settings. Note that the DataGrid is surrounded by a server-side form (lines 30 and 46); with the code given in Listing 6.1 this Web form is superfluous, but it will be needed as we build on this code, adding command buttons. Figure 6.1 shows a screenshot of the code in Listing 6.1 when viewed through a browser.

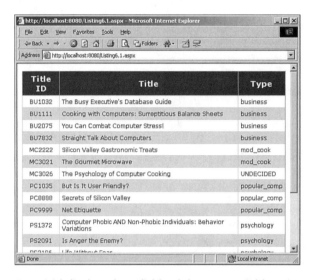

FIGURE 6.1   A DataGrid displays three fields of the titles table.

By inspecting Figure 6.1 you might be able to see that, for the rows in the titles table, the type column contains one of six values: "business," "mod_cook," "popular_comp," "psychology," "trad_cook," or "UNDECIDED." When providing filtering buttons, one option would be to create seven such buttons—one to show all results, and one for each of the type values. That is, we'd have a button labeled Show ALL Books, one labeled Show Books of Type business, another one labeled Show Books of Type mod_cook, and so on, one for each type value listed.

The problem with this approach is that it will only allow the filtering of the six hard-coded type values. What happens if a week from now, a new batch of books is entered into the database with a type value of Travel? Ideally, the filter buttons would be dynamically generated, based upon the values of the type field in the database.

We'll examine how to dynamically add such command buttons shortly. First, let's examine what the code would look like if we were satisfied with just hard-coding the potential type values.

Before we examine any code, take a moment to think what must happen when one of the filtering buttons is clicked. As we want to filter the results of the DataGrid, when the event handler is clicked, the DataGrid will need to have its DataSource repopulated with just the results matching the specified filter. This DataSource will then need to be rebound to the DataGrid (via the DataGrid's DataBind() method). In examining Listing 6.1, you can see that we already have a function that does a very similar task: the BindData() function (lines 11–27 in Listing 6.1) populates a SqlDataReader with the SELECT * FROM titles SQL query, and then binds it to the DataGrid. As we'll see in Listing 6.2, we can make a few small changes to this function to incorporate the needed filtering SQL queries.

LISTING 6.2   Seven Command Buttons Have Been Added to Allow for Filtering

```
1: <%@ import Namespace="System.Data" %>
2: <%@ import Namespace="System.Data.SqlClient" %>
3: <script runat="server" language="VB">
4:    Sub Page_Load(sender as Object, e as EventArgs)
5:     If Not Page.IsPostBack then
6:      BindData(String.Empty)
7:     End If
8:    End Sub
9:
10:
11:    Sub BindData(filterValue as String)
12:     DisplayViewingTypeMessage(filterValue)
13:
14:     '1. Create a connection
15:     Const strConnString as String = "server=localhost;uid=sa;pwd=;
➥database=pubs"
16:     Dim objConn as New SqlConnection(strConnString)
17:
18:
19:     'Create an appropriate SQL command string
20:     Dim strSQL as String
21:     If filterValue = String.Empty then
22:      strSQL = "SELECT * FROM titles"
23:     Else
24:      'SQL needs WHERE clause
25:      strSQL = "SELECT * FROM titles WHERE type = @TYPE"
```

LISTING 6.2　Continued

```
26:    End If
27:
28:    '2. Create a command object for the query
29:    Dim objCmd as New SqlCommand(strSQL, objConn)
30:
31:    'Add parameter for WHERE clause if needed
32:    If strSQL <> String.Empty then
33:    Dim filterParam as New SqlParameter("@TYPE", SqlDbType.Char, 12)
34:    filterParam.Value = filterValue
35:    objCmd.Parameters.Add(filterParam)
36:    End If
37:
38:    objConn.Open()   'Open the connection
39:
40:    'Finally, specify the DataSource and call DataBind()
41:    dgTitles.DataSource = objCmd.ExecuteReader(CommandBehavior.CloseConnection)
42:    dgTitles.DataBind()
43:
44:    objConn.Close()   'Close the connection
45:    End Sub
46:
47:
48:    Sub FilterData(sender as Object, e as CommandEventArgs)
49:    BindData(e.CommandArgument)
50:    End Sub
51:
52:
53:    Sub DisplayViewingTypeMessage(filterValue as String)
54:    If filterValue = String.Empty then
55:    lblViewingMsg.Text = "You are viewing all books..."
56:    Else
57:    lblViewingMsg.Text = "You are viewing books of type " & filterValue
58:    End If
59:    End Sub
60: </script>
61:
62: <form runat="server">
63:  <asp:Button Text="View ALL Books" runat="server"
64:      CommandArgument="" OnCommand="FilterData" />
65:  <asp:Button Text="View Books of Type business" runat="server"
66:      CommandArgument="business" OnCommand="FilterData" />
```

LISTING 6.2   Continued

```
67:  <asp:Button Text="View Books of Type mod_cook" runat="server"
68:      CommandArgument="mod_cook" OnCommand="FilterData" />
69:  <asp:Button Text="View Books of Type popular_comp" runat="server"
70:      CommandArgument="popular_comp" OnCommand="FilterData" />
71:  <asp:Button Text="View Books of Type psychology" runat="server"
72:      CommandArgument="psychology" OnCommand="FilterData" />
73:  <asp:Button Text="View Books of Type trad_cook" runat="server"
74:      CommandArgument="trad_cook" OnCommand="FilterData" />
75:  <asp:Button Text="View Books of Type UNDECIDED" runat="server"
76:      CommandArgument="UNDECIDED" OnCommand="FilterData" />
77:  <p>
78:  <asp:label id="lblViewingMsg" runat="server" Font-Name="Verdana"
79:      Font-Italic="True" Font-Color="Red" />
80:  </p>
81:  <asp:DataGrid runat="server" id="dgTitles"
82:    AutoGenerateColumns="False" CellPadding="5"
83:    Font-Name="Verdana" Font-Size="9pt"
84:    AlternatingItemStyle-BackColor="#dddddd">
85:
86:    <HeaderStyle BackColor="Navy" ForeColor="White" Font-Size="13pt"
87:        Font-Bold="True" HorizontalAlign="Center" />
88:
89:    <Columns>
90:    <asp:BoundColumn DataField="title_id" HeaderText="Title ID"
91:        ItemStyle-HorizontalAlign="Center" />
92:    <asp:BoundColumn DataField="title" HeaderText="Title" />
93:    <asp:BoundColumn DataField="type" HeaderText="Type" />
94:    </Columns>
95:  </asp:DataGrid>
96:  </form>
```

The first thing you should take note of is the altered BindData(*filterValue*) function (lines 11–36). The new version accepts a single string input parameter, filterValue, which specifies the value of the type field to filter on. If an empty string is passed in (either "" or String.Empty), the filtering logic is not applied. For example, in the Page_Load event handler, BindData(String.Empty) is called on the page's first load (line 6), which retrieves all the rows from the title table.

In addition to grabbing the specified subset of title table rows, the BindData(*filterValue*) function also makes a call to the helper function DisplayViewingTypeMessage(*filterValue*)—the call to

DisplayViewingTypeMessage(*filterValue*) is made on line 12, and the helper function itself is contained from lines 53 to 59. DisplayViewingTypeMessage(*filterValue*) accepts a single string parameter, the name of the type value being filtered, and simply sets the ASP.NET Label lblViewingMsg's Text property. This serves as a helpful message to users, so that they realize they are viewing a particular subset of the titles table. (The lblViewingMsg Label control is defined on lines 78 and 79.)

To provide filtering functionality, we need command buttons for each of the filtering options. Because there are seven options (no filtering being one, and then a filtering option for each of the six type values), seven Button controls have been added, spanning lines 63 through 76. I decided to use Button controls, but they need only be command buttons—you could use LinkButton or ImageButton controls.

Each command button's Command event is assigned to the same event handler, FilterData. To uniquely identify each Button, the CommandArgument property has been set to the value of the type field that is to be filtered on when the command button is clicked. Because our BindData(*filterValue*) function is expecting a single string parameter specifying the value of the type field to filter on, our FilterData event handler is quite simple. The FilterData event handler (lines 48–50) has a single line of code: a call to the BindData(*filterValue*) function, passing in the value of the clicked command button's CommandArgument property.

Figure 6.2 shows a screenshot of Listing 6.2 when viewed through a browser. Note that when a filter button is clicked, the ASP.NET Web page is posted back and the DataGrid is rebound with the filtered data. Additionally, a helpful message appears informing the user what subset of the titles table she is viewing.

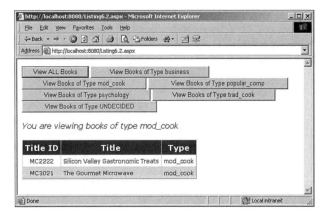

FIGURE 6.2   Clicking a filter button causes only a subset of the rows of the titles table to be displayed.

When reviewing Listing 6.2, did you wonder why the seven command buttons all had their `Command` event wired up to the same event handler (`FilterData`)? We could have opted to have each Button trigger a unique event handler, in which the proper call to `BindData(filterValue)` was made. This course of action was not chosen for two reasons: First, it would require seven one-line event handlers as opposed to one, thereby bloating the code and making it less readable; second, using just one event handler is needed when dynamically adding the filtering buttons, which we'll be doing in the next section.

Dynamically Creating the Filtering Buttons

Listing 6.2 demonstrates how to provide filtering on the values of a particular database field. However, the values that can be filtered have been hard-coded as a series of Button controls. This approach would be satisfactory for scenarios where the column being filtered on could only have a certain set of values. For example, if you wanted to sort an employee table by gender, there will obviously never be more than two potential values; hence, in this situation, adding two hard-coded command buttons would be understandable.

The `type` field in the `titles` table can have more than just the six values currently in the table. That is, new books may be added to the table with `type` values that can't be determined at this point in time. To provide filtering support for database fields whose sets of potential values are unknown, it is best to dynamically add the filtering buttons based upon the current values of the database field.

In all our examples thus far, we've created our Web controls by explicitly adding the proper control tag in our HTML section. For example, to add an ASP.NET Label control in a particular place in the HTML page, we simply added

```
<asp:label runat="server" ... />
```

wherever it was we wanted the Label displayed. In addition to adding Web controls to an ASP.NET page in this way, we can also add them dynamically by programmatically creating an instance of the control's corresponding class, setting its properties, and then adding it to the `Controls` collection of a PlaceHolder control on the page.

NOTE

The PlaceHolder control is an ASP.NET control used to indicate where dynamically-added controls should appear on the ASP.NET Web page. For more information on the PlaceHolder control, be sure to read the article "Working with Dynamically Created Controls" mentioned in the "On the Web" section at the end of this chapter.

For example, if we want to add a Button control to an ASP.NET Web page in a specific position, we would first create a PlaceHolder to specify exactly where the dynamically added Button should go. Next, we would add code to the Page_Load event handler to add the Button to the PlaceHolder's Controls collection. The following code snippet illustrates these two steps:

```
<script language="VB" runat="server">
 Sub Page_Load(sender as Object, e as EventArgs)
  ' Create a button control programmatically
  Dim myButton as Button

  ' Add the button to the PlaceHolder
  placeButtonHere.Controls.Add(myButton)

  ' Now set the button properties
  myButton = New Button()
  myButton.Text = "Click Me!"
 End Sub
</script>


Click the button below!
<asp:PlaceHolder runat="server" id="placeButtonHere" />
```

A thorough discussion of adding controls dynamically is beyond the scope of this book. However, there are two articles on this topic worth reading in the "On the Web" section at the end of this chapter. If you have not had experience with adding controls dynamically, you might want to read these recommended articles before continuing.

Listing 6.3 enhances Listing 6.2 by dynamically adding filter buttons for each distinct value of the type field. Note that the BindData(*filterValue*) and DisplayViewingTypeMessage(*filterValue*) functions and the FilterData event handler have not changed from Listing 6.2 to Listing 6.3. Furthermore, the output and functionality of Listings 6.2 and 6.3 are identical; therefore, to see a screenshot of Listing 6.3 when viewed through a browser, refer back to Figure 6.2.

LISTING 6.3   The Filter Buttons Displayed Are Dynamically Added on Each Page Load

```
1: <%@ import Namespace="System.Data" %>
2: <%@ import Namespace="System.Data.SqlClient" %>
3: <script runat="server" language="VB">
4: ' ... The BindData and DisplayViewingTypeMessage functions have
5:    been omitted for brevity. See Listing 6.2 for their details ...
6:
```

LISTING 6.3   Continued

```
 7:   Sub Page_Load(sender as Object, e as EventArgs)
 8:    AddFilterButtons()
 9:
10:    If Not Page.IsPostBack then
11:     'Populate the DataGrid
12:     BindData(String.Empty)
13:    End If
14:   End Sub
15:
16:
17:   Sub FilterData(sender as Object, e as CommandEventArgs)
18:    BindData(e.CommandArgument)
19:   End Sub
20:
21:
22:   Sub AddFilterButtons()
23:    'Dynamically add the control buttons
24:    '1. Create a connection
25:    Const strConnString as String = "server=localhost;uid=sa;pwd=;
➥database=pubs"
26:    Dim objConn as New SqlConnection(strConnString)
27:
28:
29:    'Create an appropriate SQL command string
30:    Const strSQL as String = "SELECT DISTINCT type FROM titles ORDER BY type"
31:
32:    '2. Create a command object for the query
33:    Dim objCmd as New SqlCommand(strSQL, objConn)
34:
35:    objConn.Open()   'Open the connection
36:    Dim dr as SqlDataReader = objCmd.ExecuteReader()
37:
38:    'Add the View ALL button
39:    Dim filterButton as New Button()
40:    filterButtonLocation.Controls.Add(filterButton)
41:    filterButton.Text = "View ALL Books"
42:    filterButton.CommandArgument = ""
43:    AddHandler filterButton.Command, AddressOf Me.FilterData
44:
45:    'Now, loop through the SqlDataReader, adding buttons
46:    While dr.Read()
```

LISTING 6.3   Continued

```
47:     filterButton = New Button()
48:     filterButtonLocation.Controls.Add(filterButton)
49:     filterButton.Text = "View Books of Type " & dr("type")
50:     filterButton.CommandArgument = dr("type")
51:
52:     AddHandler filterButton.Command, AddressOf Me.FilterData
53:     End While
54:
55:     objConn.Close()  'Close the connection
56:     End Sub
57:
58: </script>
59:
60: <form runat="server">
61:   <asp:PlaceHolder runat="server" id="filterButtonLocation" />
62:   <p>
63:    <asp:label id="lblViewingMsg" runat="server" Font-Name="Verdana"
64:       Font-Italic="True" Font-Color="Red" />
65:   </p>
66:   <asp:DataGrid runat="server" id="dgTitles"
67:     AutoGenerateColumns="False" CellPadding="5"
68:     Font-Name="Verdana" Font-Size="9pt"
69:     AlternatingItemStyle-BackColor="#dddddd">
70:
71:    <HeaderStyle BackColor="Navy" ForeColor="White" Font-Size="13pt"
72:       Font-Bold="True" HorizontalAlign="Center" />
73:
74:    <Columns>
75:     <asp:BoundColumn DataField="title_id" HeaderText="Title ID"
76:        ItemStyle-HorizontalAlign="Center" />
77:     <asp:BoundColumn DataField="title" HeaderText="Title" />
78:     <asp:BoundColumn DataField="type" HeaderText="Type" />
79:    </Columns>
80:   </asp:DataGrid>
81: </form>
```

When dynamically adding controls to an ASP.NET Web page, it often helps to
provide a PlaceHolder control, so that you know precisely where the newly added
controls will appear. Such a PlaceHolder control, `filterButtonLocation`, has been
declared on line 61. This control does nothing but serve as the location where our
filtering buttons will be dynamically added.

The `AddFilterButtons()` function performs the work needed to add the filter buttons to the ASP.NET Web page (see lines 22–56). This function is called on each page load, and it is therefore called from the `Page_Load` event handler (line 8). Because we do not know what values the `type` field might have, the `AddFilterButtons()` function must find out what potential values are in the field and create a Button control for each distinct value. In addition to this, the `AddFilterButtons()` function should create a filter button to display all books.

To retrieve the values of the `type` field, a `SELECT DISTINCT type FROM titles` SQL query is used to populate a `SqlDataReader` (lines 25 through 36). Following that, the filter buttons are added to the `filterButtonLocation` PlaceHolder, starting with the View ALL Books Button (lines 40 through 43). To add a Button to the page, we create a new instance of the `Button` class (see lines 39 and 47) and then set its `Text` and `CommandArgument` properties accordingly (see lines 41–42 and 49–50). We then add it to the PlaceHolder control's `Controls` collection (see lines 40 and 48). Finally, we have to wire up the Button's `Command` event to the `FilterData` event handler. This is accomplished by using Visual Basic .NET's `AddHandler` function, as can be seen on lines 43 and 52.

NOTE

To add an event handler to the Button's `Command` event in C#, you would use the following syntax:

```
filterButton.Command += new CommandEventHandler(this.FilterData);
```

To learn more about consuming events, be sure to consult the "Consuming Events" article presented in the "On the Web" section at the end of this chapter.

The output for Listing 6.3 is identical to that of Listing 6.2 (assuming that no new values for the `type` field appear). Hence, you can refer back to Figure 6.2 for a screenshot of Listing 6.3.

NOTE

Our examples in this section have examined adding filtering buttons to a DataGrid control. However, filtering buttons can also be used to work with both the DataList and Repeater controls. The server-side code presented in Listings 6.2 and 6.3 will work with any data Web control.

A-Z Filter Buttons

An example of filter button usage in a production Web site can be seen at Microsoft's ASP.NET Forums Member List page at http://www.asp.net/Forums/User/ShowAllUsers.aspx. The ASP.NET Forums, which is an online messageboard site for

ASP.NET and ASP.NET-related questions, contains (at the time of this writing) more than 80,000 registered users. Obviously, it is implausible to display all 80,000 users on one Web page. One option would be to just display the 80,000 or so members in a DataGrid using pagination, displaying, say, 50 users per page. The downside to this approach is that if a Web visitor wishes to find a particular user, he might have to page through up to 1,600 pages!

The solution employed by the creators of the ASP.NET Forums was to, by default, list all the users ordered by the date which they signed up for a free user account on the ASP.NET Forums. Visitors can page through this data one at a time if they like. Alternatively, at the top of the page are the letters of the alphabet rendered as hyperlinks. By clicking on a particular letter, only those users whose username begins with that letter are displayed.

The ASP.NET Forum source code creates the 26 hard-coded filter buttons in much the same way that the seven filter buttons of Listing 6.2 (lines 63–76) were created, except that the ASP.NET Forums use LinkButton controls for the 26 filter buttons instead of Button controls. Just like with Listing 6.2, the ASP.NET Forums has each of the 26 filter buttons' Command events handled by one event handler, with each filter button's CommandArgument property set to the letter that the usernames are to be filtered on.

NOTE

To learn more about the ASP.NET Forums (or to post your questions on ASP.NET), visit http://www.asp.net/Forums/. You can even download the complete source code for the ASP.NET Forums. Visit http://www.asp.net/Forums/Download/ to download the code and to learn more about the system requirements for running the ASP.NET Forums on your computer.

A More Optimized Approach to Filtering

In Listings 6.2 and 6.3, each time a filter button is clicked, the ASP.NET Web page is posted back, the DataSource is repopulated with the filtered results, and the DataGrid's DataBind() method is recalled. This means that each time a filter button is clicked, a database access occurs.

At first glance, this might seem less than ideal. After all, on the first page visit, we retrieve *all* the rows from the titles table. After clicking on a filter button, we want to display a subset of that data. It seems wasteful to have to go back to the database and get the data that we already have! (Granted, we don't have exactly the information we want to display, but the information we want to display is contained in the information we have on hand.)

If you've had much experience with the DataSet object, you're likely aware that a DataSet has a property called `Tables`, which is a collection of `DataTable` objects. Each of these `DataTable` objects represents structured data, such as a database table. Each `DataTable` object has a `DefaultView` property, which returns a `DataView` object. A `DataView` can be thought of as a "window" into a `DataTable`. It is through this window that we access the items in the `DataTable`. A `DataView`, among other things, can be used to view records of a `DataTable` that match certain criteria. That is, using the `DataView`'s `RowFilter` property, we can provide a filtered view of a `DataTable`, meaning that we can provide a filtered view of our DataSet.

Unfortunately, the DataSet does not natively survive postbacks like the Web controls, with their ViewState, can. If the DataSet cannot survive postbacks, that means we will need to repopulate the DataSet on each postback, which is what we're trying to avoid! To get around this, we can programmatically add the DataSet to the ViewState, as we'll see in Listing 6.4.

To provide a more optimized approach to filtering results in a data Web control, we can start by using a DataSet instead of a DataReader. Upon the page's first load, this DataSet is populated with all of the `title` table's rows. Furthermore, this DataSet will need to be added to the page's ViewState so that it can survive postbacks.

When the user clicks a filter button, the ASP.NET Web page will be posted back and the `FilterData` event handler will be executed. Here, rather than calling `BindData(filterValue)`, we'll want to pull the DataSet out from the ViewState, alter the proper `DataTable`'s `DefaultView`'s `RowFilter` property, and then rebind this DataSet to the DataGrid.

This series of actions will save a database access with each filtering button-click. That is, the only database access will occur on the first visit to the page.

Listing 6.4 illustrates a few of the server-side functions that are needed to perform this optimization. The code listing builds naturally from Listing 6.3, and doesn't add any user-level functionality; hence, you can refer back to Figure 6.2 for a screenshot of Listing 6.4 in action.

LISTING 6.4   A DataSet Is Cached in the ViewState to Save Database Accesses

```
 1: <%@ import Namespace="System.Data" %>
 2: <%@ import Namespace="System.Data.SqlClient" %>
 3: <script runat="server" language="VB">
 4:   Sub Page_Load(sender as Object, e as EventArgs)
 5:     AddFilterButtons()
 6:
 7:     If Not Page.IsPostBack then
 8:       'Populate the DataGrid
 9:       BindData()
```

LISTING 6.4   Continued

```
10:     End If
11:     End Sub
12:
13:
14:     Sub BindData()
15:       '1. Create a connection
16:       Const strConnString as String = "server=localhost;uid=sa;pwd=;
➥database=pubs"
17:       Dim objConn as New SqlConnection(strConnString)
18:
19:
20:       'Create an appropriate SQL command string
21:       Const strSQL as String = "SELECT * FROM titles"
22:
23:       '2. Create a command object for the query
24:       Dim objCmd as New SqlCommand(strSQL, objConn)
25:
26:       '3. Create a DataAdapter and Fill the DataSet
27:       Dim objDA as New SqlDataAdapter()
28:       objDA.SelectCommand = objCmd
29:
30:       Dim objDS as New DataSet()
31:       objDA.Fill(objDS, "titles")
32:
33:       'Add the DataSet to the ViewState
34:       ViewState.Add("TitlesDataSet", objDS)
35:
36:       'Finally, specify the DataSource and call DataBind()
37:       dgTitles.DataSource = ViewState("TitlesDataSet")
38:       dgTitles.DataBind()
39:
40:       objConn.Close()   'Close the connection
41:     End Sub
42:
43:
44:     Sub FilterData(sender as Object, e as CommandEventArgs)
45:       'Inform the user what filtering is being performed
46:       DisplayViewingTypeMessage(e.CommandArgument)
47:
48:       'Get the DataSet out of the ViewState
49:       Dim objDS as DataSet = ViewState("TitlesDataSet")
50:
```

LISTING 6.4 Continued

```
51:     'Apply the filtering
52:     If e.CommandArgument = String.Empty then
53:       objDS.Tables("titles").DefaultView.RowFilter = ""
54:     Else
55:       objDS.Tables("titles").DefaultView.RowFilter =
➥"type = '" & e.CommandArgument & "'"
56:     End If
57:
58:     'Now, bind the DataGrid to the filtered DataSet
59:     dgTitles.DataSource = objDS.Tables("titles").DefaultView
60:     dgTitles.DataBind()
61:   End Sub
62:
63:   ...
64: </script>
```

In Listing 6.4, the BindData() function has been altered to no longer accept a
filterValue parameter. Rather, BindData(), which is only called on the first load of
the page (that is, not on any postbacks), starts by populating a DataSet with the
results of a SELECT * FROM titles SQL query (lines 15–31). Specifically, the Fill
method of the SqlDataAdapter adds a DataTable to the DataSet with the name
"titles" (line 31). After this populated DataTable has been added to the DataSet, the
DataSet is added to the ViewState (line 34). Next, the DataGrid's DataSource property
is set to this DataSet and the DataBind() method is called.

By storing the DataSet in the ViewState on line 34, we are essentially storing the
DataSet in a page-level cache. This cache is local to this particular page visited by
this particular user. It consumes no server-resident resources, just some extra HTML
in the _VIEWSTATE hidden form field.

CAUTION

For large DataGrids with many columns and rows, the _VIEWSTATE hidden form field can
grow to be very large, on the order of tens of kilobytes. A large _VIEWSTATE increases the total
size of the page, requiring longer download times, which could negatively affect a dial-up
user's experience. In such cases, you can store the DataGrid's data using ASP.NET's data
cache. For more information on this technology, be sure to read the "Caching with ASP.NET"
article referenced in the "On the Web" section at the end of this chapter.

When a filtering button is clicked, the ASP.NET page is posted back and the
FilterData event handler is executed. Here the DataSet is retrieved from the

ViewState (line 49) and the DataTable "titles"'s DefaultView's RowFilter property is set so that only rows whose type field has the value specified by the command button's CommandArgument property are shown. The RowFilter property expects input in the form

FieldName <operator> Value

FieldName is the name of a field of the DataTable (type, in our example); <operator> is a comparison operator, like =, <, <>, >=, and so on; Value is a value that FieldName is compared against using the <operator>. For fields of a string type (such as Text, varchar, char, and so on), the Value portion must be surrounded by quotes or a single apostrophe. Hence, on line 55 you'll note that I set the RowFilter property to

"type = '" & e.CommandArgument & "'"

If e.CommandArgument equals, say, "popular_comp", the RowFilter property will equal "type = 'popular_comp'". In the event that the View All Records button is clicked, the CommandArgument property will have a blank string as its value. In this case, we want to reset the RowFilter property so that all rows are displayed. The RowFilter property can be reset by assigning it an empty string, as shown on line 53.

After this RowFilter property has been set, all that remains is binding the filtered DataView to the DataGrid. This last step is accomplished on lines 59 and 60.

CAUTION

Whenever you use a cache to reduce database accesses, realize that the data you are displaying on the page can become stale. That is, if the user spends 15 minutes on this page, continually filtering data from the cached DataSet, the data she is seeing is data that is 15 minutes old. Additions, updates, and removals of data from the underlying data store that have occurred in this time period will not be reflected in the ASP.NET Web page. If the data you are providing is rarely updated or is not time-sensitive, this will likely not be a concern.

The concepts we've just discussed cover a lot of intermediate to advanced material that is outside the scope of this book. This includes more advanced features of the DataSet and using the ViewState as a page-level cache. Rather than delve into these topics here, I encourage you to read the related resources in the "On the Web" section at the end of this chapter.

Doing a Batch Update

In Chapter 9, "Editing the DataGrid Web Control," we'll examine how to use the DataGrid and DataList's editing capabilities. The built-in editing support provides editing on a row-level basis. That is, the entire contents of a DataGrid are displayed to the user with each row containing an Edit button. When the Edit button is clicked, the row whose Edit button was clicked has its various columns converted into TextBoxes or DropDownLists, or whatever editing interface you choose. Additionally, the row's Edit button is replaced by Update and Cancel buttons. After updating the data and clicking the Update button, the data is saved to the underlying data store and the DataGrid is displayed as it was originally, but with the updated row information.

This row-level editing is useful if you plan on only occasionally changing the data, or if when you plan on having to update the database table, you expect to only have to update a couple of rows at most. However, if you know that you will need to edit, say, 20 rows, it can be quite annoying to have to click the Edit button, make your changes, and then click the Update button 20 times. In such a scenario, it would be nice to have the *entire* data Web control appear in its edit mode, with one button on the page labeled Update ALL Changes Made.

Clearly, this Update ALL Changes Made command button is a standard ASP.NET Web control external to the DataGrid or DataList it operates on. When this button is clicked, the data Web control's contents need to be iterated through, updating the underlying data store to reflect the changes to each row. (This update would be an UPDATE SQL statement if the data store was a relational database; it might be some set of XML commands if the underlying data store were an XML file.)

Let's look at an example of this idea. The `titles` table in the `pubs` database contains a `price` field, which represents the selling price of the book. Imagine that your boss has asked you to construct a Web interface that displays all the books and their prices. From this interface, each price should be displayed as an editable TextBox, enabling the user to change the price of zero to many books at a time. At the top of the Web page should be an Update ALL Prices button that updates the underlying database with any changes to book prices.

As in the previous section's examples in which we used a DataGrid Web control, let's turn to the DataList Web control for this exercise. Listing 6.5 contains the code to allow for batch updates. The `Page_Load` event handler and `BindData()` functions have been omitted for brevity. Because we are not using filter buttons here, the `BindData()` method does not take any filtering parameter. The code for the `Page_Load` event handler and `BindData()` functions can be found by referring back to Listing 6.1, lines 4–8 and 11–27, respectively.

LISTING 6.5   Clicking the Update ALL Prices Button Updates All Rows in the DataList

```
1: <%@ import Namespace="System.Data" %>
2: <%@ import Namespace="System.Data.SqlClient" %>
3: <script runat="server" language="C#">
```

LISTING 6.5   Conitnued

```
4:   ' ... The Page_Load event handler and BindData functions
5:   ' have been omitted for brevity. See Listing 6.1 for details ...
6:
7:   void updatePrices(object sender, EventArgs e)
8:   {
9:     // 1. Create a connection
10:    const string strConnString = "server=localhost;uid=sa;pwd=;database=pubs";
11:    SqlConnection objConn = new SqlConnection(strConnString);
12:
13:    // Create an appropriate UPDATE statement
14:    const string strSQL = "UPDATE titles SET price = @price WHERE title_id =
➥@titleID";
15:
16:    // Create a command object for the query
17:    SqlCommand objCmd = new SqlCommand(strSQL, objConn);
18:    objConn.Open();
19:
20:    string titleID, strPrice;
21:
22:    // iterate through the DataList's TextBoxes
23:    foreach (DataListItem dlItem in dlTitles.Items)
24:    {
25:      // reference the TextBox
26:      TextBox txtPrices = (TextBox) dlItem.FindControl("txtPrice");
27:
28:      // Grab the value
29:      strPrice = txtPrices.Text;
30:
31:      // Get the title_id from DataKeys
32:      titleID = dlTitles.DataKeys[dlItem.ItemIndex].ToString();
33:
34:      // Now, update the parameters
35:      SqlParameter priceParam = new SqlParameter("@price", SqlDbType.Money);
36:      if (strPrice == String.Empty)
37:        // we need to insert a NULL
38:        priceParam.Value = DBNull.Value;
39:      else
40:        priceParam.Value = strPrice;
41:      objCmd.Parameters.Add(priceParam);
42:
43:      SqlParameter titleIDParam = new SqlParameter("@titleID",
➥SqlDbType.VarChar, 6);
```

LISTING 6.5   Conitnued

```
44:       titleIDParam.Value = titleID;
45:       objCmd.Parameters.Add(titleIDParam);
46:
47:       // now, execute the query
48:       objCmd.ExecuteNonQuery();
49:
50:       // Clear the parameters
51:       objCmd.Parameters.Clear();
52:     }
53:
54:    objConn.Close();   // close the connection
55:    }
56: </script>
57:
58: <form runat="server">
59: <asp:Button Text="Update ALL Prices" runat="server"
60:    OnClick="updatePrices" />
61: <p>
62: <asp:DataList runat="server" id="dlTitles"
63:    CellPadding="5" BorderStyle="Inset"
64:    Font-Name="Verdana" Font-Size="9pt"
65:    AlternatingItemStyle-BackColor="#dddddd"
66:    DataKeyField="title_id">
67:
68:   <ItemTemplate>
69:   <b>Title:</b> <%# DataBinder.Eval(Container.DataItem, "title") %>
70:   <br /><b>Price:</b>
71:   <asp:TextBox runat="Server" id="txtPrice" Columns="5"
72:    Text='<%# DataBinder.Eval(Container.DataItem, "price") %>' />
73:   </ItemTemplate>
74: </asp:DataList>
75: </form>
```

Let's start by dissecting the DataList declaration starting at line 62. First notice that we set the DataKeyField property to the titles table's primary key field, title_id (line 66). In the ItemTemplate, we use data-binding syntax to display the title of the book, along with a TextBox listing its price. For some reason, the titles table allows NULLs in the price field. If the price field is NULL, the value returned by the DataBinder.Eval() method will be a blank string.

When the user visits the page, he will be shown a list of the titles and prices of all the books in the `titles` database. The price will be listed in an editable TextBox. After the user has updated any price values, he needs a way to save the changes back to the database. The Update ALL Prices Button control on lines 59 and 60 provides this functionality. This Button control has its `Click` event wired up to the `updatePrices` event handler (lines 7–55), which we will examine in a moment. For now, realize that when this button is clicked, the ASP.NET page is posted back and the code in the `updatePrices` event handler is executed.

The task the `updatePrices` event handler is faced with sounds like a simple one—it must update the database with the new values entered by the user. This task, however, requires a bit of code. First, we must create a connection to the database. Lines 9 through 18 create a connection to the `pubs` database and prepare a `SqlCommand` object with a SQL UPDATE command. The UPDATE string (line 14) uses parameters to specify the `price` and `title_id` field values.

After we have established a connection, we are ready to iterate through the rows of the DataList, reading in the value of the `txtPrice` TextBox and updating the database with the corresponding value. To iterate through the rows of the DataList, we iterate through the `DataListItem` instances returned by the `Items` property of the DataList (line 23). For each iteration, we need to perform the following tasks:

1. Read in the value of the `txtPrice` TextBox.

2. Determine the `title_id` value for the row being updated.

3. Update the database.

On line 26 we reference the `txtPrice` TextBox through the `FindControl` method. As we examined in Chapter 5, the `FindControl` method returns the child control whose `ID` is equal to the string parameter passed into the `FindControl` method. The return type of `FindControl` is `Control`, which is the base type of all ASP.NET Web controls. However, we are assigning the result of the `FindControl` method to a variable of type `TextBox`. In Visual Basic .NET, we do not need to explicitly cast the return value of `FindControl` to a `TextBox`, but Listing 6.5 is written in C#, which requires such practices. The `(TextBox)` code on line 26 casts the return value of `FindControl` to that of type `TextBox`.

After we have this TextBox control referenced by the `txtPrices` variable, we can find the value of the TextBox control by referencing its `Text` property (see line 29).

NOTE

If `FindControl` cannot find a control with the `ID` value specified as its input parameter, a value of `null` (or `Nothing` in Visual Basic .NET) is returned. A more robust implementation of Listing 6.5 would include a conditional statement to check whether `txtPrices` was equal to `null` before attempting to de-reference it on line 29.

With these two lines of code (lines 26 and 29), we have completed step 1. Now we must determine the value of the title_id field for the particular row. We do this by consulting the DataKeys collection. Line 32 retrieves the proper item from the DataKeys collection and assigns it to the titleID local variable. This concludes step 2.

All that remains now is to update the database. Because we are using a parameterized query, the first step is to add the parameters to our SqlCommand object (objCmd). If the txtPrice TextBox is empty, we want to update the row with a NULL value. This check is made on line 36. After we've added the parameters to the objCmd (lines 41 and 45), we can execute the query using the ExecuteNonQuery() method of the SqlCommand class (line 48). (The ExecuteNonQuery() method is optimized for database calls that do not return any values.) Finally, on line 51 we clear the SqlCommand object's Parameters collection, because we are reusing the same SqlCommand object through each iteration of the loop.

Figure 6.3 shows a screenshot of Listing 6.5 when viewed through a browser.

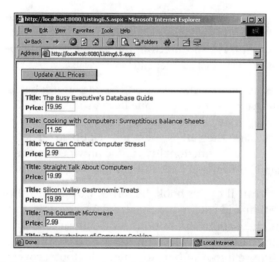

FIGURE 6.3   A DataList displays each book's price in an editable TextBox.

Note that the code in Listing 6.5 makes a database call for each row in the DataList, regardless of whether it has been changed. In cases where the user has made a change to only one or two of the rows out of perhaps 50, it might seem grossly inefficient to perform 50 database updates calls when in fact only two were needed.

Realistically, these additional database accesses are unlikely to negatively affect the overall performance of your Web site. After all, how often are you going to be performing batch updates of this kind? Most likely, you'll only allow a small subset of total users to even access this page, and even those users will likely only use such functionality rarely.

If for some reason the extraneous database calls are of chief concern, one option would be to store the values of the prices before being edited, so that they can be compared to the new values. One way to accomplish this would be to create a DataList identical to the one that displays the titles and editable prices of each book. Set this DataList's `Visible` property to `False`, so that it won't appear on the ASP.NET Web page. Then, in the `updatePrices` event handler, you can check the value of the current DataList row being iterated through, with its corresponding row in the invisible DataList. If the values are the same, you can forgo the database update call.

Summary

In this chapter, we looked at two real-world examples that involved using command buttons external to the data Web controls. These external command buttons affect the data Web control in some way.

We first looked at creating filtering buttons. Filtering buttons are command buttons that show only a subset of the data Web control's total data. Although we looked at adding command buttons to a DataGrid, the same logic could be applied in adding such filter buttons to DataLists or Repeaters.

We also examined using external Web controls to perform batch updates. Editing the DataGrid or DataList involves editing one item in a DataGrid row at a time. There are scenarios, however, where we'd like to let users edit *all* the rows of the DataGrid or DataList at once, and then allow them to click on an Update All button and have all the results saved. Such functionality can be provided by the use of templates, an external command button, and code to iterate through the updated values.

This chapter ends Part II of this book. In Part II, we looked at how to add command buttons, both within and external to the data Web controls. In the examples we worked through, these command buttons provided varying functions, from listing the details about a particular row, to adjusting the data displayed in the data Web control. In Part III, we'll look at how to extend the topics covered in Part II to provide more common functionality—the sorting, paging, and editing of a DataGrid's contents.

On the Web

For more information on the topics discussed in this chapter, consider perusing the following online resources:

- "Dynamic Controls in ASP.NET"—`http://aspnet.4guysfromrolla.com/articles/081402-1.aspx`

- "Working with Dynamically Created Controls"—`http://aspnet.4guysfromrolla.com/articles/082102-1.aspx`

- "Consuming Events"—`http://msdn.microsoft.com/library/default.asp?url=/library/en-us/cpguide/html/cpconeventsoverview.asp`

- "A Forum for Discussion of the ASP.NET Forums Source Code"—`http://www.asp.net/Forums/ShowForum.aspx?ForumID=66`

- "Using ViewState"—`http://docs.aspng.com/quickstart/aspplus/doc/stateoverview.aspx#viewstate`

- "ViewState Tutorials"—`http://www.123aspx.com/directory.aspx?dir=125`

- "Sorting and Filtering Data Using a DataView"—`http://msdn.microsoft.com/library/default.asp?url=/library/en-us/cpguide/html/cpconsortingfilteringdatausingdataview.asp`

- "Wielding the Power of the DataView"—`http://www.asp101.com/articles/stuart/dataview/default.asp`

- "Caching with ASP.NET"— `http://aspnet.4guysfromrolla.com/articles/022802-1.aspx`

- "Working with the ADO.NET Data Model"—`http://www.microsoft.com/usa/presentations/Working_w_the_ADO.NET_Object_Model.ppt`

- "Serve Dynamic Pages Quickly"—`http://www.devx.com/upload/free/features/vbpj/2002/04apr02/an0402/an0402-1.asp`

PART III

In Part I, we examined the basics of the data Web controls, which included a high-level introduction to the data Web controls, followed by a thorough examination of binding data to these controls. We also looked at how to display data with the data Web controls, and how to customize their HTML output through the use of display properties and templates.

In Part II, we turned our attention to adding both internal and external command buttons that affected the data Web controls. For example, in Chapter 4, we looked at how to provide buttons and hyperlinks to each row of a DataGrid Web control. We looked at how to wire server-side code to the ItemCommand event raised when a command button is clicked. We also looked at adding command buttons via templates (Chapter 5) and enhancing the functionality of the data Web controls by using external command buttons (Chapter 6).

We will now extend the lessons learned from Part II to provide sorting, pagination, and editing capabilities in the DataGrid. Each of these three topics has its own chapter in Part III. In Chapter 7, "Sorting the DataGrid's Data," we will examine just how to sort data in a DataGrid; likewise, in Chapter 8, "Providing DataGrid Pagination," we will look at adding pagination support to the DataGrid, ignoring the task of paging through sorted data.

In Chapter 10, "Putting it All Together: A Real-World Example," we will see how to meld the concepts learned in Chapters 7, 8, and 9. This chapter will present a single ASP.NET Web page that allows the user to sort, page through, edit, delete, and add additional data. By the end of Part III, you will have mastered the more useful and advanced features of the DataGrid Web control.

7

Sorting the DataGrid's Data

In previous code examples, we have demonstrated listing the contents of the pubs database's titles table. Recall that the titles table contains information about various books, such as their title, the price, the publication date, and so on. Now, imagine that we want to display the contents of the titles table in a data Web control with the results ordered alphabetically by the book's title.

This task may seem quite trivial: All we would need to do is alter our SQL query, adding an ORDER BY clause that specifies a proper ordering. For example, the following SQL query would suffice:

```
SELECT title, price, royalty, pubdate
FROM titles
ORDER BY title
```

By populating a DataSet or DataReader with this SQL query, then setting the data Web control's DataSource property to the resulting DataSet or DataReader, and finally calling the data Web control's DataBind() method, we would have a listing of the books in the titles table ordered alphabetically.

This approach, unfortunately, doesn't give much flexibility to the user visiting the Web page. What if he wants to view the contents of the titles table ordered by the price of the book, from the most expensive to the least expensive? Or maybe he wants to view the books from the most recently published book to the least recently published one. To provide such functionality, we could create a set of external sorting command buttons, much like we did in the last chapter to create the external filtering buttons.

Fortunately, the DataGrid Web control provides built-in sorting functionality. As we will see in this chapter, the DataGrid's sorting functionality adds a HyperLink command button to each column's header. When this command button is clicked, the DataGrid's SortCommand event is raised. By providing an event handler for this event, we can determine when the user opts to sort the DataGrid's data. At that point, we can re-query the database, retrieve the data in the desired sort order, and then rebind the data to the DataGrid.

NOTE

Alternatively, as we saw in Chapter 6, "Using External Web Controls to Achieve Effects on a Data Web Control," we can use ViewState caching techniques to cache the DataGrid's data and then sort that cached version, which ends up saving a database call. We will examine both approaches again in this chapter.

Providing Simple Sorting Support in the DataGrid Web Control

Recall from Chapter 1, "An Introduction to the DataGrid, DataList, and Repeater," that the DataGrid contains an AutoGenerateColumns property that defaults to True. When AutoGenerateColumns is True, a column is added to the DataGrid control for each field in the DataSource. In the vast majority of our DataGrid examples up to this point, we've set the AutoGenerateColumns property to False and explicitly specified the columns we want to appear in our DataGrid using BoundColumns and TemplateColumns.

The steps required for providing sorting support for a DataGrid whose AutoGenerateColumns property is set to True differs from the steps required for a DataGrid whose AutoGenerateColumns property is set to False. In the next two subsections, we will examine sorting a DataGrid whose AutoGenerateColumns property is set to True (the default). In the "Sorting a DataGrid with AutoGenerateColumns Set to False" section, we'll look at how to provide sorting capabilities to a DataGrid whose AutoGenerateColumns property is set to False.

Using the DataGrid's AllowSorting Property

Providing sorting support in a DataGrid whose AutoGenerateColumns property is set to True is fairly straightforward, requiring the following three steps:

1. Set the DataGrid's `AllowSorting` property to `True`.

2. Provide an event handler for the DataGrid's `SortCommand` event. This event handler should obtain the data in the properly sorted order and rebind the data to the DataGrid.

3. Wire up the DataGrid's `SortCommand` event to the event handler you authored in step 2.

Recall that the typical DataGrid displays the heading of each column as a simple textual label, displaying the name of the `DataSource` field that the column represents. However, when providing sorting support, we want each column's textual header to be converted into a hyperlink, so that when a particular row's header's hyperlink is clicked, the DataGrid's contents are sorted by that particular column's values.

Converting the DataGrid's column headers from textual labels to hyperlinks is quite simple: All we have to do is set the `AllowSorting` property to `True`. When the `AutoGenerateColumns` property is set to `True`, setting the `AllowSorting` property to `True` will convert the DataGrid's column header portion to a HyperLink command button. Listing 7.1 illustrates this concept.

LISTING 7.1 When `AllowSorting` Is Set to True, the DataGrid's Column Headers Become Hyperlinks

```
 1: <%@ import Namespace="System.Data" %>
 2: <%@ import Namespace="System.Data.SqlClient" %>
 3: <script runat="server" language="VB">
 4:
 5:     Sub Page_Load(sender as Object, e as EventArgs)
 6:        If Not Page.IsPostBack then
 7:          BindData()
 8:        End If
 9:     End Sub
10:
11:
12:     Sub BindData()
13:        '1. Create a connection
14:        Const strConnString as String = "server=localhost;uid=sa;pwd=;
➥database=pubs"
15:        Dim objConn as New SqlConnection(strConnString)
16:
17:        '2. Create a command object for the query
18:        Const strSQL as String = "SELECT title, price, pubdate FROM titles"
```

LISTING 7.1   Continued

```
19:        Dim objCmd as New SqlCommand(strSQL, objConn)
20:
21:        objConn.Open()    'Open the connection
22:
23:        'Finally, specify the DataSource and call DataBind()
24:        dgTitles.DataSource = objCmd.ExecuteReader(CommandBehavior.
➥CloseConnection)
25:        dgTitles.DataBind()
26:
27:        objConn.Close()    'Close the connection
28:     End Sub
29:
30: </script>
31: <form runat="server">
32:   <asp:DataGrid runat="server" id="dgTitles"
33:       Font-Name="Verdana" Font-Size="9pt" CellPadding="5"
34:       AlternatingItemStyle-BackColor="#dddddd"
35:       AllowSorting="True" AutoGenerateColumns="True">
36:
37:     <HeaderStyle BackColor="Navy" ForeColor="White" Font-Size="13pt"
38:              Font-Bold="True" HorizontalAlign="Center" />
39:   </asp:DataGrid>
40: </form>
```

The key line in Listing 7.1 is line 35, where the DataGrid's AllowSorting and AutoGenerateColumns DataGrid properties are set to True.

> **NOTE**
>
> We didn't need to explicitly set the AutoGenerateColumns property to True; rather, we could have simply omitted the property from the DataGrid's declaration, as it defaults to True.

By simply setting the AllowSorting and AutoGenerateColumns DataGrid properties to True, the default header labels for each DataGrid column are turned into HyperLink command buttons. Figure 7.1 displays a screenshot of Listing 7.1 when viewed through a browser. Note that each DataGrid column header is underlined, signifying a hyperlink.

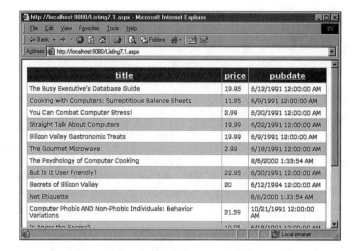

FIGURE 7.1 With AllowSorting set to True, hyperlinks are displayed in the headers of each DataGrid column.

To implement sorting in a DataGrid whose AutoGenerateColumns property is set to True, we need to perform the following steps:

1. Set the DataGrid's AllowSorting property to True.

2. Provide an event handler for the DataGrid's SortCommand event. This event handler should obtain the data in the properly sorted order and rebind the data to the DataGrid.

3. Wire up the DataGrid's SortCommand event to the event handler you authored in step 2.

Listing 7.1 accomplishes step 1. At this point, if a user clicks on one of these hyperlinks, the ASP.NET page is posted back and the DataGrid's SortCommand event is raised. Because we have yet to complete parts 2 and 3, nothing happens from the user's perspective. Now we need to tackle part 2: writing an event handler for the SortCommand event.

Writing a SortCommand Event Handler

To actually have anything happen when a DataGrid column's sort header hyperlink is clicked, we need to provide a SortCommand event handler. This event handler will fire every time one of the DataGrid's column's sort header hyperlinks is clicked.

The SortCommand event handler must have the following signature:

```
Sub EventHandlerName(sender as Object, e as DataGridSortCommandEventArgs)
```

In this event handler, we need to reissue our SQL query using an appropriate ORDER BY clause. This new SQL query should then be used to populate a DataSet or DataReader, which is then set to our DataGrid's DataSource property. Finally, we need to rebind the DataGrid by calling its DataBind() method.

NOTE

Each time a user clicks on one of the DataGrid's columns' sort hyperlinks to sort the DataGrid, the DataSource must be adjusted so that its contents are correctly sorted, and the DataGrid must be rebound to the DataSource. Typically, re-sorting the DataSource requires that the SQL query used to populate the DataSource be reissued. However, in the section "Caching the DataGrid's DataSource at the Page-Level," we will discuss how to cache the DataSource so that re-sorting the DataSource does not require an additional database query.

To accomplish this, it is clear that in the event handler we'll need some way of determining what DataGrid column was clicked. To aid with this need, the DataGridColumn class, which abstractly defines a DataGrid's column, contains a SortExpression property. When a particular DataGrid column's header's sort hyperlink is clicked, the DataGrid columns SortExpression value is passed along to the SortCommand event handler. To facilitate this, the DataGridSortCommandEventArgs class contains a SortExpression property that contains this value.

With the AutoGenerateColumns property set to True, each column has its SortExpression property automatically set to the name of the DataSource field the column represents. In Listing 7.1, the SortExpression value for the price DataGrid column is price, while the SortExpression value for the pubdate column is pubdate.

Hence, our SortCommand event handler will have to do the following:

1. Create a SQL query whose ORDER BY clause is determined by the SortExpression property of the event handler's DataGridSortCommandEventArgs parameter.

2. Populate a DataSet or DataReader with the SQL query from step 1.

3. Set the DataGrid's DataSource property to the DataSet or DataReader generated in step 2.

4. Call the DataGrid's DataBind() method.

It should be clear that the tasks our SortCommand event handler needs to perform are nearly identical to those performed by the BindData() subroutine (see lines 12–28 in Listing 7.1). Specifically, the BindData() subroutine in Listing 7.1 performs steps 2, 3, and 4, but not step 1; that is, the BindData() subroutine does not contain a variable ORDER BY clause. However, if we make some small changes to our BindData() subroutine so that it does perform step 1, our SortCommand event handler will be quite simple indeed—all it will need to do is defer to the BindData() subroutine.

To accomplish this, our BindData() subroutine will have to take as an input parameter a string indicating the name of the database field that we want to order our SQL results upon. Listing 7.2 contains the new code for our BindData(SortFieldName) subroutine.

LISTING 7.2   The BindData(SortFieldName) Subroutine Sorts the SQL Results by a Specified Field Name

```
 1:   Sub BindData(SortFieldName as String)
 2:      '1. Create a connection
 3:      Const strConnString as String = "server=localhost;uid=sa;pwd=;
➥database=pubs"
 4:      Dim objConn as New SqlConnection(strConnString)
 5:
 6:      '2. Create a command object for the query
 7:      Dim strSQL as String
 8:      strSQL = "SELECT title, price, pubdate " & _
 9:              "FROM titles " & _
10:              "ORDER BY " & SortFieldName
11:
12:      Dim objCmd as New SqlCommand(strSQL, objConn)
13:
14:      objConn.Open()    'Open the connection
15:
16:      'Finally, specify the DataSource and call DataBind()
17:      dgTitles.DataSource = objCmd.ExecuteReader(CommandBehavior.
➥CloseConnection)
18:      dgTitles.DataBind()
19:
20:      objConn.Close()    'Close the connection
21:   End Sub
```

Note that on line 1 the definition of the BindData(SortFieldName) subroutine has been altered to accept a string input parameter SortFieldName, which is the name of the DataSource field that we want to sort the results on. To accomplish this, the SQL statement (lines 8 through 10) adds an ORDER BY clause, with the order based upon the value of the string variable SortFieldName (line 10). The remainder of the code in the BindData(SortFieldName) subroutine is the same as it was in Listing 7.1.

With the new BindData(SortFieldName) subroutine, our SortCommand event handler becomes one single line of code—we simply need to call BindData(SortFieldName), passing in the value of the SortExpression of the DataGridSortCommandEventArgs parameter. Listing 7.3 contains the complete source code needed to provide a sortable DataGrid.

LISTING 7.3   With the Modified BindData(SortFieldName) Subroutine, the SortCommand Event Handler Is Quite Simple

```
 1: <%@ import Namespace="System.Data" %>
 2: <%@ import Namespace="System.Data.SqlClient" %>
 3: <script runat="server" language="VB">
 4:     ' The BindData(SortFieldName) subroutine has been omitted for brevity ...
 5:     ' ... see Listing 7.2 for details ...
 6:
 7:     Sub Page_Load(sender as Object, e as EventArgs)
 8:       If Not Page.IsPostBack then
 9:         BindData("title")
10:       End If
11:     End Sub
12:
13:
14:     Sub SortDataGrid(sender as Object, e as DataGridSortCommandEventArgs)
15:       BindData(e.SortExpression)
16:     End Sub
17: </script>
18:
19: <form runat="server">
20:   <asp:DataGrid runat="server" id="dgTitles"
21:       Font-Name="Verdana" Font-Size="9pt" CellPadding="5"
22:       AlternatingItemStyle-BackColor="#dddddd"
23:       AllowSorting="True" AutoGenerateColumns="True"
24:       OnSortCommand="SortDataGrid">
25:
26:     <HeaderStyle BackColor="Navy" ForeColor="White" Font-Size="13pt"
27:                  Font-Bold="True" HorizontalAlign="Center" />
28:   </asp:DataGrid>
29: </form>
```

There are just three lines of code in Listing 7.3 that are worthy of our attention. The first is line 9, where we call the BindData(SortFieldName) subroutine on the first page load. Note that here we pass in "title" as the SortFieldName parameter, which initially sorts the DataGrid by the title of the books. We could have provided a different titles field name, but, with the way we coded BindData(*SortFieldName*), we would need to provide *some* field name.

The second is the SortCommand event handler's code on line 15. Note that with our new BindData(SortFieldName) subroutine, our SortCommand event handler only needs this one line of code. It simply calls BindData(*SortFieldName*), passing in the SortExpression value of the DataGrid whose column sort header was clicked. Because the SortExpression of each DataGrid column is set equal to the DataSource field name whose data fills the column, we can simply pass in this SortExpression property into the BindData(SortFieldName) subroutine.

The final line of code to examine is line 24. This ties the DataGrid's SortCommand event to the SortDataGrid event handler (lines 14 through 16).

Figures 7.2 and 7.3 illustrate Listing 7.3 in action. Figure 7.2 shows the DataGrid when the page is first loaded. Note that the DataGrid is sorted alphabetically by the books' titles. Figure 7.3 is the output when the Price column sort hyperlink is clicked. Note that the DataGrid is sorted by price, from the lowest to the highest values.

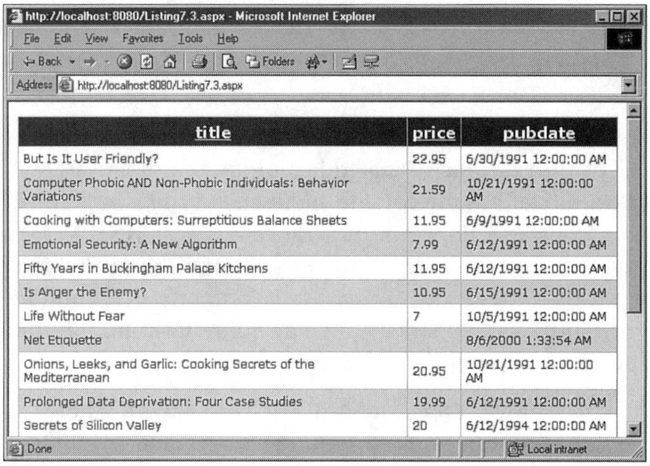

FIGURE 7.2   The initial ordering of the DataGrid is by the title field.

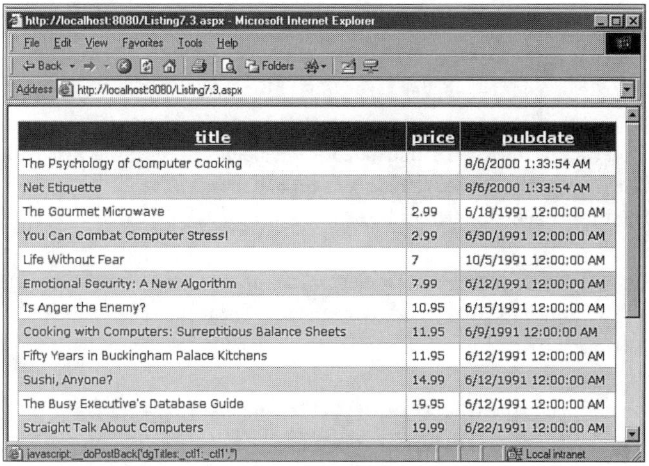

FIGURE 7.3   When the Price column's sort header hyperlink is clicked, the DataGrid's data is ordered by the price field.

Sorting a DataGrid with `AutoGenerateColumns` Set to `False`

As we saw in the last two sections, when both the `AutoGenerateColumns` and `AllowSorting` properties are set to `True`, the DataGrid automatically converts every field in the `DataSource` into a column in the DataGrid, making each column sortable by converting the column's header from a textual label to a hyperlink. Although this is very handy, there are instances when we want to specify the columns to appear in our DataGrid through the use of BoundColumn controls. By using BoundColumn controls, we can specify things like what fields of the `DataSource` should appear in the columns of the DataGrid (as well as in what order), and the display properties for each column, such as background color, horizontal alignment, and formatting. With these advantages, it is clear that there are times when we'd like to provide sorting support to a DataGrid that has its `AllowSorting` property set to `True`, but its `AutoGenerateColumns` property set to `False`.

When both the `AutoGenerateColumns` and `AllowSorting` properties are set to `True`, the `SortExpression` property of each DataGrid column is automatically set to the `DataSource`'s field name that the column represents. When we want to provide sorting support to a DataGrid whose `AutoGenerateColumns` is set to `False`, we need to explicitly provide the `SortExpression` property. All the column types derived from the `DataGridColumn` class contain the `SortExpression` property. The column types, which we've examined in previous chapters, include BoundColumn, ButtonColumn, HyperLinkColumn, and TemplateColumn.

Listing 7.4 illustrates how to provide sorting for a DataGrid whose `AutoGenerateColumns` property is set to `True`. The server-side script block in Listing 7.4 has been omitted for brevity—it is identical to that in Listing 7.3.

LISTING 7.4   A DataGrid Whose `AutoGenerateColumns` Property Is Set to True Can Be Sorted as Well

```
 1: <form runat="server">
 2:   <asp:DataGrid runat="server" id="dgTitles"
 3:       Font-Name="Verdana" Font-Size="9pt" CellPadding="5"
 4:       AlternatingItemStyle-BackColor="#dddddd"
 5:       AllowSorting="True" AutoGenerateColumns="False"
 6:       OnSortCommand="SortDataGrid">
 7:
 8:     <HeaderStyle BackColor="Navy" ForeColor="White" Font-Size="13pt"
 9:             Font-Bold="True" HorizontalAlign="Center" />
10:
11:     <Columns>
12:       <asp:BoundColumn DataField="title" HeaderText="Title"
13:             SortExpression="title" />
14:       <asp:BoundColumn DataField="price" HeaderText="Price"
```

LISTING 7.4   Continued

```
15:             SortExpression="price" DataFormatString="{0:c}"
16:             ItemStyle-HorizontalAlign="Right" />
17:      <asp:BoundColumn DataField="pubdate" HeaderText="Published Date" />
18:    </Columns>
19:  </asp:DataGrid>
20: </form>
```

The first thing to note is that the AutoGenerateColumns property has been set to False, and the AllowSorting property has been set to True (line 5). Additionally, the DataGrid's SortCommand event has been wired up to the SortDataGrid event handler on line 6. To see the code for the SortDataGrid event handler, refer back to Listing 7.3, lines 14–16.

The DataGrid's columns are specified on lines 12 through 17. Note that the first two BoundColumn controls—the Title and Price columns, lines 12 through 16—contain a SortExpression property that has been set to the DataSource field name the column represents. However, the third BoundColumn, Published Date (line 17), does *not* have a SortExpression property. When setting AutoGenerateColumns to False, you can specify which columns are sortable: To make a column sortable, simply provide a SortExpression property value; to make a column unsortable, simply omit the SortExpression property from the BoundColumn.

Figure 7.4 illustrates this concept. Note that the Published Date column's header is a text label and *not* a hyperlink, whereas the Title and Price columns' headers are indeed hyperlinks. This makes both the Title and Price columns sortable, and the Published Date column unsortable.

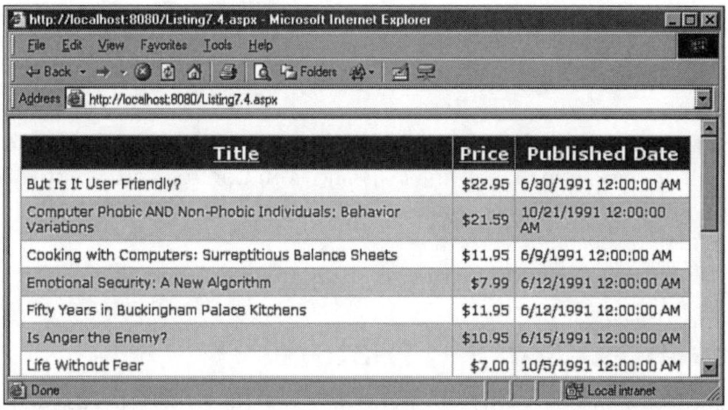

FIGURE 7.4   Lacking the SortExpression property, the Published Date column is unsortable.

Note that the `SortExpression` property values for the Title and Price columns are equivalent to the `DataSource` field name the column represents. This is important because our `BindData(SortFieldName)` subroutine expects as its input parameter the specific `DataSource` field name that the results are to be ordered by. Hence, if we give the Title column a `SortExpression` value of, say, TitleSort, we would get a runtime error when trying to sort the Title column because the `BindData(SortFieldName)` subroutine would be trying to execute the following SQL statement:

```
SELECT title, price, pubdate
FROM titles
ORDER BY TitleSort
```

Because `TitleSort` is not the name of a field in the `SELECT` clause, SQL Server will raise an error. Of course, we could set the Title column's `SortExpression` property to something like `TitleSort` and then alter our `SortDataGrid` event handler to check the `SortExpression` property and, based on the value, call the `BindData(SortFieldName)` subroutine with the appropriate field name. This might look like

```
Sub SortDataGrid(sender as Object, e as DataGridSortCommandEventArgs)
   If e.SortExpression = "TitleSort" then
      BindData("title")
   ElseIf e.SortExpression = "PriceSort" then
      BindData("price")
   End If
End Sub
```

This approach seems overly verbose and anything but robust. Clearly, the cleanest method is to just use the approach shown in Listing 7.4, where the `SortDataGrid` event handler is one line of code and the BoundColumns' `SortExpression` properties are set to the `DataSource` field name they represent.

> **NOTE**
>
> For more information on the basics of sorting a DataGrid's contents, be sure to check out the article "An Extensive Examination of the DataGrid Web Control: Part 4" listed in the "On the Web" section at the end of this chapter.

Adding Advanced Sorting Features

So far, we have seen how to add very simple sorting support to a DataGrid control. Although the sorting capabilities we have examined thus far are nice, they lack more advanced features that users are often accustomed to. For example, in Listing 7.4, the user can sort the DataGrid's data alphabetically by the title or by the price in ascending order. But what if the user wants to view the data by price in descending order?

Or what if she wants to view the price in ascending order? What if two or more books have the same price, and she wants to have those books sorted alphabetically?

With some additional programming, we can build a DataGrid that supports these advanced features. In the next section, we'll look at how to provide the ability for a particular DataGrid column to be sorted in either ascending or descending order. In the section "Providing Multi-Column Sorting," we'll examine how to sort the contents of the DataGrid on one column, breaking ties by a sorting a different column.

Before we begin addressing how to add these two advanced features, let's take a moment to quickly review over what is happening behind the scenes when a user opts to sort a DataGrid column by clicking on the column's sort header. Specifically, in Listing 7.4, when the sort header hyperlink of either the Title or Price column is clicked, the following events occur:

1. The ASP.NET Web page is posted back.

2. The DataGrid's `SortCommand` event is raised.

3. The `SortDataGrid` event handler, which is wired up to the DataGrid's `SortCommand` event, is executed.

4. The `BindData(SortFieldName)` subroutine is called, passing in the `SortExpression` property of the column whose sort header hyperlink was clicked.

5. A SQL query is formed that orders the results by the `DataSource` field represented by the `SortFieldName` input parameter to the `BindData(SortFieldName)` subroutine.

6. The SQL query is used to populate a `SqlDataReader` object.

7. The DataGrid's `DataSource` property is set to the `SqlDataReader` object from step 6, and the DataGrid's `DataBind()` method is called.

8. The DataGrid is displayed to the user sorted in ascending order by the DataGrid column whose sort header was clicked.

This chain of events always leads to the columns being sorted in ascending order, because in our `BindData(SortFieldName)` subroutine, we built up our SQL query by simply appending the name of the field we want to order the results by to the end of the SQL query. That is, if the user clicks on the Title column, which has a `SortExpression` property value of `"title"`, the SQL query becomes

```
SELECT title, price, pubdate
FROM titles
ORDER BY title
```

With SQL, the default sorting order is ascending. Of course, you can specify the sorting order using either the ASC or DESC keywords, for ascending and descending, respectively. If we want to sort the titles in reverse alphabetical order (descending order), we would need to adjust our SQL query so that it looks like this:

```
SELECT title, price, pubdate
FROM titles
ORDER BY title DESC
```

To sort the results in alphabetical order (ascending order), we could leave off any specification on the sort order:

```
SELECT title, price, pubdate
FROM titles
ORDER BY title
```

We could also specify that the sort be done in ascending order by adding the ASC keyword:

```
SELECT title, price, pubdate
FROM titles
ORDER BY title ASC
```

Now that we have a good understanding of the process that occurs when a DataGrid column's sort header hyperlink is clicked, we're ready to learn how to sort a DataGrid column in both ascending and descending order.

Supporting Ascending and Descending Sorting Orders

Before providing the capability to sort a DataGrid column in both ascending and descending order, it is important that we take a moment to decide on the user interface. For our first example, we'll simply use the standard sort header hyperlinks. That is, the first time a DataGrid column's sort header hyperlink is clicked, the results are displayed in ascending order. If a particular row's sort order is ascending and the sort header hyperlink is clicked again, the results are displayed in descending order. Similarly, if a particular row's sort order is descending and the sort header hyperlink is clicked again, the results are displayed in ascending order.

To accomplish this, we need some way to keep track of how a row should be sorted if its sort header hyperlink is clicked. This information needs to persist across postbacks. With classic ASP, we might opt to store such information in the Session object, and this is also an option with ASP.NET. However, because we only need to store this information on a page-level basis as opposed to a user session-level basis, it would be wiser to use the ViewState.

NOTE

For more information on the `ViewState`, check out Susan Warren's article "Taking a Bite Out of ASP.NET `ViewState`." You can find a reference to the article in the "On the Web" section at the end of this chapter.

For each sortable DataGrid column, we will add a string variable in the `ViewState` that indicates whether the column needs to be displayed in ascending or descending order when the column's sort header hyperlink is clicked. Listing 7.5 illustrates how we can enable DataGrid columns to be sorted both in ascending and descending order. Note that the `BindData(SortFieldName)` subroutine from Listing 7.5 has been omitted for brevity; to review the `BindData(SortFieldName)` subroutine code, refer back to Listing 7.3. Additionally, the DataGrid declaration in Listing 7.5 has been omitted as well—it is the same as the DataGrid declaration in Listing 7.4.

LISTING 7.5   Each Column's Sort Direction Is Stored in a `ViewState` Variable

```
1: <%@ import Namespace="System.Data" %>
2: <%@ import Namespace="System.Data.SqlClient" %>
3: <script runat="server" language="VB">
4:     '... The BindData method has been omitted for brevity ...
5:     '... Refer back to Listing 7.3 for its details ...
6:
7:     Sub Page_Load(sender as Object, e as EventArgs)
8:       If Not Page.IsPostBack then
9:         ViewState("titleSortDirection") = "ASC"
10:        ViewState("priceSortDirection") = "ASC"
11:
12:        BindData("title " & ViewState("titleSortDirection"))
13:
14:        SwapDirection("titleSortDirection")
15:      End If
16:     End Sub
17:
18:
19:     Sub SwapDirection(viewStateKey as String)
20:       If ViewState(viewStateKey) = "ASC" then
21:         ViewState(viewStateKey) = "DESC"
22:       Else
23:         ViewState(viewStateKey) = "ASC"
24:       End If
25:     End Sub
26:
27:
```

LISTING 7.5   Continued

```
28:     Sub SortDataGrid(sender as Object, e as DataGridSortCommandEventArgs)
29:         BindData(e.SortExpression & " " & ViewState(e.SortExpression &
➡"SortDirection"))
30:
31:         SwapDirection(e.SortExpression & "SortDirection")
32:     End Sub
33: </script>
34:
35:   <%-- The DataGrid declaration has been omitted for brevity
36:         Refer back to Listing 7.4 for its details...   --%>
```

The key pieces of Listing 7.5 can be found in the Page_Load event handler (lines 9 through 14), the SwapDirection(*ViewStateKey*) subroutine (lines 19 through 25), and the code in the SortDataGrid event handler (lines 29 and 31) .

CAUTION

When storing a variable in the ViewState, realize that the key used to retrieve and store the variable is case sensitive. That is, ViewState("titleSortDirection") and ViewState("TitleSortDirection") reference *two different* variables in the ViewState (because the latter example has its first character capitalized, and the former does not).

Let's first look at what happens when the page is visited for the first time. Recall that for each sortable column, we need to store a string variable in the ViewState that indicates how the column should be sorted when its sort header hyperlink is clicked. Because we only have two sortable columns in our DataGrid, the Title and Price columns, we create two such ViewState variables on lines 9 and 10 in our first visit to the page, setting the variables to "ASC", the direction we want to have the columns sorted by default. Next, a call to the BindData(*SortFieldName*) subroutine is made on line 12. Instead of just passing in a DataSource field name, we pass in both the field name and the direction we want the results sorted. Hence, on line 12 the *SortFieldName* parameter is passed in as a value of "title ASC", which sorts the results by the title field in ascending order.

After making a call to the BindData(*SortFieldName*) subroutine on line 12, a call to the SwapDirection(*ViewStateKey*) is made on line 14. The SwapDirection(*ViewStateKey*) subroutine accepts a ViewState key name (a string) as its input parameter. It then checks to see whether the value of the particular ViewState variable is "ASC" (line 20); if it is, it changes the value to "DESC". If the value of the ViewState variable is *not* "ASC", SwapDirection(*ViewStateKey*) changes the value back to "ASC" (lines 20–24). This toggling of the ViewState variable has the effect of changing the column's sort order each time the column's sort header hyperlink is clicked.

The SortDataGrid event handler (lines 28 through 32) first makes a call to the BindData(SortFieldName) subroutine on line 29, passing in an appropriate string by concatenating the SortExpression property value with a blank space and the value of the particular column's ViewState variable. Finally, on line 31, a call to the SwapDirection(*ViewStateKey*) subroutine is made, swapping the sort order for the column whose sort header hyperlink was just clicked.

To clear any confusion that may exist, let's run through the code's execution life cycle when a column's sort header hyperlink is clicked. First the ASP.NET Web page is posted back, and the DataGrid's SortCommand event is fired. This in turn executes the SortDataGrid event handle, which calls the BindData(SortFieldName) subroutine. Imagine that the Title column was the column that had its sort header hyperlink clicked. Then the value of e.SortExpression is "title", so the call to BindData(*SortFieldName*) on line 29 is passed in the value of e.SortExpression, concatenated with a blank string, and then concatenated with the ViewState variable whose name is the value of e.SortExpression combined with the string "SortDirection". Because the value of e.SortExpression is "Title", we are grabbing the ViewState variable "titleSortDirection". The ViewState variable "titleSortDirection" will have a value of either "ASC" or "DESC", meaning that the string passed into the BindData(SortFieldName) subroutine will be either "title ASC" or "title DESC", depending on the current value of the ViewState variable "titleSortDirection". Assuming the input to the BindData(SortFieldName) subroutine was "title DESC", the following SQL query is used in repopulating the DataGrid:

```
SELECT title, price, pubdate
FROM titles
ORDER BY title DESC
```

NOTE

Note that when choosing the ViewState variable names in the Page_Load event handler (lines 9 and 10), I was careful to choose the names so that they followed the pattern *FieldName*SortDirection. Using this technique, I can then query the value of the proper ViewState variable by using the SortExpression concatenated with the string "SortDirection" because the SortExpression values for the columns are equal to the field names the columns represent.

After the call to the BindData(SortFieldName) subroutine is made, a call to the SwapDirection(*ViewStateKey*) subroutine is made (line 31). This call changes the sort order for the Title column from "DESC" to "ASC" or vice versa, depending upon the current value of the titleSortDirection ViewState variable.

Figures 7.5 and 7.6 depict the code from Listing 7.5 in action. Figure 7.5 shows the page when the Price sort header hyperlink has been clicked for the first time—note that the DataGrid is sorted in ascending order by price. Figure 7.6 illustrates what happens when the Price column's sort header is clicked again. This time, the DataGrid is sorted by price in descending order.

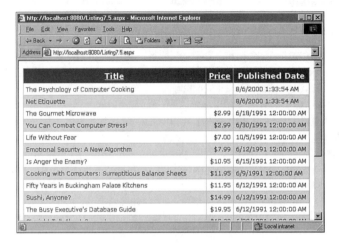

FIGURE 7.5   The DataGrid is ordered by price in ascending order.

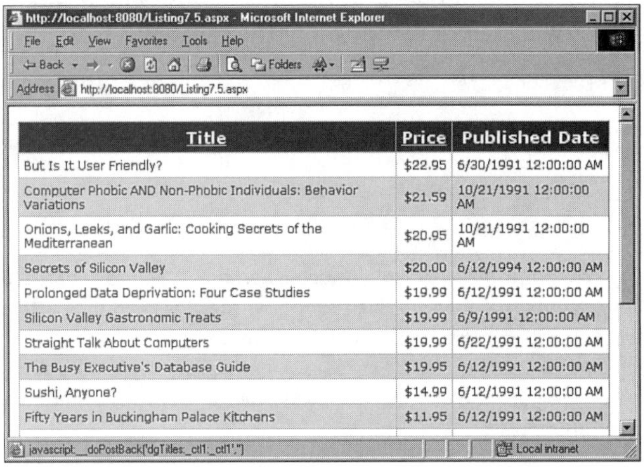

FIGURE 7.6   The DataGrid is ordered by price in descending order.

Improvements to the User Interface

One downside to the user interface we just examined is that, from the user's perspective, it's difficult to determine what column has been sorted on and in what direction. Granted, through simple inspection, it wouldn't take an average user long to determine what column of the DataGrid had been sorted and in what order. Nevertheless, it would be helpful to have some sort of visual cue to indicate this information. For example, if you use Microsoft Outlook, you'll likely have noticed that you can sort a list of emails in a folder by clicking on the From, Subject, or Date Received headers. When clicking on such a field, a small up or down arrow appears next to the field name, indicating that the results are sorted by that column and in what direction (an up arrow indicates ascending order, a down arrow indicates descending order).

It would be nice to provide a similar user interface to our DataGrid control. There are a number of ways to accomplish this task. Personally, I think the easiest would be to create a number of images, three for each sortable DataGrid column. Each sortable DataGrid column would need an image with only the name of the column, an image with the name of the column and a down arrow next to it, and an image with the name of the column and an up arrow next to it. For our Title table, we would have an image reading Title, an image reading Title with an up arrow next to the word Title, and an image reading Title with a down arrow next to the word Title. Similarly, we would have these three images for our Price column as well. These images should be named *ColumnName*Plain.gif for the image with just the name of the column, *ColumnName*ASC.gif for the image with the name of the column and an up arrow, and *ColumnName*DESC.gif for the image with the name of the column and a down arrow.

Next, in our DataGrid declaration, for our sortable DataGrid columns we would replace the HeaderText property in the BoundColumn control with the HeaderImageUrl property, whose value is set to the image without the arrow for that column. That is, in Listing 7.4, our DataGrid declaration had the following BoundColumns:

```
<asp:BoundColumn DataField="title" HeaderText="Title"
        SortExpression="title" />
<asp:BoundColumn DataField="price" HeaderText="Price"
        SortExpression="price" DataFormatString="{0:c}"
        ItemStyle-HorizontalAlign="Right" />
<asp:BoundColumn DataField="pubdate" HeaderText="Published Date" />
```

We would replace the HeaderText property in the Title and Price BoundColumns with the HeaderImageUrl property:

```
<asp:BoundColumn DataField="title" HeaderImageUrl="TitlePlain.gif"
        SortExpression="title" />
<asp:BoundColumn DataField="price" HeaderImageUrl="PricePlain.gif"
        SortExpression="price" DataFormatString="{0:c}"
        ItemStyle-HorizontalAlign="Right" />
<asp:BoundColumn DataField="pubdate" HeaderText="Published Date" />
```

This would display the Title image and Price image in the header of the Title and Price columns. These images, when clicked, would cause a postback, raising the DataGrid's SortCommand event just as in Listings 7.4 and 7.5, when the HeaderText property was used instead.

Whenever the SortDataGrid event handler is fired, we need to call a subroutine that iterates through the columns of the DataGrid, setting each column's HeaderImageUrl property accordingly. Specifically, the column whose sort header hyperlink was just clicked would have its HeaderImageUrl changed to the appropriate up or down arrow version, whereas all other sortable columns would have their HeaderImageUrl changed back to the plain image. Listing 7.6 provides the code needed to produce such a user interface.

LISTING 7.6   An Up or Down Arrow Is Used to Illustrate How the DataGrid's Data Is Sorted

```
 1: <%@ import Namespace="System.Data" %>
 2: <%@ import Namespace="System.Data.SqlClient" %>
 3: <script runat="server" language="VB">
 4:    ' ... The BindData and SwapDirections subroutines have been
 5:    ' ... omitted for brevity.  Refer back to Listings 7.3 and 7.5,
 6:          ' ... respectively, for details ...
 7:
 8:    Sub Page_Load(sender as Object, e as EventArgs)
 9:      If Not Page.IsPostBack then
10:        ViewState("titleSortDirection") = "ASC"
11:        ViewState("priceSortDirection") = "ASC"
12:
13:        BindData("title " & ViewState("titleSortDirection"))
14:        ChangeHeaderImageUrl("title", "ASC")
15:        SwapDirection("titleSortDirection")
16:      End If
17:    End Sub
18:
19:
20:    Sub ChangeHeaderImageUrl(fieldName as String, sortDirection as String)
21:      ' Loop through all of the DataGrid columns
22:      Dim iLoop as Integer
23:      Dim column as DataGridColumn
24:      Dim dgRow as DataGridItem = dgTitles.Controls(0).Controls(0)
25:      Dim sortButton as ImageButton
26:
27:      For iLoop = 0 to dgTitles.Columns.Count - 1
28:
29:        column = dgTitles.Columns(iLoop)
30:
```

LISTING 7.6   Continued

```
31:          ' See if the column has a SortExpression property
32:          If column.SortExpression <> String.Empty then
33:            'Now, check if the SortExpression equals the fieldName
34:
35:            sortButton = dgRow.Cells(iLoop).Controls(0)
36:
37:            If column.SortExpression = fieldName then
38:              'We need to apply a new arrow direction
39:              column.HeaderImageUrl = fieldName & sortDirection & ".gif"
40:              sortButton.ImageUrl = column.HeaderImageUrl
41:            Else
42:              'This column wasn't sorted, we need to display the
43:              'standard image url
44:              column.HeaderImageUrl = column.SortExpression & "Plain.gif"
45:              sortButton.ImageUrl = column.HeaderImageUrl
46:            End If
47:          End If
48:       Next iLoop
49:     End Sub
50:
51:
52:     Sub SortDataGrid(sender as Object, e as DataGridSortCommandEventArgs)
53:         BindData(e.SortExpression & " " & ViewState(e.SortExpression &
➥"SortDirection"))
54:         ChangeHeaderImageUrl(e.SortExpression, ViewState(e.SortExpression &
➥"SortDirection"))
55:         SwapDirection(e.SortExpression & "SortDirection")
56:     End Sub
57: </script>
58:
59: <form runat="server">
60:   <asp:DataGrid runat="server" id="dgTitles"
61:       Font-Name="Verdana" Font-Size="9pt" CellPadding="5"
62:       AlternatingItemStyle-BackColor="#dddddd"
63:       AllowSorting="True" AutoGenerateColumns="False"
64:       OnSortCommand="SortDataGrid">
65:
66:     <HeaderStyle BackColor="Navy" ForeColor="White" Font-Size="13pt"
67:             Font-Bold="True" HorizontalAlign="Center" />
68:
69:     <Columns>
70:       <asp:BoundColumn DataField="title" HeaderImageUrl="TitlePlain.gif"
71:             SortExpression="title" />
```

LISTING 7.6   Continued

```
72:        <asp:BoundColumn DataField="price" HeaderImageUrl="PricePlain.gif"
73:              SortExpression="price" DataFormatString="{0:c}"
74:              ItemStyle-HorizontalAlign="Right" />
75:        <asp:BoundColumn DataField="pubdate" HeaderText="Published Date" />
76:      </Columns>
77:    </asp:DataGrid>
78: </form>
```

The first thing to note is that the BoundColumns for the Title and Price columns both have their HeaderImageUrl property set to the "plain" versions of the image files, the ones without an up or down arrow next to the image title (lines 70 and 72, respectively). The Page_Load event handler for Listing 7.6 is nearly identical to that of Listing 7.5; the only difference is that after calling the BindData(SortFieldName) subroutine and before calling SwapDirection(ViewStateKey), we call a new subroutine, ChangeHeaderImageUrl(FieldName, SortDirection) (line 14).

The new subroutine, ChangeHeaderImageUrl(FieldName, SortDirection) (lines 11 through 28), is called on the first page load, as well as each time one of the DataGrid's column's sort header hyperlinks is clicked. This subroutine is responsible for updating the HeaderImageUrl property of each of the sortable columns in the DataGrid, as well as the ImageUrl property of the ImageButton control that makes up the actual image in the DataGrid column header.

The FieldName input parameter to the ChangeHeaderImageUrl(FieldName, SortDirection) subroutine specifies what column has just had its sort header hyperlink clicked. The ChangeHeaderImageUrl(FieldName, SortDirection) subroutine iterates through each column in the DataGrid's Columns collection using a For... Next loop starting on line 27. Before that, however, a number of variables are declared. On line 22, iLoop, a simple integer looping variable, is declared. On line 23, column is declared as a DataGridColumn instance. This variable is used in the For ... Next loop to reference the current DataGrid column that is being iterated over. On line 24, a variable of type DataGridItem called dgRow is created and assigned to the first DataGridItem in the DataGrid, the header row that contains the sort header hyperlinks (as ImageButtons) for each of the sortable columns. To retrieve this header row, we have to first reference the first (0th) child control of the DataGrid, which is a DataGridTable object. The children controls of the DataGridTable are the rows of the DataGrid. Because we want to retrieve the first (0th) row, we reference the DataGridTable's 0th child control. Hence, in the end, we want the 0th child control of the 0th child control of the DataGrid, or dgTitles.Controls(0).Controls(0) (line 24) .

Note that we are only concerned with altering the HeaderImageUrl property and ImageButton ImageUrl property of those columns that are sortable. In each iteration of our For ... Next loop, we set the current column to a local variable column (line 29). On line 32, we then check the column's SortExpression property to determine whether the DataGrid column is sortable. Recall that to make a column sortable when the AutoGenerateColumns property is set to False, you have to specify a SortExpression property for the column. Hence, columns whose SortExpression is a blank string are not sortable. Therefore, lines 33 through 46 will only be reached if the current column being examined is a sortable column.

Assuming the column is sortable, we first grab an instance of the ImageButton used to represent the sort header for the particular column. When supplying a HeaderImageUrl property for a DataGrid column, the header is displayed via an ImageButton control. To physically alter the image displayed by the header, we must directly reference this ImageButton and tweak its ImageUrl property. Line 35 references the ImageButton for the current column being iterated through and assigns it to the local variable sortButton. Note that dgRow.Cells(iLoop) retrieves the particular column we're currently iterating over from the header DataGridItem row; the Controls(0) retrieves the first (0th) child control from this row's column, which is an ImageButton control (because the HeaderImageUrl property was set for this row) .

After referencing the ImageButton control, we check to see whether the column's SortExpression property is identical to the *FieldName* input parameter (line 37). If it is, we need to set the column's HeaderImageUrl property and the ImageButton's ImageUrl property to the appropriate image. For example, if we are displaying the Title column in ascending order, we want to change the HeaderImageUrl property to "TitleASC.gif". On lines 39 and 40, we set the HeaderImageUrl and ImageUrl properties accordingly; the correct image URL can be determined by concatenating the value of the *FieldName* input parameter with the *SortDirection* input parameter, followed by the extension .gif. (The *SortDirection* input parameter will have the value "ASC" or "DESC".)

If, on the other hand, the current column being iterated over is *not* the column whose sort header ImageButton was clicked, we want to convert the ImageButton's ImageUrl back to the "plain" image. This is accomplished in the Else statement on lines 44 and 45.

Note that in the SortDataGrid event handler, we make a call to the ChangeHeaderImageUrl(*FieldName*, *SortDirection*) subroutine each time after BindData(*SortFieldName*) and before calling SwapDirection(*ViewStateKey*) (line 54) .

Figures 7.7 and 7.8 show Listing 7.6 when viewed through a browser. Specifically, Figure 7.7 shows the page on the first page view, when the DataGrid is sorted alphabetically (in ascending order) by the Title column. Figure 7.8 shows what happens after the Title sort header is clicked, which reverses the sort order for the Title column. Note that the arrow in the Title image in Figure 7.7 points up, whereas the arrow in the Title image in Figure 7.8 points down. Furthermore, note that the Price image has no arrows, because we are sorting by the Title column.

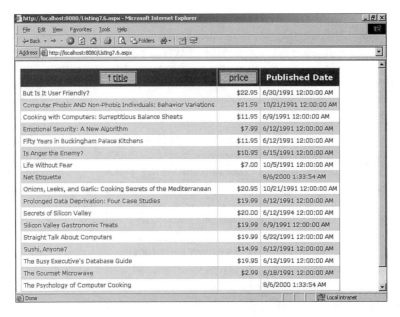

FIGURE 7.7   An up arrow indicates that the DataGrid is sorted in ascending order by the Title column.

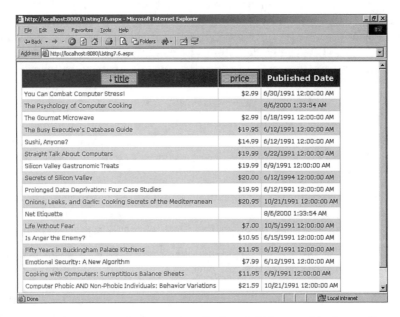

FIGURE 7.8   A down arrow indicates that the DataGrid is sorted in descending order by the Title column.

Providing Multi-Column Sorting

Now that we know how to provide both ascending and descending support for a single column, let's examine how to provide sorting across multiple columns. That is, how can we have it so that when one column is sorted, any ties are broken by a sort order on another column? A specific example of this occurs when sorting the books in Listing 7.6 by price: If two books have the same price, they are ordered alphabetically.

Let's take the code from Listing 7.6 and extend it so that whenever the Price column is sorted, ties are broken by sorting the titles of the tied books in alphabetical order. For simplicity's sake, let's not concern ourselves with breaking ties when sorting the Title column.

Currently when the Price column's sort header is clicked the first time, the DataGrid's data is sorted by the price in ascending order. This is accomplished via the following SQL query:

```
SELECT title, price, pubdate
FROM titles
ORDER BY price ASC
```

When the Price column's sort header is clicked a second time, the DataGrid is sorted by the price in descending order, which is accomplished via the following SQL query:

```
SELECT title, price, pubdate
FROM titles
ORDER BY price DESC
```

To sort the Price column in either ascending or descending order with ties being broken by the values of the Title column, we need to use one of the following two ORDER BY clauses in our SQL statement:

```
-- for ordering by price in ascending order, breaking ties
-- alphabetically on the title
ORDER BY price ASC, title ASC
```

```
-- for ordering by price in descending order, breaking ties
-- alphabetically on the title
ORDER BY price DESC, title ASC
```

Currently we are determining the sorting by passing in the field name and sort direction for the ORDER BY clause through the input parameter of the BindData(SortFieldName) subroutine. For our example, we'll need to call BindData(SortFieldName) like so:

```
BindData("price ASC, title ASC")
```

In the `SortDataGrid` event handler in Listing 7.6, we determined the input parameter to `BindData(`*SortFieldName*`)` by concatenating the value of the clicked DataGrid column's `SortExpression`, along with the proper `ViewState` variable that indicates in what direction the data is to be sorted. It is clear that to allow for multi-column sorting, we will need to enhance this call to `BindData(`*SortFieldName*`)` in some manner, so that when sorting by the Price column, either `price ASC, title ASC` or `price DESC, title ASC` gets passed in to the `BindData(SortFieldName)` subroutine, depending upon what direction the Price column data needs to be sorted.

As you can see in Listing 7.7, the solution uses a new subroutine, `PrepareBindData(`*FieldName*`, `*SortDirection*`)` (lines 20–26), which is called in place of `BindData(`*SortFieldName*`)` in the `SortDataGrid` event handler. It is the `PrepareBindData(`*FieldName*`, `*SortDirection*`)` subroutine that makes the appropriate call to `BindData(`*SortFieldName*`)` when the Price column is being sorted.

LISTING 7.7   Ties in the Price Are Broken by Sorting the Titles Alphabetically

```
 1: <%@ import Namespace="System.Data" %>
 2: <%@ import Namespace="System.Data.SqlClient" %>
 3: <script runat="server" language="VB">
 4:   ' ... The BindData, SwapDirections, and ChangeHeaderImageUrl
 5:   ' ... subroutines have been omitted for brevity.  Refer back
 6:   ' ... to Listings 7.3, 7.5, and 7.6 respectively, for details
 7:
 8:   Sub Page_Load(sender as Object, e as EventArgs)
 9:     If Not Page.IsPostBack then
10:       ViewState("titleSortDirection") = "ASC"
11:       ViewState("priceSortDirection") = "ASC"
12:
13:       PrepareBindData("title", ViewState("titleSortDirection"))
14:       ChangeHeaderImageUrl("title", "ASC")
15:       SwapDirection("titleSortDirection")
16:     End If
17:   End Sub
18:
19:
20:   Sub PrepareBindData(fieldName as String, sortDirection as String)
21:     If fieldName = "price" then
22:       BindData(fieldName & " " & sortDirection & ", title ASC")
23:     Else
24:       BindData(fieldName & " " & sortDirection)
25:     End If
26:   End Sub
```

LISTING 7.7   Continued

```
27:
28:
29:     Sub SortDataGrid(sender as Object, e as DataGridSortCommandEventArgs)
30:         PrepareBindData(e.SortExpression, ViewState(e.SortExpression &
➥"SortDirection"))
31:         ChangeHeaderImageUrl(e.SortExpression, ViewState(e.SortExpression &
➥"SortDirection"))
32:         SwapDirection(e.SortExpression & "SortDirection")
33:     End Sub
34: </script>
35:
36:   <%-- The DataGrid declaration has been for brevity.
37:        Refer back to Listing 7.6 for details ...   --%>
```

Note that the call to BindData(*SortFieldName*) has been replaced with a call to PrepareBindData(*FieldName*, *SortDirection*) on line 30 in the SortDataGrid event handler and on line 13 in the Page_Load event handler. The PrepareBindData(*FieldName*, *SortDirection*) subroutine (lines 20 through 26) is fairly simple. It checks whether the field to sort on is the price field (line 21); if it is, a call to BindData(*SortFieldName*) is made as it normally would, with "title ASC" appended to the end. This will cause our SQL statement's ORDER BY clause in BindData(*SortFieldName*) to have the form

```
ORDER BY price direction, title ASC
```

Here *direction* is either "ASC" or "DESC", depending on the value of the *SortDirection* parameter passed in to the PrepareBindData(*FieldName*, *SortDirection*) subroutine. If, on the other hand, we are not sorting on the Price column, we simply call BindData(*SortFieldName*), as we did in Listing 7.6 (line 24). Hence, the PrepareBindData(*FieldName*, *SortDirection*) subroutine manages to perform multi-column sorting when sorting on the Price column, and regular single-column sorting when sorting via the Title column.

Figure 7.9 illustrates the DataGrid being sorted by the Price column. Note that in instances where there are tied prices, such as *Cooking with Computers* and *Fifty Years in Buckingham Palace Kitchens*, both priced at $11.95, the books are sorted in alphabetical order. Compare this to Figure 7.6, which shows the DataGrid ordered by the Price column, but with single-column ordering. Note that in that example, the *Fifty Years in Buckingham Palace Kitchens* title precedes the *Cooking with Computers* title, showing up in reverse alphabetical order.

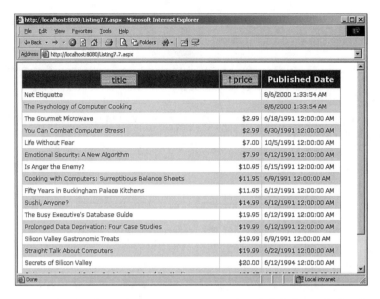

FIGURE 7.9   Books that have the same price are ordered alphabetically by their titles.

NOTE

For more information on sorting in ascending and descending order and in using multi-column sorting techniques, refer to Dino Espisito's "Effective Sorting in ASP.NET DataGrids" article mentioned in the "On the Web" section at the end of this chapter.

Caching the DataGrid's DataSource at the Page Level

In Chapter 6, we examined how to use external command buttons to provide filtering buttons. When initially presenting code to provide filtering button support, each time a filtering button is clicked, a database call is made, grabbing a portion of the total data depending on the filtering conditions.

In our discussions on this matter, we realized that each call out to the database is a bit wasteful. After all, on the first visit to the page, we display *all* the records from the table. Hence, it contains the records for any particular filter, and doesn't require a database access every time a filter button is clicked.

To overcome this, we use a DataSet for the data Web control's DataSource and then cache the DataSet in the ViewState. When a filter button is clicked, we can retrieve the DataSet from the ViewState, apply the filter, and rebind the filtered data to the data Web control. This approach eliminates the unneeded database accesses, but has two potential downsides. First, there is the potential for the cached data to become stale. That is, because the data being filtered is cached data from the page's first load, if records are added, updated, or deleted from the underlying database, the cached DataSet won't reflect those changes. Second, because the ViewState is maintained as a hidden HTML field, adding large objects to the ViewState can add several kilobytes. For example, a DataSet containing just the titles table from the pubs database will add roughly 20 kilobytes (20KB) to the HTML produced by the ASP.NET Web page when added to the ViewState.

In the previous code listings in this chapter, each time a sort header is clicked, we run a new SQL query, requiring a database access. As with the filtering buttons example, this database access might be superfluous if the database data does not change frequently. If the database is fairly static, the information retrieved when the page is first visited can be cached in the ViewState. When a DataGrid column's sort header is clicked, this cached data can be reordered and bound to the DataGrid.

As with caching a DataSet in the filter button example, this approach will save us a database access each time a DataGrid column's sort header is clicked. Of course, this approach carries with it the two aforementioned disadvantages: the cached data can become stale, and caching a DataSet in the ViewState will unquestionably lead to an increase in the HTML produced by the ASP.NET Web page.

To cache the data pulled in from the first page load, we need to use a DataSet in place of the SqlDataReader we have been using for our examples thus far. This is because a DataSet is designed as a disconnected data source, whereas the DataReader objects require an active connection to a data store. Furthermore, the DataSet contains a DefaultView property that is an instance of the DataView class. The DataView class is designed to provide a customizable view of a DataTable class instance to allow for sorting, filtering, and searching. (For an example of caching a DataSet, refer back to Chapter 6, Listing 6.4.)

To provide page-level caching support, we only need to make a change to one subroutine on the page: BindData(SortFieldName). Listing 7.8 provides altered version of this subroutine. To integrate Listing 7.8 with the code from Listing 7.7, simply replace the BindData(SortFieldName) subroutine in Listing 7.7 with the version presented in Listing 7.8.

LISTING 7.8   The DataGrid Data Is Cached in a ViewState Variable to Save Database Accesses

```
1:    Sub BindData(SortFieldName as String)
2:      'Check to see if we have a DataSet in the Viewstate
3:      Dim objDS as DataSet
4:
5:      If ViewState("TitlesDataSet") is Nothing then
6:        '1. Create a connection
```

LISTING 7.8   Continued

```
 7:        Const strConnString as String = "server=localhost;uid=sa;pwd=;
➥database=pubs"
 8:        Dim objConn as New SqlConnection(strConnString)
 9:
10:        '2. Create a command object for the query
11:        Dim strSQL as String
12:        strSQL = "SELECT title, price, pubdate " & _
13:                "FROM titles " & _
14:                "ORDER BY " & SortFieldName
15:
16:        Dim objCmd as New SqlCommand(strSQL, objConn)
17:
18:        '3. Create a DataAdapter and Fill the DataSet
19:        Dim objDA as New SqlDataAdapter()
20:        objDA.SelectCommand = objCmd
21:
22:        objDS = New DataSet()
23:        objDA.Fill(objDS, "titles")
24:
25:        objConn.Close()
26:
27:        'Add the DataSet to the ViewState
28:        ViewState.Add("TitlesDataSet", objDS)
29:      Else
30:        'Get the DataSet out of the ViewState
31:        objDS = ViewState("TitlesDataSet")
32:
33:        'Apply the sorting
34:        objDS.Tables("titles").DefaultView.Sort = SortFieldName
35:      End If
36:
37:      'Finally, specify the DataSource and call DataBind()
38:      dgTitles.DataSource = objDS.Tables("titles").DefaultView
39:      dgTitles.DataBind()
40:    End Sub
```

The BindData(*SortFieldName*) subroutine in Listing 7.8 starts by declaring a DataSet variable, objDS, on line 3. Recall that to cache data, we need to use a DataSet as opposed to a SqlDataReader, which we used in our previous examples in this chapter.

The BindData(*SortFieldName*) subroutine is called the first time in the Page_Load event handler when the page is loaded for the first time. It is also called each time one of the DataGrid column's sort headers is clicked. The BindData(*SortFieldName*) subroutine must be able to determine whether there is a cached DataSet in the ViewState. Line 5 makes this check—if there is *not* a cached DataSet, lines 7 through 28 are executed; otherwise, the Else portion is executed (lines 30 through 34) .

If there is no cached DataSet, the code from lines 7–28 fills a DataSet with the appropriate SQL query. This code is roughly equivalent to the BindData(*SortFieldName*) in Listing 7.7—the major difference is that in Listing 7.8 we are using a DataSet instead of a SqlDataReader. This filled DataSet is then added to the ViewState (line 28).

On the other hand, if a cached DataSet is found—that is, if ViewState("TitlesDataSet") is not equal to Nothing—we use the DefaultView on the DataSet to provide a sorted view of the data. We start on line 31 by referencing the cached DataSet by the local variable objDS. Next, the DataSet's DefaultView's Sort property is set to the *SortFieldName* input parameter (line 34).

Regardless of whether we fill a DataSet from the database or we retrieve it from the ViewState cache, we set the DataGrid's DataSource property to the DataSet's DefaultView (line 38) and call the DataGrid's DataBind() method (line 39).

This approach requires that the ASP.NET Web page perform only one database access: when the page is first loaded. The downside of caching data in this manner is that the cached data can become stale and caching the data in the ViewState results in a larger HTML output of the ASP.NET page. The penalty from this larger page size is felt twice—it yields longer times for the client to download the page from the Web server, as well as longer times when performing postbacks, because the ViewState is maintained as a hidden form field that must be passed back to the server when the form is submitted.

When caching the DataSet at the page level, you might see some slight improvement in the Web server's performance. However, from the user's perspective, it will likely result in degraded performance, because he will have to wait longer to download the Web page and perform postbacks. The time the user spends waiting to download and upload the additional bytes will likely outweigh the extra time required for the Web server to make an extra database call. Therefore, I would suggest that this page-level caching technique only be used when the following two conditions hold:

1. All the Web site's users are on a high-speed connection. For example, if you are deploying a Web application on an intranet, you can rest assured that the extra kilobytes added in the ViewState will not seriously hamper the overall performance of the Web application.

2. The cost of a database access is too high. In the majority of cases, database access is quite fast. However, there are certain cases where database accesses can

take up to several seconds to complete. For example, the Web server may reside in an office building in Los Angeles, while the company's master database that your Web site needs to access is located in the company's headquarters in Washington, D.C. Also, the query that needs to be run might be quite complex, or might be operating on a table with millions of records.

If both of these conditions hold true, you should consider using page-level caching techniques. More often than not, these two conditions will not be true, and therefore the standard "database access for every postback" model that we used in Listing 7.7 is preferred.

What About Using the Data Cache?

The .NET Framework provides a wonderful caching API, commonly referred to as the *data cache*, that allows for in-memory caching on the Web server. The caching API is fairly powerful—when inserting items into the cache, you can specify that they exist for an absolute duration or a sliding duration. An absolute duration specifies how long an item should stay in the cache after it's placed there, regardless of its usage pattern. A sliding duration specifies how long an item should stay in the cache since its last use.

We have seen how to cache the DataSet in a page-level cache using the ViewState; we could opt to use the data cache instead. Through the use of the data cache, we would remove the two disadvantages of using the ViewState to cache a DataSet.

Because the data cache stores its contents on the Web server's memory, it adds any additional bytes to the ViewState—this eliminates the problem of the additional page size. By using the data cache, the disadvantage of stale data can be removed as well. Items inserted into the cache can exist for an absolute or sliding time interval. In addition to this, items inserted into the data cache can have a caching dependency, such as when a particular file on the Web server's filesystem changes. That is, if an item in the cache has a file as its dependency, whenever that file is modified, the item whose dependency relies on that file will be evicted from the cache. Using this technique, a clever developer can make an item in the cache dependent upon when a particular row in the database. See the article "Invalidating an ASP.NET Cache Item from SQL Server" in the "On the Web" section at the end of this chapter for more information on this topic.

By tying a cached DataSet to a change in its underlying database table (an insert, update, or delete), any time the data is changed, the DataSet is evicted from the cache. Hence, when a call to the BindData(*SortFieldName*) subroutine occurs, the DataSet is repopulated from the database, removing any chance of stale data.

Although using the data cache to store the DataSet might seem like an ideal option, it has one key drawback. Because the data cache's backing store is the Web server's memory, there is limited space. Imagine that you have a Web site with 25 pages that make database accesses, and the results of these accesses are dynamic, based on user input. Because these pages are dependent upon user input, you would need to cache a DataSet for each user. If you have, on average, say, 1,000 users visiting and using these data-bound pages, and your average DataSet requires, say, 50KB of memory, the total amount of memory needed to keep all this information in the data cache amounts to 50KB × 1,000 × 25 = 1,250,000KB, or 1.25GB.

The two conditions that make page-level caching in the ViewState worthwhile are users on a high-speed network, and a slow database connection. Data caching, on the other hand, should be used when the following two conditions hold:

1. Not all users are on a high-speed network. Some users might be accessing the data from a distant location, or could be using low-bandwidth devices, such as modems.

2. The cost of a database access is unacceptably high.

If condition 1 holds, it's clear that caching the DataSet in the ViewState is not an option, because of the bloated page size. If condition 2 holds, it's clear that simply making database accesses every time a user opts to sort the data differently is going to reduce performance. In this situation, caching the DataSet in the data cache would be ideal.

If, however, there is a low cost for a database access, you might find there is only a negligible performance gain (if any) when using data caching. For this unnoticeable performance gain, you will be taxing your Web server's free memory reserves, as well as providing less data cache memory to other ASP.NET pages in your Web application.

Summary

In this chapter, we examined how to sort the data in a DataGrid. We started by employing the simplest sorting techniques, which involves setting the AllowSorting and AutoGenerateColumns properties of the DataGrid to True and providing a SortCommand event handler.

Next, we studied how to sort a DataGrid whose AutoGenerateColumns property is set to False. We also looked at adding more advanced features to our sorting, such as allowing users to sort a DataGrid's column's data both in ascending and descending order.

The chapter concluded with a demonstration on how to cache the DataGrid's DataSource at the page level. By caching the DataSource, we can retrieve the DataGrid's data in one trip to the database. When the user opts to sort the

DataGrid's data on different criteria, the cached `DataSource` can be reordered and bound back to the DataGrid, saving a trip to the database. Although this approach saves database accesses, its disadvantages include stale data and increased page size.

In the next chapter, we will examine how to display the data of a DataGrid in multiple pages. This is a very useful technique when you need to display hundreds or thousands of records, because it allows for the vast number of records to be displayed in smaller chunks, making the data easier to read and comprehend.

On the Web

For more information on the topics discussed in this chapter, consider perusing the following online resources:

- "An Extensive Examination of the DataGrid Web Control: Part 4"— `http://aspnet.4guysfromrolla.com/articles/052202-1.aspx`

- "Effective Sorting in ASP.NET DataGrids"—`http://msdn.microsoft.com/msdnnews/2001/sept/Sorting/Sorting.asp`

- "ASP.NET DataGrid Column Sorting"—`http://www.dotnetjunkies.com/tutorials.aspx?tutorialid=52`

- "Taking a Bite Out of ASP.NET ViewState"—`http://msdn.microsoft.com/library/default.asp?url=/library/en-us/dnaspnet/html/asp11222001.asp`

- "Invalidating an ASP.NET Cache Item from SQL Server"— `http://www.dotnetjunkies.com/tutorials.aspx?tutorialid=385`

8

Providing DataGrid Pagination

The examples we've looked at throughout the past seven chapters have displayed small amounts of data, usually around 25 database records. These examples displayed all of the data at one time. Although such an approach is sensible when dealing with manageable amounts of data, imagine if we displayed 500 database records all on one page. There would simply be too much data for the user to digest.

When presenting large amounts of data, many Web sites break the data up into pages. For example, doing a search for "DataGrid" on Google.com returns an estimated 114,000 results. Of course, I am not shown *all* 114,000 results at once, just 10 at a time. At the bottom of the page is a list of page numbers, allowing me to advance to the next page, or to one of the next 10 pages.

Google, obviously, is not the only Web site that breaks up large amounts of data into readable pages. All search engines do this, whether the search engine searches the entire World Wide Web or only a particular Web site. For example, searching for products by a keyword on Amazon.com will display all matching products 10 at a time.

In Chapter 7, "Sorting the DataGrid's Data," we looked at the DataGrid's built-in properties to aid with sorting. These included the AllowSorting property and the SortCommand event. As we'll see in this chapter, the DataGrid also provides a number of properties and events to assist with paging.

Adding Paging Support to the DataGrid

As we saw in Chapter 7, the first step to add sorting support to the DataGrid is to set the AllowSorting property to True. Not surprisingly, the DataGrid contains a similar property to enable paging: AllowPaging. As with sorting, this property needs to be explicitly set to True to enable the DataGrid's paging features.

Along with the AllowPaging property, there is a PageSize property that specifies how many records to display per page. This property has a default value of 10. By just setting the AllowPaging property to True and (optionally) setting the PageSize property, the DataGrid displays only the first PageSize number of rows from the DataSource. Additionally, beneath the displayed rows is a row that has < and > characters, which are rendered as hyperlinks. The previous page can be reached by clicking the < link, and the next page can be reached by clicking the > link. Figure 8.1 contains a screenshot of a DataGrid with its AllowPaging property set to True and its PageSize property set to 5 (see line 47 in Listing 8.1).

> **NOTE**
>
> As Figure 8.1 shows, when the page is first loaded, the < character is simply a text character, *not* a hyperlink. This is because when the page is first loaded, we are displaying the first page of data. Therefore, there is no way the user can view the previous page.

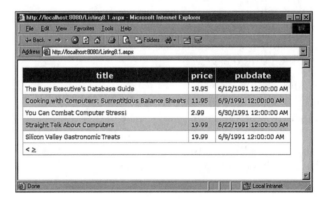

FIGURE 8.1   Setting AllowPaging to True displays only the PageSize records per page.

Listing 8.1 contains the source code used for the ASP.NET Web page shown in Figure 8.1. The code is similar to previous examples we've looked at throughout this book.

LISTING 8.1   The DataGrid's AllowPaging and PageSize Properties Are Set

```
1: <%@ import Namespace="System.Data" %>
2: <%@ import Namespace="System.Data.SqlClient" %>
3: <script runat="server" language="VB">
```

LISTING 8.1   Continued

```
 4:      Sub Page_Load(sender as Object, e as EventArgs)
 5:        If Not Page.IsPostBack then
 6:          BindData()
 7:        End If
 8:      End Sub
 9:
10:
11:      Sub BindData()
12:        '1. Create a connection
13:        Const strConnString as String = "server=localhost;uid=sa;pwd=;
➥database=pubs"
14:        Dim objConn as New SqlConnection(strConnString)
15:
16:        '2. Create a command object for the query
17:        Dim strSQL as String
18:        strSQL = "SELECT title, price, pubdate " & _
19:                 "FROM titles "
20:
21:        Dim objCmd as New SqlCommand(strSQL, objConn)
22:
23:        '3. Create a DataAdapter and Fill the DataSet
24:        Dim objDA as New SqlDataAdapter()
25:        objDA.SelectCommand = objCmd
26:
27:        objConn.Open()
28:
29:        Dim objDS as DataSet = New DataSet()
30:        objDA.Fill(objDS, "titles")
31:
32:        objConn.Close()
33:
34:        'Finally, specify the DataSource and call DataBind()
35:        dgTitles.DataSource = objDS
36:        dgTitles.DataBind()
37:
38:        objConn.Close()    'Close the connection
39:      End Sub
40: </script>
41:
42: <form runat="server">
43:   <asp:DataGrid runat="server" id="dgTitles"
```

LISTING 8.1   Continued

```
44:        Font-Name="Verdana" Font-Size="9pt" CellPadding="5"
45:        AlternatingItemStyle-BackColor="#dddddd"
46:        AutoGenerateColumns="True"
47:        AllowPaging="True"  PageSize="5">
48:
49:     <HeaderStyle BackColor="Navy" ForeColor="White" Font-Size="13pt"
50:             Font-Bold="True" HorizontalAlign="Center" />
51:    </asp:DataGrid>
52: </form>
```

On line 47, you can see that the DataGrid's AllowPaging property has been set to True, and its PageSize property has been set to 5.

One important difference to note between many of our previous examples and Listing 8.1 is that instead of populating our SQL query in a SqlDataReader, we are using a DataSet (lines 29 through 35). The reason we are using a DataSet is because when using the default paging, the DataSource must be set to an object that implements the ICollection interface. The DataSet implements this interface, but the DataReader classes (SqlDataReader, OleDbDataReader, and so on) do not. The default DataGrid paging requires that its DataSource implement ICollection because the DataGrid needs to be able to calculate the total number of records to determine how many total pages there are for the given DataSource. Unfortunately, the only way to determine how many total records are in a DataReader class is to iterate completely through the DataReader's rows, incrementing some counter variable, after which you cannot return to previous records.

> **NOTE**
>
> Although the DataGrid's default paging requires that the DataSource implement the ICollection interface, the DataGrid also offers custom paging. When using custom paging, the DataSource need not implement ICollection. We will examine custom paging later in this chapter.

Allowing the User to Page Through the Data

Unfortunately, getting the DataGrid to page the data is a bit more complicated than simply setting the AllowPaging and PageSize properties. In fact, the DataGrid displayed in Figure 8.1 doesn't perform any sort of paging. If you click the > hyperlink to advance to the next page, nothing happens. That is, the ASP.NET Web page is posted back, but the exact same data is displayed again.

The good news is that only a few lines of code are needed to provide full paging support. Before we examine the code, though, let's take a brief moment to discuss how the DataGrid knows what page of data is currently being displayed, along with what happens when one of the < or > hyperlinks is clicked.

Determining the Number of Pages and the Current Page

The DataGrid has two properties that can be used to determine what page of data is currently being displayed and how many pages of data there are.

The CurrentPageIndex property is an integer value that indicates what page is currently being displayed. This index is zero-based, meaning that when the first page of data is being displayed, CurrentPageIndex equals zero. More generally, when the nth page of data is being displayed, CurrentPageIndex equals $n - 1$.

The PageCount property indicates how many total pages there are; the value of PageCount is equal to the number of records in the DataSource divided by the number of records you are showing per page (the value of the PageSize property). If there is any remainder left over, the PageCount value is incremented to the nearest integer. That is, if the DataSource has nine records and the PageSize property is set to 5, PageCount will equal 2, because 9 divided by 5 is 1.8; because there is a remainder, the answer is incremented to 2. There would be two pages: The first would display records 1, 2, 3, 4, and 5, and the second would display records 6, 7, 8, and 9.

> **NOTE**
>
> In mathematical terms, the PageCount is the ceiling of the number of records in the DataSource divided by PageSize.
>
> Because the CurrentPageIndex property specifies what page of data is being displayed in the DataGrid, CurrentPageIndex should always be between 0 and PageCount − 1.

When one of the paging hyperlinks is clicked, the ASP.NET Web page performs a postback. (Remember that your DataGrid must be placed within a Web form, as in Listing 8.1, line 42.) When the page posts back, the DataGrid's PageIndexChanged event is raised.

Our task will be to provide an event handler and wire it up to the PageIndexChanged event. All that this event handler will have to do is update the DataGrid's CurrentPageIndex property and rebind the DataSource to the DataGrid.

> **CAUTION**
>
> It is vitally important that you remember to rebind the DataGrid in the PageIndexChanged event handler. If you fail to do this, when attempting to navigate to a different page, you will still be shown the first page of data. This happens because when moving to a different page of data, the ASP.NET page is posted back, the PageIndexChanged event fires, and the PageIndexChanged event handler executes. If this event handler does not rebind the DataGrid data, the DataGrid will be rendered using the ViewState, which will redisplay the DataGrid's first page output. Therefore, as you can in line 9 in Listing 8.2, the last line of the PageIndexChanged event handler is a call to the BindData() subroutine.

The `PageIndexChanged` event handler must have the following definition:

```
Sub EventHandler(sender as Object, e as DataGridPageChangedEventHandler)
```

The `DataGridPageChangedEventHandler` class contains a `NewPageIndex` property that specifies what page the user wants to view. If the user clicks the < hyperlink, the value of the `DataGridPageChangedEventHandler`'s parameter `NewPageIndex` property will be the value of the `CurrentPageIndex` property minus 1. If the user clicks the > hyperlink, the value of the `DataGridPageChangedEventHandler`'s parameter `NewPageIndex` property will be the value of the `CurrentPageIndex` property plus 1.

As mentioned previously, all we need to do in the event handler is update the DataGrid's `CurrentPageIndex` property and rebind the `DataSource` to the DataGrid. This simply involves setting the DataGrid's `CurrentPageIndex` to the `NewPageIndex` property of the `DataGridPageChangedEventHandler` parameter and then calling the `BindData()` subroutine. The complete code for the `PageIndexChanged` event handler can be seen here:

```
Sub dgTitles_Paging(sender As Object, e As DataGridPageChangedEventArgs)
    dgTitles.CurrentPageIndex = e.NewPageIndex
    BindData()
End Sub
```

All that remains is to wire up the `dgTitles_Paging` event handler to the DataGrid's `PageIndexChanged` event. This can be done through the DataGrid's declaration. Listing 8.2 illustrates how to accomplish this.

LISTING 8.2   Add an Event Handler for the DataGrid's `PageIndexChanged` Event

```
 1: <%@ import Namespace="System.Data" %>
 2: <%@ import Namespace="System.Data.SqlClient" %>
 3: <script runat="server" language="VB">
 4:   ' ... The Page_Load event handler and BindData() subroutine
 5:   '    have been omitted for brevity.  Refer back to Listing 8.1 ...
 6:
 7:     Sub dgTitles_Paging(sender As Object, e As DataGridPageChangedEventArgs)
 8:         dgTitles.CurrentPageIndex = e.NewPageIndex
 9:         BindData()
10:     End Sub
11: </script>
12:
13: <form runat="server">
14:   <asp:DataGrid runat="server" id="dgTitles"
15:       Font-Name="Verdana" Font-Size="9pt" CellPadding="5"
16:       AlternatingItemStyle-BackColor="#dddddd"
```

LISTING 8.2   Continued

```
17:        AutoGenerateColumns="True"
18:        PageSize="5" AllowPaging="True"
19:        OnPageIndexChanged="dgTitles_Paging">
20:
21:    <HeaderStyle BackColor="Navy" ForeColor="White" Font-Size="13pt"
22:            Font-Bold="True" HorizontalAlign="Center" />
23:  </asp:DataGrid>
24: </form>
```

Listing 8.2 contains the dgTitles_Paging event handler we looked at previously (lines 7 through 10). It also wires up the dgTitles_Paging event handler to the DataGrid's PageIndexChanged event (line 19). As with Listing 8.1, the AllowPaging and PageSize properties are set to True and 5, respectively (line 18).

With this added event handler, the ASP.NET page in Listing 8.2 pages through the data one page at a time as the user clicks the < and > hyperlinks. You can refer back to Listing 8.1 to see a screenshot of the ASP.NET Web page when you first visit it. Figure 8.2 contains a screenshot of the page after the > hyperlink has been clicked once. Note that the records displayed in Figure 8.2 are different than those in Figure 8.1. Specifically, they are records 6–10 from the titles database table.

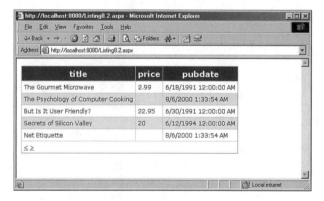

FIGURE 8.2   When the user clicks the > hyperlink, the second page of data is shown.

Providing a More Elegant Paging Interface

The paging interface of Figures 8.1 and 8.2 was a simple pair of < and > hyperlinks at the bottom of the DataGrid. This interface has a set of stylistic properties much like the DataGrid's. For example, the paging interface has properties like BackColor, BorderStyle, Font, ForeColor, HorizontalAlign, Width, and others. The DataGrid's

`PagerStyle` property can be used to set visual properties for the pager interface. Like the `ItemStyle`, `HeaderStyle`, and other "style" properties, the `PagerStyle` property is an instance of a class—specifically the `DataGridPagerStyle` class. The `DataGridPagerStyle` class has a number of properties that can be set, such as `BackColor`, `Font`, and `Width`. As with the DataGrid's other "style" properties, you set the `PagerStyle` instance's properties using the following notation:

```
<asp:DataGrid runat="server" id="MyDataGrid"
      PagerStyle-BackColor="Blue"
      PagerStyle-Font-Name="Verdana"
      ... />
```

Alternatively, you can set `PagerStyle` properties using the following notation:

```
<asp:DataGrid runat="server" id="MyDataGrid"
   ...>
  <PagerStyle BackColor="Blue" Font-Name="Verdana" />
   ...
</asp:DataGrid>
```

Table 8.1 gives a quick rundown of the more useful properties of the `DataGridPagerStyle` class. Not all properties of the `DataGridPagerStyle` class are displayed in Table 8.1—just the more commonly used ones, including the ones we'll be examining in this chapter. For the full list of the `DataGridPagerStyle` class properties, be sure to refer to the technical documentation provided in the "On the Web" section at the end of this chapter.

TABLE 8.1   The `DataGridPagerStyle` Properties

Property	Description
BackColor	Specifies the background color of the pager row.
Font	Specifies the font's name, size, and style options (bolded, italicized, underlined, and so on).
ForeColor	The foreground color of the pager row.
HorizontalAlign	The horizontal alignment of the pager row—can be Left, Right, or Center.
Mode	Specifies whether the pager should be displayed as a Next/Previous set of hyperlinks or a list of links for each page. The default is to display Next/Previous hyperlinks.
NextPageText	The text to display for the Next hyperlink when Mode is set to display Next/Previous hyperlinks. The default is >.
PrevPageText	The text to display for the Next hyperlink when Mode is set to display Next/Previous hyperlinks. The default is <.
PageButtonCount	If Mode is set to display a list of links for each page, specifies how many pages of links to display. Defaults to 10. If this property is set to a value less than the total number of pages, after the last page link, an ellipsis (. . .) is displayed.

TABLE 8.1   Conitnued

Property	Description
Position	Specifies where the paging hyperlinks should appear. Options include Bottom, Top, and TopAndBottom.
Width	The width of the pager row. Can be in pixels or percentages.

Displaying the Paging Interface as Next/Previous Hyperlinks

The < and > hyperlinks we saw in Figure 8.1 and 8.2 can easily be changed to Next and Prev hyperlinks by simply setting the PagerStyle's NextPageText and PrevPageText to "Next" and "Prev", respectively. We can right-align or center-align these hyperlinks by setting the PagerStyle's HorizontalAlign property to Right or Center, respectively. In addition, we can specify the pager's font, background color, and foreground color by setting the Font, BackColor, and ForeColor properties.

Listing 8.3 provides an alternative pager interface from Listing 8.2. It utilizes the exact same server-side Visual Basic .NET code from Listing 8.2; the only changes are in the DataGrid's declaration.

LISTING 8.3   The Pager Interface Is Highly Customizable

```
 1: The server-side code block has been omitted for brevity.
 2: Refer back to Listing 8.2 and 8.1 for its details.
 3:
 4: <form runat="server">
 5:   <asp:DataGrid runat="server" id="dgTitles"
 6:       Font-Name="Verdana" Font-Size="9pt" CellPadding="5"
 7:       AlternatingItemStyle-BackColor="#dddddd"
 8:       AutoGenerateColumns="True"
 9:       PageSize="5" AllowPaging="True"
10:       OnPageIndexChanged="dgTitles_Paging">
11:
12:     <HeaderStyle BackColor="Navy" ForeColor="White" Font-Size="13pt"
13:             Font-Bold="True" HorizontalAlign="Center" />
14:
15:     <PagerStyle BackColor="Navy" ForeColor="White" Font-Size="8pt"
16:             Font-Bold="True" HorizontalAlign="Right"
17:             NextPageText="Next >" PrevPageText="< Prev"
18:             Position="TopAndBottom" />
19:   </asp:DataGrid>
20: </form>
```

The PagerStyle properties in Listing 8.3 are set on lines 15 through 18. The BackColor and ForeColor are set to Navy and White (line 15), to match the colors of the DataGrid's header. The paging hyperlinks are right-aligned (line 16), and the next and previous hyperlinks are denoted by "Next >" and "< Prev" (line 17).

In addition, the Position property is set to TopAndBottom (line 18). The property specifies where the pager interface should appear on the DataGrid. Its default is Bottom, which places the pager interface after the DataGrid's Footer row; if the DataGrid's ShowFooter property is False (the default), the pager interface appears after the last Item row. If the Position property is set to Top, the pager interface is placed before the Header row; if the DataGrid's ShowHeader property is set to False, the pager interface appears after the last Item row. Finally, if the Position property is set to TopAndBottom, as in Listing 8.3, the pager interface is displayed both above and below the DataGrid's Header and Footer rows.

Figure 8.3 illustrates the placement of the pager interface when the Position property is set to TopAndBottom.

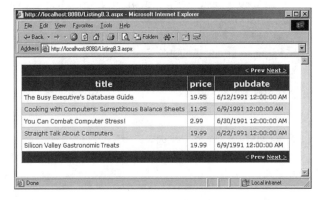

FIGURE 8.3   The pager interface is displayed both above and below the DataGrid Header and Footer rows.

Displaying the Paging Interface as Hyperlinks for Each Page

The Next/Previous hyperlink interface is a good paging interface to use when the user is presented with a relatively small amount of data that he will likely want to step through in sequential order. However, if your DataGrid will contain tens or hundreds of pages, or if you expect your users will want to step through the pages in a random order, you might want to consider using an alternative paging interface.

By setting the PagerStyle's Mode property to NumericPages, the paging interface changes from a Next/Previous hyperlink model to one that contains a number of hyperlinks for the various pages. For example, if you have four pages in your DataGrid and set the Mode property to NumericPages in place of the Next/Previous hyperlinks, the user will see four numbers: 1, 2, 3, and 4. Three of these numbers will be hyperlinks that display the specific page; of the four pages, the one currently being visited is displayed as text, not as a hyperlink.

You might be wondering what will be displayed if the DataGrid has, say, 50 pages. Will there be a hyperlink for each of the 50 pages? To control how many hyperlinks will be displayed, you can set the PagerStyle's PageButtonCount property, which has a default value of 10. If you set the PageButtonCount property to 10 for a DataGrid that has 50 pages, initially only hyperlinks 1 through 10 will be displayed. After the 10 will be a hyperlinked ellipsis (...). If you click on, say, the 5 hyperlink, the fifth page of data will be displayed, along with the 1 to 10 hyperlinks at the bottom. If you click on the ellipsis hyperlink, page 10 will be shown. Additionally, the labels at the bottom will change to list links 10 to 20, with ellipses both before 10 and after 20.

The preceding description of how the PagerStyle's PageButtonCount property works might be a bit confusing. A sample should clear things up. Listing 8.4 contains a DataGrid declaration that sets the PagerStyle's Mode property to NumericPages. Because the data we are displaying is broken up into four pages, the PageButtonCount property has been set to 3 to illustrate the functionality of the NumericPages hyperlink interface.

LISTING 8.4   The NumericPages Mode Displays Three Hyperlinks at the Bottom of Each Page

```
 1: <form runat="server">
 2:   <asp:DataGrid runat="server" id="dgTitles"
 3:       Font-Name="Verdana" Font-Size="9pt" CellPadding="5"
 4:       AlternatingItemStyle-BackColor="#dddddd"
 5:       AutoGenerateColumns="True"
 6:       PageSize="5" AllowPaging="True"
 7:       OnPageIndexChanged="dgTitles_Paging">
 8:
 9:     <HeaderStyle BackColor="Navy" ForeColor="White" Font-Size="13pt"
10:             Font-Bold="True" HorizontalAlign="Center" />
11:
12:     <PagerStyle BackColor="Navy" ForeColor="White" Font-Size="8pt"
13:             Font-Bold="True" HorizontalAlign="Right"
14:             Mode="NumericPages" PageButtonCount="3" />
15:   </asp:DataGrid>
16: </form>
```

The pager interface is set on lines 12 through 14 in Listing 8.4. The important properties to focus on are Mode and PageButtonCount on line 14. The Mode property specifies that we are to use a NumericPages hyperlink interface, while the PageButtonCount indicates that three hyperlinks should be displayed per page.

When the code in Listing 8.4 is visited in a browser for the first time, the DataGrid's first page of data is displayed as shown in Figure 8.4. The pager interface lists the first three pages at the bottom—1, 2, and 3, with 2 and 3 as hyperlinks, and 1 as text (because we're currently on the first page). Additionally, after the 3 hyperlink, an ellipsis hyperlink is displayed.

If the ellipsis hyperlink is clicked, page 4 of the DataGrid's data is displayed. The pager interface lists three pages at the bottom—2, 3, and 4, with 2 and 3 as hyperlinks, and 4 as text (as we're currently on the fourth page). Additionally, before the 2 hyperlink is an ellipsis hyperlink that takes the user back to the first page.

Figure 8.4 illustrates the DataGrid displaying the first page of data, as seen when the page is first visited. Figure 8.5 shows the output if the user clicks the ellipsis hyperlink from Figure 8.4. In Listing 8.4, the fourth page of data is being displayed, and the pager interface contains references to pages 2, 3, and 4, with an ellipsis before the 2 hyperlink.

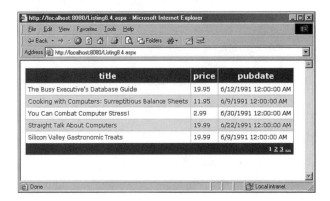

FIGURE 8.4   The first page of data is displayed.

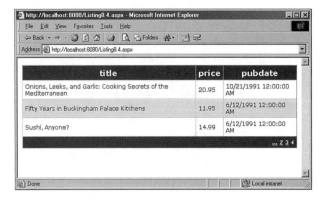

FIGURE 8.5   By clicking on the ellipsis hyperlink, the fourth page of data is displayed.

Paging Through the DataGrid Using Custom Paging

Recall that whenever the user clicks a pager hyperlink, the ASP.NET Web page is posted back and the DataGrid's PageIndexChanged event is fired. When using the DataGrid's default paging mechanism, we need to provide an event handler for this event that performs the following two steps:

1. Update the DataGrid's CurrentPageIndex property.

2. Rebind the DataSource to the DataGrid by calling the BindData() subroutine.

These two steps lead to a rather simple and concise event handler. The problem is that every time the user requests a new page of data, the BindData() subroutine reads the entire contents of the DataSource, even though only a subset of records are being displayed. For example, the entire contents of the titles table will be retrieved each time the user clicks on a paging link.

To understand the implications of this, imagine that your DataSource is comprised of 5,000 records, and you are displaying 15 records per page. When the user first visits the page, all 5,000 records will be retrieved from the database, but only the first 15 will be shown. When the user clicks to visit the next page of data, all 5,000 records will again be retrieved from the database, but only records 16 through 30 will be shown. If the user steps through, say, 10 pages, she will have seen a total of 150 records, but we will have actually retrieved 50,000 records from the database!

Retrieving 5,000 records per page is clearly inefficient if we only want to display 15 records. If there was some way we could only retrieve the 15 needed records, we'd be able to dramatically reduce the total number of records transmitted from the database to the ASP.NET Web page. Fortunately, there is such a way—it's called custom paging.

Remember that the default paging mechanism needs to have the entire contents of the query that's to be paged through each time the DataGrid is rendered so that it can correctly determine how many pages the data can be broken up into. Essentially, it needs to know how many total records we're paging through. As we'll see in the next section, when employing custom paging we will be returning only those records that need to be displayed on the current page of data being viewed; however, we will also need to let the DataGrid know the number of total records in the DataSource that the query being paged through consists of.

Examining Custom Paging

With custom paging, only the records that need to be displayed on a particular page are returned—this is the benefit of custom paging over the DataGrid's default paging. However, as we pointed out at the end of the last section, the DataGrid needs to know how many records are to be paged through. However, because the DataGrid needs to calculate the number of pages based on the number of records, we must explicitly specify this value. We accomplish this by setting the DataGrids' VirtualItemCount property.

To help clarify things a bit, let's consider an example. Imagine that we have a Web page that allows visitors to add their name and a brief comment, similar to a guestbook. To facilitate this, we would create a database table named Comments with the fields CommentID, Name, Comment, and DateAdded, which would be of types integer primary key, varchar(50), varchar(255), and datetime, respectively. In addition to this, we'd need to provide an ASP.NET Web page that would allow users to add entries to the guestbook. (This is left as an exercise to the reader.)

In addition to allowing a user to add a comment to the guestbook, we'd like to allow users to view the contents of the guestbook. If we have a popular Web site, the number of people leaving comments might be quite large, and the Comments database table could quickly grow to hundreds, thousands, or tens of thousands of records. We obviously need to provide pagination through this data, because it would be impractical to present the user with all the potential thousands of guestbook entries on one page.

It would be wise to decide to implement custom paging to reduce the total number of records that must be brought from the database to the ASP.NET Web page as the user pages through the guestbook comments.

In implementing custom paging, we are faced with two challenges:

1. Determining the total number of records we want to page through

2. Querying the database for only those records that we need on a particular page

We need to be able to accomplish the first task to properly set the DataGrid's VirtualItemCount property, so that the paging interface is able to be correctly displayed. Accomplishing the second task is fundamental to the motivation behind custom paging—retrieving only the rows from the database that are needed for displaying the current page.

In the next two subsections, we will look at how to accomplish these two tasks.

Obtaining the Number of Records

The first task can be accomplished by issuing a SQL query that uses the SQL COUNT aggregate function. In general, to obtain the number of total records that need to be paged through, we can use

```
SELECT COUNT(*)
FROM TableName
WHERE OptionalWhereClause
```

In our example, if we want to page through all the records in the Comments table, we would use

```
SELECT COUNT(*)
FROM Comments
```

If, on the other hand, we only want to page through those comments that were left by a visitor named Scott, we could use

```
SELECT COUNT(*)
FROM TableName
WHERE Name = 'Scott'
```

> **NOTE**
>
> If you've not seen the COUNT aggregate function before, you might want to take a moment to read up on it. There are a couple of good online articles referenced in the "On the Web" section at the end of this chapter.

Retrieving Only the Needed Records via a Stored Procedure

The benefit of using custom paging is that we only need to retrieve the records to be displayed on the page of data that the user is currently viewing. But how can we construct a SQL query that retrieves just the needed rows?

Imagine that for each record of the data we want to page through, we add an integer field named IncreasingID to the data, such that the ith row in the data has a value of i. To clarify this concept, let's look at an example. Assume that the data we want to allow the end user to page through is shown in Figure 8.6. Now, imagine that we have some way to augment the data shown in Figure 8.6 to contain the additional field IncreasingID, as shown in Figure 8.7.

	CommentID	Name	Comment	DateAdded
1	1	Scott	Wassup?	2002-10-03 10:09:08.813
2	2	Steve	How does this thing work?	2002-10-03 10:09:18.737
3	3	John	Hey, how's everyone doing?	2002-10-03 10:09:34.620
4	5	Sue	I look forward to learning abou...	2002-10-03 10:09:54.940
5	6	Jisun	Hi everyone, how long have you ...	2002-10-03 10:10:09.430
6	7	Scott	Hi Jisun, I've been using ASP.N...	2002-10-03 10:10:34.497
7	9	John	Hi there, Frank. Hi Jisun, hi ...	2002-10-03 10:10:59.853
8	10	Mike	Wow, there's a lot of people sa...	2002-10-03 10:11:12.400
9	12	Steve	Good one, Julia, but you haven'...	2002-10-03 10:11:34.763
10	13	Julia	Oh yes, sorry about that.	2002-10-03 10:11:40.050
11	14	Steve	Uh... you still haven't said hi...	2002-10-03 10:11:49.803
12	15	Julia	I know!	2002-10-03 10:11:55.663
13	16	Julia	Ok...	2002-10-03 10:11:58.207
14	17	Julia	HELLO EVERYONE!	2002-10-03 10:12:03.403
15	18	Mike	There are some pretty crazy peo...	2002-10-03 10:12:15.380
16	19	Scott	Mike, just ignore Julia, she's ...	2002-10-03 10:12:24.073
17	20	Ned	I think you mean crazy, she's c...	2002-10-03 10:12:31.133

FIGURE 8.6   The data from the Comments table that is to be paged through.

	IncreasingID	CommentID	Name	Comment	DateAdded
1	1	1	Scott	Wassup?	2002-10-03 10:09:08.813
2	2	2	Steve	How does this thing work?	2002-10-03 10:09:18.737
3	3	3	John	Hey, how's everyone doing?	2002-10-03 10:09:34.620
4	4	5	Sue	I look forward to learning abou...	2002-10-03 10:09:54.940
5	5	6	Jisun	Hi everyone, how long have you ...	2002-10-03 10:10:09.430
6	6	7	Scott	Hi Jisun, I've been using ASP.N...	2002-10-03 10:10:34.497
7	7	9	John	Hi there, Frank. Hi Jisun, hi ...	2002-10-03 10:10:59.853
8	8	10	Mike	Wow, there's a lot of people sa...	2002-10-03 10:11:12.400
9	9	12	Steve	Good one, Julia, but you haven'...	2002-10-03 10:11:34.763
10	10	13	Julia	Oh yes, sorry about that.	2002-10-03 10:11:40.050
11	11	14	Steve	Uh... you still haven't said hi...	2002-10-03 10:11:49.803
12	12	15	Julia	I know!	2002-10-03 10:11:55.663
13	13	16	Julia	Ok...	2002-10-03 10:11:58.207
14	14	17	Julia	HELLO EVERYONE!	2002-10-03 10:12:03.403
15	15	18	Mike	There are some pretty crazy peo...	2002-10-03 10:12:15.380
16	16	19	Scott	Mike, just ignore Julia, she's ...	2002-10-03 10:12:24.073
17	17	20	Ned	I think you mean crazy, she's c...	2002-10-03 10:12:31.133

FIGURE 8.7   The augmented data from Figure 8.6, which includes an IncreasingID field.

Note that the CommentID fields in Figure 8.6 have holes in them. That is, there is no record where CommentID equals 4. Perhaps this was an offensive guestbook entry that the site's administrator deleted. Figure 8.6 has two other holes—it's missing records with CommentIDs 8 and 11, as well.

The purpose of the IncreasingID field is to fill these holes. As Figure 8.7 shows, the IncreasingID has no holes, and for any given row i, the value of IncreasingID is i.

When you have such an IncreasingID, you can use custom paging with either the Next/Previous paging interface, or the paging interface that consists of links for each page. In general, to retrieve the records for the kth page of data, where you are displaying i records per page, the following SQL query can be used:

```
SELECT ColumnList
FROM TableName
WHERE IncreasingID > k * i AND IncreasingID <= (k+1) * i
```

For example, let's say that we want to show 10 records per page—here, i would equal 10. When displaying the first page of data, k will equal 0, meaning we can retrieve the proper subset of rows for the first page by using

```
SELECT ColumnList
FROM TableName
WHERE IncreasingID > 0 * 10 AND IncreasingID <= (0+1) * 10
```

This will get the records whose IncreasingID is between 1 and 10, inclusive. To display the third page of data, k will equal 2, and our SQL statement will look like

```
SELECT ColumnList
FROM TableName
WHERE IncreasingID > 2 * 10 AND IncreasingID <= (2+1) * 10
```

This will get the records whose IncreasingID is between 21 and 30, inclusive.

One problem remains: how do we augment our data so that it increases an IncreasingID field? Intuitively, you might reason that your database table's primary key column already exhibits the properties of an IncreasingID field. You might reason that because your database table has an integer primary key that is an auto-increment value starting at 1 and incrementing by 1 for each record, that this primary key field can be used in place of the IncreasingID field in the SQL queries given previously. Such a primary key field can be used as the IncreasingID field, but only if there are no holes in the primary key values, such as the ones shown in Figure 8.6.

Holes can also appear when records are deleted. When confronted with holes, there are two options. The first is to compact the holes, which requires some tricky SQL that is beyond the scope of this book. Furthermore, this process needs to be done whenever a hole is created. The second approach is to use an IncreasingID field, as shown in Figure 8.7.

When we add an IncreasingID field, we are not adding a new field to the database table. Rather, we are constructing a SQL resultset that has the fields of the table along with an additional field. To add an IncreasingID field, you should use a SQL stored procedure to build a temporary table that contains two fields: an auto-incrementing integer field with initial and incremental values of 1 called IncreasingID, and an integer field called OtherID. After the temporary table is created, it should be populated by the SQL query that we want to page through. That is, if we want to construct a SQL resultset that contains an IncreasingID and the records of the Comments database table, we'd populate the temporary table with the primary key values from the Comments table (CommentID) using the following SQL:

```
-- Create the temporary table
CREATE TABLE #CommentTempTable
(
  IncreasingID       int      IDENTITY(1,1),
  OtherID        int
)

-- Now, populate the temporary table
INSERT INTO #CommentTempTable (OtherID)
SELECT CommentID
FROM Comments
ORDER BY CommentID ASC
```

After we have populated the temporary table, all that remains is to return the correct resultset. This is accomplished by doing a SELECT query on the temporary table, returning the temporary table's primary key value as well as the fields of the Comments table. An inner join should be performed, joining the temporary table to the Comments table on the temporary table's second field and the Comment table's primary key field. The final SQL SELECT statement should return only those rows whose corresponding IncreasingID is within the range specified by the page number being displayed (see lines 25 and 26 in Listing 8.5) .

The complete code for such a stored procedure is shown in Listing 8.5.

LISTING 8.5   Adding an IncreasingID Field via a Temporary Table

```
 1: CREATE PROCEDURE sp_PageThroughData
 2: (
 3:     @PageSize    int,
 4:     @CurrentPage    int
 5: )
 6: AS
 7:
 8: CREATE TABLE #CommentTempTable
 9: (
10:    IncreasingID        int     IDENTITY(1,1),
11:    OtherID        int
12: )
13:
14: -- Now, populate the temporary table
15: INSERT INTO #CommentTempTable (OtherID)
16: SELECT CommentID
17: FROM Comments
18: ORDER BY CommentID ASC
19:
20: -- Finally, return the records
21: SELECT IncreasingID, Comments.*
22: FROM #CommentTempTable
23:    INNER JOIN Comments ON
24:      Comments.CommentID = #CommentTempTable.OtherID
25: WHERE IncreasingID > @PageSize * @CurrentPage
26:      AND IncreasingID <= @PageSize * (@CurrentPage+1)
```

The stored procedure in Listing 8.5 takes two input parameters: @PageSize, which specifies how many records the stored procedure should return, and @CurrentPage, which indicates what page of data is currently being requested. These parameters allow the stored procedure to return only those records that we are interested in displaying in our DataGrid. That is, if @PageSize is set to 10, then the stored procedure will return 10 records, perhaps fewer if we want to view the records on the last page.

Although only the needed records are transmitted from the database server to the ASP.NET Web page, the stored procedure itself must take the time to create a temporary table and populate it with the entire contents of the SQL query (see the INSERT statement, lines 15 through 18). This means that if the Comments table contains 5,000 rows, each time the user pages through the DataGrid's data, 5,000 rows are copied into a temporary table. Of course, the stored procedure returns only the needed rows to the ASP.NET Web page.

The differences between the stored procedure option and the DataGrid's default paging are subtle. With the default paging approach, we copy all the rows from the database to the ASP.NET Web page. With the stored procedure approach, all of the records are copied to a temporary table on the database server, and then only those needed rows are copied to the ASP.NET Web page. While both approaches seem to do the same thing, the stored procedure route will likely provide better performance because it's copying less data across application boundaries.

NOTE

We'll take a closer look at the advantages and disadvantages of the stored procedure approach for custom paging later in this chapter.

Now that we've examined this stored procedure, let's create an ASP.NET Web page that allows the user to page through the Comments table. Listing 8.6 contains the code and HTML for an ASP.NET page that uses the stored procedure from Listing 8.5.

LISTING 8.6   Using a Stored Procedure and Custom Paging

```
 1: <%@ import Namespace="System.Data" %>
 2: <%@ import Namespace="System.Data.SqlClient" %>
 3: <script runat="server">
 4:     Sub Page_Load(sender as Object, e as EventArgs)
 5:       If Not Page.IsPostBack then
 6:         dgCommentsdgComments.VirtualItemCount = GetTotalItemsInQuery()
 7:         dgCommentsdgComments.CurrentPageIndex = 0
 8:
 9:         BindData()
10:       End If
11:     End Sub
12:
13:
```

LISTING 8.6   Continued

```
14:     Sub BindData()
15:       'Create a connection to the DB
16:       Const strConnString as String = "server=localhost;uid=sa;pwd=;
➥database=pubs"
17:       Dim objConn as New SqlConnection(strConnString)
18:
19:       Const strSQL as String = "sp_PageThroughData"
20:
21:       Dim objCmd as New SqlCommand(strSQL, objConn)
22:       objCmd.CommandType = CommandType.StoredProcedure
23:
24:       Dim pageSizeParam as New SqlParameter("@PageSize", SqlDbType.Int, 4)
25:       pageSizeParam.Value = dgComments.PageSize
26:       objCmd.Parameters.Add(pageSizeParam)
27:
28:       Dim currentPageParam as New SqlParameter("@CurrentPage",
➥SqlDbType.Int, 4)
29:       currentPageParam.Value = dgComments.CurrentPageIndex
30:       objCmd.Parameters.Add(currentPageParam)
31:
32:       objConn.Open()    'Open the connection
33:
34:       'Finally, specify the DataSource and call DataBind()
35:       dgComments.DataSource = objCmd.ExecuteReader(CommandBehavior.
➥CloseConnection)
36:       dgComments.DataBind()
37:
38:       objConn.Close()    'Close the connection
39:     End Sub
40:
41:
42:     Sub dgComments_Paging(sender As Object, e As DataGridPageChangedEventArgs)
43:       dgComments.CurrentPageIndex = e.NewPageIndex
44:       BindData()
45:     End Sub
46:
47:
48:     Function GetTotalItemsInQuery()
49:       '1. Create a connection
50:       Const strConnString as String = "server=localhost;uid=sa;pwd=;
➥database=pubs"
```

LISTING 8.6   Continued

```
51:        Dim objConn as New SqlConnection(strConnString)
52:
53:        '2. Create a command object for the query
54:        Dim strSQL as String
55:        strSQL = "SELECT COUNT(*) FROM Comments"
56:
57:        Dim objCmd as New SqlCommand(strSQL, objConn)
58:
59:        objConn.Open()    'Open the connection
60:
61:        ' Get the number of records
62:        Dim recCount as Integer
63:        recCount = objCmd.ExecuteScalar()
64:
65:        objConn.Close()
66:
67:        Return recCount
68:     End Function
69: </script>
70:
71: <form runat="server">
72:    <asp:DataGrid runat="server" id="dgComments"
73:        Font-Name="Verdana" Font-Size="9pt" CellPadding="5"
74:        AlternatingItemStyle-BackColor="#dddddd"
75:        AutoGenerateColumns="True" Width="75%"
76:        PageSize="10" AllowPaging="True"
77:        OnPageIndexChanged="dgComments_Paging"
78:        AllowCustomPaging="True">
79:
80:      <HeaderStyle BackColor="Navy" ForeColor="White" Font-Size="13pt"
81:              Font-Bold="True" HorizontalAlign="Center" />
82:
83:      <PagerStyle BackColor="Navy" ForeColor="White" Font-Size="8pt"
84:              Font-Bold="True" HorizontalAlign="Right"
85:              Mode="NumericPages" />
86:    </asp:DataGrid>
87: </form>
```

Recall that with custom paging, we need to set the DataGrid's `VirtualItemCount`
property to the number of records we plan on paging through. We do this on line 5

in the page's Page_Load event handler when the page is first visited (when Page.IsPostBack is False). Note that the DataGrid's VirtualItemCount property is set to the return value of a function, GetTotalItemsInQuery(). This function, which can be found spanning lines 48 to 68, performs a SQL COUNT query (line 55) to calculate this number of total records that will be paged through.

After the VirtualItemCount property is set in the Page_Load event handler, the BindData() subroutine is called. BindData() has the same semantics in this ASP.NET Web page as it has always had: to bind the appropriate data to the DataGrid. To retrieve the appropriate data, the sp_PageThroughData store procedure, which was presented in Listing 8.5, needs to be called. In calling this stored procedure, we must specify two input parameters: @PageSize and @CurrentPage. The values we need to pass in for these two parameters are simply the values of the DataGrid's PageSize and CurrentPageIndex properties. On lines 24 through 30, we create the needed SqlParameter instances, set the parameters to the proper values, and add them to the SqlCommand object objCmd. The BindData() subroutine finishes by opening the database connection (line 32), setting the DataGrid's DataSource to the SqlDataReader returned by the ExecuteReader(CommandBehavior.CloseConnection) method (line 35), calling the DataGrid's DataBind() method (line 36), and closing the connection (line 28) .

NOTE

Note that the BindData() subroutine uses a DataReader object. Because we are using custom paging, we are not required to use a DataSet, as we were with the DataGrid's default paging.

---

dgComments_Paging, the event handler for the DataGrid's PageIndexChanged event (lines 42–45) is identical to the version of dgComments_Paging in previous examples in this chapter. It simply updates the DataGrid's CurrentPageIndex property and calls the BindData() method. Figure 8.8 is a screenshot of the code in Listing 8.6 in action.

To summarize, to select only those records for a particular page of data, we add an IncreasingID field to the data that we want to page through. This can be accomplished via a stored procedure that creates a temporary table with an auto-increment field and an integer field. This table is then populated with the primary key field of the records that are to be paged through. After this temporary table has been populated, a SQL SELECT clause can be used to extract the correct set of primary key values from the table, which, via a join, can be paired with the other fields of the table that is being paged through.

The stored procedure approach provides better performance than the default paging approach, which must copy all the rows to be paged through from the database server to the ASP.NET Web page. Yet, creating a temporary table and populating it with *all* the rows from the table each time the user requests to view a different page of data seems a bit inefficient. Although there is a bit of a performance hit with inserting all the rows of the desired table into a temporary table, it is not severe for smaller tables.

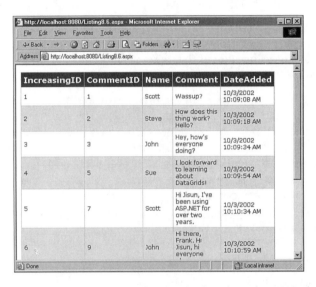

FIGURE 8.8   Only the records that need to be displayed on the particular page of data are returned from the stored procedure.

For example, on the Web site I run, 4GuysFromRolla.com, there is an `Articles` database table that has a row for each article written on 4Guys. When a user wants to search 4GuysFromRolla.com, this `Articles` table is searched, and the results are sent back to the Web page using the stored procedure approach we just discussed. The performance of this stored procedure approach is nothing to scoff at, running through the query analyzer in less than one second. Keep in mind, though, that the `Articles` table is by no means a large table—it is comprised of about 1,500 rows.

For large tables that might contain hundreds of thousands or millions of rows, copying over all the records from the table that you want to page through to the temporary table might incur an overhead of several seconds, or even minutes! For example, using the stored procedure on my personal computer for a table with 250,000 records took five seconds to complete. Clearly, the stored procedure isn't viable for larger tables.

Fortunately, there is another option that involves paging through the data using the data's primary key values. We'll examine this option in detail in the next section.

Retrieving Only the Needed Records Using Primary Key Values

In the previous section, we saw that if we had an `IncreasingID` field we could display any particular page of data by using a simple formula: to view the *k*th page of data, where each page of data displays *i* records, we choose `IncreasingIDs` between *k* * *i* + 1 and (*k*+1) * *i*, inclusive.

If we have a database table that has an integer with an auto-increment primary key value, we can apply this formula only if it is guaranteed that there are no "holes" in the auto-increment values. Recall that a hole can occur by having one or more records deleted.

There is, however, a way to page through the data using auto-incremented primary key information regardless of the presence of holes. The secret is to save the first and last auto-incremented primary key values each time a page is displayed. That is, if we are viewing a page of data that displays 10 records, starting with record 17 and ending with record 28 (signifying that two records between 17 and 28 must have been deleted at sometime), we save the values 17 and 28 in the `ViewState`. If the user opts to view the previous page, we get only the first 10 records whose primary key is less than 17; if the user opts to view the next page, we get only the first 10 records whose primary key is greater than 28.

> **TIP**
>
> To get the first *n* records from a SQL query, we can use the SQL keyword `TOP`. This can be used in a SQL SELECT query like so:
>
> ```
> SELECT TOP N ColumnList
> FROM TableName
> ```
>
> For more information on `TOP`, please refer to the article "Limit Your Resultset with TOP or SET ROWCOUNT" in the "On the Web" section at the end of this chapter.

A quick example is in order. Imagine that we want to page through our `Comments` table, part of which was shown in Figure 8.6. The data shown in Figure 8.6 contained holes in the auto-incremented primary key field, `CommentID`. Specifically, there is no record where `CommentID` equals 4, 8, or 11. Now, imagine that we want to page through the comments five at a time. Recall that we keep two variables in the ASP.NET Web page's `ViewState`—the first and last primary key values that have been displayed. On the first visit to the page, these values are defaulted to 0. Hence, our initial SQL query for the first page will look like this:

```
SELECT TOP 5 CommentID, Name, Comment, DateAdded
FROM Comments
WHERE CommentID > 0
ORDER BY CommentID ASC
```

Note that we use a TOP 5 because we're interested in displaying five records per page. This query will return the first five records from the Comments table whose CommentID is greater than 0 (1, 2, 3, 5, and 6). At this point, we need to store the first and last primary key values in the ViewState; that is, we'll store 1 in a ViewState variable named LowID, and we'll store 6 in a ViewState variable named HighID.

When the user opts to view the next page of data, our SQL query will become

```
SELECT TOP 5 CommentID, Name, Comment, DateAdded
FROM Comments
WHERE CommentID > 6
ORDER BY CommentID ASC
```

We know to retrieve records from the Comments table whose CommentID is greater than 6, because that was the CommentID of the last record in the previous page. The preceding SQL query will return five records namely(7, 9, 10, 12, and 13). The LowID ViewState variable would be assigned the value 7, whereas the HighID ViewState variable would be assigned the value 13.

If the user opts to view the previous page at this point, the SQL query used to grab the particular records will be as follows:

```
SELECT TOP 5 CommentID, Name, Comment, DateAdded
FROM Comments
WHERE CommentID < 7
ORDER BY CommentID DESC
```

This will return the five rows from the Comments table that need to be displayed.

It is important to note that the SQL query's ORDER BY clause is slightly different, depending on whether we're retrieving the records for the next or previous page. When obtaining records for the next page, the ORDER BY clause sorts the results by CommentID in ascending order; when obtaining records for the previous page, the ORDER BY clause sorts the results by CommentID in descending order. The reason these ORDER BY clauses must be included is because if they are not, there is no guarantee that we'll get the five records we want. For example, imagine that we have a SQL query to retrieve the records for the previous page that do not include an ORDER BY clause, and look like

```
SELECT TOP 5 CommentID, Name, Comment, DateAdded
FROM Comments
WHERE CommentID < 100
```

Without the ORDER BY clause, we could theoretically get back any five records less than 100, such as records 1, 2, 3, 5, and 6. By using the ORDER BY clause, we are guaranteed to get the records 99, 98, 97, 96, and 95.

Listing 8.7 contains the code to implement this form of custom paging. Note that
the GetTotalItemsInQuery() function has been omitted from Listing 8.7 for brevity;
it is identical to the GetTotalItemsInQuery() function presented in Listing 8.6, lines
48 through 68.

LISTING 8.7   Paging Through Data Using the Primary Key Method

```
 1: <%@ import Namespace="System.Data" %>
 2: <%@ import Namespace="System.Data.SqlClient" %>
 3: <script runat="server" language="VB">
 4:   '... The GetTotalItemsInQuery() function has been omitted for brevity.
 5:   ' ... Refer back to Listing 8.6 for details on this function ...
 6:
 7:     Sub Page_Load(sender as Object, e as EventArgs)
 8:       If Not Page.IsPostBack then
 9:         dgComments.VirtualItemCount = GetTotalItemsInQuery()
10:         ViewState("LowID") = 0
11:
12:         Const strConnString as String = "server=localhost;uid=sa;pwd=;
➥database=pubs"
13:         Dim objConn as New SqlConnection(strConnString)
14:         Dim strSQL as String
15:
16:         strSQL = "SELECT TOP " & dgComments.PageSize & " CommentID,
➥Name, " & _
17:                 "Comment, DateAdded " & _
18:                 "FROM Comments " & _
19:                 "WHERE CommentID > 0 " & _
20:                 "ORDER BY CommentID ASC"
21:
22:         'Get the results
23:         Dim objCmd as New SqlCommand(strSQL, objConn)
24:
25:         objConn.Open()
26:         BindData(objCmd)
27:         objConn.Close()
28:       End If
29:     End Sub
30:
31:
32:     Sub BindData(objCmd as SqlCommand)
33:       'Create a DataAdapter and Fill the DataSet
34:       Dim objDA as New SqlDataAdapter()
```

LISTING 8.7   Continued

```
35:        objDA.SelectCommand = objCmd
36:
37:        Dim objDS as DataSet = New DataSet()
38:        objDA.Fill(objDS, "titles")
39:
40:        'Get a DataView from the DataSet's "titles" DataTable
41:        Dim myDataView as DataView = New DataView(objDS.Tables("titles"))
42:
43:        'Sort the DataView on the commentID
44:        myDataView.Sort = "CommentID ASC"
45:
46:        'Bind the dataView to the DataGrid
47:        dgComments.DataSource = myDataView
48:        dgComments.DataBind()
49:
50:        'Now, get the high and low IDs
51:        ViewState("LowID") = myDataView(0)("CommentID")
52:        ViewState("HighID") = myDataView(myDataView.Count-1)("CommentID")
53:    End Sub
54:
55:
56:    Sub dgComments_Paging(sender As Object,
➥e As DataGridPageChangedEventArgs)
57:        'See if the user is visiting the next page or previous page
58:        'Create a connection
59:        Const strConnString as String = "server=localhost;uid=sa;pwd=;
➥database=pubs"
60:        Dim objConn as New SqlConnection(strConnString)
61:        Dim strSQL as String
62:        Dim objCmd as New SqlCommand()
63:        Dim IDParam as New SqlParameter("@IDParam", SqlDbType.Int, 4)
64:
65:        If dgComments.CurrentPageIndex = e.NewPageIndex - 1 then
66:          'The user wants to see the next page
67:          strSQL = "SELECT TOP " & dgComments.PageSize & " CommentID,
➥Name, " & _
68:                "Comment, DateAdded " & _
69:                "FROM Comments " & _
70:                "WHERE CommentID > @IDParam " & _
71:                "ORDER BY CommentID ASC"
72:
```

LISTING 8.7   Continued

```
73:              IDParam.Value = ViewState("HighID")
74:          Else
75:              'The user wants to see the previous page
76:              strSQL = "SELECT TOP " & dgComments.PageSize & " CommentID,
➥Name, " & _
77:                  "Comment, DateAdded " & _
78:                  "FROM Comments " & _
79:                  "WHERE CommentID < @IDParam " & _
80:                  "ORDER BY CommentID DESC"
81:
82:              IDParam.Value = ViewState("LowID")
83:          End If
84:
85:          'Set the CurrentPageIndex property
86:          dgComments.CurrentPageIndex = e.NewPageIndex
87:
88:          'Get the results
89:          objCmd.Parameters.Add(IDParam)
90:
91:          objCmd.CommandText = strSQL
92:          objCmd.Connection = objConn
93:
94:          objConn.Open()
95:          BindData(objCmd)
96:          objConn.Close()
97:      End Sub
98: </script>
99:
100: <form runat="server">
101:    <asp:DataGrid runat="server" id="dgComments"
102:        Font-Name="Verdana" Font-Size="9pt" CellPadding="5"
103:        AlternatingItemStyle-BackColor="#dddddd"
104:        AutoGenerateColumns="True" Width="75%"
105:        PageSize="10" AllowPaging="True"
106:        OnPageIndexChanged="dgComments_Paging"
107:        AllowCustomPaging="True">
108:
109:    <HeaderStyle BackColor="Navy" ForeColor="White" Font-Size="13pt"
110:              Font-Bold="True" HorizontalAlign="Center" />
111:
112:    <PagerStyle BackColor="Navy" ForeColor="White" Font-Size="8pt"
```

LISTING 8.7 Continued

```
113:                Font-Bold="True" HorizontalAlign="Right"
114:                Mode="NextPrev" NextPageText="Next >" PrevPageText="< Prev" />
115:    </asp:DataGrid>
116: </form>
```

The code in Listing 8.7 is quite lengthy, especially when compared to the custom paging code that utilized the stored procedure (see Listing 8.6). Let's turn our attention first to the Page_Load event handler (lines 7–29), which only executes instructions on the page's first load, when Page.IsPostBack is False (line 8). On line 9, the DataGrid's VirtualItemCount is set to the value returned by the GetTotalItemsInQuery() function.

NOTE

This GetTotalItemsInQuery() function has been omitted from Listing 8.7 for brevity, but was presented in Listing 8.6. Essentially, it returned the number total records in the data to be paged through by using the following SQL query:

```
SELECT COUNT(*) FROM Comments
```

On line 10, we set the ViewState variable LowID to its initial value of 0. Next, on lines 12 through 23 a connection to the database is established, and a SqlCommand object created using the SQL query spelled out on lines 16–20. The SQL query uses the TOP keyword to grab the first dgComments.PageSize number of records from the Comments table, where the CommentID is greater than 0. It then orders the results by the DateAdded field. After we have this SqlCommand object and have opened the database connection, we call BindData(objCmd), passing in the SqlCommand object (line 26).

The BindData(objCmd) subroutine in Listing 8.7 can be found spanning lines 32 to line 53. The BindData(objCmd) subroutine starts by filling a DataSet using the passed in SqlCommand object. On line 34 the SqlDataAdapter object is created, and on line 35, its SelectCommand property is set to the passed-in SqlCommand object objCmd. A DataSet, objDS, is created on line 37, and is filled on line 38.

Next, we need to create a DataView object from the DataSet (line 41). The DataView class has a Sort property that allows us to sort the contents contained in the DataView; on line 44, we sort the results on the CommentID field in ascending order. The reason we need to use a DataView is because we need to sort the results by the CommentID in ascending order when the user opts to view the previous page of data the results are sorted in descending order. For example, if the user is viewing a page of data whose first record has CommentID 100, and then the user opts to view the previous page of data, the following SQL query will be issued:

```
SELECT TOP 5 CommentID, Name, Comment, DateAdded
FROM Comments
WHERE CommentID < 100
ORDER BY CommentID DESC
```

This will retrieve records 99, 98, 97, 96, and 95, in that order. However, we want to show them in ascending order (95, 96, 97, 98, and 99). To accommodate this, we use a DataView and sort its results on the CommentID field in ascending order.

The BindData(*objCmd*) subroutine next binds the sorted DataView to the DataGrid (lines 47 and 48). It completes by setting the values of the LowID and HighID ViewState variables. On line 51, ViewState("LowID") is set to the CommentID field of the first record in the DataView. Similarly, on line 52 ViewState("HighID") is set to the CommentID field of the last record in the DataView. These primary key values written to the ViewState are used in SQL queries issued by the dgComments_Paging event handler. Recall that the dgComments_Paging event handler is the event handler for the DataGrid's PageIndexChanged event, which fires every time the user clicks either the Next or Previous hyperlink.

The dgComments_Paging event handler, which can be found starting on line 56, is responsible for forming the correct SQL query based on whether the user wants to view the next or previous page. On lines 59 through 63, the needed SqlConnection, SqlCommand, and SqlParameter classes are created. On line 65, we check to see whether the user has opted to view the next page by checking whether the current page is one less than the page the user is requesting to view. Lines 66 through 73 build up the proper SQL for viewing the next page. The SQL query used includes a parameter, @IDParam, which is set to ViewState("HighID") on line 73. If, on the other hand, the user has opted to view the previous page, the code from lines 75 through 82 is executed. An appropriate SQL query is constructed (lines 76 through 80), and the @IDParam parameter is set to the value of ViewState("LowID") on line 82.

After the dgComments_Paging event handler has formed the correct SQL statement, we can update the DataGrid's CurrentPageIndex to the NewPageIndex (line 86), add the IDParam SqlParameter to the SqlCommand objCmd (line 89), and set objCmd's CommandText and Connection properties (lines 91 and 92). At this point, all that we need to do is open the connection (line 94) and call the BindData(*objCmd*) subroutine, passing in the objCmd SqlCommand object (line 95). In calling BindData(*objCmd*), the DataGrid will be bound to the records for the requested page and the LowID and HighID ViewState variables will be updated.

Lines 100 through 116 contain the DataGrid declaration, which is enclosed in a Web form. This declaration is nearly identical to the one in Listing 8.6. The important difference is that this DataGrid uses the Next/Previous paging interface, as opposed to a list of hyperlinks of pages. Although the stored procedure approach to custom paging can support either the Next/Previous interface or the hyperlinked list of pages, when using the primary key method, you *must* use the Next/Previous interface. This is because with the primary key method, there might be holes in the primary key value, which means there isn't a simple function we can use to precisely grab the records for any given page. Rather, we have to know the last primary key value of the current page to get the next page of data, or the first primary key value of the current page to get the previous page of data.

Figure 8.9 contains a screenshot of Listing 8.7 in action. Note that the DataGrid includes the CommentID field of each comment, and that there are some holes in the CommentIDs. Regardless, precisely 10 records are shown per page.

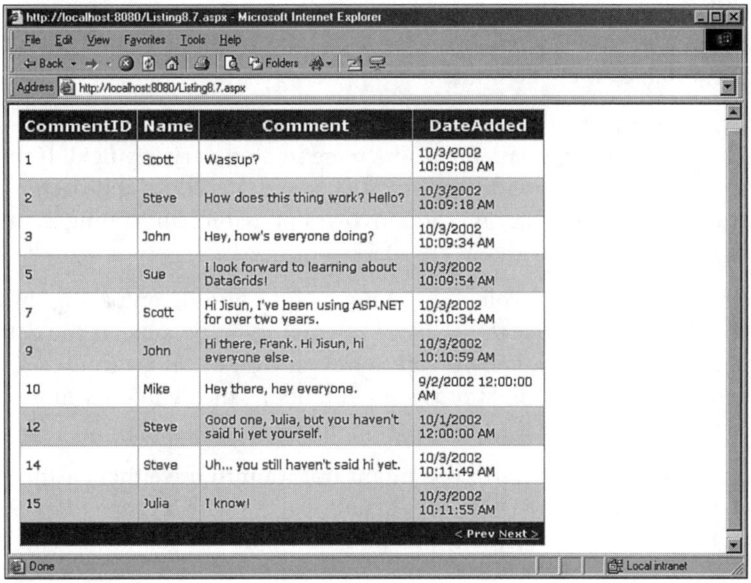

FIGURE 8.9   Custom paging can be efficiently accomplished by using the primary key method.

The Stored Procedure Method Versus the Primary Key Method—Which Is Better?

In the last two sections, we examined two methods for employing custom paging: using a stored procedure to add an IncreasingID field to the data to be paged through; and storing the auto-incremented primary key value for each page being displayed in order to correctly determine the subset of records to retrieve when the user opts to view the next or previous page. Both of these approaches have their advantages and disadvantages, which we'll examine here.

The stored procedure option allows for the most flexibility in the paging interface. With the stored procedure approach, either the Next/Previous or the hyperlinked list of pages interfaces can be used. With the primary key method, however, only the Next/Previous paging interface is an option. Additionally, the stored procedure method moves most of the complexity involved in selecting the correct subset of the records to be displayed to the database. This leads to a shorter, cleaner, and more readable ASP.NET Web page.

The big disadvantage of the stored procedure method is that each time the user requests to see a new page of data, *all* the records from the underlying database table must be copied into a temporary table. As mentioned before, this operation can take several seconds or even minutes on sufficiently large tables. For example, using the stored procedure method on a table with 250,000 rows on my personal computer required five seconds, a painfully long time to have to wait for a Web page to start loading. The TOP *N* SQL query, however, took a fraction of a second to run on the 250,000 row table on my computer.

Despite the performance advantages of the primary key method, it requires that the data to be paged through has an auto-incremented primary key field. If this is not the case, you will have to resort to using the stored procedure approach. Furthermore, the primary key method involves more difficult coding than the stored procedure counterpart.

So which approach should you choose? If you are planning on paging through a large table, by all means use the primary key method if possible. If the data to page through is small, however, and you are certain it won't start growing in size, there's no reason not to use the stored procedure method, which will offer more manageable code and more features in the paging interface.

If performance is a key concern, you might not want to use either custom paging method, but rather use the DataGrid's default paging with a cached DataSet. We'll examine how to do this in the next section.

Paging Through a Cached DataSet

As we saw earlier in this chapter, one of the downsides with the default paging functionality provided by the DataGrid is that each time a user views a different page of data, the BindData() subroutine must be called, which retrieves *all* the records from the database. One possible remedy of this problem is to use custom paging. Recall that custom paging can be employed to greatly reduce the amount of records being passed from the database server to the ASP.NET Web page each time the user views a different page of data.

Although custom paging can provide a substantial reduction in the amount of data being passed back and forth from the database to the ASP.NET Web page, it still has its shortcomings. Imagine that our DataSource has 40 records; displaying it in a DataGrid whose PageSize is set to 10 will result in a DataGrid with four pages. Assume that the user opts to view page 1, then page 2, and then page 1 again. With default paging, each time the user moves from viewing one page of DataGrid data to the next, 40 rows must be transmitted from the database to the ASP.NET Web page; in viewing three pages of data, 120 records must be transmitted. With custom paging, each time a user views a page, only 10 records are transmitted between the database and ASP.NET Web page. In viewing three pages, even when two of the pages viewed are the same page, a total of 30 records will be transmitted.

There are certain scenarios in which we might not need to go back to the database at all, instead using the data cache to store a DataSet populated with the database data. A specific scenario in which this would be advantageous involves displaying data that doesn't change often and is shown the same to all users. For example, imagine that an e-commerce site wants to have a page that displays the 100 top-selling items for the past week.

To allow a user to page through a cached DataSet, we can simply employ the default paging approach. The only change would be that in the `BindData()` subroutine, we'd bind the DataGrid to the DataSet retrieved from the cache; if the DataSet is not in the cache (either because it has been evicted, or has yet to be placed in the cache), we would need to populate the DataSet from the database and then insert it into the cache.

In the section "Caching the DataGrid's `DataSource`" from Chapter 7, we discussed how to cache a DataSet in the data cache. This same technique can be used to allow a user to page through a cached DataSet.

NOTE

For more information on this technique, be sure to read the article ".NET Data Caching" listed in the "On the Web" section at the end of this chapter. This article discusses the .NET data cache in detail, and includes an example that illustrates how to page through a cached DataSet.

Summary

In this chapter, we examined how to provide pagination support for the DataGrid Web control. The DataGrid Web control provides a default paging mechanism that can be employed by following two steps:

1. Set the DataGrid's `AllowPaging` property to `True`.

2. Create an event handler for the DataGrid's `PageIndexChanged` event. This event handler should update the DataGrid's `CurrentPageIndex` property and rebind the data to the DataGrid.

The default paging mechanism only works with `DataSources` that implement the `ICollection` interface, such as the DataSet or any class from the `System.Collections` namespace, which include `ArrayLists`, `Hashtables`, and so on. The DataReader classes, such as `SqlDataReader` and `OleDbDataReader`, do not implement the `ICollection` interface, and therefore cannot be used as `DataSoruces` for the DataGrid's default paging. In addition to requiring that its `DataSource` implement `ICollection`, the entire data to be paged through must be retrieved each time the user steps through the pages of the DataGrid.

With custom paging, however, the `DataSource` need only contain those records that will be displayed on the current page of data the user is viewing. This can greatly reduce the number of records that must be transmitted from the database server to the ASP.NET Web page as the user steps through the pages of data. The prime challenge with custom paging is constructing the needed SQL queries to extract the right subset of data from the database for the particular page of data being rendered. This approach can be done with a stored procedure that builds up a temporary table, or with more complex code in your ASP.NET Web page, assuming that the database table being paged through has either a primary key field or an auto-increment field with no holes.

In the next chapter, we'll look at how to allow the user to interactively edit the contents of the DataGrid. In Chapter 10, "Putting it All Together: A Real-World Example," we'll take the lessons we've learned to create a powerful user interface that allows users to add, edit, delete, sort, and page through the contents of a DataGrid!

On the Web

For more information on the topics discussed in this chapter, consider perusing the following online resources:

- "The `DataGridPagerStyle` Class's Technical Documentation"—
  http://msdn.microsoft.com/library/default.asp?url=/library/en-us/
  cpref/html/frlrfsystemwebuiwebcontrolsdatagridpagerstyleclasstopic.asp

- ".NET Data Caching"—http://aspnet.4guysfromrolla.com/articles/
  100902-1.aspx

- "The `COUNT` Aggregate Function"—http://msdn.microsoft.com/library/
  default.asp?url=/library/en-us/tsqlref/ts_ca-co_5790.asp

- "Using Aggregate SQL Functions"—http://www.aspalliance.com/aspxtreme/
  ado/structuredquerylanguagebasics.aspx?pageno=8

- "The DataGrid's `AllowCustomPaging` Attribute"—http://www.aspalliance.com/
  aspxtreme/sys/Web/UI/WebControls/DataGridClassAllowCustomPaging.aspx

- "Paging Through the Records of a Stored Procedure"—http://www.4guysfrom-
  rolla.com/webtech/062899-1.shtml

- "Limit Your Resultset with TOP or SET ROWCOUNT"—
  http://www.inquiry.com/techtips/thesqlpro/10min/10min0600.asp

9

Editing the DataGrid Web Control

The visitors to a Web site can typically be partitioned into two groups: the users of the Web site, and the administrators of the Web site. When talking about data-driven Web sites, typically the users are only allowed to view data, while administrators are allowed to edit, add, and remove data. For example, consider any popular e-commerce Web site. The users (shoppers) cannot add items to the Web site's database or adjust the prices or items; only administrators can perform these tasks. The users are limited to viewing the data and using it in predefined ways (such as adding a product to a shopping cart). In the past two chapters, we examined ways to enhance users' viewing of the data by providing sorting and pagination support.

How do administrators interact with the data to make edits, remove existing items, or add new ones? One way is to require them to log into the database server and issue the proper SQL INSERT, UPDATE, and DELETE SQL statements. However, such a requirement would allow only SQL-savvy individuals to be administrators, and would reduce the efficiency of data administration. In this chapter, we'll look at how to provide an enhanced editing user interface for administrators by providing mechanisms allowing the DataGrid's data to be edited. (We'll look at enhancing the user interface for adding and deleting records in Chapter 10, "Putting it All Together: A Real-World Example.")

The DataGrid's Editing Interface

Editing the DataGrid can be an incredibly easy feature to add for certain data, but can be quite intricate for other types of data. For example, adding editing support is a breeze if the DataGrid is being used to display data that has no foreign keys, and whose data can easily be edited through the use of a standard TextBox Web control. However, if the DataGrid has foreign key constraints or data that cannot easily be edited in the form of a TextBox, including editing support, while possible, is more of a challenge. Because of the difference in the degree of difficulty depending on the DataGrid's data, this chapter will be arranged such that the simpler cases are examined first, working up to more complex scenarios.

Before we dive into providing editing capabilities for various types of data, let's first take a look at the editing interface provided by the DataGrid. To use the DataGrid's default editing interface, we add an EditCommandColumn column to our DataGrid. This column displays an Edit button for each row in the DataGrid. This enables a user to edit one row of the DataGrid at a time. To edit a particular row, the user must click the Edit button for the row he wants to edit.

> **NOTE**
>
> The Edit button can be created as a typical HTML button, or as a hyperlink. A hyperlinked image can be used as well. We will examine how to choose how the Edit button is rendered in this chapter.

When a particular row's Edit button is clicked, the ASP.NET Web page is posted back, and the DataGrid's EditCommand event is fired. It is our responsibility to provide an event handler for this event. This event handler needs to indicate which row is the row that is to be edited by setting the DataGrid's EditItemIndex property to the index of the row whose Edit button was clicked. The following code snippet, which is taken from the EditCommand event handler from Listing 9.1 (lines 31 to 34), illustrates how the DataGrid's EditItemIndex property can be set to the row whose Edit button was clicked.

```
Sub dgComments_EditRow(sender As Object, e As DataGridCommandEventArgs)
    dgComments.EditItemIndex = e.Item.ItemIndex
    ...
```

When the DataGrid is rendered, the row index that corresponds to the value of the EditItemIndex property in each column of the row is rendered in its edit mode. The default edit mode for a column is a TextBox Web control. Additionally, when a row is rendered in edit mode, the Edit button is replaced with two new buttons: Update and Cancel. The user can then make changes to the data in the column; when she's done, she can click the Update button to save the data to the database, or Cancel to cancel the editing. Clicking either of these buttons causes a postback, and either the DataGrid's UpdateCommand or CancelCommand event is fired, depending on what button was clicked. The event handlers for the UpdateCommand event must update the database with the new values. Both event handlers should conclude by resetting the DataGrid's `EditItemIndex` property back to –1, which will render every row in the DataGrid in its usual non-edit mode.

NOTE

Recall from Chapter 4, "Adding Buttons and HyperLinks to the DataGrid Web Control," that when *any* button in a DataGrid is clicked, the DataGrid's `ItemCommand` event is fired. This means that when the Edit, Update, or Cancel button is clicked, the `ItemCommand` event is fired along with the `EditCommand`, `UpdateCommand`, or `CancelCommand` event.

Let's take a moment to examine a couple of screenshots of the DataGrid's editing features in action. Figure 9.1 contains a view of an editable DataGrid as displayed when the page is first visited, or whenever the DataGrid's `EditItemIndex` property is set to –1 (the default).

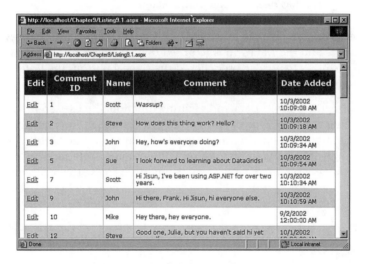

FIGURE 9.1   An editable DataGrid with each row displaying an Edit hyperlink.

When the user clicks the Edit button for a particular row, that row becomes the row being edited. Each column of the row is rendered in its edit mode, and the Edit button is replaced by a pair of Update and Cancel buttons. Figure 9.2 shows the DataGrid after a row has been selected to be edited. Note that it is possible not to have all the columns of the edited row enter their edit mode. Columns that refrain from entering an edit mode are read-only; we'll examine how to specify a column as read-only in the next section.

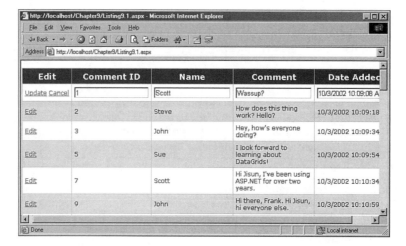

FIGURE 9.2   A row has been selected to be edited.

After a user makes his changes and clicks the Update button, the changes are saved to the database and the DataGrid is returned to its previous form as shown in Figure 9.1. If, on the other hand, the user clicked the Cancel button, the DataGrid is returned to its previous form without saving any of the changes.

To summarize, the built-in DataGrid's editing functionality uses an interface that allows the user to edit one row at a time. You can create an interface that, say, lets the user edit all rows at once with an Update All button at the bottom of the page; however, you will be on your own for providing such an interface. To accomplish this custom interface and updating, you would need to use the techniques discussed in Part II.

Editing Data with No Foreign Keys That Can Be Edited in a TextBox

Providing editing support is quite simple if the data has no foreign keys and can easily be edited using a simple TextBox Web control. Recall that when a DataGrid row is selected to be edited, the columns of the rows that are not marked read-only are rendered in edit mode. We can specify the HTML that should be used to render a particular column in edit mode; however, the DataGrid can do this for us as well, rendering each editable column as a TextBox Web control. Because the DataGrid can provide the editing interface for editable columns for us free of charge, adding editing support for types of data that do not have foreign keys and can be edited well using a TextBox is simple.

NOTE

The reason editing data with foreign keys can be more difficult is because you want to restrict the user's editing choices, which is impossible with a TextBox control. You want to restrict the user's editing choices to the set of potential values the foreign key field can accept. This is typically done through a DropDownListBox Web control; we'll see an example of using the DropDownList for this purpose later in this chapter.

Before we examine code that provides DataGrid editing support, let's first enumerate the code pieces that need to be included:

- The DataGrid declaration needs to include an EditCommandColumn column, which will produce the Edit, Update, and Cancel buttons.

- An event handler for the DataGrid's EditCommand event. This event handler should simply set the DataGrid's EditItemIndex property to the index of the row whose Edit button was clicked, and then rebind the DataGrid.

- An event handler for the DataGrid's UpdateCommand event. This event handler should read in the values the user enters into the editable columns' edit interfaces. It should then update the database with these new values. Finally, it needs to set the DataGrid's EditItemIndex property to –1 and rebind the DataGrid.

- An event handler for the DataGrid's CancelCommand event. This event handler simply needs to set the DataGrid's EditItemIndex property to –1 and rebind the DataGrid.

Listing 9.1 contains the server-side code and HTML content for an ASP.NET Web page that provides editing support for the Comments database table. It does not fully implement the UpdateCommand event handler—we'll look at how to read the values from the edited row's columns shortly.

NOTE

Recall that we examined the Comments database table in Chapter 8, "Providing DataGrid Pagination." Specifically, the Comments table is *not* part of the pubs database, but is a table we added on our own to simulate an online guestbook application. This custom table will be used extensively for this chapter, Chapter 10, and Chapter 12.

LISTING 9.1   This DataGrid Is Editable, But Does Not Save the Changes Made

```
1: <%@ import Namespace="System.Data" %>
2: <%@ import Namespace="System.Data.SqlClient" %>
3: <script runat="server" language="VB">
```

LISTING 9.1   Continued

```
4:      Sub Page_Load(sender as Object, e as EventArgs)
5:        If Not Page.IsPostBack then
6:          BindData()
7:        End If
8:      End Sub
9:
10:
11:     Sub BindData()
12:       '1. Create a connection
13:       Const strConnString as String = "server=localhost;uid=sa;pwd=;
➥database=pubs"
14:       Dim objConn as New SqlConnection(strConnString)
15:
16:       '2. Create a command object for the query
17:       Const strSQL as String = _
18:         "SELECT CommentID, Name, Comment, DateAdded FROM Comments
➥ORDER BY CommentID"
19:       Dim objCmd as New SqlCommand(strSQL, objConn)
20:
21:       objConn.Open()    'Open the connection
22:
23:       'Finally, specify the DataSource and call DataBind()
24:       dgComments.DataSource = objCmd.ExecuteReader(CommandBehavior.
➥CloseConnection)
25:       dgComments.DataBind()
26:
27:       objConn.Close()    'Close the connection
28:     End Sub
29:
30:
31:     Sub dgComments_EditRow(sender As Object, e As DataGridCommandEventArgs)
32:       dgComments.EditItemIndex = e.Item.ItemIndex
33:       BindData()
34:     End Sub
35:
36:     Sub dgComments_UpdateRow(sender As Object, e As DataGridCommandEventArgs)
37:       'Get information from columns...
38:       'Update the database...
39:
```

LISTING 9.1 Continued

```
40:        dgComments.EditItemIndex = -1
41:        BindData()
42:     End Sub
43:
44:     Sub dgComments_CancelRow(sender As Object, e As DataGridCommandEventArgs)
45:        dgComments.EditItemIndex = -1
46:        BindData()
47:     End Sub
48:
49: </script>
50: <form runat="server">
51:   <asp:DataGrid runat="server" id="dgComments"
52:        Font-Name="Verdana" Font-Size="9pt" CellPadding="5"
53:        AlternatingItemStyle-BackColor="#dddddd"
54:        AutoGenerateColumns="False" DataKeyField="CommentID"
55:        OnEditCommand="dgComments_EditRow"
56:        OnUpdateCommand="dgComments_UpdateRow"
57:        OnCancelCommand="dgComments_CancelRow">
58:
59:     <HeaderStyle BackColor="Navy" ForeColor="White" Font-Size="13pt"
60:              Font-Bold="True" HorizontalAlign="Center" />
61:
62:     <Columns>
63:       <asp:EditCommandColumn ButtonType="LinkButton" HeaderText="Edit"
64:            EditText="Edit" UpdateText="Update" CancelText="Cancel" />
65:       <asp:BoundColumn DataField="CommentID" HeaderText="Comment ID" />
66:       <asp:BoundColumn DataField="Name" HeaderText="Name" />
67:       <asp:BoundColumn DataField="Comment" HeaderText="Comment" />
68:       <asp:BoundColumn DataField="DateAdded" HeaderText="Date Added" />
69:     </Columns>
70:   </asp:DataGrid>
71: </form>
```

The Page_Load event handler (lines 4 through 8) and the BindData() subroutine (lines 11 through 28) should look very similar—the majority of the examples in this book have used identical code. Nevertheless, let's take a brief moment to review these two parts of Listing 9.1. The Page_Load event handler simply calls the BindData() subroutine on the page's first load (line 6). The BindData() subroutine populates a `SqlCommand` with the contents of the `Comments` table, and then binds the resulting `SqlDataReader` to the `dgComments` DataGrid (lines 24 and 25).

Let's now turn our attention to the DataGrid's declaration, which spans line 51 to line 70. First, note that we add an EditCommandColumn (lines 63–64); this column is rendered as the Edit hyperlink shown in Figure 9.1, and the Update and Cancel hyperlinks in Figure 9.2. Note that we can specify whether the Edit, Update, and Cancel buttons should be hyperlinks or standard HTML buttons with the `ButtonType` property. By setting it to `LinkButton`, a hyperlink is used (this is also the default); to have the Edit, Update, and Cancel buttons rendered as HTML buttons, set the `ButtonType` property to `PushButton`.

The `EditText`, `UpdateText`, and `CancelText` properties of the EditCommandColumn specify the text that should appear in the button or hyperlink for the Edit, Update, and Cancel buttons.

CAUTION

If you fail to set the `EditText`, `UpdateText`, or `CancelText` properties, the buttons will not appear in the DataGrid. Therefore, remember to set these properties when adding an EditCommandColumn to a DataGrid!

If you want the Edit, Update, and Cancel buttons to be graphical images, set the `ButtonType` property to `LinkButton`, and then enter the HTML for an `IMG` tag in the `EditText`, `UpdateText`, and `CancelText` properties. For example, to have the Edit button display an image found at `/images/editButton.gif`, the `EditText` property should be set to:

```
EditText="<img src='/images/editButton.gif' alt='Edit this row' />
```

The other germane pieces of Listing 9.1 are the three event handlers spanning line 31 to line 47. These are the event handlers that fire when the user clicks on the Edit, Update, or Cancel buttons. Note that these event handlers have the following definition:

```
Sub EventHandler(sender as Object, e as DataGridCommandEventArgs)
```

Each event handler has a different task to accomplish. Recall from our discussion in the section "The DataGrid's Editing Interface" that the event handler for the Edit button needs to set the DataGrid's `EditItemIndex` property to the row whose Edit button was clicked, and then rebind the DataGrid data. The dgComments_EditRow event handler (lines 31 through 34), which fires whenever the Edit button for a row is clicked, does exactly that. On line 32 the `EditItemIndex` property is set to the index of the row that was clicked, and on line 33 the `BindData()` subroutine is called, rebinding the DataGrid.

The dgComments_UpdateRow event handler (lines 36 through 42), which fires whenever the Update button for a row is clicked, must read the values from the edited row's columns and update the database. (Listing 9.1 has omitted these actions for the time being.) After the data is added to the database, the dgComments_UpdateRow event handler needs to return the DataGrid to its pre-editing state, which it does by setting the EditItemIndex property to –1 (line 40) and rebinding the DataGrid (line 42).

The dgComments_CancelRow event handler (lines 44 through 47), which fires whenever the Cancel button for a row is clicked, simply returns the DataGrid to its pre-editing state by setting the EditItemIndex property to –1 (line 45) and rebinding the DataGrid (line 46).

To have these event handlers fire at the appropriate time, we have to wire them up to the associated DataGrid events, which we do in lines 55 through 57.

Let's quickly summarize the actions that occur when a user opts to edit a row in an editable DataGrid. First, the user must click the Edit button of a particular DataGrid row. When this happens, the ASP.NET Web page is posted back and the DataGrid's EditCommand event handler is fired, causing the dgComments_EditRow event handler to execute. The dgComments_EditRow event handler sets the DataGrid's EditItemIndex property to the index of the row that was selected to be edited, and then calls the BindData() subroutine, rebinding the DataGrid. When the DataGrid is rendered in the BindData() subroutine, it renders the columns of the row whose index matches the EditItemIndex in edit mode. In addition, for the row being edited, the Edit button will be replaced by two buttons: Update and Cancel. The default edit mode is a TextBox for each column, as shown in Figure 9.3.

After the user has updated the row with its new values, she can click either the Update or Cancel button. Either button will cause the ASP.NET page to be posted back; if the Update button is clicked, the DataGrid's UpdateCommand event is fired, while the CancelCommand event is fired if the Cancel button is clicked. If the UpdateCommand event is fired, the dgComments_UpdateRow event handler is also fired. The dgComments_UpdateRow event handler updates the database and returns the DataGrid to its pre-editing mode by setting the EditItemIndex to a value that cannot possibly be an index value for an existing DataGrid row (such as –1). If the CancelCommand event is fired, the dgComments_CancelRow event handler is fired, which returns the DataGrid to its pre-editing mode.

Figure 9.3 shows a screenshot of Listing 9.1 when the user has clicked the Edit button.

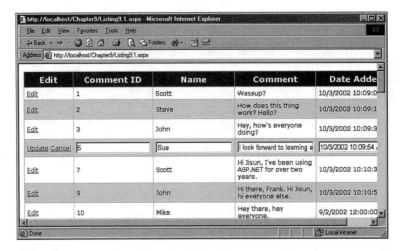

FIGURE 9.3   When a row is edited, all columns are rendered in edit mode.

Creating Read-Only Columns

In Listing 9.1, we saw how to provide the base code needed to turn on a DataGrid's editing features. Figure 9.3 shows a screenshot of Listing 9.1 when the user has clicked the Edit button for a particular row. Note that when a row is being edited, *all* columns in the row being edited are displayed in edit mode.

Often, we do not want to let the user edit all the rows. For example, in Listing 9.1 we display the CommentID field from the Comments table, which is a primary key value. Obviously, we don't want to allow the user to edit this field.

Fortunately, the DataGrid makes it easy to specify that a column should be non-editable. To mark a column non-editable, simply set the ReadOnly property of the BoundColumn to True (the default is False).

Listing 9.2 contains an alternative DataGrid declaration from Listing 9.1. The DataGrid declaration in Listing 9.2 makes both the CommentID and DateAdded columns read-only. Figure 9.4 contains a screenshot of the code from Listing 9.2 when the user has clicked the Edit button for a row. Note that the user is unable to edit either the CommentID or DateAdded columns for the row being edited.

LISTING 9.2   The CommentID and DateAdded Columns Are No Longer Editable

```
1: <asp:DataGrid runat="server" id="dgComments"
2:     Font-Name="Verdana" Font-Size="9pt" CellPadding="5"
3:     AlternatingItemStyle-BackColor="#dddddd"
4:     AutoGenerateColumns="False" DataKeyField="CommentID"
```

LISTING 9.2   Continued

```
5:     OnEditCommand="dgComments_EditRow"
6:     OnUpdateCommand="dgComments_UpdateRow"
7:     OnCancelCommand="dgComments_CancelRow">
8:
9: <HeaderStyle BackColor="Navy" ForeColor="White" Font-Size="13pt"
10:             Font-Bold="True" HorizontalAlign="Center" />
11:
12: <Columns>
13:     <asp:EditCommandColumn ButtonType="LinkButton" HeaderText="Edit"
14:         EditText="Edit" UpdateText="Update" CancelText="Cancel" />
15:     <asp:BoundColumn DataField="CommentID"
16:             HeaderText="Comment ID" ReadOnly="True" />
17:     <asp:BoundColumn DataField="Name" HeaderText="Name" />
18:     <asp:BoundColumn DataField="Comment" HeaderText="Comment" />
19:     <asp:BoundColumn DataField="DateAdded" HeaderText="Date Added"
20:             ReadOnly="True" />
21: </Columns>
22: </asp:DataGrid>
```

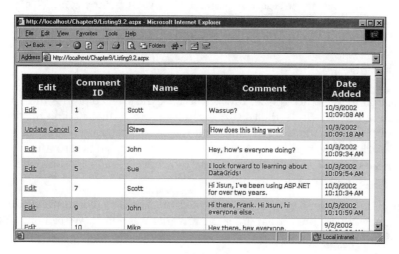

FIGURE 9.4   The `CommentID` and `DateAdded` columns are not editable.

Updating the Database with the Altered Values

In Listing 9.1, we saw how to provide the Edit, Update, and Cancel buttons for each row, and how to have a selected row enter an editing mode when the row's Edit button is clicked. In Listing 9.2, we saw how to make certain columns read-only. The only task that remains for creating a fully functional editable DataGrid is adding code to the dgComments_UpdateRow event handler to actually update the database with the changes.

The real challenge involved in this aspect is retrieving the altered data from the edited row. After we have this data, updating the database is simply a matter of constructing an appropriate parameterized SQL statement.

Recall that when a user clicks an Edit button for a row, the row is converted into edit mode, and each column that has not been marked as read-only is converted into a TextBox. In the dgComments_UpdateRow event handler, which fires after the user clicks the Update button, we need to extract the values entered into the TextBoxes. This can be accomplished by referencing the Cells collection of the DataGridItem that was edited; the edited DataGridItem can be referenced by the DataGridCommandEventArgs parameter's Item property.

Each editable TableCell in the Cells collection will have a TextBox child control, which can be referenced via the TableCells Controls collection. For example, in the DataGrid in Listing 9.2, we can reference the TextBox control for the Name column by using

```
Sub dgComments_UpdateRow(sender As Object, e As DataGridCommandEventArgs)
  Dim nameTextBox as TextBox
  nameTextBox = e.Item.Cells(2).Controls(0)

  ...
End Sub
```

The reason we reference the Cells(2) is because the Name column is the third column in the DataGrid—the EditCommandColumn is the first, and the CommentID column is the second. (Keep in mind that the Cells collection is indexed starting at zero, which is why we refer to the *third* cell as the using Cells(2).) After we have referenced the Name column TextBox, we can extract its value by using the Text property, as in nameTextBox.Text.

We need to use a similar approach to extract the Comment column's TextBox value. In addition, we need the CommentID for the row that was edited. We can obtain this in one of two ways:

1. By extracting the Text of the CommentID column—e.Item.Cells(1).Text.

2. By using the DataKeys collection. (Note that we set the DataKeyField to CommentID in both Listings 9.1 (line 54) and 9.2 (line 4).

I will use option 2 because I find it to be a cleaner and more readable approach.

Listing 9.3 contains the completed code for the dgComments_UpdateRow event handler. With this updated event handler, when the user edits a row, the row's changes are persisted to the database.

LISTING 9.3   The Updated dgCommand_UpdateRow Event Handler Persists the User's Edits to the Database

```
 1: Sub dgComments_UpdateRow(sender As Object, e As DataGridCommandEventArgs)
 2:      'Get information from columns...
 3:      Dim nameTextBox as TextBox = e.Item.Cells(2).Controls(0)
 4:      Dim commentTextBox as TextBox = e.Item.Cells(3).Controls(0)
 5:
 6:      Dim iCommentID as Integer = dgComments.DataKeys(e.Item.ItemIndex)
 7:
 8:
 9:      'Update the database...
10:      Dim strSQL as String
11:      strSQL = "UPDATE Comments SET Name = @NameParam, " & _
12:              "Comment = @CommentParam WHERE CommentID = @CommentIDParam"
13:
14:      Const strConnString as String = "server=localhost;uid=sa;pwd=;
➥database=pubs"
15:      Dim objConn as New SqlConnection(strConnString)
16:
17:      Dim objCmd as New SqlCommand(strSQL, objConn)
18:
19:      Dim nameParam as New SqlParameter("@NameParam", SqlDbType.VarChar, 50)
20:      Dim commentParam as New SqlParameter("@CommentParam",
➥SqlDbType.VarChar, 255)
21:      Dim commentIDParam as New SqlParameter("@CommentIDParam",
➥SqlDbType.Int, 4)
22:
23:      nameParam.Value = nameTextBox.Text
24:      objCmd.Parameters.Add(nameParam)
25:
26:      commentParam.Value = commentTextBox.Text
27:      objCmd.Parameters.Add(commentParam)
28:
29:      commentIDParam.Value = iCommentID
30:      objCmd.Parameters.Add(commentIDParam)
31:
32:      'Issue the SQL command
33:      objConn.Open()
```

LISTING 9.3   Continued

```
34:       objCmd.ExecuteNonQuery()
35:       objConn.Close()
36:
37:       dgComments.EditItemIndex = -1
38:       BindData()
39: End Sub
```

To retrieve the values of the TextBox Web controls, we reference the `Controls` collection of the appropriate `TableCell` for the row being edited, as previously discussed. On line 3 we retrieve a reference to the `Name` column's TextBox; on line 4 we retrieve a reference to the `Comment` column's TextBox. In addition to the `Name` and `Comment` TextBox values, we need to know the `CommentID` of the row that was just edited. We retrieve this on line 6 using the `DataKeys` collection. (Recall that we discussed the `DataKeys` collection in Chapter 4.)

After we have these values, we're ready to issue a parameterized SQL statement. This SQL statement is constructed on lines 11 and 12. On lines 14 and 15, the database connection is established. Lines 17 through 30 create the `SqlCommand` and add the necessary parameters. Finally, on lines 33 through 35 we use the `Open()` method to open the database connection and execute the command before closing the connection. After this, we set the DataGrid's `EditItemIndex` to –1 and rebind the DataGrid data.

With this amended `dgComments_UpdateRow` event handler, the changes made to a DataGrid row are persisted to the database.

Using Other Controls to Edit Data

As we saw in Figures 9.1 through 9.4, the DataGrid provides a TextBox Web control as a default editing interface for a column. However, there are times when the data we are editing cannot be easily edited via a simple TextBox. For example, we might want to use a multiline TextBox, or perhaps a DropDownList, or CheckBoxList. In addition, we might want to add validation controls to the editing interface, which are not added by the DataGrid's default editing interface.

Our DataGrid's `Comment` column is a good example of when a standard TextBox Web control might not be the optimal editing interface. Because the `Comment` column can accept inputs of up to 255 characters, it might be better to use a multiline TextBox.

We can specify the HTML and Web controls to be used for a column's editing interface by using a TemplateColumn control instead of a BoundColumn control. Recall from Chapter 3, "Customizing the HTML Output," that the TemplateColumn control can contain a number of templates. The ItemTemplate, for example, is the template used when the column is rendered in a standard row. The TemplateColumn can also include an EditItemTemplate, which, as its name suggests, is the template used when a column is rendered in edit mode.

Listing 9.4 contains the source code for an ASP.NET Web page that uses a custom editing interface for the Comment column. Most of the code in Listing 9.4 is identical to that in Listing 9.3, and has therefore been omitted for brevity. The only parts new to Listing 9.4 are the DataGrid declaration (specifically the change from a BoundColumn control to a TemplateColumn control for the Comment column) and the dgComment_UpdateRow event handler. Because of the change in the Comment column, we have to alter the way we reference the TextBox for the Comment column in the dgComment_UpdateRow event handler.

LISTING 9.4   A Custom Editing Interface Is Employed for the Comment Column

```
 1: <%@ import Namespace="System.Data" %>
 2: <%@ import Namespace="System.Data.SqlClient" %>
 3: <script runat="server" language="VB">
 4:    ' ... The Page_Load event handler, BindData() subroutine,
 5:    ' ... dgComment_EditRow, and dgComment_CancelRow event handlers
 6:    ' ... are identical to the ones presented in Listing 9.3 ...
 7:
 8:    Sub dgComments_UpdateRow(sender As Object, e As DataGridCommandEventArgs)
 9:       'Get information from columns...
10:       ...
11:       Dim commentTextBox as TextBox = e.Item.Cells(3).
➥FindControl("txtComment")
12:       ...
13:
14:       ' The remainder of the dgComment_UpdateRow eventhandler is identical
15:       ' to the dgComment_UpdateRow event handler in Listing 9.3 ...
16:    End Sub
17: </script>
18:
19: <form runat="server">
20:    <asp:DataGrid runat="server" id="dgComments"
21:        Font-Name="Verdana" Font-Size="9pt" CellPadding="5"
22:        AlternatingItemStyle-BackColor="#dddddd"
23:        AutoGenerateColumns="False" DataKeyField="CommentID"
24:        OnEditCommand="dgComments_EditRow"
25:        OnUpdateCommand="dgComments_UpdateRow"
26:        OnCancelCommand="dgComments_CancelRow">
27:
```

LISTING 9.4   Continued

```
28:     <HeaderStyle BackColor="Navy" ForeColor="White" Font-Size="13pt"
29:             Font-Bold="True" HorizontalAlign="Center" />
30:
31:     <Columns>
32:       <asp:EditCommandColumn ButtonType="LinkButton" HeaderText="Edit"
33:           EditText="Edit" UpdateText="Update" CancelText="Cancel" />
34:       <asp:BoundColumn DataField="CommentID"
35:               HeaderText="Comment ID" ReadOnly="True" />
36:       <asp:BoundColumn DataField="Name" HeaderText="Name" />
37:       <asp:TemplateColumn HeaderText="Comment">
38:         <ItemTemplate>
39:           <%# DataBinder.Eval(Container.DataItem, "Comment") %>
40:         </ItemTemplate>
41:         <EditItemTemplate>
42:           <asp:TextBox runat="server" id="txtComment" TextMode="MultiLine"
43:               Columns="40" Rows="6" MaxLength="255"
44:               Text='<%# DataBinder.Eval(Container.DataItem, "Comment")
➥%>' />
45:         </EditItemTemplate>
46:       </asp:TemplateColumn>
47:       <asp:BoundColumn DataField="DateAdded" HeaderText="Date Added"
48:               ReadOnly="True" />
49:     </Columns>
50:   </asp:DataGrid>
51: </form>
```

Let's first look at the differences in the DataGrid's declaration. The Data declaration in Listing 9.4 is identical to that in Listing 9.3 save for lines 37 through 46, which specify that the DataGrid's Comment column should be rendered using a TemplateColumn as opposed to a BoundColumn.

Recall that a TemplateColumn can have multiple templates. The ItemTemplate is the template used when rendering the column for a normal row. The Comment column's ItemTemplate is defined on lines 38 through 40. This ItemTemplate is quite simple, it just emits the value of the Comment field from the DataSource. (If you need to brush up on the data-binding syntax (<%# ... %>), consider looking over Chapters 2 and 3 once again.)

The EditItemTemplate (lines 41 through 45) is the template used when the column is being rendered in edit mode. This occurs when the index of the DataGrid row being rendered is equal to the DataGrid's EditItemIndex property. In Listing 9.4, the

EditItemTemplate specifies that a multiline TextBox control with 40 characters and 6 rows should be used. Furthermore, the TextBox's `MaxLength` property is set to 255, which is an attribute recognized by later versions of Internet Explorer that limits the user's input to 255 characters.

On line 44, the TextBox's `Text` property is set to the value of the `Comment` field of the `DataSource` using data-binding syntax. By setting the `Text` property, when the user opts to edit a particular row, the value of the row's `Comment` field will appear in the multiline TextBox.

CAUTION

If you forget to set TextBox's `Text` property as was done on line 44, when the user clicks a row's Edit button, the multiline TextBox representing the value of the `Comment` field will be blank.

Also note that in the multiline TextBox we specify the TextBox's `ID` property, setting it to `txtComment`. We do this so that the `TextBox` control can be easily referenced in the `dgComments_UpdateRow` event handler. (Recall that we need to reference this TextBox's value in the `dgComments_UpdateRow` event handler so that the database can be updated with the values entered by the user.)

TIP

To make a TemplateColumn read-only, just don't provide an EditItemTemplate for the TemplateColumn.

The other interesting part to the code in Listing 9.4 is in the `dgComments_UpdateRow` event handler. Because the `Comment` column uses a TemplateColumn as opposed to a BoundColumn, the syntax for retrieving the value of the `Comment` column's TextBox is a bit different. The reason is because the TemplateColumn is rendered as a series of controls that are then added to the DataGrid's corresponding `TableCell`. All HTML content in a TemplateColumn's template is rendered as a LiteralControl. Therefore, the EditItemTemplate in Listing 9.4 is comprised of three child controls: a LiteralControl, representing the HTML whitespace that appears before the TextBox Web control; the TextBox Web control `txtContent`; and a LiteralControl, representing the HTML whitespace that appears after the TextBox Web control.

Recall that the code used to retrieve the TextBox value in Listing 9.3 was as follows:

```
Dim commentTextBox as TextBox = e.Item.Cells(3).Controls(0)
```

However, because the first control of the `Comments TableCell` is a LiteralControl representing the whitespace before the TextBox, `e.Item.Cells(3).Controls(0)` will return a LiteralControl, not a TextBox control.

Although we could adjust the dgComments_UpdateRow event handler code to use

```
Dim commentTextBox as TextBox = e.Item.Cells(3).Controls(1)
```

This code might need to be changed if we add more HTML or Web controls to the Comment column's EditItemTemplate. A more elegant solution is to use the FindControl(*controlID*) method to explicitly reference the TableCell's child control, whose ID is set to txtComment. This is accomplished in the dgComments_UpdateRow event handler in Listing 9.4 on line 11.

The remaining code for the dgComments_UpdateRow event handler is the same as it was in Listing 9.3. That is, after we have correctly referenced the Comment column's TextBox, we proceed as we did in Listing 9.3 in updating the database with the changes.

Figure 9.5 contains a screenshot of Listing 9.4 in action. Note that the Comment column's editing interface is rendered as a multiline TextBox.

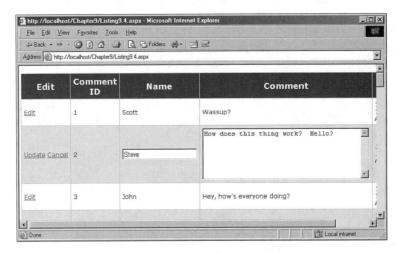

FIGURE 9.5   The Comment column uses a customized editing interface.

Listing 9.4 illustrates how to add a custom editing interface to a particular DataGrid column. Note that when adding the custom editing interface, you need to be certain to do two things.

First, you must be certain that the custom editing interface is correctly set to the value in the corresponding DataSource field when it's selected for editing. For example, in Listing 9.4 we set the TextBox's Text property to the value of the DataSource's Comment field so that when the user edited a particular row, the row's Comment value would appear in the multiline TextBox. Regardless of what custom editing interface you provide, you will need to be certain to set its initial value to the value of the field it's representing.

Second, you must make certain that you correctly reference the custom editing interface's data in the event handler that is executed when the Update button is clicked. For example, in Listing 9.4 we needed to use the FindControl method to get a reference to the Comment column's TextBox.

A DataGrid column's custom editing interface is limited only by your imagination and programming skills. You can add TextBoxes, DropDownLists, RadioButtons, CheckBoxes, CheckBoxLists, RadioButtonLists, and so on. In fact, in the next section we will examine how to add a Calendar Web control to a DataGrid column's custom editing interface. Regardless of the editing interface you think up, just be certain that you are able to set its initial value to the value of the corresponding DataSource field, and after the user clicks Update, you are able to read its data.

Using a Calendar Control in a Customized Editing Interface

If the data we are displaying in the DataGrid has a column that is a date, we can provide a rich customized editing interface to the date column by utilizing the ASP.NET Calendar control. The ASP.NET Calendar Web control displays a calendar in month form, enabling the user to select a particular day of any month of any year. (If you are not familiar with the Calendar control, you might want to read "The Calendar Web Control" referenced in the "On the Web" section at the end of this chapter before continuing.)

For our Comments table, there is a DateAdded field that is a DateTime field in SQL Server. However, let's imagine that we are only interested in the actual date the comment was posted, not the date and time. In this scenario, we could use a Calendar Web control for the editing interface for this column.

NOTE

If we were interested in both the date and time, we might want to use two Web controls in the editing interface: a Calendar Web control, enabling the user to select the date, and a some other Web control to enable the user to select the time. This other Web control could be as simple as a TextBox, or as involved as a custom Web control written expressly for time inputs.

Recall that to provide a customized editing interface, we have to use a TemplateColumn as opposed to a BoundColumn. Hence, our first step is altering our DataGrid's declaration from Listing 9.4 to use a TemplateColumn for the DateAdded column as opposed to a BoundColumn. In this TemplateColumn, we might want to have the ItemTemplate display only the date part of the DateAdded field, as opposed to the date and time. In our EditItemTemplate, we will use a Calendar Web control. The updated DataGrid declaration can be found in Listing 9.5.

LISTING 9.5   The DataGrid Declaration Has Been Altered to Include a TemplateColumn for the DateAdded Column

```
 1: <form runat="server">
 2:   <asp:DataGrid runat="server" id="dgComments"
 3:       Font-Name="Verdana" Font-Size="9pt" CellPadding="5"
 4:       AlternatingItemStyle-BackColor="#dddddd"
 5:       AutoGenerateColumns="False" DataKeyField="CommentID"
 6:       OnEditCommand="dgComments_EditRow"
 7:       OnUpdateCommand="dgComments_UpdateRow"
 8:       OnCancelCommand="dgComments_CancelRow">
 9:
10:     <HeaderStyle BackColor="Navy" ForeColor="White" Font-Size="13pt"
11:             Font-Bold="True" HorizontalAlign="Center" />
12:
13:     <Columns>
14:       <asp:EditCommandColumn ButtonType="LinkButton" HeaderText="Edit"
15:             EditText="Edit" UpdateText="Update" CancelText="Cancel" />
16:       <asp:BoundColumn DataField="CommentID"
17:             HeaderText="Comment ID" ReadOnly="True" />
18:       <asp:BoundColumn DataField="Name" HeaderText="Name" />
19:       <asp:TemplateColumn HeaderText="Comment">
20:         <ItemTemplate>
21:           <%# DataBinder.Eval(Container.DataItem, "Comment") %>
22:         </ItemTemplate>
23:         <EditItemTemplate>
24:           <asp:TextBox runat="server" id="txtComment" TextMode="MultiLine"
25:               Columns="40" Rows="6" MaxLength="255"
26:               Text='<%# DataBinder.Eval(Container.DataItem, "Comment")
➥ %>' />
27:         </EditItemTemplate>
28:       </asp:TemplateColumn>
29:       <asp:TemplateColumn HeaderText="Date Added"
30:           ItemStyle-HorizontalAlign="Center">
31:         <ItemTemplate>
32:           <%# String.Format("{0:d}", Convert.ToDateTime
➥(DataBinder.Eval(Container.DataItem, "DateAdded"))) %>
33:         </ItemTemplate>
34:         <EditItemTemplate>
35:           <asp:Calendar id="calDate" runat="server"
```

LISTING 9.5   Continued

```
36:                     SelectedDate='<%# Convert.ToDateTime
➡(DataBinder.Eval(Container.DataItem, "DateAdded")) %>'
37:                     VisibleDate='<%# Convert.ToDateTime
➡(DataBinder.Eval(Container.DataItem, "DateAdded")) %>' />
38:             </EditItemTemplate>
39:           </asp:TemplateColumn>
40:       </Columns>
41:     </asp:DataGrid>
42: </form>
```

The added TemplateColumn can be found in lines 29 through 39. Note that in the DateAdded column's ItemTemplate, we format the value of the DateAdded field so that only the date part is displayed. To accomplish this, we use the String.Format method (line 32).

Recall that when providing a customized editing interface, there are two tasks we must concern ourselves with. The first is ensuring that the Web control (or controls) used to implement the customized editing interface have their initial value set to the value of the DataSource field they are representing. We accomplish this with the Calendar control in lines 36 and 37, where we set the SelectedDate and VisibleDate properties.

The SelectedDate property indicates what date is selected by default on the Calendar Web control. Clearly, we want the Calendar's SelectedDate property set to the current value of the row's DateAdded field. The VisibleDate property specifies what month and year are displayed in the Calendar control; we want this property also set to the current value of the row's DateAdded field so that the month and year of the DateAdded field is displayed in the Calendar.

CAUTION

If you fail to set the VisibleDate property, the Calendar control will display the current month and year by default, regardless of the value of the SelectedDate property. That is, even if the SelectedDate property is set to October 10, 2002, if the current date is April 1, 2003, the Calendar control will display the calendar for April 2003. Of course, the user can cycle back to October 2002, but this would likely be inconvenient.

By setting these two properties of the Calendar control, we have achieved our first goal: ensuring that the Web control used to implement the customized editing interface has its initial value set to the value of the DataSource field it is representing.

At this point, when the user clicks the Edit button for a row in the DataGrid, the row will become editable. The Name column will have a standard TextBox, the Comment column will have a multiline TextBox (refer back to Listing 9.4 for more information), and the DateAdded column will have a Calendar Web control displayed. The user can switch the months of the Calendar Web control and click on the various days. Each time the user switches to a different Calendar month or selects a date from the Calendar control, the ASP.NET Web page is posted back. However, the row being edited remains in editing mode, because the DataGrid's EditItemIndex property has not changed.

Each time the user clicks a specific date in the Calendar, the Calendar control's SelectedDate property is updated to reflect the currently selected date. After the user has chosen an appropriate date (as well as updated the Name and/or Comment columns if so desired), he can click the Update button to commit the changes to the database. Clicking the Update button will cause the ASP.NET Web page to be posted back and the DataGrid's UpdateCommand event to fire. This will cause the dgComments_UpdateRow event handler to execute.

Recall that when adding a customized editing interface, our second task is to alter the event handler that fires when the Update button is clicked, so that the value entered for the customized editing interface can be read and inserted into the database. To accomplish this, we need to update our dgComments_UpdateRow event handler. Specifically, we need to provide a means by which the Calendar control can be accessed and have its SelectedDate property read.

The code in Listing 9.6 contains the updated code for the dgComments_UpdateRow event handler.

LISTING 9.6   The SelectedDate Property of the Calendar Control Is Used to Update the Database

```
1:     Sub dgComments_UpdateRow(sender As Object, e As DataGridCommandEventArgs)
2:        'Get information from columns...
3:        Dim nameTextBox as TextBox = e.Item.Cells(2).Controls(0)
4:        Dim commentTextBox as TextBox = e.Item.Cells(3).
➥FindControl("txtComment")
5:        Dim dateAdded as Calendar = e.Item.Cells(4).FindControl("calDate")
6:
7:        Dim iCommentID as Integer = dgComments.DataKeys(e.Item.ItemIndex)
8:
9:
10:       'Update the database...
11:       Dim strSQL as String
12:       strSQL = "UPDATE Comments SET Name = @NameParam, DateAdded =
➥@DateAddedParam, " & _
13:               "Comment = @CommentParam WHERE CommentID = @CommentIDParam"
14:
```

LISTING 9.6 Continued

```
15:        Const strConnString as String = "server=localhost;uid=sa;pwd=;
➥database=pubs"
16:        Dim objConn as New SqlConnection(strConnString)
17:
18:        Dim objCmd as New SqlCommand(strSQL, objConn)
19:
20:        Dim nameParam as New SqlParameter("@NameParam", SqlDbType.VarChar, 50)
21:        Dim commentParam as New SqlParameter("@CommentParam", SqlDbType.
➥VarChar, 255)
22:        Dim dateAddedParam as New SqlParameter("@DateAddedParam", SqlDbType.
➥DateTime)
23:        Dim commentIDParam as New SqlParameter("@CommentIDParam",
➥SqlDbType.Int, 4)
24:
25:        nameParam.Value = nameTextBox.Text
26:        objCmd.Parameters.Add(nameParam)
27:
28:        commentParam.Value = commentTextBox.Text
29:        objCmd.Parameters.Add(commentParam)
30:
31:        dateAddedParam.Value = dateAdded.SelectedDate
32:        objCmd.Parameters.Add(dateAddedParam)
33:
34:        commentIDParam.Value = iCommentID
35:        objCmd.Parameters.Add(commentIDParam)
36:
37:        'Issue the SQL command
38:        objConn.Open()
39:        objCmd.ExecuteNonQuery()
40:        objConn.Close()
41:
42:        dgComments.EditItemIndex = -1
43:        BindData()
44:    End Sub
```

The bold lines in Listing 9.6 represent the lines of code updated from the
dgComments_UpdateRow event handler from Listing 9.4.

On line 5, the Calendar Web control is referenced by the local variable dateAdded.
The FindControl(*controlID*) technique is used here as it was to reference the
Comment column TextBox (see Listing 9.4, or line 4 in Listing 9.6). The SQL statement

on lines 12 and 13 is also updated to update the selected database record's `DateAdded` field.

Because the SQL statement is parameterized, we need to create a parameter for the `@DateAddedParam` parameter. This is accomplished on line 22. On lines 31 and 32, we set the `Value` of this parameter to the `SelectedDate` property of the Calendar control and then add the parameter to the `Parameters` collection of the `SqlCommand` object `objCmd`. The remainder of the `dgComments_UpdateRow` event handler is identical to that in Listing 9.4.

Figure 9.6 shows a screenshot of the updated code presented in Listings 9.5 and 9.6. Specifically, the screenshot is of when a user has clicked on the Edit button for a row. Note that the `DateAdded` column is rendered as a Calendar Web control. Also notice that the `DateAdded` column values that are not being edited display only the date part, not the date and time.

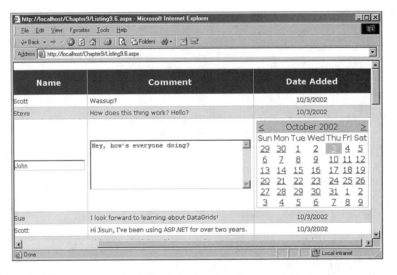

FIGURE 9.6   The customized editing interface for the `DateAdded` column uses a Calendar control.

Editing Data That Has Foreign Key Constraints

In relational databases—such as Microsoft SQL Server, Microsoft Access, or Oracle, among others—it is quite common for tables to have fields that serve as a foreign key to other tables. For example, in the pubs database, the `titles` database table has a `pub_id` field, which is a foreign key into the primary key field `pub_id` of the `publishers` table. The `pub_id` in the `titles` table maps a particular book to a particular publisher.

A foreign key constraint requires that the value entered into the foreign key is equal to the value of the primary key field in the table that the foreign key maps to. That is, in the `titles` table, the `pub_id` foreign key value must be set to a value that exists in the `publishers` table's `pub_id` field.

NOTE

Foreign keys and foreign key constraints help maintain relational integrity in a relational database system. The topic of the semantics and syntax of foreign keys is well beyond the scope of this book—if you're not familiar with foreign keys, consider perusing the references in the "On the Web" section at the end of this chapter.

When providing editing support for data that contains foreign keys, it is vital that the user only be allowed to select a valid entry for the foreign key fields. There are a number of foreign key relationships employed by various tables in the `pubs` database, such as the `pub_id` field in the `titles` table, which specifies the publisher for each book. For example, for the book *The Busy Executive's Database Guide*, the `pub_id` field has a value of 1389. This maps to a primary key value in the `publishers` table for the publisher Algodata Infosystems. When editing this book, the user might want to change the publisher to Ramona Publishers, which has a `pub_id` of 1756. Clearly, you can't expect the user to have these cryptic numbers memorized.

NOTE

The `pub_id` field in the `publishers` and `titles` tables are `char(4)` data types. Although foreign keys are most commonly integer data types, they can be of other types, so long as each foreign key value maps to an existing primary key value in the corresponding table.

To summarize, when a user is allowed to enter a foreign key field, she must only be allowed to change the foreign key value to a legal value. It is our job to ensure that this is the case. Additionally, we should allow the user to choose from, perhaps, the name of the publisher, as opposed to the actual `pub_id`.

The DropDownList Web control is well suited for the editing constraints imposed by a foreign key. The DropDownList requires that the user select from a predetermined list of items, such as the list of all publishers in the `publishers` table. Furthermore, the text that appears in the DropDownList can be the value of the `publisher` table's `pub_name` field, while the value for each DropDownList item can be the `pub_id`. Given this, we can allow the editing of data containing a foreign key by implementing a customized editing interface for the foreign key column (or columns) that consists of a data-bound DropDownList.

NOTE

A DropDownList is a Web control rendered as an HTML list box that can only have one item selected from it at a time. It is equivalent to the ListBox Web control when the ListBox's SelectionMode property is set to Single.

Recall the two challenges we are faced with when providing a customized editing interface: setting the editing interface's initial value to the value of the DataSource field that the column being edited is representing, and obtaining the value the user entered in the event handler that fires when the Update button is clicked.

With the customized editing interface for our foreign key DataGrid column, the second task is fairly trivial—the real challenge involved is in assigning the value of the edited row's pub_id field to the default value to the DropDownList.

Listing 9.7 contains the server-side code and HTML content needed for an ASP.NET Web page that allows the editing of the pubs database's titles table. A data-bound DropDownList is used for the DataGrid's pub_id customized editing interface.

LISTING 9.7   A Data-Bound DropDownList Is Used to Edit a Foreign Key Column

```
 1: <%@ import Namespace="System.Data" %>
 2: <%@ import Namespace="System.Data.SqlClient" %>
 3: <script runat="server" language="VB">
 4:     Dim ddlDataSet as DataSet = New DataSet()
 5:
 6:     Sub Page_Load(sender as Object, e as EventArgs)
 7:       If Not Page.IsPostBack then
 8:         BindData()
 9:       End If
10:     End Sub
11:
12:
13:     Sub BindData()
14:       '1. Create a connection
15:       Const strConnString as String = "server=localhost;uid=sa;pwd=;
➥database=pubs"
16:       Dim objConn as New SqlConnection(strConnString)
17:
18:       '2. Create a command object for the query
19:       Dim strSQL as String = _
20:         "SELECT title_id, title, t.pub_id, p.pub_name, price FROM
➥titles t " & _
21:         "INNER JOIN publishers p ON t.pub_id = p.pub_id ORDER BY title"
```

LISTING 9.7   Continued

```
22:        Dim objCmd as New SqlCommand(strSQL, objConn)
23:
24:        objConn.Open()    'Open the connection
25:
26:        'Finally, specify the DataSource and call DataBind()
27:        dgTitle.DataSource = objCmd.ExecuteReader(CommandBehavior.
➥CloseConnection)
28:        dgTitle.DataBind()
29:
30:        objConn.Close()    'Close the connection
31:    End Sub
32:
33:
34:    Function GetPublishers() as DataSet
35:        '1. Create a connection
36:        Const strConnString as String = "server=localhost;uid=sa;pwd=;
➥database=pubs"
37:        Dim objConn as New SqlConnection(strConnString)
38:
39:        '2. Create a command object for the query
40:        Const strSQL as String = _
41:          "SELECT pub_id, pub_name FROM publishers ORDER BY pub_name"
42:
43:        Dim myDataAdapter as SqlDataAdapter
44:        myDataAdapter = New SqlDataAdapter(strSQL, objConn)
45:
46:        'Fill the DataSet
47:        objConn.Open()    'Open the connection
48:        myDataAdapter.Fill(ddlDataSet, "Publishers")
49:        objConn.Close()    'Close the connection
50:
51:        Return ddlDataSet 'Return the DataSet
52:    End Function
53:
54:
55:    Function GetSelectedIndex(pub_id as String) as Integer
56:        'Loop through the DataSet ddlDataSet
57:        Dim iLoop as Integer
58:        Dim dt as DataTable = ddlDataSet.Tables("Publishers")
59:        For iLoop = 0 to dt.Rows.Count - 1
60:          If pub_id = dt.Rows(iLoop)("pub_id").ToString() then
```

LISTING 9.7   Continued

```
61:           Return iLoop
62:         End If
63:       Next iLoop
64:     End Function
65:
66:
67:     Sub dgTitle_EditRow(sender As Object, e As DataGridCommandEventArgs)
68:       dgTitle.EditItemIndex = e.Item.ItemIndex
69:       BindData()
70:     End Sub
71:
72:     Sub dgTitle_UpdateRow(sender As Object, e As DataGridCommandEventArgs)
73:       'Get information from columns...
74:       Dim ddlPublishers as DropDownList = e.Item.Cells(2).
➥FindControl("ddlPublisher")
75:
76:       Dim titleID as String = dgTitle.DataKeys(e.Item.ItemIndex)
77:
78:
79:       'Update the database...
80:       Dim strSQL as String
81:       strSQL = "UPDATE titles SET pub_id = @pubIDParam " & _
82:               "WHERE title_id = @titleIDParam"
83:
84:       Const strConnString as String = "server=localhost;uid=sa;pwd=;
➥database=pubs"
85:       Dim objConn as New SqlConnection(strConnString)
86:
87:       Dim objCmd as New SqlCommand(strSQL, objConn)
88:
89:       Dim pubIDParam as New SqlParameter("@pubIDParam", SqlDbType.Char, 4)
90:       Dim titleIDParam as New SqlParameter("@titleIDParam", SqlDbType.
➥VarChar, 6)
91:
92:       pubIDParam.Value = ddlPublishers.SelectedItem.Value
93:       objCmd.Parameters.Add(pubIDParam)
94:
95:       titleIDParam.Value = titleID
96:       objCmd.Parameters.Add(titleIDParam)
97:
98:       'Issue the SQL command
```

LISTING 9.7   Continued

```
 99:        objConn.Open()
100:        objCmd.ExecuteNonQuery()
101:        objConn.Close()
102:
103:        dgTitle.EditItemIndex = -1
104:        BindData()
105:      End Sub
106:
107:      Sub dgTitle_CancelRow(sender As Object, e As DataGridCommandEventArgs)
108:        dgTitle.EditItemIndex = -1
109:        BindData()
110:      End Sub
111:
112: </script>
113: <form runat="server">
114:   <asp:DataGrid runat="server" id="dgTitle"
115:        Font-Name="Verdana" Font-Size="9pt" CellPadding="5"
116:        AlternatingItemStyle-BackColor="#dddddd"
117:        AutoGenerateColumns="False" DataKeyField="title_id"
118:        OnEditCommand="dgTitle_EditRow"
119:        OnUpdateCommand="dgTitle_UpdateRow"
120:        OnCancelCommand="dgTitle_CancelRow">
121:
122:      <HeaderStyle BackColor="Navy" ForeColor="White" Font-Size="13pt"
123:              Font-Bold="True" HorizontalAlign="Center" />
124:
125:      <Columns>
126:        <asp:EditCommandColumn ButtonType="LinkButton" HeaderText="Edit"
127:            EditText="Edit" UpdateText="Update" CancelText="Cancel" />
128:        <asp:BoundColumn DataField="title"
129:                HeaderText="Title" ReadOnly="True" />
130:        <asp:TemplateColumn HeaderText="Publisher">
131:          <ItemTemplate>
132:            <%# DataBinder.Eval(Container.DataItem, "pub_name") %>
133:          </ItemTemplate>
134:          <EditItemTemplate>
135:            <asp:DropDownList id="ddlPublisher" runat="server"
136:                DataTextField="pub_name"
137:                DataValueField="pub_id"
138:                DataSource="<%# GetPublishers() %>"
139:                SelectedIndex='<%# GetSelectedIndex(Container.
➥DataItem("pub_id")) %>'
```

LISTING 9.7   Continued

```
140:                    />
141:              </EditItemTemplate>
142:           </asp:TemplateColumn>
143:           <asp:BoundColumn DataField="price" DataFormatString="{0:c}"
144:                    HeaderText="Price" ReadOnly="True" />
145:        </Columns>
146:     </asp:DataGrid>
147: </form>
```

The first thing you'll probably notice about Listing 9.7 is its length. Although it might be a bit daunting at first, realize that the majority of the code in the listing is code we've examined in previous code listings.

The DataGrid rendered by Listing 9.7 contains four columns: an EditCommandColumn (lines 126–127), a Title column (lines 128–129), a Publisher column (lines 130–142), and a Price column (lines 143–144). To simplify the exercise, and because we're only concerned with demonstrating how to provide editing for foreign key columns, only the Publisher column is made editable. The other columns in the DataGrid could easily be made editable through techniques we learned earlier in this chapter.

Note that the Publisher column displays the name of the book's publisher, not the actual foreign key value. This is done by using an INNER JOIN in the SQL statement to obtain the fields form the publishers table that correspond to pub_id field for each row in the titles table. This SQL statement can be found on lines 19 through 21 in the BindData() subroutine. Specifically, the pub_name field from the publishers table is included in each record of our query's resultset, which corresponds to the name of the publisher for the particular book.

The customized editing interface for the DataGrid's Publisher column is defined in the EditItemTemplate (lines 134–141). The customized editing interface is simply a DropDownList Web control. The DropDownList Web control can be data-bound; that is, we can supply DataTextField, DataValueField, and DataSource properties for the DropDownList. When the DropDownList is rendered, the items in the DropDownList are made up from the records in the specified DataSource. The DataTextField property specifies the DataSource field whose value should be displayed as the text for each DropDownList item, while the DataValueField property specifies the DataSource field whose value should be the value of the DropDownList item.

In Listing 9.7, we set the DataTextField to pub_name because we want to display the publisher's name as the text of each item of the DropDownList (line 136). The

DataValueField property is set to pub_id (line 137), because this is the information we need to update the pub_id field of the titles table when the user clicks the Update button.

The DataSource is specified via data-binding syntax, because we have to provide code to construct an appropriate DataSource. Specifically, we want to create an object that can be used as a DataSource containing the pub_id and pub_name fields for each record from the publishers table. The DataSource for the DropDownList is returned by the function GetPublishers(), which we need to write and include in our server-side code.

The GetPublishers() function (lines 34–52) accepts no parameters and returns a DataSet. The code for this function is fairly straightforward–a connection to the database is opened, and a DataSet is filled with the results of a SQL query. Specifically, the SQL query retrieves the rows of the publishers table (lines 40 and 41). After we have filled the DataSet (line 48), the connection is closed and the DataSet is returned (line 51) .

Note that the DataSet that is filled in the GetPublishers() function is declared outside the GetPublishers() function on line 4. You might be wondering why we would want to declare the DataSet outside the of the GetPublishers() function. We will examine the rationale behind this in a bit. For now, just be cognizant of the fact that the DataSet populated in the GetPublishers() function has been declared external to the function.

By setting the DataTextField, DataValueField, and DataSource properties in the DropDownList, we have managed to add a data-bound DropDownList to the Publisher column's editing interface. When the user clicks the Edit button, he will see a DropDownList with the list of available publishers. However, recall the first task involved in creating a customized editing interface: The editing interface must default to the value of the DataSource field it is representing. In just providing the DataTextField, DataValueField, and DataSource properties, our DropDownList doesn't do this. That is, regardless of what publisher the book *Emotional Security: A New Algorithm* has, when its Edit button is clicked, the DropDownList of publishers would have the first publisher selected by default (Algodata Infosystems in our example, because the SQL query in the GetPublishers() function orders the results alphabetically by the publisher's name).

To have the DropDownList automatically select the row's publisher, we must correctly set the DropDownList's SelectedIndex property. We do this on line 139 by using data-binding syntax to call a function GetSelectedIndex(*publisherID*). Like the GetPublishers() function, we must create the GetSelectedIndex(*publisherID*) function and include it in our ASP.NET code section.

The GetSelectedIndex(*publisherID*) function accepts as input the pub_id value of the book that's being edited. Its task is to determine what index in the

DropDownList the specified pub_id resides in. That is, if the book that's being edited has a pub_id field value of 0736 for New Moon Books, the GetSelectedIndex(*publisherID*) function must determine the index of the item in the DropDownList that has the value 0736 (or whose text is New Moon Books).

The GetSelectedIndex(*publisherID*) function can be found spanning line 55 to line 64. Because the DropDownList's SelectedIndex property is an integer property, the GetSelectedIndex(*publisherID*) function returns an integer. To determine the index of the DropDownList item that corresponds to the passed-in pub_id, the GetSelectedIndex(*publisherID*) function iterates through the ddlDataSet that was populated in the GetPublishers() function. Specifically, the ddlDataSet's Publishers DataTable is referenced as a local variable dt (line 58), which is then enumerated over. At each iteration, the passed-in pub_id value is compared to the value of the DataRow's pub_id field. If they match up, the current value of iLoop is immediately returned (line 61).

We can iterate through the DataSet of publishers to determine the index of the DropDownList item that has the corresponding pub_id value because the DropDownList was constructed with the same DataSet from the GetPublishers() function. Hence, the ordering of the rows in ddlDataSet is identical to the ordering of the items in the DropDownList control. The reason the GetPublishers() function used a globally scoped DataSet instead of creating a local DataSet was so that the GetSelectedIndex(*publisherID*) function could access the same DataSet without having to query the database again.

NOTE

Intuitively, it might seem that the GetSelectedIndex(*publisherID*) function should be able to reference the DropDownList in the EditItemTemplate and iterate through its Items collection, rather than using the abstruse DataSet method. However, we cannot use this approach, because when the GetSelectedIndex(*publisherID*) function executes, the actual DropDownList has yet to be added to the DataGrid's row's TableCell. Because it has not been added yet, it cannot yet be referenced.

With the DropDownList's SelectedIndex property properly set, we've completed the first task of providing a customized editing interface. All we have left to do is provide the code to retrieve the value chosen by the user from the editing interface, and update the database with this information. This occurs in the dgTitle_UpdateRow event handler (lines 72–105).

On line 74, the local variable ddlPublishers is used to reference the DropDownList in the editing interface. The FindControl(*controlID*) method we examined earlier is employed here to retrieve the DropDownList. On lines 81 and 82, a parameterized UPDATE statement is provided that updates the particular book's pub_id field. Two SqlParameter objects, pubIDParam and titleIDParam, are created on lines 89 and 90, and their `Value` properties are set on lines 92 and 95. The `pubIDParam`'s `Value` is set to the `Value` of the `SelectedItem` from the DropDownList, while the `Value` of the `titleIDParam` is set to the correct `title_id` field using the `DataKeys` collection. On line 100, the actual SQL `UPDATE` statement is executed, thereby updating the database with the user's edits.

NOTE

Note that the data type of the `pubIDParam` is declared to be of type `char(4)` (line 89), because the foreign key data type is a `char(4)`, not an `int`.

Figure 9.7 contains a screenshot of Listing 9.7 when the Edit button for a particular row is clicked. Note that a DropDownList Web control is provided in the Publisher column's editing interface, and that it defaults to the current publisher of the book whose Edit button was clicked.

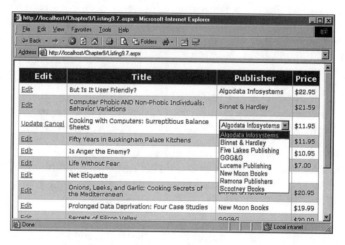

FIGURE 9.7　When edited, the Publisher column is displayed as a data-bound DropDownList of all existing publishers.

Extending the Editing Interface to Allow for NULL Values

When using foreign keys in a database model, sometimes you might want to allow a foreign key to contain NULL values. For example, the `titles` table allows for the `pub_id` column to contain NULLs; books whose `pub_id` is NULL might be books that are still in the conceptual stages and have yet to garnish interest from any particular publisher.

We'd like to be able to extend the code from Listing 9.7 to allow the user to select an option from the DropDownList that corresponds to a NULL value. Perhaps a

DropDownList item might read "No Publisher Yet," or something similar. Similarly, we'd like to be able to display a DropDownList item for those titles whose pub_id field is NULL. With our code in Listing 9.7, there is no way to give a title a NULL-value publisher. Furthermore, there is no way to edit a title that has a NULL-value publisher, because the SQL statement on lines 19–21 in Listing 9.7 uses an INNER JOIN to merge the publisher table with the title table. Because there cannot be a publisher with a NULL pub_id, the INNER JOIN precludes any titles with a NULL-value publisher from ending up in the final resultset.

To enable the user to edit books with NULL publisher values, and to allow a book to be altered to contain a NULL publisher value, we'll have to make the following high-level changes to the code in Listing 9.7:

- The SQL query used for grabbing the DataGrid's data must use a LEFT JOIN to include those titles with a NULL-value publisher.

- The GetPublishers() function must alter the ddlDataSet DataSet so that it includes an additional row for the NULL-value option. This row will need to be given a pub_id and pub_name. The pub_id must be chosen so that it will never conflict with an existing publisher—a value of –1 should suffice. The pub_name used will be "No Publisher Yet."

- The GetSelectedIndex(*publisherID*) function must be updated to accept a parameter of type Object rather than type String. It must also check to see whether the passed-in pub_id is NULL; if it is, it must return the index where the "No Publisher Yet" item was placed in the DropDownList.

- The dgTitle_UpdateRow event handler must check to see whether the user opts for the "No Publisher Yet" option. If this is the case, a different SQL UPDATE statement must be issued that updates the particular titles row with a NULL-valued pub_id.

As you can see, there are quite a number of changes needed to the code in Listing 9.7. Listing 9.8 contains the enhanced code to enable the Publisher column editing interface to support NULL-valued publishers.

LISTING 9.8   The User Can Edit Titles That Have a NULL-Valued Publisher

```
1: <%@ import Namespace="System.Data" %>
2: <%@ import Namespace="System.Data.SqlClient" %>
3: <script runat="server" language="VB">
4:    ' ... The Page_Load, dgTitle_EditRow, and dgTitle_CancelRow
5:      ' ... event handlers have been omitted for brevity.
6:      ' ... Refer back to Listing 9.7 for details ...
7:
```

LISTING 9.8 Continued

```
 8:      Dim ddlDataSet as DataSet = New DataSet()
 9:
10:      Sub BindData()
11:        '1. Create a connection
12:        Const strConnString as String = "server=localhost;uid=sa;pwd=;
➥database=pubs"
13:        Dim objConn as New SqlConnection(strConnString)
14:
15:        '2. Create a command object for the query
16:        Dim strSQL as String = _
17:          "SELECT title_id, title, t.pub_id, p.pub_name,
➥price FROM titles t " & _
18:          "LEFT JOIN publishers p ON t.pub_id = p.pub_id ORDER BY title"
19:        Dim objCmd as New SqlCommand(strSQL, objConn)
20:
21:        objConn.Open()    'Open the connection
22:
23:        'Finally, specify the DataSource and call DataBind()
24:        dgTitle.DataSource = objCmd.ExecuteReader(CommandBehavior.
➥CloseConnection)
25:        dgTitle.DataBind()
26:
27:        objConn.Close()    'Close the connection
28:      End Sub
29:
30:
31:      Function GetPublishers() as DataSet
32:        '1. Create a connection
33:        Const strConnString as String = "server=localhost;uid=sa;pwd=;
➥database=pubs"
34:        Dim objConn as New SqlConnection(strConnString)
35:
36:        '2. Create a command object for the query
37:        Const strSQL as String = _
38:          "SELECT pub_id, pub_name FROM publishers ORDER BY pub_name"
39:
40:        Dim myDataAdapter as SqlDataAdapter
41:        myDataAdapter = New SqlDataAdapter(strSQL, objConn)
42:
43:        'Fill the DataSet
44:        objConn.Open()    'Open the connection
```

LISTING 9.8   Continued

```
45:        myDataAdapter.Fill(ddlDataSet, "Publishers")
46:        objConn.Close()    'Close the connection
47:
48:        'Add the NULL option to the DataSet
49:        Dim dt as DataTable = ddlDataSet.Tables("Publishers")
50:        Dim NULLRow as DataRow = dt.NewRow()
51:        NULLRow("pub_id") = -1
52:        NULLRow("pub_name") = "No Publisher Yet"
53:
54:        dt.Rows.InsertAt(NULLRow, 0)   'Insert the row at the front
55:
56:        Return ddlDataSet 'Return the DataSet
57:    End Function
58:
59:
60:    Function GetSelectedIndex(pub_id as Object) as Integer
61:        If pub_id.Equals(DBNull.Value) then
62:          Return 0
63:        Else
64:          Dim strPubID as String = pub_id.ToString()
65:
66:          'Loop through the DataSet ddlDataSet
67:          Dim iLoop as Integer
68:          Dim dt as DataTable = ddlDataSet.Tables("Publishers")
69:          For iLoop = 0 to dt.Rows.Count - 1
70:            If strPubID = dt.Rows(iLoop)("pub_id").ToString() then
71:              Return iLoop
72:            End If
73:          Next iLoop
74:        End If
75:    End Function
76:
77:    Function EmitPublisherName(pub_name as Object) as String
78:        If pub_name.Equals(DBNull.Value) then
79:          Return "No Publisher Yet"
80:        Else
81:          Return pub_name.ToString()
82:        End If
83:    End Function
84:
85:
```

LISTING 9.8   Continued

```
86:      Sub dgTitle_UpdateRow(sender As Object, e As DataGridCommandEventArgs)
87:          'Get information from columns...
88:          Dim ddlPublishers as DropDownList = e.Item.Cells(2).FindControl
➡️("ddlPublisher")
89:          Dim titleID as String = dgTitle.DataKeys(e.Item.ItemIndex)
90:
91:          'Update the database...
92:          Dim strSQL as String
93:          Dim pubIDParam as New SqlParameter("@pubIDParam", SqlDbType.Char, 4)
94:          Dim titleIDParam as New SqlParameter("@titleIDParam", SqlDbType.
➡️VarChar, 6)
95:          Const strConnString as String = "server=localhost;uid=sa;pwd=;
➡️database=pubs"
96:          Dim objConn as New SqlConnection(strConnString)
97:          Dim objCmd as New SqlCommand()
98:
99:          'Determine if we are dealing with a NULL or not...
100:         If ddlPublishers.SelectedItem.Value = -1 then
101:            'We are dealing with a NULL
102:            strSQL = "UPDATE titles SET pub_id = NULL " & _
103:                     "WHERE title_id = @titleIDParam"
104:         Else
105:            strSQL = "UPDATE titles SET pub_id = @pubIDParam " & _
106:                     "WHERE title_id = @titleIDParam"
107:
108:            pubIDParam.Value = ddlPublishers.SelectedItem.Value
109:            objCmd.Parameters.Add(pubIDParam)
110:         End If
111:
112:         titleIDParam.Value = titleID
113:         objCmd.Parameters.Add(titleIDParam)
114:
115:         objCmd.CommandText = strSQL
116:         objCmd.Connection = objConn
117:
118:         'Issue the SQL command
119:         objConn.Open()
120:         objCmd.ExecuteNonQuery()
121:         objConn.Close()
122:
123:         dgTitle.EditItemIndex = -1
```

LISTING 9.8   Continued

```
124:        BindData()
125:     End Sub
126: </script>
127: <form runat="server">
128:    <asp:DataGrid runat="server" id="dgTitle"
129:        Font-Name="Verdana" Font-Size="9pt" CellPadding="5"
130:        AlternatingItemStyle-BackColor="#dddddd"
131:        AutoGenerateColumns="False" DataKeyField="title_id"
132:        OnEditCommand="dgTitle_EditRow"
133:        OnUpdateCommand="dgTitle_UpdateRow"
134:        OnCancelCommand="dgTitle_CancelRow">
135:
136:      <HeaderStyle BackColor="Navy" ForeColor="White" Font-Size="13pt"
137:              Font-Bold="True" HorizontalAlign="Center" />
138:
139:      <Columns>
140:        <asp:EditCommandColumn ButtonType="LinkButton" HeaderText="Edit"
141:            EditText="Edit" UpdateText="Update" CancelText="Cancel" />
142:        <asp:BoundColumn DataField="title"
143:                HeaderText="Title" ReadOnly="True" />
144:        <asp:TemplateColumn HeaderText="Publisher">
145:          <ItemTemplate>
146:            <%# EmitPublisherName(DataBinder.Eval(Container.DataItem,
➥"pub_name")) %>
147:          </ItemTemplate>
148:          <EditItemTemplate>
149:            <asp:DropDownList id="ddlPublisher" runat="server"
150:                DataTextField="pub_name"
151:                DataValueField="pub_id"
152:                DataSource="<%# GetPublishers() %>"
153:                SelectedIndex='<%# GetSelectedIndex(Container.DataItem
➥("pub_id")) %>'>
154:            </asp:DropDownList>
155:          </EditItemTemplate>
156:        </asp:TemplateColumn>
157:        <asp:BoundColumn DataField="price" DataFormatString="{0:c}"
158:                HeaderText="Price" ReadOnly="True" />
159:      </Columns>
160:    </asp:DataGrid>
161: </form>
```

The SQL query that populated our DataGrid in Listing 9.7 did not include those titles whose pub_id was NULL because an INNER JOIN was used, and there are no publishers with a NULL pub_id value. To be able to retrieve those titles that have a pub_id field with the value NULL, we need to use a LEFT JOIN, as opposed to an INNER JOIN, for the SQL query that populates the DataGrid. The BindData() subroutine in Listing 9.8 has been altered to use this new SQL statement (lines 16–18).

> **NOTE**
>
> A LEFT JOIN returns *all* rows from the left table in the join (titles), regardless of whether there's a matching publishers.pub_id for the titles.pub_id. For more information on LEFT JOINs and RIGHT JOINs, see the links in the "On the Web" section at the end of this chapter.

Although this SQL query will retrieve all the titles, the value of the returned pub_name field will be NULL for those titles that have a NULL value for pub_id. Because this is the field we are displaying in the DataGrid's Publisher column, we need to update the Publisher column's ItemTemplate. If we fail to update the ItemTemplate, those titles that have the value NULL for pub_id will display a blank string for the Publisher name. Rather than having a blank string displayed, we'd like to have a message No Publisher Yet displayed.

To accomplish this, let's update the Publisher column's ItemTemplate to call a custom function. On line 146, the data-binding syntax has been changed from Listing 9.7 from

```
<%# DataBinder.Eval(Container.DataItem, pub_name) %>
```

to

```
<%# EmitPublisherName(DataBinder.Eval(Container.DataItem, "pub_name")) %>
```

The EmitPublisherName(*pubName*) is a function we must write and include in the code section for our ASP.NET page. This function needs to accept an input parameter of type Object, because we don't know if the value returned by DataBinder.Eval(Container.DataItem, "pub_name") will be a string value or a DbNull value.

The EmitPublisherName(*pubName*) function (lines 77–83) is fairly simple. It checks to see whether the pass-in Object parameter is equal to the type DBNull (line 78). If it is, it returns the string No Publisher Yet. If the Object parameter is not NULL, we know it contains the name of the book's publisher and can simply return this string (line 81).

The next task we are faced with involves updating the GetPublishers() function so that the ddlDataSet DataSet has a new row added to it that represents the NULL option. Recall that the `ddlDataSet` DataSet is the specified `DataSource` for the data-bound DropDownList in the Publisher column's editing interface. Because we want this DropDownList to include an item for the NULL option, we must add an appropriate record to the `ddlDataSet` DataSet prior to returning the DataSet.

This is accomplished on lines 49 through 54. The `DataTable` of the DataSet is referenced on line 49, and a new `DataRow` is created on line 50. The pub_id and pub_name fields are then set in line 51 and 52, respectively. Finally, the row is added to the front of the `DataTable`'s `Rows` collection on line 54.

At this point, we have altered the DropDownList in the Publisher column's editing interface to include an option for the user to specify that a book should have a NULL value for the pub_id field. However, we also need to update the `GetSelectedIndex(`*`publisherID`*`)` function. In Listing 9.7, this function accepted a single input parameter of type String because it expected a valid pub_id of type char(4). However, we need to accept an input parameter of type Object in case the pub_id value is NULL.

The updated `GetSelectedIndex(`*`publisherID`*`)` function can be found starting a line 60. Note that its input parameter, pub_id, is of type Object. On line 61, we check to see whether this input parameter is of type `DBNull`. If it is, we return 0, because the `No Publisher Yet` option is the first option in the DropDownList. (The reason the `No Publisher Yet` option is the first option in the DropDownList is because in the `GetPublishers()` function, we added this option as the first row in the DataSet's Publishers `DataTable`.) If, however, the pub_id input parameter is not NULL, we convert it to an `Int32` (line 64) and then use the code we used earlier to iterate through the `ddlDataSet` DataSet.

The final change we need to implement to support NULL-value pub_id fields is updating the `dgTitle_UpdateRow` event handler so that it is able to update the database with a NULL value for pub_id. We need to issue one of two SQL UPDATE statements, depending on whether the user has set the Publisher column's DropDownList to the NULL option. If the Publisher column's DropDownList has been set to the NULL option, the `Value` of the DropDownList's `SelectedItem` will be –1. On line 100 we check to see whether this is the case. If the `Value` is –1, the user wants to set the title's pub_id to NULL. That is, the "No Publisher Yet" item from the DropDownList has been selected.

In this event, we use the SQL UPDATE statement defined on lines 102 and 103. If, on the other hand, the user has set the book's pub_id field to a specific publisher, we need to use a SQL UPDATE statement that has a parameter for the pub_id. The SQL UPDATE statement on lines 105 and 106 is identical to the SQL UPDATE statement in the `dgTitle_UpdateRow` event handler of Listing 9.7. On line 108, the `SqlParameter` pubIDParam has its `Value` set to the `Value` of the DropDownList's `SelectedItem`; on line 109, the pubIDParam is added to the `Parameters` collection of the `objCmd` object.

The remainder of the dgTitle_UpdateRow event handler simply issues the SQL UPDATE statement (lines 112–121) and returns the DataGrid to its pre-edited state (lines 123 and 124).

Figure 9.8 contains a screenshot of Listing 9.8 when viewed through a browser. Specifically, Figure 9.8 captures the screen after the user has clicked Edit for a particular row. Note that the DropDownList in the Publisher column for the row being edited contains the "No Publisher Yet" option. Furthermore, books that are not being edited and have a NULL-value publisher show the text No Publisher Yet in their Publisher column.

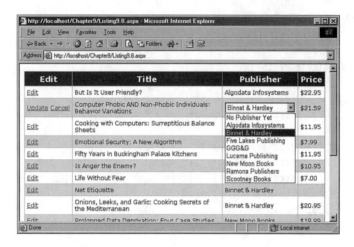

FIGURE 9.8   The DropDownList includes a "No Publisher Yet" option.

Adding Validation Controls to the Editing Interface

In the examples we have seen in this chapter, we have omitted any kind of form field validation. With ASP.NET, form validation is quite easy thanks to the powerful validation Web controls; however, how can we add these validation controls to the editing interfaces of an editable DataGrid? Unfortunately, we cannot add validation controls to the default DataGrid editing interface—we must instead supply a customized editing interface.

For example, in Listing 9.4 we used a DataGrid to display the information from the Comments database table. The DataGrid's Comment column had a customized editing interface that utilized a multiline TextBox. (Refer back to Figure 9.5 for a screenshot of the multiline TextBox in action.) We might want to require the user to enter a value for this multiline TextBox. That is, if the user clicks the Update button, we don't want to permit the update unless the user has supplied a value for the Comment field.

Adding form field validation to a customized editing interface is quite simple and involves two straightforward steps. First, we have to add the appropriate validation control (or controls) to the particular column's EditItemTemplate. For example, to require that the user supply a value for the Comment field, we'd want to add a RequiredFieldValidator validation control to the Comment column's editing interface, like so:

```
<asp:DataGrid runat="server" id="dgComments" ... >
  <Columns>

    ...

    <asp:TemplateColumn HeaderText="Comment">
      <ItemTemplate>
        <%# DataBinder.Eval(Container.DataItem, "Comment") %>
      </ItemTemplate>
      <EditItemTemplate>
        <asp:TextBox runat="server" id="txtComment" TextMode="MultiLine"
                Columns="40" Rows="6" MaxLength="255"
                Text='<%# DataBinder.Eval(Container.DataItem, "Comment") %>' />

        <asp:RequiredFieldValidator runat="server"
                ControlToValidate="txtComment" Display="Dynamic"
                ErrorMessage="<br /><i>You must provide a Comment.</i>" />
      </EditItemTemplate>
    </asp:TemplateColumn>

    ...

  </Columns>
</asp:DataGrid>
```

Note that we added a RequiredFieldValidator and set its ControlToValidate property to the ID of the multiline TextBox also defined in the EditItemTemplate.

To complete this exercise, we need to add one more line of code. In the event handler that fires when the Update button is clicked, we need to add a line that will check to see whether the Page.IsValid property is False. If this property is False, it indicates that a validation control on the page contains an invalid value. If this is the case, rather than updating the database and resetting the DataGrid to its pre-editing state, the event handler must simply exit. This can be accomplished by adding the following line of code to the proper event handler:

```
Sub dgComments_UpdateRow(sender As Object, e As DataGridCommandEventArgs)
  If Not Page.IsValid Then Return False

  ...
End Sub
```

It is vital that this line of code be included for the validation to work for down-level browsers. Validation Web controls utilize client-side validation code for up-level browsers, but not for down-level browsers. Therefore, if a user is visiting with a down-level browser and you omit the `Page.IsValid` check from the Update button event handler, the user will be able to update the database using a blank value for the `Comment` field.

If this sounds a bit confusing, you can see what I mean by omitting the preceding line from the Update button event handler and then setting the `@Page` directive's `ClientTarget` attribute to `DownLevel`, as was discussed in Chapter 3. You'll notice that without the `Page.IsValid` check in the Update button's event handler, you can enter a blank value into the `Comment` TextBox and have the data updated in the database when clicking the Update button.

NOTE

Up-level browsers will enjoy the benefits of client-side validation. If a user with an up-level browser fails to enter a value for the `Comment` TextBox, an error message will dynamically appear when she clicks the Update button without requiring a postback.

Listing 9.9 contains code updated from Listing 9.4 that provides a RequiredFieldValidator for the `Comment` column's multiline TextBox. (The majority of the code in Listing 9.9 has been omitted because it is identical to that in Listing 9.4.) Figure 9.9 contains a screenshot of the code in Listing 9.9 when the user clicks the Update button after not having entered a value into the `Comment` TextBox.

LISTING 9.9   A RequiredFieldValidator Ensures That the User Enters a Value for the Comment Column's TextBox

```
 1: <%@ import Namespace="System.Data" %>
 2: <%@ import Namespace="System.Data.SqlClient" %>
 3: <script runat="server" language="VB">
 4: '  ... The Page_Load, dgComments_EditRow, and dgComments_CancelRow event
 5: '  ... handlers have been omitted for brevity.  Also, the BindData()
 6: '  ... subroutine has been omitted.  Refer back to Listing 9.4  ...
 7:
 8:    Sub dgComments_UpdateRow(sender As Object, e As DataGridCommandEventArgs)
 9:       'Make sure the Page is Valid!
10:       If Not Page.IsValid then Exit Sub
11:
12:       '  ... The remainder of the dgComments_UpdateRow event handler
13:       '  ... can be found in Listing 9.4 ...
14:    End Sub
```

LISTING 9.9   Continued

```
15: </script>
16: <form runat="server">
17:   <asp:DataGrid runat="server" id="dgComments"
18:       Font-Name="Verdana" Font-Size="9pt" CellPadding="5"
19:       AlternatingItemStyle-BackColor="#dddddd"
20:       AutoGenerateColumns="False" DataKeyField="CommentID"
21:       OnEditCommand="dgComments_EditRow"
22:       OnUpdateCommand="dgComments_UpdateRow"
23:       OnCancelCommand="dgComments_CancelRow">
24:
25:     <HeaderStyle BackColor="Navy" ForeColor="White" Font-Size="13pt"
26:              Font-Bold="True" HorizontalAlign="Center" />
27:
28:     <Columns>
29:       <asp:EditCommandColumn ButtonType="LinkButton" HeaderText="Edit"
30:            EditText="Edit" UpdateText="Update" CancelText="Cancel" />
31:       <asp:BoundColumn DataField="CommentID"
32:                HeaderText="Comment ID" ReadOnly="True" />
33:       <asp:BoundColumn DataField="Name" HeaderText="Name" />
34:       <asp:TemplateColumn HeaderText="Comment">
35:         <ItemTemplate>
36:           <%# DataBinder.Eval(Container.DataItem, "Comment") %>
37:         </ItemTemplate>
38:         <EditItemTemplate>
39:           <asp:TextBox runat="server" id="txtComment" TextMode="MultiLine"
40:                  Columns="40" Rows="6" MaxLength="255"
41:                  Text='<%# DataBinder.Eval(Container.DataItem,
➥"Comment") %>' />
42:
43:             <asp:RequiredFieldValidator runat="server"
44:                  ControlToValidate="txtComment" Display="Dynamic"
45:                  ErrorMessage="<br /><i>You must provide a Comment.</i>" />
46:         </EditItemTemplate>
47:       </asp:TemplateColumn>
48:       <asp:BoundColumn DataField="DateAdded" HeaderText="Date Added"
49:                ReadOnly="True" />
50:     </Columns>
51:   </asp:DataGrid>
52: </form>
```

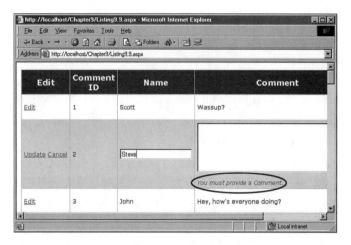

FIGURE 9.9   An error message is displayed if the user clicks the Update button without supplying a value for the Comment TextBox.

Summary

In this chapter, we examined the DataGrid's built-in editing functionality. When using the DataGrid's editing functionality, an EditCommandColumn column needs to be added to the DataGrid; this special column type adds an Edit button next to each row. When the Edit button is clicked, the ASP.NET Web page is posted back and the DataGrid's EditCommand event is fired. We then need to provide an event handler for the event that sets the DataGrid's EditItemIndex property to the index of the row we want to edit. Doing this transforms the particular row into an editable row, converting the Edit button to Update and Cancel buttons, and converting each column in the row into the column's editing interface.

By default, a column's editing interface is a simple TextBox. However, we can specify a customized editing interface in the EditItemTemplate of a TemplateColumn. For example, in this chapter, we saw how to add a multiline TextBox, a Calendar control, and a data-bound DropDownList to the editing interface of various columns in a DataGrid. Additionally, we examined how to add validation controls to the interface.

In the next chapter, we will meld the lessons learned in this chapter and the last two. We will see how, using just a DataGrid, we can create a user interface that supports sorting and paging through data, as well as adding, editing, and deleting information!

On the Web

For more information on the topics discussed in this chapter, consider perusing the following online resources:

- "An Extensive Examination of the DataGrid Web Control: Employing Simple Editing"—http://aspnet.4guysfromrolla.com/articles/071002-1.aspx

- "DataGrid In-Place Editing"—http://msdn.microsoft.com/msdnmag/issues/01/06/cutting/cutting0106.asp

- "The Calendar Web Control"—http://samples.gotdotnet.com/quickstart/aspplus/samples/webforms/ctrlref/webctrl/calendar/doc_cal.aspx

- "Referential Integrity in SQL Server"—http://www.sqlmag.com/Articles/Index.cfm?ArticleID=8687

- "An Extensive Examination of the DataGrid Web Control: Editing Data with Foreign Keys"—http://aspnet.4guysfromrolla.com/articles/080702-1.aspx

- "Additional Criteria in the JOIN Clause"—http://sqlteam.com/item.asp?ItemID=11122

- "Server Control Form Validation"—http://docs.aspng.com/quickstart/aspplus/doc/webvalidation.aspx

10

Putting It All Together: A Real-World Example

In the past three chapters, we have examined how to use the DataGrid's sorting, pagination, and editing features. In each chapter, however, we studied these features independent of one another; that is, in the chapter on pagination, we did not examine how to enable the user to sort the data being paged through. In this chapter, we will tie together the concepts discussed in the last three chapters, building a rich ASP.NET Web page that will enable an administrative user to edit and delete data, as well as page and sort through the existing data.

This chapter intends to present a real-world example of using the DataGrid Web control and its impressive feature set. We will focus on using the lessons learned in the previous chapters in unison to provide a very powerful, robust, and useful ASP.NET Web page.

An Overview on Providing Sorting, Paging, and Data Modification Features for a Single DataGrid

Adding sorting, paging, or editing features to a DataGrid usually involves a few simple steps. For example, to sort the contents of a DataGrid, we set the DataGrid's `AllowSorting` property to `True` and provide an event handler for the DataGrid's `SortCommand` event. To include pagination support, we set the DataGrid's `AllowPaging` property to `True` and provide an event handler for the DataGrid's `PageIndexChanged` event.

Adding both sorting and pagination abilities to one DataGrid is, unfortunately, not as simple as just setting the

`AllowSorting` and `AllowPaging` properties to `True` and writing the two needed event handlers. Instead, a bit more care needs to be taken. For example, as we saw in Chapter 7, "Sorting the DataGrid's Data," typically when sorting, we include a modified version of the `BindData()` subroutine—`BindData(sortExpression)`—that takes a string input parameter that specifies what column of the DataGrid to sort the contents on. However, with the pagination examples, we used the parameter-less version of `BindData()`. This is one example where we must take care when providing multiple features for a single DataGrid.

In this chapter we will look first at creating a DataGrid that supports both sorting and pagination. After we have accomplished this, we'll examine how to also allow the data to be modified (edited and deleted).

Providing Sorting and Pagination Support in a Single DataGrid

When building a DataGrid that supports multiple features, I find that it helps to start by implementing one feature completely before beginning to tackle the next one. This approach works well when implementing features that are not dependent on one another. However, in the previous section I forewarned that the sorting, paging, and data modification functionalities were not independent—you cannot simply add one feature on top of the other without any changes and expect it to work.

Given this, you might be quite perplexed as to why I am planning to tackle these features one at a time. The reason is because these features, while somewhat dependent, are more independent than not. Furthermore, it has been my personal experience that in real-world settings, you might be asked to implement a particular feature (say, pagination support), and it's not until after you complete the task that you are requested to add another, potentially dependent feature (such as sorting). Therefore, I think it will be worthwhile to approach this problem in this manner.

Having said that, let's start by creating a DataGrid that will display the contents of the `Comment table` and provide pagination support. (Recall that we examined the `Comments` database table in Chapter 8, "Providing DataGrid Pagination," and Chapter 9, "Editing the DataGrid Web Control.") As we saw in Chapter 8, you can provide pagination support either through the DataGrid's default paging or through custom paging.

With default paging, the complete data that is to be paged through must be loaded into an object that implements the `ICollection` interface, such as the DataSet. When the DataGrid is rendered, only a portion of this data is displayed. The portion being displayed is dependent upon what page of data the user is viewing and how many records per page are being displayed. The downside of default paging is that each time the user steps through a page of data, the *entire* contents of the data being paged through must be retrieved from the database.

Custom paging, on the other hand, circumvents this extraneous data retrieval by allowing only those specific records to be displayed on the current DataGrid page to be retrieved from the database. As we saw in Chapter 8, retrieving the correct subset of rows from the database can be a bit tricky. One approach is to implement a stored procedure that builds a temporary table and completely copies the data being paged through into this temporary table. Then it can selectively pick out the rows that the DataGrid needs to display, and send only these rows to the ASP.NET Web page. If the data being displayed has an auto-incremented primary key value, the primary key method can be employed to provide pagination.

Intuitively, you might opt to provide pagination support using the primary key method, as we did in the "Retrieving Only the Needed Records Using Primary Key Values" section in Chapter 8. This method is the most efficient in terms of retrieving only the records needed and not succumbing to unneeded copying, as with the stored procedure method. Unfortunately, the primary key method cannot be used when we want to include sorting support as well. If you were to do so, to also add sorting support for the DataGrid, you would need to redo the paging, either using the stored procedure method or the DataGrid's default paging.

The custom paging primary key method will not work with sorting because the data must be displayed in order of its primary key values for the primary key approach to work. That is, if we want to provide pagination for data that has an integer, auto-increment, primary key field, the data must be displayed in order of either increasing or decreasing primary key values. Recall that when using the primary key method, we determined the subset of records to retrieve for the next or previous page by examining the primary key value of the first or last row in the DataGrid for the current page. If the data is not sorted by this primary key value, we cannot use this logic. Therefore, we cannot provide both sorting and pagination when using the primary key method for custom paging because the user can't sort on any DataGrid column other than the one that contains the primary key value.

The stored procedure method for pagination can be used in tandem with sorting, but it is not very pretty code. Specifically, the stored procedure must accept an additional input parameter: the name of the field to sort by. When issuing the INSERT statement to populate the temporary table, a SQL dynamic statement must be created that sorts on the field passed in by the user. This dynamic SQL statement can be executed using the EXEC function.

NOTE

For more information on executing dynamic SQL statements in a stored procedure, consult the references in the "On the Web" section at the end of this chapter.

Rather than bog ourselves down with the stored procedure method details, we'll use the DataGrid's default paging method. Although this isn't the optimal approach, it is the easiest and quickest.

Adding Pagination Support

Having decided to implement pagination support for our DataGrid using the default DataGrid paging method, we're ready to examine the code for a pageable DataGrid that displays the contents of the Comment table 10 records at a time. Listing 10.1 contains the necessary code and DataGrid declaration. The Next/Previous hyperlinks paging interface is used in Listing 10.1, although the list of hyperlinks paging interface could also have been used. In addition to the standard pagination, the user is shown a helpful message indicating what page of data is being viewed, and how many total pages the data is divided up into.

LISTING 10.1   A DataGrid with Pagination Support

```
 1: <%@ import Namespace="System.Data" %>
 2: <%@ import Namespace="System.Data.SqlClient" %>
 3: <script runat="server" language="VB">
 4:     Sub Page_Load(sender as Object, e as EventArgs)
 5:       If Not Page.IsPostBack then
 6:         BindData()
 7:       End If
 8:     End Sub
 9:
10:
11:     Sub BindData()
12:       '1. Create a connection
13:       Const strConnString as String = "server=localhost;uid=sa;pwd=;
➥database=pubs"
14:       Dim objConn as New SqlConnection(strConnString)
15:
16:       '2. Create a command object for the query
17:       Dim strSQL as String
18:       strSQL = "SELECT CommentID, Name, Comment, DateAdded " & _
19:               "FROM Comments"
20:
21:       Dim objCmd as New SqlCommand(strSQL, objConn)
22:
23:       '3. Create a DataAdapter and Fill the DataSet
24:       Dim objDA as New SqlDataAdapter()
25:       objDA.SelectCommand = objCmd
26:
```

LISTING 10.1   Continued

```
27:        objConn.Open()
28:
29:        Dim objDS as DataSet = New DataSet()
30:        objDA.Fill(objDS, "titles")
31:
32:        objConn.Close()
33:
34:        'Finally, specify the DataSource and call DataBind()
35:        dgComments.DataSource = objDS
36:        dgComments.DataBind()
37:
38:        objConn.Close()    'Close the connection
39:
40:        ShowPageInformation()
41:     End Sub
42:
43:
44:     Sub ShowPageInformation()
45:        'This sub displays paging information in the appropriate label
46:        lblPagingInfo.Text = "Displaying Page " & _
47:            (dgComments.CurrentPageIndex+1).ToString() & " of " & _
48:            dgComments.PageCount
49:     End Sub
50:
51:
52:     Sub dgComments_Paging(sender As Object, e As DataGridPageChangedEventArgs)
53:        dgComments.CurrentPageIndex = e.NewPageIndex
54:        BindData()
55:     End Sub
56: </script>
57:
58: <form runat="server">
59:   <asp:DataGrid runat="server" id="dgComments"
60:        Font-Name="Verdana" Font-Size="9pt" CellPadding="5"
61:        AlternatingItemStyle-BackColor="#dddddd"
62:        AutoGenerateColumns="False" Width="75%"
63:        PageSize="10" AllowPaging="True"
64:        OnPageIndexChanged="dgComments_Paging">
65:
66:     <HeaderStyle BackColor="Navy" ForeColor="White" Font-Size="13pt"
67:             Font-Bold="True" HorizontalAlign="Center" />
68:
```

LISTING 10.1   Continued

```
69:      <PagerStyle BackColor="Navy" ForeColor="White" Font-Size="8pt"
70:              Font-Bold="True" HorizontalAlign="Right"
71:              NextPageText="Next >" PrevPageText="< Prev" />
72:
73:      <Columns>
74:        <asp:BoundColumn DataField="Name" HeaderText="Name"
75:            SortExpression="Name" />
76:        <asp:BoundColumn DataField="Comment" HeaderText="Comment"
77:            SortExpression="Comment" />
78:        <asp:BoundColumn DataField="DateAdded" HeaderText="Date Added"
79:            SortExpression="DateAdded"
80:            ItemStyle-HorizontalAlign="Center" DataFormatString="{0:d}" />
81:      </Columns>
82:    </asp:DataGrid>
83:    <asp:label id="lblPagingInfo" runat="server" Font-Name="Verdana"
84:       Font-Size="9pt" Font-Italic="True" Width="75%" HorizontalAlign="Right" />
85: </form>
```

Although Listing 10.1 contains 85 lines of code and DataGrid declaration content, the majority of it is code we've examined before. Recall that to provide pagination support, we must set the DataGrid's `AllowSorting` property to `True`, which is done on line 63. Next, we must provide an event handler for the DataGrid's `PaegIndexChanged` event. On line 64, we wire this event to the event handler `dgComments_Paging`.

Paging using the DataGrid's default paging is fairly simple and straightforward. In the `dgComments_Paging` event handler (lines 52–55) we specify what page of data the user wants to view by setting the DataGrid's `CurrentPageIndex` property to the value of the `NewPageIndex` property of the event handler's `DataGridPageChangedEventArgs` parameter (line 53). Next, the `BindData()` subroutine is called (line 54).

The `BindData()` subroutine (lines 11–41) fills a DataSet with the entire results of the SQL query that the user can page through; namely, all the records in the `Comment` table (see lines 18 and 19). This DataSet is then assigned to the DataGrid's `DataSource` property (line 35) and the DataGrid's `DataBind()` method is called (line 36).

Note that in addition to performing these tasks, the `BindData()` subroutine also makes a call to the `ShowPageInformation()` subroutine (line 40). The `ShowPageInformation()` subroutine (lines 44–49) displays a message indicating what page of data the user is currently viewing, and the total number of pages. It accomplishes this by setting the `Text` property of the Label `lblPagingInfo` to a string that includes the `CurrentPageIndex` and `PageCount` properties of the DataGrid. The `lblPageInfo` Label is defined in the HTML section on lines 83 and 84.

NOTE

Note that in the `ShowPageInformation()` subroutine we display the current page of data the user is viewing by emitting the value of the DataGrid's `CurrentPageIndex` property plus 1 (see line 47). The reason we add 1 to the value of the `CurrentPageIndex` property is because the `CurrentPageIndex` property is indexed at zero, meaning when the user is viewing the first page of data, `CurrentPageIndex` equals zero. By adding 1, the user is shown a message such as "Displaying Page 1 of 6" instead of "Displaying Page 0 of 6."

A screenshot of the code in Listing 10.1 can be seen in Figure 10.1. Note that with our inclusion of the `lblPageInfo` Label and `ShowPageInformation()` subroutine, the user is shown a message indicating what page of data she's viewing and how many total pages of data exist.

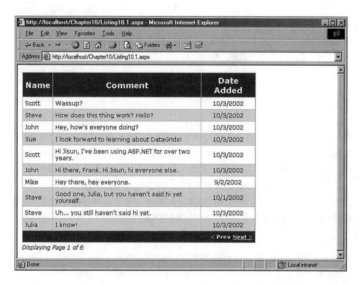

FIGURE 10.1   The user can page through the contents of the `Comment` table.

Adding Sorting Support to a Pageable DataGrid

Now that we have a DataGrid with paging support, let's see what we need to do to also include sorting support. In the code examples in Chapter 7, where we discussed the DataGrid's sorting features, we used a modified version of the `BindData()` subroutine we've been using throughout this book. Specifically, our `BindData()` subroutine accepted a string input parameter, *sortExpression*, which indicated the

field by which to order the SQL results. With this version of the
BindData(*sortExpression*) subroutine, the code to provide sorting is trivial. All we
have to do is set the DataGrid's AllowSorting property to True and provide an event
handler for the DataGrid's SortCommand event. This event handler need only call the
BindData(*sortExpression*) subroutine, passing in the value of the SortExpression
the user wants to sort by. (For a sorting code example, refer back to Chapter 7.)

To add sorting to a DataGrid that already supports pagination, we must alter the
BindData() subroutine used by the pageable DataGrid so that it accepts a
sortExpression input parameter. This modified BindData(*sortExpression*) subroutine would look identical to the original BindData() subroutine, save for one important difference: the SQL query would contain an ORDER BY clause based on the
sortExpression parameter. For example, the new BindData(*sortExpression*)
subroutine might look like this:

```
Sub BindData(sortExpr as String)
    ...

    Dim strSQL as String
    strSQL = "SELECT CommentID, Name, Comment, DateAdded " & _
             "FROM Comments ORDER BY " & sortExpr


    ...
End Sub
```

In addition to this small change in the BindData() subroutine, the code from Listing
10.1 will need to have its Page_Load and dgComments_Paging event handlers updated,
because two event handlers call the BindData() subroutine (see lines 6 and 54 in
Listing 10.1). In the Page_Load event handler, we might opt to replace the call to
BindData() with a call to BindData("DateAdded ASC"), which will have the data in
the DataGrid initially ordered by the DateAdded field in chronologically increasing
order.

But what parameter value do we pass into the new BindData(*sortExpression*)
subroutine from the dgComments_Paging event handler? Imagine that the user has
first visited the page, meaning we want to sort the results by CommentID in ascending
order. When the user clicks the Next hyperlink to view the second page of data, we
need to have the BindData(*sortExpression*) subroutine grab the data in the correct
order—that is, we still must sort by DateAdded in ascending order. Similarly, if a user
clicks the hyperlink in a particular DataGrid's column's header to sort by that particular column, each time the user pages through the data, the dgComments_Paging
event handler is executed, which must call the BindData(*sortExpression*) subroutine passing in the proper sort expression.

To know the proper sort expression to pass into the BindData(*sortExpression*) subroutine from the dgComments_Paging event handler, we must have some way of saving the current sort expression across postbacks. Sounds like a job for a ViewState variable!

Each time the user opts to sort on a particular column, our code must set some ViewState variable to the SortExpression property of the sorted column. Then, in the dgComments_Paging event handler, the call to BindData(*sortExpression*) must pass in the value of this ViewState variable. When the user is paging through the data, the ordering of the data can be "remembered" across postbacks in this manner. Listing 10.2 contains the source code for a DataGrid that supports both paging and sorting.

LISTING 10.2   This DataGrid Provides Both Pagination and Sorting Capabilities

```
 1: <%@ import Namespace="System.Data" %>
 2: <%@ import Namespace="System.Data.SqlClient" %>
 3: <script runat="server" language="VB">
 4: ' ... The ShowPageInformation() subroutine has been omitted for brevity ...
 5:   ' ... Refer back to Listing 10.1 for its details ...
 6:
 7:    Sub Page_Load(sender as Object, e as EventArgs)
 8:      If Not Page.IsPostBack then
 9:        ViewState("SortExpr") = "DateAdded ASC"
10:        BindData(ViewState("SortExpr"))
11:      End If
12:    End Sub
13:
14:
15:    Sub BindData(sortExpr as String)
16:      '1. Create a connection
17:      Const strConnString as String = "server=localhost;uid=sa;pwd=;
➥database=pubs"
18:      Dim objConn as New SqlConnection(strConnString)
19:
20:      '2. Create a command object for the query
21:      Dim strSQL as String
22:      strSQL = "SELECT CommentID, Name, Comment, DateAdded " & _
23:              "FROM Comments ORDER BY " & sortExpr
24:
25:      Dim objCmd as New SqlCommand(strSQL, objConn)
26:
27:      '3. Create a DataAdapter and Fill the DataSet
```

LISTING 10.2   Continued

```
28:         Dim objDA as New SqlDataAdapter()
29:         objDA.SelectCommand = objCmd
30:
31:         objConn.Open()
32:
33:         Dim objDS as DataSet = New DataSet()
34:         objDA.Fill(objDS, "titles")
35:
36:         objConn.Close()
37:
38:         'Finally, specify the DataSource and call DataBind()
39:         dgComments.DataSource = objDS
40:         dgComments.DataBind()
41:
42:         objConn.Close()    'Close the connection
43:
44:         ShowPageInformation()
45:       End Sub
46:
47:
48:       Sub dgComments_Paging(sender As Object, e As
        ➥DataGridPageChangedEventArgs)
49:         dgComments.CurrentPageIndex = e.NewPageIndex
50:         BindData(ViewState("SortExpr"))
51:       End Sub
52:
53:
54:       Sub dgComments_Sorting(sender as Object, e as
        ➥DataGridSortCommandEventArgs)
55:         'Set the sortExpr ViewState variable accordingly
56:         ViewState("SortExpr") = e.SortExpression
57:
58:         'Reset the data to show the FIRST page of data
59:         dgComments.CurrentPageIndex = 0
60:
61:         'Bind the data!
62:         BindData(ViewState("SortExpr"))
63:       End Sub
64:
65: </script>
66: <form runat="server">
```

LISTING 10.2   Continued

```
67:    <asp:DataGrid runat="server" id="dgComments"
68:       Font-Name="Verdana" Font-Size="9pt" CellPadding="5"
69:       AlternatingItemStyle-BackColor="#dddddd"
70:       AutoGenerateColumns="False" Width="75%"
71:       PageSize="10" AllowPaging="True"
72:       OnPageIndexChanged="dgComments_Paging"
73:       AllowSorting="True" OnSortCommand="dgComments_Sorting">
74:
75:       <HeaderStyle BackColor="Navy" ForeColor="White" Font-Size="13pt"
76:                Font-Bold="True" HorizontalAlign="Center" />
77:
78:       <PagerStyle BackColor="Navy" ForeColor="White" Font-Size="8pt"
79:                Font-Bold="True" HorizontalAlign="Right"
80:                NextPageText="Next >" PrevPageText="< Prev" />
81:
82:       <Columns>
83:         <asp:BoundColumn DataField="Name" HeaderText="Name"
84:             SortExpression="Name" />
85:         <asp:BoundColumn DataField="Comment" HeaderText="Comment"
86:             SortExpression="Comment" />
87:         <asp:BoundColumn DataField="DateAdded" HeaderText="Date Added"
88:             SortExpression="DateAdded"
89:             ItemStyle-HorizontalAlign="Center" DataFormatString="{0:d}" />
90:       </Columns>
91:    </asp:DataGrid>
92:    <asp:label id="lblPagingInfo" runat="server" Font-Name="Verdana"
93:       Font-Size="9pt" Font-Italic="True" Width="75%" HorizontalAlign="Right" />
94: </form>
```

The code in Listing 10.2 builds upon the code presented in Listing 10.1 by adding sorting support to the DataGrid. Recall that to provide sorting support, the DataGrid's AllowSorting property must be set to True, and an event handler for the DataGrid's SortCommand event must be specified (line 73). Additionally, when explicitly listing the DataGrid columns in a Columns tag, as is the case here (lines 82–90), those columns that are sortable must have their SortExpression property provided (see lines 84, 86, and 88). As discussed in Chapter 7, when a particular DataGrid column's sorting hyperlink is clicked, the ASP.NET Web page is posted back and the DataGrid's SortCommand event is fired, causing the specified event handler to fire (dgComments_Sorting in Listing 10.2, lines 54–63). The event handler is passed a DataGridSortCommandEventArgs parameter that includes a SortExpression property. The value of this parameter's SortExpression property is assigned the

`SortExpression` property value of the DataGrid column whose sorting hyperlink was clicked.

To enable both paging and sorting support for a DataGrid, the `BindData()` subroutine from Listing 10.1 has to be updated to accept an input parameter. The updated version, `BindData(sortExpression)`, is included in Listing 10.2 and can be found spanning line 15 to line 45. This subroutine is essentially the same as it was in Listing 10.1, except for one very important part—the SQL query, constructed on lines 22 and 23, orders the query results by the field specified by the *sortExpression* parameter.

With this altered `BindData(sortExpression)` subroutine, the event handlers that call the subroutine must be updated so that they pass in a parameter to sort the results by. The `Page_Load` event handler (lines 7–12) passes in the value `DateAdded ASC`, which initially sorts the comments by the date they were made in chronologically increasing order. Note that the `ViewState` variable `SortExpr` is assigned the value `DateAdded ASC` (line 9). Recall from our discussion prior to Listing 10.2 that we need to be able to persist the sort expression across postbacks to the page, which we accomplish by using a `ViewState` variable. The `dgComments_Paging` event handler, which fires every time the user navigates from one page to another, sets the DataGrid's `CurrentPageIndex` property on line 49, as it did in Listing 10.1, and then calls the `BindData(sortExpression)` subroutine, passing in as the *sortExpression* the value of the `ViewState` variable `SortExpr` (line 50) .

Finally, an event handler for the DataGrid's `SortCommand` event is needed. This event handler, `dgComments_Sorting` (lines 54–63), assigns the new `SortExpression` value to `ViewState("SortExpr")` (line 56), sets the DataGrid's `CurrentPageIndex` property to 0 (line 59), and rebinds the DataGrid by calling the `BindData(sortExpression)` subroutine, passing in the value of the new `SortExpression` (line 62).

You might be wondering why the `dgComments_Sorting` event handler sets the DataGrid's `CurrentPageIndex` property to 0. Imagine for a moment that we didn't reset the DataGrid's `CurrentPageIndex` property to 0 and the following events transpired: The user visits our page and is shown the data in chronologically increasing order. He pages through the first few pages of comments and is viewing page four of six when he decides he wants to see the results ordered by the Name column. When he clicks the Name column, he sees comments from Ned, Sally, and Scott (as opposed to comments from other posters whose names come sooner in the alphabet, such as Dave, Frank, and Jisun). Why is this?

In our example, the user pages to the fourth page of data before opting to sort the results. However, if the DataGrid's `CurrentPageIndex` property is not reset to 0, when the user clicks on the Name column's sorting hyperlink, he will be shown the fourth page of data as sorted by the DataGrid's Name column. Such behavior will undoubtedly confuse users. When a user opts to sort data by a particular field, he expects to start viewing the sorted data starting from the beginning of the data, not somewhere in the middle. By resetting the `CurrentPageIndex` property to 0, the user is shown the first page of the sorted data.

Figures 10.2 and 10.3 contain screenshots of Listing 10.2. Note that in both screenshots, the DataGrid column headers are hyperlinks, indicating that the columns are sortable. Figure 10.2 shows a screenshot of the fourth page of data being displayed when the DataGrid is sorted by the Date Added column in ascending order (the default sort order). Figure 10.3 shows a screenshot of the second page of data being displayed when the DataGrid is sorted by the Name column.

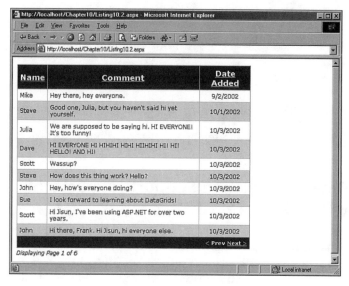

FIGURE 10.2   The DataGrid is sorted by the Date Added column.

ADDING ENHANCED SORTING FEATURES

In Chapter 7 we examined how to implement the DataGrid's standard sorting functionality, which is what is used in Listing 10.2. We also looked at how to provide more advanced sorting features, such as allowing each DataGrid column to be sortable in both ascending and descending order. To accomplish this, we used a `ViewState` variable that indicates whether the data is to be sorted in ascending or descending order. If a user clicks repeatedly on one particular DataGrid column's sorting hyperlink, the sort order for that column is toggled between ascending and descending order.

These advanced sorting features can be added to DataGrids that also support pagination, and can be added using the same code we used in Chapter 7. One thing to be aware of: The user might click the Next/Previous buttons between clicking the sorting hyperlinks. Therefore, if you have any information that needs to be maintained across multiple postbacks (such as the `sortExpression` value in Listing 10.2), you'll need to store such information in a `ViewState` variable.

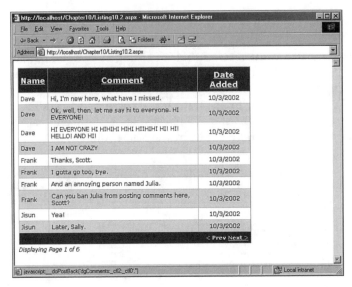

FIGURE 10.3   The DataGrid is sorted by the Name column.

Adding Data Modification Support to a Sortable and Pageable DataGrid

Now that we've seen how to meld both the sorting and paging features inherent in the DataGrid control into a single control, it's time to turn our attention to how to enable the modification of the data in such a DataGrid. In Chapter 9, we saw how to use the DataGrid's built-in editing features, which we'll now add to a pageable, sortable DataGrid. We'll also examine how to provide delete functionality. This all-in-one DataGrid, which allows for updating, deleting, modifying, sorting, and paging through data, serves quite nicely as an administration interface for a data-driven Web site.

We'll look at adding editing and deleting support to our DataGrid one feature at a time, starting with adding an editing interface. In Chapter 9, we thoroughly examined the DataGrid's editing features. Furthermore, if you'll recall back to Chapter 4, "Adding Buttons and HyperLinks to the DataGrid Web Control," we saw how to add a Delete button to a DataGrid. (Specifically, we looked at the example of a DataGrid being used to display a shopping cart that includes Remove and Details buttons for every item in the DataGrid.)

Because we've already seen examples of editing and deleting from a DataGrid, we won't spend too much time examining the details of providing such features to a pageable, sortable DataGrid. Rather, we'll focus on what issues arise when attempting to add such features to a DataGrid that already supports sorting and paging.

NOTE

Because the DataGrid was designed for displaying, editing, sorting, and paging records, we will not spend time discussing how to use the DataGrid to add records, although there are clever tricks you can employ to use the DataGrid interface for adding data. For more information on these techniques, be sure to read the "Quickly Adding a New Row in a DataGrid" article, referenced in the "On the Web" section at the end of this chapter.

Typically, if you want to allow the insertion of data into the Comment table, you would provide a separate ASP.NET Web page that simply displays a Web form with the needed input fields, and, once filled out and submitted, inserts the information into the database. Although this can be done on the same page as the DataGrid, it can lead to complications if validation controls are used both for the editing interface and for the data-inserting section on the page. Furthermore, placing both data display and data insertion features on one page leads to a cluttered interface that your users might find confusing or difficult to navigate.

Adding Editing Support to a Sortable, Pageable DataGrid

Recall from Chapter 9 that to add editing support for a DataGrid, we need to perform three steps:

1. Add an EditCommandColumn to the DataGrid. (The EditCommandColumn is rendered into an Edit button for each DataGrid row, or an Update and Cancel button for the row that is currently being edited.)

2. For any columns that require a custom editing interface, use a TemplateColumn with an EditItemTemplate to provide the needed editing interface.

3. Provide event handlers for the DataGrid's EditCommand, UpdateCommand, and CancelCommand events, which fire when the user clicks the Edit, Update, and Cancel buttons, respectively.

What changes to these steps are needed to provide editing capabilities to a DataGrid that already supports sorting and paging?

The DataGrid determines what row to render in edit mode based on the value of the EditItemIndex property. In the event handler for the EditCommand, you must set this property to the index of the row whose Edit button was clicked, and then rebind the DataGrid. With the CancelCommand event, you must reset the DataGrid's EditItemIndex property to –1 and rebind the DataGrid. Finally, with the UpdateCommand event, you must update the database with new values the user has entered and then reset the DataGrid's EditItemIndex property to –1 and rebind the DataGrid.

The rebinding of the DataGrid in all three event handlers requires a call to the BindData() subroutine, but the BindData() subroutine has been updated to accept an string input parameter, *sortExpression*. One such change that must be made, as was done in Listing 10.2, is that whenever the EditCommand, UpdateCommand, or CancelCommand event handler needs to call BindData(*sortExpression*), it will have to pass in the value of the SortExpr ViewState variable (ViewState("SortExpr")).

Another consideration that must be kept in mind when a DataGrid that already supports paging and sorting has editing support added is the following: Imagine that a user clicks the Edit button for a particular row in the DataGrid. As we know, the ASP.NET page will be posted back and the DataGrid will be redrawn with the particular row whose Edit button was clicked being displayed in its edit mode. Imagine at this point that the user clicks one of the sorting hyperlinks, or one of the Next/Previous hyperlinks in the paging interface. What will happen?

As you already know, the ASP.NET Web page will be posted back and the DataGrid's SortCommand event will fire (assuming the user clicked one of the sorting hyperlinks). The event handler for the SortCommand event, dgComments_Sorting, as defined in Listing 10.2, line 54, will reset the ViewState("SortExpr") variable to the new SortExpression, reset the DataGrid's CurrentPageIndex property to 0, and then rebind the DataGrid. This will result in the DataGrid being sorted by the specified column, with the first page of data showing. However, recall that prior to sorting, the user clicked the Edit button for a row, which had the effect of setting the DataGrid's EditItemIndex property to that row's index. This means that if we don't reset the DataGrid's EditItemIndex property when the first page of the new sorted data is displayed, one of the rows will be rendered as if the user had clicked the Edit button! Therefore, it is vital that both the dgComments_Sorting and the dgComments_Paging event handlers reset the DataGrid's EditItemIndex property to –1.

To summarize, the only two changes we need to make to incorporate editing support into a pageable/sortable DataGrid are to update the call to the BindData(*sortExpression*) subroutine in the EditCommand, UpdateCommand, and CancelCommand event handlers, and update the dgComments_Sorting and dgComments_Paging event handlers to reset the DataGrid's EditItemIndex property to –1.

Listing 10.3 contains an updated version of Listing 10.2, which includes editing support. Note that all three columns in the DataGrid employ a customized editing interface. The Name column uses a simple TextBox; the Comment column uses a multi-line TextBox as we saw in Chapter 9, Listing 9.4; and the Date Added column uses a Calendar Web control, as we saw in Chapter 9, Listing 9.5. Additionally, the Name and Comment columns use a RequiredFieldValidator validation control, as was shown in Chapter 9, Listing 9.9.

LISTING 10.3   The Sortable/Pageable DataGrid Is Now Also Editable

```
 1: <%@ import Namespace="System.Data" %>
 2: <%@ import Namespace="System.Data.SqlClient" %>
 3: <script runat="server" language="VB">
 4: '... The Page_Load event handler and the BindData(sortExpression)
 5:    '... and ShowPageInformation() subroutine has been omitted for brevity
 6:    '... Refer back to Listing 10.2 for details ...
 7:
 8:     Sub dgComments_Paging(sender As Object, e As
➥DataGridPageChangedEventArgs)
 9:        'Turn off editing
10:        dgComments.EditItemIndex = -1
11:
12:        dgComments.CurrentPageIndex = e.NewPageIndex
13:        BindData(ViewState("SortExpr"))
14:     End Sub
15:
16:
17:     Sub dgComments_Sorting(sender as Object, e as
➥DataGridSortCommandEventArgs)
18:        'Set the sortExpr ViewState variable accordingly
19:        ViewState("SortExpr") = e.SortExpression
20:
21:        'Reset the data to show the FIRST page of data
22:        dgComments.CurrentPageIndex = 0
23:
24:        'Turn off editing
25:      · dgComments.EditItemIndex = -1
26:
27:        'Bind the data!
28:        BindData(ViewState("SortExpr"))
29:     End Sub
30:
31:
32:     Sub dgComments_EditRow(sender As Object, e As DataGridCommandEventArgs)
33:        dgComments.EditItemIndex = e.Item.ItemIndex
34:        BindData(ViewState("SortExpr"))
35:     End Sub
36:
37:     Sub dgComments_UpdateRow(sender As Object, e As DataGridCommandEventArgs)
38:        'Make sure the Page is Valid
```

LISTING 10.3   Continued

```
39:        If Not Page.Isvalid Then Exit Sub
40:
41:        'Get information from columns...
42:        Dim nameTextBox as TextBox = e.Item.Cells(1).FindControl("txtName")
43:        Dim commentTextBox as TextBox = e.Item.Cells(2).
➥FindControl("txtComment")
44:        Dim dateAdded as Calendar = e.Item.Cells(3).FindControl("calDate")
45:
46:        Dim iCommentID as Integer = dgComments.DataKeys(e.Item.ItemIndex)
47:
48:
49:        'Update the database...
50:        Dim strSQL as String
51:        strSQL = "UPDATE Comments SET Name = @NameParam, DateAdded =
➥@DateAddedParam, " & _
52:                    "Comment = @CommentParam WHERE CommentID = @CommentIDParam"
53:
54:        Const strConnString as String = "server=localhost;uid=sa;pwd=;
➥database=pubs"
55:        Dim objConn as New SqlConnection(strConnString)
56:
57:        Dim objCmd as New SqlCommand(strSQL, objConn)
58:
59:        Dim nameParam as New SqlParameter("@NameParam", SqlDbType.VarChar, 50)
60:        Dim commentParam as New SqlParameter("@CommentParam", SqlDbType.
➥VarChar, 255)
61:        Dim dateAddedParam as New SqlParameter("@DateAddedParam",
➥SqlDbType.DateTime)
62:        Dim commentIDParam as New SqlParameter("@CommentIDParam",
➥SqlDbType.Int, 4)
63:
64:        nameParam.Value = nameTextBox.Text
65:        objCmd.Parameters.Add(nameParam)
66:
67:        commentParam.Value = commentTextBox.Text
68:        objCmd.Parameters.Add(commentParam)
69:
70:        dateAddedParam.Value = dateAdded.SelectedDate
71:        objCmd.Parameters.Add(dateAddedParam)
72:
73:        commentIDParam.Value = iCommentID
```

LISTING 10.3   Continued

```
74:          objCmd.Parameters.Add(commentIDParam)
75:
76:          'Issue the SQL command
77:          objConn.Open()
78:          objCmd.ExecuteNonQuery()
79:          objConn.Close()
80:
81:          dgComments.EditItemIndex = -1
82:          BindData(ViewState("SortExpr"))
83:       End Sub
84:
85:       Sub dgComments_CancelRow(sender As Object, e As DataGridCommandEventArgs)
86:          dgComments.EditItemIndex = -1
87:          BindData(ViewState("SortExpr"))
88:       End Sub
89: </script>
90: <form runat="server">
91:    <asp:DataGrid runat="server" id="dgComments"
92:        Font-Name="Verdana" Font-Size="9pt" CellPadding="5"
93:        AlternatingItemStyle-BackColor="#dddddd"
94:        AutoGenerateColumns="False" Width="75%"
95:        PageSize="10" AllowPaging="True"
96:        OnPageIndexChanged="dgComments_Paging"
97:        AllowSorting="True" OnSortCommand="dgComments_Sorting"
98:        OnEditCommand="dgComments_EditRow"
99:        OnUpdateCommand="dgComments_UpdateRow"
100:       OnCancelCommand="dgComments_CancelRow"
101:       DataKeyField="CommentID">
102:
103:       <HeaderStyle BackColor="Navy" ForeColor="White" Font-Size="13pt"
104:             Font-Bold="True" HorizontalAlign="Center" />
105:
106:       <PagerStyle BackColor="Navy" ForeColor="White" Font-Size="8pt"
107:             Font-Bold="True" HorizontalAlign="Right"
108:             NextPageText="Next >" PrevPageText="< Prev" />
109:
110:       <Columns>
111:         <asp:EditCommandColumn EditText="Edit" UpdateText="Update"
112:             CancelText="Cancel" ButtonType="LinkButton" />
113:         <asp:TemplateColumn HeaderText="Name" SortExpression="Name">
114:           <ItemTemplate>
115:             <%# DataBinder.Eval(Container.DataItem, "Name") %>
```

LISTING 10.3   Continued

```
116:          </ItemTemplate>
117:          <EditItemTemplate>
118:            <asp:TextBox runat="server" id="txtName" Columns="15"
119:                MaxLength="50" Font-Name="Verdana" Font-Size="9pt"
120:                Text='<%# DataBinder.Eval(Container.DataItem, "Name") %>' />
121:            <asp:RequiredFieldValidator runat="server"
122:                ControlToValidate="txtName" Display="Dynamic"
123:                ErrorMessage="<br />You must provide a Name." />
124:          </EditItemTemplate>
125:        </asp:TemplateColumn>
126:        <asp:TemplateColumn HeaderText="Comment" SortExpression="Comment">
127:          <ItemTemplate>
128:            <%# DataBinder.Eval(Container.DataItem, "Comment") %>
129:          </ItemTemplate>
130:          <EditItemTemplate>
131:            <asp:TextBox runat="server" id="txtComment" Width="95%"
132:                MaxLength="255" Font-Name="Verdana" Font-Size="9pt"
133:                TextMode="MultiLine" Rows="5"
134:                Text='<%# DataBinder.Eval(Container.DataItem, "Comment") %>' />
135:            <asp:RequiredFieldValidator runat="server"
136:                ControlToValidate="txtComment" Display="Dynamic"
137:                ErrorMessage="<br />You must provide a Comment." />
138:          </EditItemTemplate>
139:        </asp:TemplateColumn>
140:        <asp:TemplateColumn HeaderText="Date Added" SortExpression="DateAdded"
141:                ItemStyle-HorizontalAlign="Center">
142:          <ItemTemplate>
143:            <%# DataBinder.Eval(Container.DataItem, "DateAdded", "{0:d}") %>
144:          </ItemTemplate>
145:          <EditItemTemplate>
146:            <asp:Calendar id="calDate" runat="server"
147:                SelectedDate='<%# Convert.ToDateTime(DataBinder.Eval
➥(Container.DataItem, "DateAdded")) %>'
148:                VisibleDate='<%# Convert.ToDateTime(DataBinder.Eval
➥(Container.DataItem, "DateAdded")) %>' />
149:          </EditItemTemplate>
150:        </asp:TemplateColumn>
151:      </Columns>
152:    </asp:DataGrid>
153:    <asp:label id="lblPagingInfo" runat="server" Font-Name="Verdana"
154:      Font-Size="9pt" Font-Italic="True" Width="75%"
➥HorizontalAlign="Right" />
155: </form>
```

As with Listing 10.2, Listing 10.3 at first appears quite formidable; however, the vast majority of the code present in Listing 10.3 has been examined thoroughly in previous chapters. The DataGrid declaration in Listing 10.3 has undergone some major work from its incarnation in Listing 10.2. Specifically, an EditCommandColumn (lines 111 and 112) has been added, and all the BoundColumns from Listing 10.2 have been converted to TemplateColumns in Listing 10.3. The reason Listing 10.3 uses TemplateColumns is because we want to provide a custom editing interface for each column.

The customized editing interfaces for each column can be found in their EditItemTemplate sections. The Name column uses a standard TextBox for its editing interface (lines 118–120), with a RequiredFieldValidator included to ensure that the user supplies a value for the Name column when editing (lines 121–123). The Comment column uses a multiline TextBox for its customized editing interface (lines 131–134) and, like the Name column, includes a RequiredFieldValidator (lines 135–137). Finally, the Date Added column's editing interface uses a Calendar Web control (lines 146–148).

In addition to providing an EditCommandColumn and editing interfaces for the editable columns, we must also wire up the DataGrid's EditCommand, UpdateCommand, and CancelCommand to appropriate event handlers. This is done on lines 98 through 100. In Chapter 9, when we first examined enabling editing support for a DataGrid, we saw that these three event handlers all ended up calling the BindData() method at some point. When using these event handlers in a DataGrid that supports paging, we must use an alternative version of BindData(), one that takes an input parameter specifying the DataSource field to sort on. Therefore, the BindData() call in these three event handlers has been replaced by a call to BindData(ViewState("SortExpr")) (see lines 34, 82, and 87), where ViewState("SortExpr") is a ViewState variable that persists what DataGrid column the results are sorted by across postbacks.

The dgComments_Sorting and dgComments_Paging event handlers from Listing 10.2 must also be updated to enable for editing support. Specifically, these two event handlers must make certain that when they are called, the DataGrid is taken out of edit mode. This is accomplished by resetting the DataGrid's EditItemIndex property to –1 (see lines 10 and 25). By setting EditItemIndex to –1, these event handlers ensure that when a user has the DataGrid in edit mode, the DataGrid gracefully exits edit mode if either a sorting hyperlink or Next/Previous paging hyperlink is clicked.

The remainder of the code in Listing 10.3 is code we have seen in previous examples in Chapter 9. Figure 10.4 contains a screenshot of Listing 10.3 when viewed through a browser. Specifically, it's a screenshot of the DataGrid after the user has opted to edit a particular row.

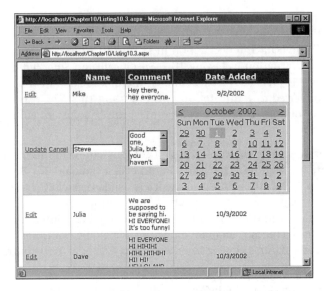

FIGURE 10.4   The user can edit the pageable/sortable DataGrid.

Providing Support to Delete Records

The DataGrid we've been working on throughout this chapter displays the contents of the Comments database table, which represents an online discussion in a guestbook or chatroom-type application. This DataGrid would be a useful tool for a site administrator, allowing all the comments to be read, sorted, edited, or selected based on the posting date or the poster. An additional feature that would be nice to include would be enabling the system administrator to delete records from the Comment table if the comment is spam or contains profanity.

To enable the deleting of data, we need to provide a Delete button in our DataGrid. In Chapter 4, we saw how to add buttons to the DataGrid through the ButtonColumn. In Chapter 5, "Adding Command Buttons to the Data Web Controls," we saw that if we add a command button to the DataGrid with a CommandName of Delete, whenever this command button is clicked, the DataGrid will fire its DeleteCommand event. These two approaches will be used to implement the deletion of data through the DataGrid. Namely, we'll use a ButtonColumn to create a command button column in the DataGrid, setting the ButtonColumn's CommandName property to "Delete". Then we'll provide an event handler for the DataGrid's DeleteCommand event; in this event handler, we'll need to determine the CommentID of the row whose Delete button was clicked, and issue a SQL statement that effectively deletes this record. The code for adding a Delete button can be seen in Listing 10.4.

LISTING 10.4   With a Delete Button, an Administrator Can Delete Database Data Via the DataGrid

```
 1: <%@ import Namespace="System.Data" %>
 2: <%@ import Namespace="System.Data.SqlClient" %>
 3: <script runat="server" language="VB">
 4: ' ... All of the subroutines and event handlers from
 5: ' ... Listing 10.3 have been omitted, since they remain
 6: ' ... unchanged here in Listing 10.4.
 7:
 8:     Sub dgComments_DeleteRow(sender As Object, e As DataGridCommandEventArgs)
 9:         'Turn off editing
10:         dgComments.EditItemIndex = -1
11:
12:         Dim iCommentID as Integer
13:         iCommentID = dgComments.DataKeys(e.Item.ItemIndex)
14:
15:         'Update the database...
16:         Dim strSQL as String
17:         strSQL = "DELETE FROM Comments WHERE CommentID = @CommentIDParam"
18:
19:         Const strConnString as String = "server=localhost;uid=sa;
➥pwd=;database=pubs"
20:         Dim objConn as New SqlConnection(strConnString)
21:
22:         Dim objCmd as New SqlCommand(strSQL, objConn)
23:
24:         Dim commentIDParam as New SqlParameter("@CommentIDParam",
➥SqlDbType.Int, 4)
25:         commentIDParam.Value = iCommentID
26:         objCmd.Parameters.Add(commentIDParam)
27:
28:         'Issue the SQL command
29:         objConn.Open()
30:         objCmd.ExecuteNonQuery()
31:         objConn.Close()
32:
33:         BindData(ViewState("SortExpr"))
34:     End Sub
35: </script>
36: <form runat="server">
37:   <asp:DataGrid runat="server" id="dgComments"
38:       Font-Name="Verdana" Font-Size="9pt" CellPadding="5"
```

LISTING 10.4   Continued

```
39:         AlternatingItemStyle-BackColor="#dddddd"
40:         AutoGenerateColumns="False" Width="75%"
41:         PageSize="10" AllowPaging="True"
42:         OnPageIndexChanged="dgComments_Paging"
43:         AllowSorting="True" OnSortCommand="dgComments_Sorting"
44:         OnEditCommand="dgComments_EditRow"
45:         OnUpdateCommand="dgComments_UpdateRow"
46:         OnCancelCommand="dgComments_CancelRow"
47:         DataKeyField="CommentID"
48:         OnDeleteCommand="dgComments_DeleteRow">
49:
50:     <HeaderStyle BackColor="Navy" ForeColor="White" Font-Size="13pt"
51:             Font-Bold="True" HorizontalAlign="Center" />
52:
53:     <PagerStyle BackColor="Navy" ForeColor="White" Font-Size="8pt"
54:             Font-Bold="True" HorizontalAlign="Right"
55:             NextPageText="Next >" PrevPageText="< Prev" />
56:
57:     <Columns>
58:       <asp:EditCommandColumn EditText="Edit" UpdateText="Update"
59:           CancelText="Cancel" ButtonType="LinkButton" />
60:       <asp:ButtonColumn Text="Delete" ButtonType="LinkButton"
61:           CommandName="Delete" />
62:
63:       '... The TemplateColumn declarations for the Name, Comments, and
64:       '... Date Added columns have been omitted for brevity.
65:       '... Refer back to Listing 10.3
66:
67:     </Columns>
68:   </asp:DataGrid>
69:   <asp:label id="lblPagingInfo" runat="server" Font-Name="Verdana"
70:      Font-Size="9pt" Font-Italic="True" Width="75%" HorizontalAlign="Right" />
71: </form>
```

Listing 10.4 contains an addition to the DataGrid declaration, as well as a new event handler to the code section. The DataGrid declaration has been updated to contain a ButtonColumn that displays a Delete button (lines 60 and 61). Because this ButtonColumn's CommandName property is set to "Delete", when the Delete button is clicked, the DataGrid's DeleteCommand event handler will fire. On line 48, we wire up this event to the dgComments_DeleteRow event handler.

NOTE

Recall from Chapters 4 and 5 that every time a command button inside a DataGrid is clicked, the DataGrid's `ItemCommand` event fires. By giving the command button the special `CommandName` value `"Delete"`, the DataGrid's `DeleteCommand` event fires as well. Note that instead of using a `CommandName` value `"Delete"` and the `DeleteCommand` event, we could have just as easily given the command button an arbitrary `CommandName` value and provided an event handler for the `ItemCommand` event.

The `dgComments_DeleteRow` event handler (lines 8–34) starts like the paging and sorting event handlers: it resets the DataGrid's `EditItemIndex` to –1 (line 10). Next, it determines the value of the `CommentID` field for the row whose Delete button was clicked (line 13) and then issues a parameterized SQL statement that deletes the specified record (lines 16 through 31). Finally, the `BindData(sortExpression)` subroutine is called on line 33. This is needed because the DataGrid's underlying data has changed, and we need to rebind the contents of the `Comment table` to the DataGrid.

Figure 10.5 contains a screenshot of the code in Listing 10.4. Note that each DataGrid row contains a Delete button. When this button is clicked, the ASP.NET Web page is posted back and the DataGrid's `DeleteCommand` event fires, causing the `dgComments_DeleteRow` event handler to execute. This deletes the specified record from the `Comments` database table, and then rebinds the DataGrid based on the proper sort criteria.

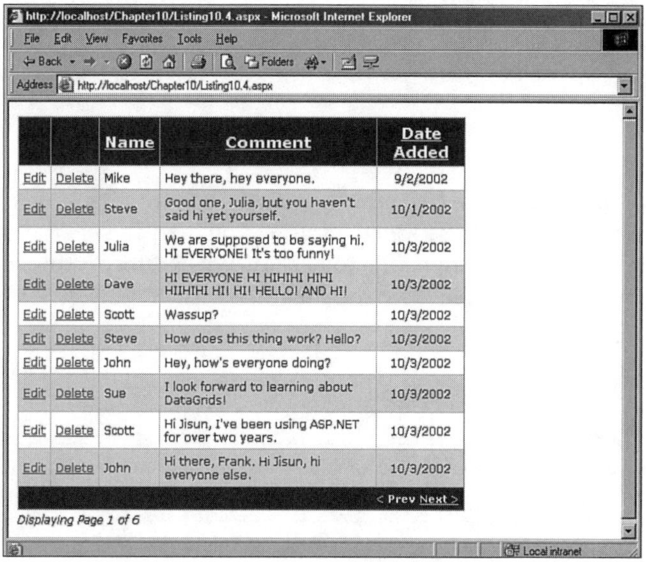

FIGURE 10.5   A system administrator can delete a database record through the DataGrid interface.

Using Client-Side Script to Ensure That the User Wants to Delete the Selected Record

Although the code in Listing 10.4 will delete a selected record, its usability leaves a bit to be desired. A common feature that is missing is a way for the user to confirm that she wants to delete a record. As soon as the user clicks the Delete button, the record is gone forever—should a user accidentally click the mouse button while it's hovering over a DataGrid row's Delete button, the record will be deleted. As this all might take place in a split second, the user might not realize what has just happened.

Rather than allowing a record to be deleted so nonchalantly, let's modify our code from Listing 10.4 to include some client-side script that will require the user to acknowledge that she does, in fact, want to delete the specified record. Specifically, we'll modify the code such that when the user clicks the Delete button, a JavaScript confirm dialog box will appear asking the user whether she wants to delete the record. This dialog box will have two buttons: OK and Cancel. The record will only be deleted if the user clicks the OK button.

To provide such functionality, we need to be able to alter the HTML output of the DataGrid's Delete button such that the Delete button has a client-side `onclick` event that runs the following client-side JavaScript code when fired:

```
return confirm("Are you sure you want to delete this record?");
```

Specifically, we'd like our Delete button's HTML to look like this:

```
<a href="JavaScript code to do the postback"
   onclick="return confirm('Are you sure you want to delete this record?')">
   Delete
</a>
```

This code will provide the desired effect, causing a modal client-side dialog box to appear when the user clicks the Delete button. Note that the `href` attribute of the a tag will contain some JavaScript code to perform this postback; this code is automatically added by ASP.NET and looks something like this:

```
javascript:__doPostBack('dgComments:_ctl2:_clt2,'').
```

NOTE

For more information on the JavaScript function `confirm`, be sure to refer to the sources listed in the "On the Web" section at the end of this chapter.

The challenge facing us is in altering HTML rendered by the Delete button so that it includes the client-side `onclick` event handler.

To help solve this problem, we can use the `Attributes` property of the Delete button. Realize that all Web controls contain an `Attributes` property that is a collection of attributes for the Web control. These attributes include client-side events like `onblur`, `onmouseover`, `onclick`, and others. We can specifically set an attribute of a Web control by programmatically setting the proper entry in the Web control's `Attributes` collection. That is, if we have a Web control, `someControl`, and we want to have a JavaScript `alert` dialog box popup whenever the user clicks the Web control, we could use the following code to specify the `onclick` attribute for the Web control:

```
someControl.Attributes("onclick") = "javascript:alert('Hello, World!');"
```

For example, if `someControl` were a Label Web control with its `Text` property set to `"Click Me"` and we added the preceding line of code to our ASP.NET Web page's `Page_Load` event handler, the HTML produced by the Label control would be as follows:

```
<span id="someControl" onclick="javascript:alert('Hello, World!');">
  Click Me
</span>
```

Using the `Attributes` collection, we can assign some client-side code to execute when the `onclick` client-side event is fired for our Delete button. However, we need some way to reference this Delete button. In Chapter 4, we saw how we could use the DataGrid's `ItemDataBound` event to programmatically set the `Text` and `NavigateUrl` properties of a HyperLinkColumn. Recall that the DataGrid's `ItemDataBound` event fires once for each row, immediately after the `DataSource` has been bound to the row.

By the time the DataGrid's `ItemDataBound` event fires, the Delete button has been created and added to the DataGridItem that constitutes the DataGrid row. Therefore, we can write an event handler for the DataGrid's `ItemDataBound` event that programmatically references the Delete button for the row and adds the client-side `onclick` event handler code using the Delete button's `Attributes` collection.

NOTE

We'll be discussing the `ItemDataBound` and `ItemCreated` events in much greater detail in the next chapter.

Listing 10.5 contains the code for the event handler for the DataGrid's `ItemDataBound` event.

LISTING 10.5   The dgComments_RowDataBound Event Handler Sets the Delete Button's Client-Side onclick Event

```
 1: Sub dgComments_RowDataBound(sender as Object, e As DataGridItemEventArgs)
 2:     If e.Item.ItemType <> ListItemType.Header AND _
 3:         e.Item.ItemType <> ListItemType.Footer then
 4:       Dim deleteButton as LinkButton = e.Item.Cells(1).Controls(0)
 5:
 6:       'We can now add the onclick event handler
 7:       deleteButton.Attributes("onclick") = "javascript:return " & _
 8:           "confirm('Are you sure you want to delete this record?');"
 9:     End If
10: End Sub
```

The dgComments_RowDataBound event handler is fairly simple. The event handler fires for both item rows in the DataGrid and header and footer rows, but because there is no Delete button in the header or footer rows, we need to ensure that we're not dealing with such a row before trying to programmatically set the Delete button's client-side onclick event. Such a check is made on line 2, determining whether the current DataGridItem's ItemType property is of the type ListItemType.Header or ListItemType.Footer. If it is neither of these, the code from lines 4 through 8 executes.

On line 4, the Delete button is referenced. Because the Delete button is in the second column of the DataGrid, we access the DataGridItem's Cells(1) property to get the second TableCell. Because the Delete button is the sole control in the column, we can reference it using the TableCell's Controls collection, Controls(0). After we have this Delete button referenced as a local variable, we can go ahead and set the button's Attributes collection so that the client-side onclick event fires a specified block of JavaScript (lines 7 and 8).

After adding the event handler in Listing 10.5 to our ASP.NET Web page from Listing 10.4, we need to wire up the DataGrid's ItemDataBound event to this event handler. This can be easily accomplished by adding the following line of code to the DataGrid declaration immediately after line 48 in Listing 10.4:

```
OnItemDataBound="dgComments_RowDataBound"
```

After the DataGrid's ItemDataBound event has been wired up to the dgComments_RowDataBound event handler, whenever a user clicks a Delete button, he will be prompted with a confirm dialog box, as shown in Figure 10.6. If the user clicks the confirm dialog box's Cancel button, the row will not be deleted.

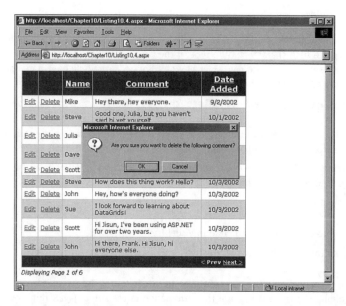

FIGURE 10.6 A client-side dialog box appears when the user clicks any Delete button.

The astute reader will have noticed that we could have added the client-side `onclick` event handler to the Delete button when the DataGrid's `ItemCreated` event fired. Although this is true, there is a benefit to setting the Delete button's `Attributes` collection in an event handler for the DataGrid's `ItemDataBound` event. The advantage is that when the `ItemDataBound` event fires, we can access the values of the `DataSource` that are being bound to this particular row. This means that we can provide a more descriptive client-side confirm dialog box.

For example, if we change lines 7 and 8 in Listing 10.5 to

```
deleteButton.Attributes("onclick") = "javascript:return " & _
    "confirm('Are you sure you want to delete the following " & _
    "comment?\n\n" & _
    Regex.Replace(DataBinder.Eval(e.Item.DataItem, "Name"), "'", "\'") & _
    "\n" & _
    Regex.Replace(DataBinder.Eval(e.Item.DataItem, "Comment"), "'", "\'") & _
    "');"
```

when the user clicks a Delete button, she will be shown a confirm dialog box that not only asks her if she wants to delete the comment, but also shows her the author of the comment and the actual comment itself, as seen in Figure 10.7.

NOTE

The `Regex.Replace` method replaces all apostrophes (`'`) with escaped apostrophes (`\'`). It is vital to replace such characters; otherwise, if the `Comment` or `Name` fields from the `DataSource` contain any apostrophes, the `confirm` call won't fire because you'll have a malformed input string to the `confirm` function. Specifically, you'll have a string like

```
'Are you sure you want to delete the following: It's nice to be here!'
```

The apostrophe between the `t` and `s` in `It's` ends the string, meaning the remaining characters are interpreted as usual JavaScript syntax.

This case is equivalent to displaying double quotes in a string in Visual Basic .NET. For example, to assign a string the value

```
Bob said, "Hi."
```

you'd have to use the following code in Visual Basic .NET:

```
SomeString = "Bob said, ""Hi."""
```

Here two successive double quotes are used to signify that it should be interpreted as a single double quote within the string, not the termination of the string. JavaScript, however, like C#, uses the backslash character (`\`) to escape apostrophes and double quotes.

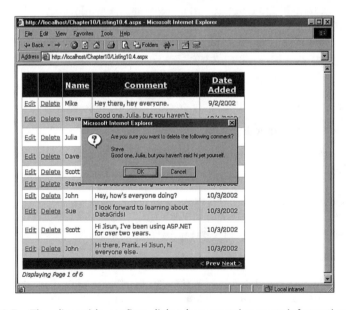

FIGURE 10.7   The client-side confirm dialog box contains more information about the comment to be deleted.

The Complete Source Code for a Multi-Functional DataGrid

Throughout this chapter, we have been building upon a single ASP.NET Web page that uses a single DataGrid to provide sorting, paging, editing, and deleting support to the Comments database table. In each of the code sections, though, we've only been examining the pertinent sections of code, leaving out code sections that we had discussed in prior code listings.

By displaying only the pertinent code in each listing, the listings were less cluttered, and allowed you to focus on the key lines of code. However, it is also helpful to see the complete source code in understanding how all the code sections fit together.

Listing 10.6 contains the complete source code for our multi-functional DataGrid. There are no comments or screenshots following the listing because we've already dissected the various pieces of the ASP.NET Web page. The listing is intended to present all the code as it would appear in your ASP.NET Web page.

LISTING 10.6   The Complete Code for the Multi-Functional DataGrid

```
 1: <%@ import Namespace="System.Data" %>
 2: <%@ import Namespace="System.Data.SqlClient" %>
 3: <script runat="server" language="VB">
 4:
 5:    Sub Page_Load(sender as Object, e as EventArgs)
 6:       If Not Page.IsPostBack then
 7:          ViewState("SortExpr") = "DateAdded ASC"
 8:          BindData(ViewState("SortExpr"))
 9:       End If
10:    End Sub
11:
12:
13:    Sub BindData(sortExpr as String)
14:       '1. Create a connection
15:       Const strConnString as String = "server=localhost;uid=sa;pwd=;
➥database=pubs"
16:       Dim objConn as New SqlConnection(strConnString)
17:
18:       '2. Create a command object for the query
19:       Dim strSQL as String
20:       strSQL = "SELECT CommentID, Name, Comment, DateAdded " & _
21:                "FROM Comments ORDER BY " & sortExpr
22:
23:       Dim objCmd as New SqlCommand(strSQL, objConn)
24:
```

LISTING 10.6   Continued

```
25:       '3. Create a DataAdapter and Fill the DataSet
26:       Dim objDA as New SqlDataAdapter()
27:       objDA.SelectCommand = objCmd
28:
29:       objConn.Open()
30:
31:       Dim objDS as DataSet = New DataSet()
32:       objDA.Fill(objDS, "titles")
33:
34:       objConn.Close()
35:
36:       'Finally, specify the DataSource and call DataBind()
37:       dgComments.DataSource = objDS
38:       dgComments.DataBind()
39:
40:       objConn.Close()    'Close the connection
41:
42:       ShowPageInformation()
43:    End Sub
44:
45:
46:    Sub ShowPageInformation()
47:      'This sub displays paging information in the appropriate label
48:      lblPagingInfo.Text = "Displaying Page " & _
49:          (dgComments.CurrentPageIndex+1).ToString() & " of " & _
50:          dgComments.PageCount
51:    End Sub
52:
53:
54:    Sub dgComments_Paging(sender As Object, e As
➥DataGridPageChangedEventArgs)
55:      'Turn off editing
56:      dgComments.EditItemIndex = -1
57:
58:      dgComments.CurrentPageIndex = e.NewPageIndex
59:      BindData(ViewState("SortExpr"))
60:    End Sub
61:
62:
63:    Sub dgComments_Sorting(sender as Object, e as
➥DataGridSortCommandEventArgs)
```

LISTING 10.6   Continued

```
64:          'Set the sortExpr ViewState variable accordingly
65:          ViewState("SortExpr") = e.SortExpression
66:
67:          'Reset the data to show the FIRST page of data
68:          dgComments.CurrentPageIndex = 0
69:
70:          'Turn off editing
71:          dgComments.EditItemIndex = -1
72:
73:          'Bind the data!
74:          BindData(ViewState("SortExpr"))
75:      End Sub
76:
77:
78:      Sub dgComments_EditRow(sender As Object, e As
➥DataGridCommandEventArgs)
79:          dgComments.EditItemIndex = e.Item.ItemIndex
80:          BindData(ViewState("SortExpr"))
81:      End Sub
82:
83:      Sub dgComments_UpdateRow(sender As Object, e As DataGridCommandEventArgs)
84:          'Make sure the Page is Valid
85:          If Not Page.Isvalid Then Exit Sub
86:
87:          'Get information from columns...
88:          Dim nameTextBox as TextBox = e.Item.Cells(1).FindControl("txtName")
89:          Dim commentTextBox as TextBox = e.Item.Cells(2).
➥FindControl("txtComment")
90:          Dim dateAdded as Calendar = e.Item.Cells(3).FindControl("calDate")
91:
92:          Dim iCommentID as Integer = dgComments.DataKeys(e.Item.ItemIndex)
93:
94:
95:          'Update the database...
96:          Dim strSQL as String
97:          strSQL = "UPDATE Comments SET Name = @NameParam, DateAdded =
➥@DateAddedParam, " & _
98:                    "Comment = @CommentParam WHERE CommentID = @CommentIDParam"
99:
100:         Const strConnString as String = "server=localhost;uid=sa;pwd=;
➥database=pubs"
```

LISTING 10.6   Continued

```
101:        Dim objConn as New SqlConnection(strConnString)
102:
103:        Dim objCmd as New SqlCommand(strSQL, objConn)
104:
105:        Dim nameParam as New SqlParameter("@NameParam", SqlDbType.VarChar, 50)
106:        Dim commentParam as New SqlParameter("@CommentParam",
➥SqlDbType.VarChar, 255)
107:        Dim dateAddedParam as New SqlParameter("@DateAddedParam",
➥SqlDbType.DateTime)
108:        Dim commentIDParam as New SqlParameter("@CommentIDParam",
➥SqlDbType.Int, 4)
109:
110:        nameParam.Value = nameTextBox.Text
111:        objCmd.Parameters.Add(nameParam)
112:
113:        commentParam.Value = commentTextBox.Text
114:        objCmd.Parameters.Add(commentParam)
115:
116:        dateAddedParam.Value = dateAdded.SelectedDate
117:        objCmd.Parameters.Add(dateAddedParam)
118:
119:        commentIDParam.Value = iCommentID
120:        objCmd.Parameters.Add(commentIDParam)
121:
122:        'Issue the SQL command
123:        objConn.Open()
124:        objCmd.ExecuteNonQuery()
125:        objConn.Close()
126:
127:        dgComments.EditItemIndex = -1
128:        BindData(ViewState("SortExpr"))
129:    End Sub
130:
131:    Sub dgComments_CancelRow(sender As Object, e As DataGridCommandEventArgs)
132:        dgComments.EditItemIndex = -1
133:        BindData(ViewState("SortExpr"))
134:    End Sub
135:
136:    Sub dgComments_DeleteRow(sender As Object, e As DataGridCommandEventArgs)
137:        'Turn off editing
138:        dgComments.EditItemIndex = -1
139:
```

LISTING 10.6   Continued

```
140:        Dim iCommentID as Integer
141:        iCommentID = dgComments.DataKeys(e.Item.ItemIndex)
142:
143:        'Update the database...
144:        Dim strSQL as String
145:        strSQL = "DELETE FROM Comments WHERE CommentID = @CommentIDParam"
146:
147:        Const strConnString as String = "server=localhost;uid=sa;pwd=;
➥database=pubs"
148:        Dim objConn as New SqlConnection(strConnString)
149:
150:        Dim objCmd as New SqlCommand(strSQL, objConn)
151:
152:        Dim commentIDParam as New SqlParameter("@CommentIDParam",
➥SqlDbType.Int, 4)
153:        commentIDParam.Value = iCommentID
154:        objCmd.Parameters.Add(commentIDParam)
155:
156:        'Issue the SQL command
157:        objConn.Open()
158:        objCmd.ExecuteNonQuery()
159:        objConn.Close()
160:
161:        BindData(ViewState("SortExpr"))
162:     End Sub
163:
164:     Sub dgComments_RowDataBound(sender as Object, e As DataGridItemEventArgs)
165:        If e.Item.ItemType <> ListItemType.Header AND _
166:              e.Item.ItemType <> ListItemType.Footer then
167:         Dim deleteButton as LinkButton = e.Item.Cells(1).Controls(0)
168:
169:         'We can now add the onclick event handler
170:         deleteButton.Attributes("onclick") = "javascript:return " & _
171:             "confirm('Are you sure you want to delete the following
➥comment?');"
172:        End If
173:     End Sub
174:
175: </script>
176: <form runat="server">
177:   <asp:DataGrid runat="server" id="dgComments"
```

LISTING 10.6   Continued

```
178:        Font-Name="Verdana" Font-Size="9pt" CellPadding="5"
179:        AlternatingItemStyle-BackColor="#dddddd"
180:        AutoGenerateColumns="False" Width="75%"
181:        PageSize="10" AllowPaging="True"
182:        OnPageIndexChanged="dgComments_Paging"
183:        AllowSorting="True" OnSortCommand="dgComments_Sorting"
184:        OnEditCommand="dgComments_EditRow"
185:        OnUpdateCommand="dgComments_UpdateRow"
186:        OnCancelCommand="dgComments_CancelRow"
187:        DataKeyField="CommentID"
188:        OnDeleteCommand="dgComments_DeleteRow"
189:        OnItemDataBound="dgComments_RowDataBound">
190:
191:    <HeaderStyle BackColor="Navy" ForeColor="White" Font-Size="13pt"
192:            Font-Bold="True" HorizontalAlign="Center" />
193:
194:    <PagerStyle BackColor="Navy" ForeColor="White" Font-Size="8pt"
195:            Font-Bold="True" HorizontalAlign="Right"
196:            NextPageText="Next >" PrevPageText="< Prev" />
197:
198:    <Columns>
199:     <asp:EditCommandColumn EditText="Edit" UpdateText="Update"
200:         CancelText="Cancel" ButtonType="LinkButton" />
201:     <asp:ButtonColumn Text="Delete" ButtonType="LinkButton"
202:         CommandName="Delete" />
203:     <asp:TemplateColumn HeaderText="Name" SortExpression="Name">
204:       <ItemTemplate>
205:         <%# DataBinder.Eval(Container.DataItem, "Name") %>
206:       </ItemTemplate>
207:       <EditItemTemplate>
208:         <asp:TextBox runat="server" id="txtName" Columns="15"
209:             MaxLength="50" Font-Name="Verdana" Font-Size="9pt"
210:             Text='<%# DataBinder.Eval(Container.DataItem, "Name") %>' />
211:         <asp:RequiredFieldValidator runat="server"
212:             ControlToValidate="txtName" Display="Dynamic"
213:             ErrorMessage="<br />You must provide a Name." />
214:       </EditItemTemplate>
215:     </asp:TemplateColumn>
216:     <asp:TemplateColumn HeaderText="Comment" SortExpression="Comment">
217:       <ItemTemplate>
218:         <%# DataBinder.Eval(Container.DataItem, "Comment") %>
```

LISTING 10.6   Continued

```
219:            </ItemTemplate>
220:            <EditItemTemplate>
221:              <asp:TextBox runat="server" id="txtComment" Width="95%"
222:                  MaxLength="255" Font-Name="Verdana" Font-Size="9pt"
223:                  TextMode="MultiLine" Rows="5"
224:                  Text='<%# DataBinder.Eval(Container.DataItem, "Comment") %>' />
225:              <asp:RequiredFieldValidator runat="server"
226:                  ControlToValidate="txtComment" Display="Dynamic"
227:                  ErrorMessage="<br />You must provide a Comment." />
228:            </EditItemTemplate>
229:          </asp:TemplateColumn>
230:          <asp:TemplateColumn HeaderText="Date Added" SortExpression="DateAdded"
231:                  ItemStyle-HorizontalAlign="Center">
232:            <ItemTemplate>
233:              <%# DataBinder.Eval(Container.DataItem, "DateAdded", "{0:d}") %>
234:            </ItemTemplate>
235:            <EditItemTemplate>
236:              <asp:Calendar id="calDate" runat="server"
237:                    SelectedDate='<%# Convert.ToDateTime(DataBinder.Eval
➥(Container.DataItem, "DateAdded")) %>'
238:                    VisibleDate='<%# Convert.ToDateTime(DataBinder.Eval
➥(Container.DataItem, "DateAdded")) %>' />
239:            </EditItemTemplate>
240:          </asp:TemplateColumn>
241:        </Columns>
242:      </asp:DataGrid>
243:      <asp:label id="lblPagingInfo" runat="server" Font-Name="Verdana"
244:          Font-Size="9pt" Font-Italic="True" Width="75%"
➥HorizontalAlign="Right" />
245: </form>
```

Summary

In this chapter, we took the lessons learned separately over the past three chapters and combined them to create a single DataGrid capable of sorting, paging, and modifying data. We examined the issues that arise when combining multiple features of the DataGrid into a single DataGrid, and looked at how to work around these potential problems. We also looked at how to use a DataGrid interface to delete and edit records in the DataGrid's underlying database table. These two tasks were accomplished using techniques learned in Chapters 4 and 5.

This chapter marks the end of Part III. Part III focused on exploring the DataGrid's useful feature set, which includes sorting, paging, and editing capabilities. In Part IV, we will turn our attention to a number of miscellaneous data Web control topics, such as using the `ItemCreated` and `ItemDataBound` events, creating custom DataGrid columns, and a look ahead to the future of the data Web controls.

On the Web

For more information on the topics discussed in this chapter, consider perusing the following online resources:

- "Running Dynamic Stored Procedures"—`http://www.4guysfromrolla.com/webtech/020600-1.shtml`

- "Using Dynamic SQL Statements in Stored Procedures"—`http://www.4guys-fromrolla.com/webtech/102300-1.shtml`

- "Quickly Adding a New Row to a DataGrid"—`http://www.dotnetbips.com/displayarticle.aspx?id=125`

- "JavaScript Confirm Form Submission"—`http://www.shiningstar.net/articles/articles/javascript/confirmsubmit.asp?ID=ROLLA`

- "Andy Smith's ConfirmedButtons Control"—`http://www.metabuilders.com/Tools/ConfirmedButtons.aspx`

- "An Extensive Examination of the DataGrid Web Control: Part 8"—`http://aspnet.4guysfromrolla.com/articles/090402-1.aspx`

PART IV

In Part IV, we will turn our attention to two topics. First, in Chapter 11, "Altering the Data Before It's Rendered," we'll look at using the `ItemCreated` and `ItemDataBound` events of the DataGrid, DataList, and Repeater controls. When a data Web control's `DataBind()` method is called, an item is added to the data Web control for each record in the specified `DataSource`. These two events fire for each row added to the data Web control. By providing event handlers for these events, we can determine the value of the data being bound to the data Web control, and alter the properties of the data Web control based on the value of the data. This has many real-world applications, such as having a DataList where items that meet a certain criteria are displayed differently. For example, imagine that you are displaying a list of stocks and their prices in a DataList. You might want to use a red-colored, bold font for those stocks whose price has changed more than 5% during the day's trading.

In Parts I, II, and III, we saw code that used the built-in DataGrid column controls, which include the BoundColumn, the TemplateColumn, the ButtonColumn, and so on. In Chapter 12, "Creating Custom Column Controls for the DataGrid," we will look at how to create our own column controls for the DataGrid. Commonly, the programming logic performed by a DataGrid custom column control can accomplished by providing code in the ASP.NET server-side code. However, by packaging the programming logic into a control, we can encapsulate the programming complexity, making our ASP.NET Web pages and server-side code more readable, reliable, and maintainable.

The two chapters in Part IV conclude this book. I hope you have enjoyed reading this book as much as I enjoyed writing it. If you have any comments or suggestions, I welcome your email at mitchell@4guysfromrolla.com. Also, for more information on the data Web controls and ASP.NET, I invite you to read the hundreds of articles found on the Web site on which I serve as editor: http://www.4GuysFromRolla.com.

Thanks for reading, and Happy Programming!

Altering the Data Before It's Rendered

One of the many advantages of the data Web controls is how easy they make it to display data on an ASP.NET Web page. If you want to display information from a database with perhaps some stylistic HTML added, only a measly two lines of code are needed: setting the data Web control's `DataSource` property to an applicable object, and then calling the `DataBind()` method. This simple approach lends itself well to displaying data from a data store "as is." But what if you want to display data differently, depending on the value of the data itself?

In previous chapters, we examined two ways to accomplish this. One method is to write a custom function that accepts a value from one or more of the `DataSource`'s fields as input and returns a string. This function would then be called using the data-binding syntax:

```
<%# YourFunction(DataBinder.Eval(Container.DataItem,
"FieldName")) %>
```

We first examined how to use this approach in Chapter 3, "Customizing the HTML Output." This approach can be used in any of the data Web controls, but recall that data-binding syntax can only be employed in a DataGrid TemplateColumn column.

The second approach is to provide event handlers for either the `ItemCreated` or `ItemDataBound` events, both of which are common to all three data Web controls. The `ItemCreated` and `ItemDataBound` events occur when the data Web control is being constructed. Specifically, the `ItemCreated` event fires when a new item (a `DataGridItem`, `DataListItem`, or `RepeaterItem`) is created for the data

Web control, while the ItemDataBound event is raised when the current row in the DataSource is bound to the data Web control item. We first examined these events in Chapter 4, "Adding Buttons and Hyperlinks to the DataGrid Web Control."

In this chapter, we will use both of these techniques to alter the data prior to displaying it, as well as examine scenarios in which one would be interested in altering the HTML output based on the value of the data. Although this chapter examines material covered in previous chapters, it looks at the material in greater depth, and in various real-world scenarios where these techniques might be used.

Using Custom Functions and Data-Binding Syntax to Modify the Display of Data Based on Its Value

Recall that the makeup of the DataGrid can be implicitly specified by setting the AutoGenerateColumns property to True (the default), which has the effect of creating a DataGrid column for each field in the DataSource; alternatively, the makeup of the DataGrid can be explicitly specified by setting the AutoGenerateColumns property to False and specifying what DataSource columns should be included through the use of the Columns tag. In the Columns tag, you can specify the type of each DataGrid column. If you create a DataGrid column of type TemplateColumn, recall that you need to provide, at minimum, an ItemTemplate tag in the TemplateColumn. This ItemTemplate tag contains HTML and data-binding syntax used when displaying each item.

With the DataList and Repeater Web controls, there is no notion of predefined column types. Rather, the makeup of these two controls is determined by their various templates. To display a set of fields from the DataSource with the DataList or Repeater, you must use data-binding syntax.

> **NOTE**
>
> Recall that data-binding syntax takes the form
>
> ```
> <%# ... %>
> ```
>
> where typically a call to the DataBinder.Eval method is found within the tags. For example, to display the value of a field named title_id using data-binding syntax, you would use:
>
> ```
> <%# DataBinder.Eval(Container.DataItem, "title_id") %>
> ```

Listing 11.1 contains a DataList that displays information about the titles table found in the pubs database. Specifically, it lists each book, its price, publish date, and year-to-date sales. (The astute reader will recall that in Chapter 3's Listing 3.4, a similar example was given. The main difference between Listing 11.1 and Listing 3.4

is that Listing 3.4 used a DataGrid as opposed to a DataList, and it did not display the pubdate field.)

LISTING 11.1   When Using a DataList, You Must Use Data-Binding Syntax to Emit the Contents of a `DataSource` Field

```
 1: <%@ import Namespace="System.Data" %>
 2: <%@ import Namespace="System.Data.SqlClient" %>
 3: <script runat="server" language="VB">
 4: Sub Page_Load(sender as Object, e as EventArgs)
 5:    If Not Page.IsPostBack then
 6:       BindData()
 7:    End If
 8: End Sub
 9:
10:
11: Sub BindData()
12:    '1. Create a connection
13:    Const strConnString as String = "server=localhost;uid=sa;pwd=;database=pubs"
14:    Dim objConn as New SqlConnection(strConnString)
15:
16:    '2. Create a command object for the query
17:    Const strSQL as String = "SELECT * FROM titles"
18:    Dim objCmd as New SqlCommand(strSQL, objConn)
19:
20:    objConn.Open() 'Open the connection
21:
22:    'Finally, specify the DataSource and call DataBind()
23:    dlTitles.DataSource = objCmd.ExecuteReader(CommandBehavior.CloseConnection)
24:    dlTitles.DataBind()
25:
26:    objConn.Close() 'Close the connection
27: End Sub
28: </script>
29:
30: <asp:DataList id="dlTitles" runat="server"
31:         Font-Name="Verdana" Font-Size="10pt" RepeatColumns="3"
32:         AlternatingItemStyle-BackColor="#eeeeee">
33:    <ItemTemplate>
34:       <b><%# DataBinder.Eval(Container.DataItem, "title") %></b><br />
35:       Retailing for <%# DataBinder.Eval(Container.DataItem, "price",
➥"{0:c}") %><br />
```

LISTING 11.1   Continued

```
36:     Published on <%# DataBinder.Eval(Container.DataItem, "pubdate",
➥"{0:d}") %><br />
37:       <%# DataBinder.Eval(Container.DataItem, "ytd_sales", "{0:#,###}") %>
➥copies sold
38:    </ItemTemplate>
39: </asp:DataList>
```

Note that the `DataBinder.Eval` statement uses an optional third parameter in the binding syntax. This parameter specifies the formatting for the data returned. Specifically, on line 35 the value of the `price` field is formatted as a currency; on line 36, the value of the `pubdate` field is formatted as a date; and on line 37, the value of the `ytd_sales` is formatted so that there will be a comma every three digits.

Figure 11.1 shows a screenshot of Listing 11.1 when viewed through a browser. Note that the `ytd_sales` field allows NULL values, so for books whose `ytd_sales` field is NULL (such as *Net Etiquette*), no amount is displayed for the number of books sold.

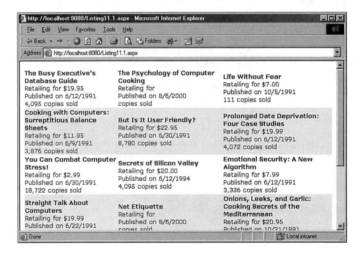

FIGURE 11.1   A three-column HTML table is used to display the books in the `titles` database table.

Displaying a Message for Books with a NULL `ytd_sales` Field

Often you will find that you want to display data differently in a data Web control, depending on what the value of the data is. In Listing 11.1, it would be nice to display a helpful message if no books have been sold. To accomplish this, we can create a custom function that takes as input the potential data type from the `DataBinder.Eval` syntax and returns a string. The return value of this function corresponds to the HTML that will be emitted. The custom function should appear in your ASP.NET Web page's server-side script block or in the code-behind page.

For our example, we'll create a custom function named `DisplaySales`, which will return a string and take an object as input. The reason this function's input parameter will be of type object is because the value of the `ytd_sales` might be one of two types: integer, when there is an integer value for the field; or `DBNull`, when the value of the field is NULL. If the `ytd_sales` field did not accept NULL values, or if we alter our SQL statement in the `BindData()` subroutine to only retrieve records that don't have NULL `ytd_sales` field values, our custom function can accept an integer input parameter. (See Listing 3.8 in Chapter 3 for an example of retrieving only those rows whose `ytd_sales` field is not NULL.)

> **NOTE**
>
> The `price` field of the `titles` table can also accept NULL values. The logic used in Listing 11.2 to display a custom message if the value of the `ytd_sales` field is NULL can be used to provide similar functionality for books with a NULL `price`.

Listing 11.2 contains an updated version of the code first presented in Listing 11.1, which displays "No copies sold" if the book's `ytd_sales` field is NULL.

LISTING 11.2 A Custom Function Is Used to Alter the Output Based Upon the Value of the Data

```
1: <%@ import Namespace="System.Data" %>
2: <%@ import Namespace="System.Data.SqlClient" %>
3: <script runat="server" language="VB">
4:
5: '... The Page_Load event handler and BindData() subroutine have been omitted
6: '... for brevity. Refer back to Listing 11.1 for details ...
7:
8:   Function DisplaySales(ytdSales as Object) as String
9:     If ytdSales.Equals(DBNull.Value) then
10:        'ytdSales is NULL
11:        Return "No copies sold"
12:     Else
13:        'ytdSales is some integer value
14:        Return String.Format("{0:#,###}", Convert.ToInt32(ytdSales)) &
➥" copies sold"
15:     End If
```

LISTING 11.2   Continued

```
16:    End Function
17: </script>
18:
19: <asp:DataList id="dlTitles" runat="server"
20:         Font-Name="verdana" Font-Size="10pt" RepeatColumns="3"
21:         AlternatingItemStyle-BackColor="#eeeeee">
22:   <ItemTemplate>
23:     <b><%# DataBinder.Eval(Container.DataItem, "title") %></b><br />
24:        Retailing for <%# DataBinder.Eval(Container.DataItem, "price",
➡"{0:c}") %><br />
25:        Published on <%# DataBinder.Eval(Container.DataItem, "pubdate",
➡ "{0:d}") %><br />
26:         <%# DisplaySales(DataBinder.Eval(Container.DataItem,
➡"ytd_sales")) %>
27:   </ItemTemplate>
28: </asp:DataList>
```

Listing 11.2 differs from Listing 11.1 in two ways. First, it contains the DisplaySales function that is responsible for displaying a helpful message if the ytd_sales field for a particular DataSource row is NULL (see lines 8 through 16). Second, the data-binding syntax in the DataList's ItemTemplate has been updated so that the data-binding syntax that displays the ytd_sales calls the DisplaySales function (line 26). Let's look at these two additions individually.

Let's turn our attention to the DisplaySales function. Note that it accepts an input parameter of type object (line 8), because we don't know whether the value of the ytd_sales column is an integer or NULL. In the DisplaySales function, we immediately check to determine whether the ytdSales input parameter is NULL (line 9). If it is, we return "No copies sold" (line 11); otherwise, ytdSales is converted to an integer (the Convert.ToInt32 call on line 14), and passed into String.Format so that it will be properly formatted with commas every three digits.

In our DataList declaration, a small change was made to the data-binding syntax on line 26. Specifically, we pass the value of the DataBinder.Eval method to the DisplaySales function. The string value returned by the DisplaySales function is then emitted as HTML.

CAUTION

Note that in Listing 11.1, the call to the DataBinder.Eval method to display the ytd_sales field had the optional third parameter, which formatted the value of ytd_sales, inserting a comma every three decimal places. In Listing 11.2, however, this was omitted from the DataBinder.Eval method call used to pass in a value to the DisplaySales function. This is because if the formatting parameter of the `DataBinder.Eval` method is present, the formatting is applied to the specified `DataSource` value and a string is returned. In our example, had we left in this formatting call, (that is, had line 26 appeared as

```
<%# DisplaySales(DataBinder.Eval(Container.DataItem, "ytd_sales",
"{0:#,###}")) %>
```

then the value passed into the `DisplaySales` function would be of type string. That is, if `ytd_sales` was NULL, then a blank string would be passed into the `DisplaySales` function. In this event, it checked on line 9 in Listing 11.2 to see whether the input parameter was of type `DBNull` would *always* be False, because the type would always be of type string. Furthermore, a runtime error would occur on line 14 when trying to convert a blank string or a string with commas in it into an `Int32`.

Figure 11.2 shows a screenshot of Listing 11.2 when viewed through a browser. Note that the books in Figure 11.1 that did not display a number of books sold now display a more sensible message: "No copies sold."

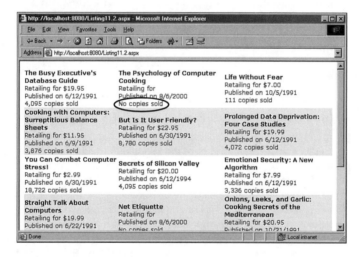

FIGURE 11.2   A helpful message is displayed for books that have a NULL `ytd_sales` field.

Using Custom Data-Binding Functions to Compute New Values

There are times when your data might not contain the precise information you want to display, but the information you do want to display can be computed from the data at hand. An everyday example would be an e-commerce Web site calculating the total cost for an order. The e-commerce database might contain information like the sales tax for each state, and the price for each item in its inventory. When a user makes a purchase, the amount to charge the user is the sum of the price of the items purchased multiplied by the applicable sales tax.

Displaying information that is computed from the values of other fields can be accomplished in two ways. One method is to perform the calculations in your SQL statement. For example, imagine for a moment that there is a book tax at 5%. If we want to display a list of books with a price that reflects the book tax, we could use the following SQL statement:

```
SELECT title, price, price * 1.05 AS PriceWithBookTax
FROM titles
```

To display the price of the book with the book tax included, we'd simply emit the value of the PriceWithBookTax field.

Another way to display computed values is to perform the computation in the ASP.NET Web page. This computed value can be performed in a function that is called via the data-binding syntax, passing in the values of the DataSource fields that are the operands in the computation. That is, we could write a function called ComputeBookPriceWithBookTax(bookPrice) that simply returns a value equal to the bookPrice input parameter times 1.05. This function could then be called in the following manner:

```
<%# ComputeBookPriceWithBookTax(DataBinder.Eval(Container.DataItem, "price")) %>
```

WHICH METHOD IS BEST? COMPUTING A VALUE IN THE SQL QUERY OR IN THE ASP.NET WEB PAGE?

Two approaches for computing a value from the values in the fields of a database table have been presented. One approach moves the work to be done to the database, while the other leaves the work to be done in the ASP.NET Web page. Which of these two options is the best choice? If the computation is performed at the database level, the ASP.NET Web page does not have to be littered by such computations. By placing this computation in a stored procedure, the computation is encapsulated from the ASP.NET Web page, meaning that if the computation ever needs to be changed (perhaps the book tax rate increases to 6.5%), the logic only needs to be altered in one place—the stored procedure. Compare that to placing the computation in the ASP.NET Web page, which would require a plethora of Web pages to be changed in the event that the logic used to perform the computation changed.

However, there are times when you, as an ASP.NET developer, cannot alter the SQL query. Perhaps you call some existing stored procedure that returns the specified data. You might want to change this stored procedure to include the computation, but the database administrator might not permit such a change. Or perhaps you are bringing in your data from an XML file, where such complex computations cannot be performed when querying.

Although the computational logic can be placed in either the SQL query (or stored procedure) or in an ASP.NET Web page, the best place for such logic, actually, is in neither the SQL query nor the ASP.NET Web page. Rather, such computations belong in a .NET component that implements the business logic for your Web site. In the article "Displaying Custom Classes in a DataGrid" (referenced in the "On the Web" section at the end of this chapter), I discuss the benefits of custom middleware objects and their benefits in designing modular Web applications. If you are unfamiliar with business objects and *n*-tier architecture, or are just interested in Web application architecture, I would encourage you to read this article as well as "Application Architecture: An N-Tier Approach" (also referenced in the "On the Web" section).

Let's look at an example of using the data-binding syntax and a custom function to generate new data that we'll display in a data Web control. Specifically, let's examine how we can display information on each book's gross income and how much money the author has made on royalties. The `titles` database table contains `advance` and `royalty` fields. `advance` is of SQL type `money`, and indicates how much money the author received as an advance. The `royalty` field is an integer type and corresponds to the percentage of each sale that the author is paid.

> **NOTE**
>
> Typically, authors only make money based on a percentage of sales of their book. The money earned from this percentage of sales is known as royalties. When the author is writing the book, the publisher commonly provides advance royalty payments to help motivate the author to continue and complete the work. These advances are borrowed against the author's future royalty earnings. Therefore, if a book has an advance value higher than the current royalty value, the publisher has paid the author more money than the author has yet earned.

In displaying the `titles` table in a data Web control, we might want to display a couple of pieces of information that aren't contained in the database table—specifically, the amount of money the book has grossed and the amount of money the author has earned from book sales. The book's gross can be computed by multiplying the price of the book times the sales (we'll assume that the `price` field indicates the price at which the publisher sells the books to the book stores, not the price at which the book stores sell the books to consumers). The amount the author has earned from royalties can be computed by multiplying the gross by the author's royalty percentage. Listing 11.3 contains the code to display these two computed values.

LISTING 11.3   The DataGrid Includes Columns for Each Book's Gross and the Royalties Earned by the Author

```
1: <%@ import Namespace="System.Data" %>
2: <%@ import Namespace="System.Data.SqlClient" %>
3: <script runat="server" language="VB">
4: '... The Page_Load event handler and BindData() subroutine have been omitted
```

LISTING 11.3   Continued

```
 5: '... for brevity. Refer back to Listing 11.1 for details ...
 6:
 7:  Function DisplaySales(ytdSales as Object) as String
 8:   If ytdSales.Equals(DBNull.Value) then
 9:       'ytdSales is NULL
10:       Return "No copies sold"
11:   Else
12:       'ytdSales is some integer value
13:       Return String.Format("{0:#,###}", Convert.ToInt32(ytdSales))
14:   End If
15:  End Function
16:
17:  Function DisplayRoyalty(royalty as Object) as String
18:   If royalty.Equals(DBNull.Value) then
19:       'royalty is NULL
20:       Return "Royalty not<br>yet determined"
21:   Else
22:       'royalty is some integer value
23:       Return royalty.ToString() & "%"
24:   End If
25:  End Function
26:
27:  Function DisplayAdvance(advance as Object) as String
28:   If advance.Equals(DBNull.Value) then
29:       'advance is NULL
30:       Return "Advance not<br>yet determined"
31:   Else
32:       'advance is some integer value
33:       Return String.Format("{0:c}", Convert.ToDouble(advance))
34:   End If
35:  End Function
36:
37:
38:  Function DisplayGross(ytdSales as Object, price as Object) as String
39:   If ytdSales.Equals(DBNull.Value) or price.Equals(DBNull.Value) then
40:       Return "$0.00"
41:   Else
42:      Dim gross as Double
43:      gross = Convert.ToDouble(price) * Convert.ToInt32(ytdSales)
44:
45:       Return String.Format("{0:c}", gross)
```

LISTING 11.3   Continued

```
46:    End If
47:  End Function
48:
49:  Function DisplayAuthorsRoyaltyTake(ytdSales as Object, price as object, _
50:                                    royalty as Object) as String
51:    If ytdSales.Equals(DBNull.Value) or price.Equals(DBNull.Value) _
52:                    or royalty.Equals(DBNull.value) then
53:      Return "$0.00"
54:    Else
55:      Dim gross as Double, authorsRoyalty as Double
56:      gross = Convert.ToDouble(price) * Convert.ToInt32(ytdSales)
57:      authorsRoyalty = gross * Convert.ToInt32(royalty) / 100
58:
59:      Return String.Format("{0:c}", authorsRoyalty)
60:    End If
61:  End Function
62: </script>
63:
64: <asp:DataGrid id="dgTitles" runat="server"
65:        Font-Name="Verdana" Font-Size="10pt"
66:        AlternatingItemStyle-BackColor="#eeeeee"
67:        AutoGenerateColumns="False" CellPadding="3"
68:
69:        HeaderStyle-HorizontalAlign="Center"
70:        HeaderStyle-Font-Bold="True"
71:        HeaderStyle-Font-Size="13pt">
72:    <Columns>
73:     <asp:BoundColumn DataField="title" HeaderText="Title" />
74:     <asp:BoundColumn DataField="price" HeaderText="Price"
75:        ItemStyle-HorizontalAlign="Right" DataFormatString="{0:c}" />
76:     <asp:TemplateColumn HeaderText="Copies Sold"
77:            ItemStyle-HorizontalAlign="Right">
78:       <ItemTemplate>
79:         <%# DisplaySales(DataBinder.Eval(Container.DataItem,
➥"ytd_sales")) %>
80:       </ItemTemplate>
81:     </asp:TemplateColumn>
82:     <asp:TemplateColumn HeaderText="Advance"
83:            ItemStyle-HorizontalAlign="Right">
84:       <ItemTemplate>
```

LISTING 11.3   Continued

```
85:              <%# DisplayAdvance(DataBinder.Eval(Container.DataItem,
➥"advance")) %>
86:          </ItemTemplate>
87:       </asp:TemplateColumn>
88:       <asp:TemplateColumn HeaderText="Royalty"
89:               ItemStyle-HorizontalAlign="Right">
90:          <ItemTemplate>
91:              <%# DisplayRoyalty(DataBinder.Eval(Container.DataItem,
➥"royalty")) %>
92:          </ItemTemplate>
93:       </asp:TemplateColumn>
94:       <asp:TemplateColumn HeaderText="Gross"
95:               ItemStyle-HorizontalAlign="Right">
96:          <ItemTemplate>
97:              <%# DisplayGross(DataBinder.Eval(Container.DataItem,
➥"ytd_sales"), _
98:              DataBinder.Eval(Container.DataItem, "price")) %>
99:          </ItemTemplate>
100:       </asp:TemplateColumn>
101:       <asp:TemplateColumn HeaderText="Royalty Payout"
102:               ItemStyle-HorizontalAlign="Right">
103:          <ItemTemplate>
104:              <%# DisplayAuthorsRoyaltyTake(DataBinder.Eval(
➥Container.DataItem, "ytd_sales"), _
105:                  DataBinder.Eval(Container.DataItem, "price"), _
106:                  DataBinder.Eval(Container.DataItem, "royalty")) %>
107:          </ItemTemplate>
108:       </asp:TemplateColumn>
109:    </Columns>
110: </asp:DataGrid>
```

The code for Listing 11.3 is lengthy, but the content is fairly simple to digest. Before tackling the code and DataGrid declaration in Listing 11.3, it might help to first take a look at the screenshot in Figure 11.3.

The DataGrid, which is declared starting on line 64, explicitly lists each column displayed via the Columns tag (starting on line 72). The title and price fields are displayed using BoundColumns (lines 73 through 75). Recall that with the DataList in Listing 11.2, to display a DataSource field we needed to use data-binding syntax. With the DataGrid, we can use BoundColumn controls if we only need to display the data "as is," or only need simple formatting applied. For example, the price field in Listing 11.3 is displayed via a BoundColumn, and is formatted as currency by specifying the DataFormatString property (line 75).

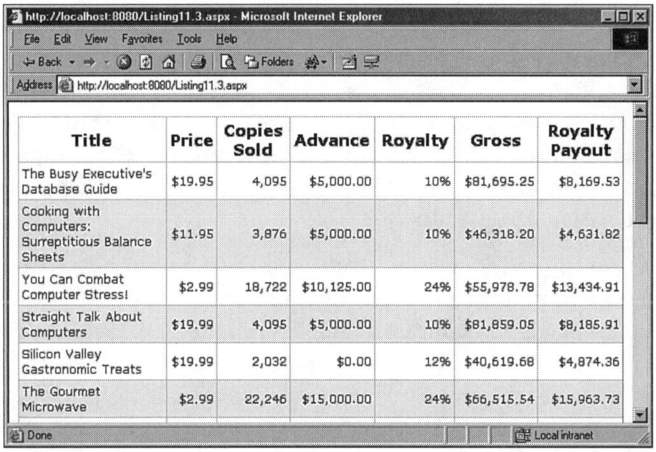

FIGURE 11.3 The Gross and Royalty Payout columns of the DataGrid are computed on the fly in the ASP.NET Web page.

The remaining five DataGrid columns are displayed using TemplateColumns. The reason TemplateColumns are used here is because we want to customize the output of the data based upon its value; hence, we need to employ data-binding syntax. To accomplish this, we have to use a TemplateColumn and specify the data-binding syntax in the TemplateColumn's ItemTemplate. For example, on lines 76 through 81 a TemplateColumn is used to display the ytd_sales field. Because this field can contain NULL values, we want to replace the values where zero copies have been sold with the text: "No copies sold." To accomplish this, we use the data-binding syntax, passing the value of the DataBinder.Eval method to the custom function DisplaySales (line 79). The DisplaySales function (lines 7–15) checks to see whether the passed-in value is NULL. If it is, the string "No copies sold" is returned (line 10); otherwise, a formatted string is returned (line 13).

NOTE

The price field might also contain NULLs. One possible enhancement to Listing 11.3 would be to have the Price column display a textual message such as "No price decided yet," as opposed to a blank string when the price field is NULL. This enhancement is left as an exercise to the reader.

Because the advance and royalty fields might also contain NULL values, the same approach is used in displaying these two fields in the DataGrid. The Advance column is specified from lines 82 through 87, and its associated display function, `DisplayAdvance`, can be found spanning lines 27 to 35. The Royalty column is specified from lines 88 to 93, and its associated display function, `DisplayRoyalty`, is defined on lines 17–25.

The next two columns in the DataGrid do not correspond to data found directly in the `DataSource`. Rather, the data in the Gross and Royalty Payout columns are computed from various fields in the `DataSource`. This computation for both columns is performed in a custom function; the Gross column value is computed in `DisplayGross`, whereas the Royalty Payout column value is computed in the `DisplayAuthorsRoyaltyTake` function.

The `DisplayGross` function, which is called in the data-binding syntax on lines 97 and 98, accepts two input parameters: the sales and price of the book. Because both of these database fields can contain NULL values, the `DisplayGross` function accepts objects as its inputs. The `DisplayGross` function, which starts on line 38, begins by checking whether either the sales or price for the book is a NULL value. If either are NULL, it returns the string "$0.00," because the book has failed to make any money at this point (line 40). If, however, neither are NULL, a local variable of type Double named `gross` is created, and assigned the value of the book's price times its sales (line 43). The function then returns the `gross` variable, formatted as a currency (line 45).

To compute the Royalty Payout column value, the `DisplayAuthorsRoyaltyTake` function is called (lines 104–106). Recall that the author's royalty earnings are computed by multiplying the book's gross by the author's royalty percentage. Because the gross is computed by multiplying the sales by the price, the `DisplayAuthorsRoyaltyTake` function needs to accept three input parameters: the sale and price, to compute the gross; and the author's royalty.

Again, all three of these fields can be NULL, so the `DisplayAuthorsRoyaltyTake` function must accept three inputs of type object. As with the `DisplayGross` function, the `DisplayAuthorsRoyaltyTake` function starts by checking whether any of its input parameters are NULL; if they are, the string "$0.00" is returned (line 53). Otherwise, first the gross is computed (line 56), and then the author's royalty is multiplied by the gross (line 57). Because the author's royalty is stored in the database as an integer, we need to divide the final result by 100 (line 57). Finally, on line 59, this computed value is formatted as a currency and returned.

Using Custom Functions to Display Non-NULL Fields

In the previous two code listings, the `DataSource` fields being passed to the custom display function could possibly contain NULL values. In light of this, we needed to have our custom display functions accept inputs of type object, and then check whether the incoming parameter was of type `DBNull`. If you want to potentially customize the display of a `DataSource` field based on its value, and the `DataSource` field cannot be a NULL value, then the custom function can specify its input parameter to be of the appropriate type.

For example, in the `titles` table, there is a field called `pubdate`, which specifies the date the book was published. Imagine that we want to display this date in a red-colored font if the `pubdate` value is more than one year ago from today. Because the `pubdate` field cannot contain NULL values, we could write our custom function to accept an input of type `DateTime` like so:

```
Function DisplayPubDate(pubdate as DateTime) as String
  If TimeSpan.Compare(DateTime.Now, pubdate.AddYears(1))
   'pubdate is more than one year ago from today
   Return "<font color=red>" & pubdate.ToString() & "</font>"
  Else
   Return pubdate.ToString()
  End If
End Function
```

To call this function from the data Web control in our ASP.NET Web page, we could use the following data-binding syntax:

```
<%# DisplayPubDate(Convert.ToDateTime(DataBinder.Eval(Container.DataItem, "pub-
date"))) %>
```

Note that a call to `Convert.ToDateTime` is made. This is needed because the return type of the `DataBinder.Eval` method is object, and the `DisplayPubDate` function expects an input of type DateTime.

NOTE

If you are using Visual Basic .NET and you do not set the `OptionStrict` property in your ASP.NET Web page or code-behind file, you can omit the explicit cast to a DateTime, because Visual Basic .NET will handle this for you automatically. However, if you are using C# or a program with Visual Basic .NET where the `OptionStrict` property is set, you will get a compile-time error if you fail to include this explicit cast.

Using the `ItemDataBound` Event to Modify the Display of Data Based on Its Value

One way to modify the display of data based on the value of the data involves using custom functions inside of data-binding syntax, as we saw in the last section. The main advantage of this approach is that it is straightforward and relatively simple to implement. To customize the display of data based on its value, simply write an appropriate function—one whose input parameter (or parameters) match the type of the value returned by the DataBinder.Eval method and whose return type is a string. This function can then be called from the data-binding syntax, as shown in Listing 11.2 and 11.3. Although this approach is easy to employ, it is limited by the fact that it can only be used to emit HTML content.

To provide a higher degree of customization of the data Web control's output based on the values of the data being bound to the control, we must provide an event handler for the control's ItemDataBound event. The ItemDataBound event is an event that all three data Web controls possess, and is raised once for each item added to the data Web control, after it has been bound to the appropriate item in the DataSource. That is, imagine we have a DataSource representing the contents of a SQL query that returned 10 rows as a result. Recall from Chapter 2, "Binding Data to the Data Controls," that when the data Web control's DataBind() method is called, the rows in the DataSource are iterated over. For each row in the DataSource, an item control is created—a DataGridItem for the DataGrid Web control, a DataListItem for the DataList, and a RepeaterItem for the Repeater—and the current row of the DataSource is bound to this newly created data Web control item. It is at this point that the ItemDataBound event is fired.

We can provide an event handler for the ItemDataBound event. The event handler definition varies slightly among the three data Web controls. For the DataGrid, the event handler must have the following definition:

```
Sub EventHandler(sender As Object, e As DataGridItemEventArgs)
  ...
End Sub
```

For the DataList, use

```
Sub EventHandler(sender As Object, e As DataListItemEventArgs)
  ...
End Sub
```

And finally, for the Repeater you must use

```
Sub EventHandler(sender As Object, e As RepeaterItemEventArgs)
  ...
End Sub
```

The second parameter contains a property named Item, which is a reference to the DataGridItem, DataListItem, or RepeaterItem that corresponds to the item that was just data-bound. Additionally, the Item contains a DataItem property, which can be used to programmatically extract items from the DataSource item that were bound to the particular Item using the DataBinder.Eval method.

Understandably, this might all sound a bit confusing. An example, though, should clear things up. Recall that in Listing 11.3 we displayed each book's gross income and the author's current royalty earnings. Imagine that rather than displaying this information in a standard DataGrid, we want to provide a Details button that displays a client-side modal dialog box with information about the particular book's gross and author royalties. To accomplish this, we need to programmatically add a call to the JavaScript function `alert` when the Details button's client-side `onclick` event fires. Listing 11.4 contains the necessary code to accomplish this.

LISTING 11.4 A Modal, Client-Side Dialog Appears When the User Clicks a Row's Details Button

```
 1: <%@ import Namespace="System.Data" %>
 2: <%@ import Namespace="System.Data.SqlClient" %>
 3: <script runat="server" language="VB">
 4: '... The Page_Load event handler, DisplaySales(), and BindData() subroutine
 5: '... have been omitted for brevity. Refer back to Listing 11.1 for details ...
 6:
 7:
 8:   Sub dgTitles_DataBound(sender as Object, e as DataGridItemEventArgs)
 9:     'Add a client-side onclick event handler to the Details button
10:     'First, make sure that we're not dealing with a header or footer item
11:     If e.Item.ItemType <> ListItemType.Header AND _
12:     e.Item.ItemType <> ListItemType.Footer then
13:
14:     Dim detailsButton as Button = e.Item.Cells(0).Controls(0)
15:
16:     'Determine the gross and author's royalties
17:     Dim gross as Double = 0.0, authorsRoyalty as Double = 0.0
18:
19:     'Make sure the values aren't null
20:     If DBNull.Value.Equals(DataBinder.Eval(e.Item.DataItem, "price")) or _
21:             DBNull.Value.Equals(DataBinder.Eval(e.Item.DataItem,
➡"ytd_sales")) or _
22:             DBNull.Value.Equals(DataBinder.Eval(e.Item.DataItem,
➡"royalty")) then
23:         'do nothing
24:     Else
25:         gross = Convert.ToDouble(DataBinder.Eval(e.Item.DataItem,
➡"price")) * _
26:             Convert.ToInt32(DataBinder.Eval(e.Item.DataItem, "ytd_sales"))
27:
28:         authorsRoyalty = gross / 100 * _
```

LISTING 11.4   Continued

```
29:          Convert.ToInt32(DataBinder.Eval(e.Item.DataItem, "royalty"))
30:     End If
31:
32:     detailsButton.Attributes("onclick") = "alert('Title: " & _
33:     DataBinder.Eval(e.Item.DataItem, "title").ToString().
➡Replace("'", "\'") & "\nGross: " & _
35:               String.Format("{0:c}", gross) & "\n" & _
36:               "Author\'s Royalties: " & _
37:               String.Format("{0:c}", authorsRoyalty) & "'); return false;"
38:     End If
39:   End Sub
40: </script>
41:
42: <form runat="server">
43:   <asp:DataGrid id="dgTitles" runat="server"
44:        Font-Name="Verdana" Font-Size="10pt"
45:        AlternatingItemStyle-BackColor="#eeeeee"
46:        AutoGenerateColumns="False" CellPadding="3"
47:
48:        OnItemDataBound="dgTitles_DataBound"
49:
50:        HeaderStyle-HorizontalAlign="Center"
51:        HeaderStyle-Font-Bold="True"
52:        HeaderStyle-Font-Size="13pt">
53:     <Columns>
54:       <asp:ButtonColumn HeaderText="Details" Text="Details"
55:           ButtonType="PushButton" ItemStyle-HorizontalAlign="Center" />
56:       <asp:BoundColumn DataField="title" HeaderText="Title" />
57:       <asp:BoundColumn DataField="price" HeaderText="Price"
58:           ItemStyle-HorizontalAlign="Right" DataFormatString="{0:c}" />
59:       <asp:TemplateColumn HeaderText="Copies Sold"
60:                       ItemStyle-HorizontalAlign="Right">
61:         <ItemTemplate>
62:             <%# DisplaySales(DataBinder.Eval(Container.DataItem,
➡"ytd_sales")) %>
63:         </ItemTemplate>
64:       </asp:TemplateColumn>
65:     </Columns>
66:   </asp:DataGrid>
67: </form>
```

Listing 11.4 creates a DataGrid that contains a Details button column that will popup a client-side alert box displaying detail information about the particular book. This is accomplished by creating a ButtonColumn in the DataGrid Web control for the Details button (lines 54 and 55). When this button is clicked, we want a client-side dialog box to appear that provides detailed information about the particular book: specifically, the book's title, gross, and author's royalty earnings. To accomplish this, we need to add client-side script to the button's client-side `onclick` event handler.

> **NOTE**
>
> Because Listing 11.4 adds a ButtonColumn to the DataGrid, we must place the DataGrid in a Web form (lines 42 and 67). If you forget to put the DataGrid in a Web form, you will receive a compile-time error indicating that to use a ButtonColumn you must place the DataGrid in a Web form.

Recall from Chapter 10, "Putting It All Together: A Real-World Example," that each Web control has an `Attributes` collection that can be used to specify client-side attributes and events. For example, in Listing 10.5 in Chapter 10, we looked at how to add a confirmation button to a Delete button. Therefore, to add a client-side `onclick`, we need to specify the value for the `onclick` event in the button's `Attributes` collection. Because the actual button control doesn't exist until the DataGrid itself is being rendered, this code needs to appear in the `ItemDataBound` event handler.

To specify an `ItemDataBound` event handler for our DataGrid, we need to create an event handler of the form

```
Sub EventHandler(sender As Object, e As DataGridItemEventArgs)
   ...
End Sub
```

The `dgTitles_DataBound` event handler (lines 8–39) provides the code to add the needed client-side `onclick` event handler to the Details button. It also contains code to compute the gross and author's royalty for the particular book. The `dgTitles_DataBound` event handler is wired up to the DataGrid's `ItemDataBound` event on line 48. This means that as the DataGrid is being rendered, after each time a new DataGridItem is bound to the current row in the `DataSource`, the `ItemDataBound` event is raised and the `dgTitles_DataBound` event handler is executed.

The dgTitles_DataBound event handler begins by checking to ensure that we're dealing with a DataGridItem that is not a header or footer, because neither the header or footer rows of the DataGrid will contain the Details button. On line 14, a local variable detailsButton is created and is used to reference the Details button. Note that to reference this button, we set detailsButton to the first (0th) control of the first (0th) column in the DataGridItem e.Item using the syntax e.Item.Cells(0).Controls(0).

Next we need to compute the gross and author's royalties, but only if the price, ytd_sales, and royalty fields of the current row in the DataSource are not NULL. Recall that the e.Item.DataItem property contains a reference to the current row of the DataSource, so to read the value of a particular field of the current DataSource row, we can use the DataBinder.Eval syntax as follows:

```
DataBinder.Eval(e.Item.DataItem, "FieldName")
```

On lines 20 through 22 we use this syntax to determine whether the price, ytd_sales, or royalty fields are NULL. If any of them are, we do nothing (line 23); otherwise we compute the gross and author's royalty (lines 25–26 and 28–29). Finally, we specify the Delete button's client-side onclick event on lines 32 through 37 using the Attributes collection. Specifically, the Delete button's onclick event causes a client-side dialog box to appear, displaying the title of the book, its gross, and the author's royalties from sales.

> **NOTE**
>
> Note that the title field, when displayed, has all apostrophes (') replaced by escaped apostrophes (\') (line 33). If this replace were omitted, any titles that contain an apostrophe would cause a client-side JavaScript error because the alert function's string input parameter is delimited by apostrophes. (This is similar to having to escape double quotes in Visual Basic .NET or VBScript with two double quotes, or having to escape double quotes in C# with \".)

On line 37, after the JavaScript call to alert, we use a return false. Recall that when adding a ButtonColumn to a DataGrid, when the ButtonColumn is clicked, the ASP.NET Web page does a postback. Because we do not want a postback to occur when the user clicks the Details button, a return false as the last statement in the client-side onclick event handler instructs the browser not to submit the form. Figure 11.4 shows the output of the code in Listing 11.4 when viewed through a browser.

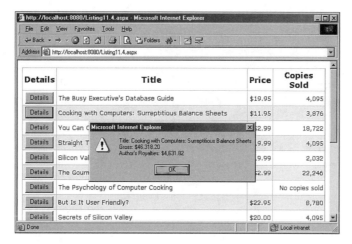

FIGURE 11.4 When the Details text is clicked, a client-side dialog box informs the user of the book's details.

Using the ItemDataBound Event to Compute Summary Data

Because the ItemDataBound event is fired for each row created, one can provide an ItemDataBound event handler that performs some form of summary computation using data in each row. For example, in Listing 11.4, the price of each book can be determined in the ItemDataBound event handler dgTitles_DataBound by using the DataBinder.Eval syntax. Using a page-level variable, we can sum up the price for each book and then compute the average price for each book.

> **NOTE**
>
> If you are using a server-side script block in your ASP.NET Web page, a *page-level variable* is a variable that is defined in the server-side script block, not one that is defined inside of a function, subroutine, or event handler. This variable, then, can be accessed by any function, subroutine, or event handler, and its value is retained until the page execution is complete. In more formal terms, it has page-level scope, and its lifetime runs through the beginning of the page execution to the end.
>
> If you are using code-behind pages, a page-level variable is a member variable of the code-behind class. A member variable can be accessed by all methods in a class, and has a lifetime equal to that of the lifetime of the class.

Listing 11.5 illustrates how to use an ItemDataBound event handler to produce summary information on the data displayed by a data Web control. (Listing 11.5 uses a DataGrid Web control, but the technique here would work equally well with a DataList or Repeater control.)

LISTING 11.5   The ItemDataBound Event's Event Handler Can Be Used to Compute Summary Information

```
1: <%@ import Namespace="System.Data" %>
2: <%@ import Namespace="System.Data.SqlClient" %>
3: <script runat="server" language="VB">
4: '... The DisplaySales() and BindData() subroutine have been omitted
5: '... for brevity. Refer back to Listing 11.1 for details ...
6:
7:    Dim totalPrice as Double = 0.0
8:    Dim numberOfBooks as Integer = 0
9:
10:    Sub Page_Load(sender as Object, e as EventArgs)
11:      If Not Page.IsPostBack then
12:        BindData()
13:
14:        'Now, display the summary data
15:        Dim avgPrice as Double = totalPrice / numberOfBooks
16:        summaryData.Text = "The average book price is: " & _
17:        String.Format("{0:c}", avgPrice)
18:      End If
19:    End Sub
20:
21:
22:    Sub dgTitles_DataBound(sender as Object, e as DataGridItemEventArgs)
23:
24:      'First, make sure that we're not dealing with a header or footer item
25:      If e.Item.ItemType <> ListItemType.Header AND _
26:        e.Item.ItemType <> ListItemType.Footer then
27:
28:        'Increment how many books we've displayed
29:        numberOfBooks += 1
30:
31:        Dim price as Object
32:        price = DataBinder.Eval(e.Item.DataItem, "price")
33:        If Not price.Equals(DBNull.Value) then
34:          totalPrice += Convert.ToDouble(price)
35:        End If
36:      End If
37:    End Sub
38: </script>
39:
40: <asp:DataGrid id="dgTitles" runat="server"
```

LISTING 11.5 Continued

```
41:        Font-Name="Verdana" Font-Size="10pt"
42:        AlternatingItemStyle-BackColor="#eeeeee"
43:        AutoGenerateColumns="False" CellPadding="3"
44:
45:        OnItemDataBound="dgTitles_DataBound"
46:
47:        HeaderStyle-HorizontalAlign="Center"
48:        HeaderStyle-Font-Bold="True"
49:        HeaderStyle-Font-Size="13pt">
50:  <Columns>
51:    <asp:BoundColumn DataField="title" HeaderText="Title" />
52:    <asp:BoundColumn DataField="price" HeaderText="Price"
53:          ItemStyle-HorizontalAlign="Right" DataFormatString="{0:c}" />
54:    <asp:TemplateColumn HeaderText="Copies Sold"
55:                    ItemStyle-HorizontalAlign="Right">
56:      <ItemTemplate>
57:        <%# DisplaySales(DataBinder.Eval(Container.DataItem,
➥"ytd_sales")) %>
58:      </ItemTemplate>
59:    </asp:TemplateColumn>
60:  </Columns>
61: </asp:DataGrid>
62:
63: <p>
64:    <asp:Label id="summaryData" runat="server"
65:              Font-Name="Verdana" Font-Italic="True" />
66: </p>
```

Listing 11.5 displays the Title, Price, and Copies Sold for each book in the `titles` table. In addition, it displays the average book price. This value is computed by summing the prices of all books and then dividing by the number of total books. To compute these two numbers, two page-level variables are created, `totalPrice` and `numberOfBooks` (lines 7 and 8). These variables are updated in the `dgTitles_DataBound` event handler, which is wired up to the DataGrid's `ItemDataBound` event on line 45. In the `dgTitles_DataBound` event handler, we first check to ensure that we're not dealing with a header or footer item (lines 25 and 26). After this has been established, we want to increment the number of books (lines 29) and then update the running total price. However, we only want to update the total if the `price` field is not NULL. This check is performed on lines 32 and 33, and if the `price` field value is not NULL, the `totalPrice` page-level variable is updated on line 34.

By placing this computation in the DataGrid's `ItemDataBound` event handler, we know that by the time the DataGrid is rendered, the page-level variable `totalPrice` will have the sum of all the prices, whereas the page-level variable `numberOfBooks` will be equal to the number of books displayed in the DataGrid. To compute the average, we just divide these two numbers. In the `Page_Load` event handler, after the call to `BindData()`, which renders the DataGrid, the average book price is computed (line 15). The Label control `summaryData` then has its `Text` property set to display this average price (the `summaryData` Label can be found in the HTML section on lines 64 and 65).

A screenshot of Listing 11.5 can be seen in Figure 11.5. Beneath the DataGrid, the average book price is displayed.

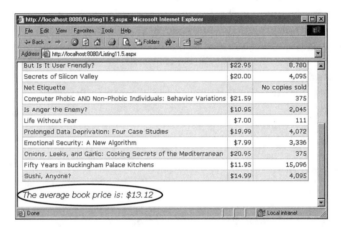

FIGURE 11.5   The average book price is computed by finding the sum of the book prices and dividing by the number of books.

Using the `ItemDataBound` Event Compared to Using SQL Query to Compute Summary Values

If you are familiar with SQL's aggregate functions such as SUM, MAX, AVG, and COUNT, you likely would have been a bit alarmed to see the average book price computed mechanically in the ASP.NET Web page in Listing 11.5. As a general rule of thumb, if a computation on some piece of data is needed and it can be performed at the database level, it is best to make the computation there as opposed to performing it in the ASP.NET Web page. That is, rather than computing the average book price in our ASP.NET Web page, it would be more sensible to use a SQL query like

```
SELECT AVG(price) FROM titles
```

This is a good rule of thumb to follow for the same reasons discussed in the sidebar earlier in this chapter. However, there are times when it might not be possible to move such an aggregate computation to a SQL query—for example, if your ASP.NET Web page must use a pre-written stored procedure that you cannot edit, or if you are using a data store that might not support such aggregate queries.

To summarize, summary calculations should, if at all possible, be performed at the database level for a myriad of reasons. However, if you cannot move such computations there for whatever reason, rest assured that you can perform these calculations by moving them to the `ItemDataBound` event's event handler.

Highlighting Data Based on Its Value

When displaying data, there is often a specific subset of the data in which the user is especially interested. A number of techniques can be used to help the user locate this information. For example, one way is to enable her to display only the data of interest; in Chapter 6, "Using External Web Controls to Achieve Effects on the Web Control," we examined how to enable the user to filter the contents of a data Web control. Another approach is to highlight the data that is of interest.

For example, imagine that we want to show the user all books in the `title` table, but also want to draw his attention to the books with a higher price. Specifically, we might want to highlight those books whose price is greater than $20.00. To accomplish this, we can use an event handler for the `ItemDataBound` event. This event handler simply needs to determine whether the `price` field is greater than $20.00; if it is, then the data Web control's item, `e.Item`, needs to have its `BackColor` property set to the highlighting color.

Listing 11.6 contains the code that lists the books in a three-column DataList. Those books that have a price greater than $20.00 are highlighted in yellow.

LISTING 11.6   Books With a Price Greater Than $20.00 Are Highlighted

```
 1: <%@ import Namespace="System.Drawing" %>
 2: <%@ import Namespace="System.Data" %>
 3: <%@ import Namespace="System.Data.SqlClient" %>
 4: <script runat="server">
 5: '... The Page_Load event handler and BindData() subroutine have been omitted
 6: '... for brevity. Refer back to Listing 11.1 for details ...
 7:
 8:    Sub dlTitles_DataBound(sender as Object, e as DataListItemEventArgs)
 9:      'Add a client-side onclick event handler to the Details button
10:      'First, make sure that we're not dealing with a header or footer item
11:      If e.Item.ItemType <> ListItemType.Header AND _
12:        e.Item.ItemType <> ListItemType.Footer then
13:        Dim price as Object
14:        price = DataBinder.Eval(e.Item.DataItem, "price")
15:
```

LISTING 11.6   Continued

```
16:        If Not price.Equals(DBNull.Value) then
17:          If Convert.ToDouble(price) > 20.0 then
18:            e.Item.BackColor = Color.Yellow
19:          End If
20:        End If
21:      End If
22:    End Sub
23: </script>
24:
25: <asp:DataList id="dlTitles" runat="server"
26:            Font-Name="verdana" Font-Size="10pt"
27:            OnItemDataBound="dlTitles_DataBound"
28:            RepeatColumns="3">
29:    ...
30:    <ItemTemplate>
31:      <b><%# DataBinder.Eval(Container.DataItem, "title") %></b><br />
32:      Retailing for <%# DataBinder.Eval(Container.DataItem, "price",
➥"{0:c}")
%><br />
33:    </ItemTemplate>
34:    ...
35: </asp:DataList>
```

The code in Listing 11.6 uses a DataList to display the books from the `titles` table in three columns (the `RepeatColumns` property is set to 3 on line 28). Specifically, each book's Title (line 31) and price (line 32) are displayed. The DataList's `ItemDataBound` event is wired up to the `dlTitles_DataBound` event handler, which starts on line 8.

The `dlTitles_DataBound` event handler first checks to make sure that we're not dealing with a header or footer item (lines 11 and 12). If this check passes, the `price` field is read and checked to see whether it is NULL (lines 13–16). If `price` is not NULL, it is converted into a Double and checked to see whether its value is greater than 20.0 (line 17). In the event that `price` is greater than 20.0, the book's DataListItem (`e.Item`) has its `BackColor` property set to the color yellow, using the `Color` structure (line 18). (The `Color` structure is found in the `System.Drawing` namespace, which is why we import this namespace on line 1.)

CAUTION

The code in Listing 11.6 will work for the DataList and DataGrid Web controls, but not for the Repeater. This is because the RepeaterItem class does not contain a `BackColor` property.

Listing 11.6, when viewed through a browser, will highlight each book whose price is greater than $20.00. To provide a more customized experience, you could add a TextBox Web control where the user can specify the price for which all books greater than that price he wants to see highlighted. This is left as an exercise to the reader.

Summary

In this chapter, we examined how to alter the data being displayed based on its value. On an ASP.NET Web page, this can be accomplished in two ways: providing a custom function that is called using the data-binding syntax and is passed the value of one or more DataSource fields; or by providing an event handler for the data Web control's ItemDataBound event.

With the custom functions in the data-binding syntax, the results of one or more fields of the current row in the DataSource can be examined to produce the output. Take, for example, an auction Web site like eBay. When a user searches on a term, the matching auctions are returned along with the time remaining in the auction. For auctions that have, say, less than one hour to go, we might want to display the remaining time in a red colored, bolded font. This can easily be accomplished using custom functions. Additionally, custom functions can be used to produce values that are computed from one or more DataSource fields, as was shown in Listing 11.3.

The data bound to each item in a data Web control can also be configured based upon its value by providing an event handler for the ItemDataBound event. Recall that the ItemDataBound event fires each time an item for a data Web control is bound to the current item of the DataSource. Customizing the output in the ItemDataBound event allows for more flexibility, because one can alter the contents of the data Web control's entire item, as opposed to just a particular DataSource field value. For example, in Listing 11.6, we saw how to highlight the item for each book whose price was greater than $20.00. Highlighting an item in this way is not possible through the custom function method.

Throughout this book, we have seen numerous examples showing how to explicitly display a DataSource field in the column of a DataGrid by using a BoundColumn or TemplateColumn. We have also examined a number of other DataGrid column types, such as the EditCommandColumn, HyperLinkColumn, and ButtonColumn. In the next chapter, "A More Advanced Examination of Using Templates," we will see how to programmatically create our own custom DataGrid columns!

On the Web

For more information on the topics discussed in this chapter, consider perusing the following online resources:

- "Displaying Custom Classes in a DataGrid"— `http://aspnet.4guysfromrolla.com/articles/102302-1.aspx`

- "Application Architecture: An N-Tier Approach"—`http://www.15seconds.com/issue/011023.htm`

- "Customizing DataBounded Output in Templates"—`http://aspnet.4guysfromrolla.com/articles/072102-1.aspx`

- "Highlighting Search Keywords in a DataGrid Web Control"—`http://aspnet.4guysfromrolla.com/articles/072402-1.aspx`

- "Recalculating Column Values in a DataGrid"—`http://www.aspnextgen.com/tutorials.aspx?tutorialid=334`

- "Dynamic Calculation in a DataGrid"—`http://www.aspnextgen.com/tutorials.aspx?tutorialid=375`

- "Displaying Hierarchical Data with the ASP.NET DataGrid"—`http://www.wimdows.net/articles/article.aspx?aid=19`

12

Creating Custom Column Controls for the DataGrid

IN THIS CHAPTER

- DataGrid Column Basics
- Steps for Creating a Robust Custom DataGrid Column
- Using Custom DataGrid Columns to Extend the Functionality of the DataGrid
- On the Web

As we've seen in numerous examples throughout this book, when using the DataGrid Web control, you can explicitly specify the columns that should appear in the DataGrid by using the Columns tag. There are a number of column types, such as the BoundColumn, which is useful for displaying data from a DataSource field, and the ButtonColumn, which creates a command button for each row. There might be times when you want to display data from a column in a certain way. You might want to display a particular column with a format not supported by the DataFormatString property of the BoundColumn, such as formatting a string as a telephone number. For example, imagine that you have a DataGrid that displays the contents of an online guestbook, as we saw in Chapter 8. One advanced formatting feature you might like to add to the column that displays the message a user adds to the guestbook is the censoring of profanity. That is, you'd like all swear words to be replaced by asterisks, such as replacing "hell" with "****".

Fortunately, you can create your own DataGrid column controls, and use them in your DataGrid, just like you use the built-in DataGrid column controls. In this chapter, we will examine how to create and use custom DataGrid column controls, and discuss the advantages of using them.

DataGrid Column Basics

Our earlier discussions examined the five provided DataGrid column controls:

- BoundColumn
- ButtonColumn
- EditCommandColumn
- HyperLinkColumn
- TemplateColumn

All of these column types are each represented by a class in the System.Web.UI.WebControls namespace with the same name. That is, the BoundColumn control is a control defined by the class System.Web.UI.WebControls. BoundColumn, the ButtonColumn control is a control defined by the class System. Web.UI.WebControls.ButtonColumn, and so on. All of these controls are derived from the DataGridColumn class, which is also found in the System.Web.UI.WebControls name-space.

NOTE

The DataGridColumn class is an abstract class, meaning that it cannot be used directly. To utilize its functionality, you must create a class that inherits the functionality of the DataGridColumn class and then use that class.

The DataGridColumn class contains the base set of properties that all DataGrid column types must include. These properties are listed in Table 12.1.

TABLE 12.1   The Properties of the DataGridColumn Class

Property	Description
ItemStyle	Specifies style information for each item of the column.
HeaderStyle	Specifies style information for the header of the column.
HeaderText	Specifies the text to appear in the header of the column.
HeaderImageUrl	Specifies an image URL to appear in the header of the column.
FooterStyle	Specifies style information for the footer of the column.
FooterText	Specifies the text to appear in the footer of the column.
SortExpression	The expression for the column that is passed to the DataGrid's SortCommand event handler when the DataGrid's AllowSorting property is set to True and the column's hyperlink sort header has been clicked.
Visible	A Boolean indicating whether the column is rendered.

The DataGridColumn class contains two important methods: Initialize() and IntializeCell(). When a DataGrid's DataBind() method is called, the Initialize() method of each column is called. This method allows for a DataGrid column to initialize any variables or data structures prior to the column being rendered. The InitializeCell() method, on the other hand, is called while the DataSource is being bound to the DataGrid. Specifically, for each row in the DataSource, the InitializeCell() method is called once for each DataGrid column. The InitializeCell() method's formal definition is given in the following:

```
Sub Overrides InitializeCell(cell as TableCell, columnIndex as Integer,
➥itemType as ListItemType)
```

When called, the InitializeCell() method's task is to add the needed content to the cell TableCell. The columnIndex and itemType input parameters are used to help determine how to render the content. The five provided DataGrid columns inherit the properties and methods of the DataGridColumn class, and extend the default functionality. For example, the BoundColumn class contains the properties listed in Table 12.1, along with the properties DataField, DataFormatString, and ReadOnly. The InitializeCell() method for the BoundColumn class needs to retrieve the DataField field from the DataSource, format it according to the DataFormatString property, and then add the formatted string to the TableCell cell.

TIP

If you are not familiar with inheritance and object-oriented design, consider reading Ian Stalling's "Using Object-Orientation in ASP.NET" article series, referenced in the "On the Web" section at the end of this chapter.

Creating Your First Custom DataGrid Column Classes

There's no reason why we can't create our own DataGrid column classes. In doing so, we must make certain that the classes are directly or indirectly derived from the DataGridColumn class, just like the five built-in DataGrid columns are.

NOTE

A class is said to be directly derived from a class if it inherits that class explicitly. For example, if you examine the ButtonColumn class's technical documentation, you'll find that it is derived from the DataGridColumn class. Therefore, it is said to be directly derived from the DataGridColumn class. However, there could exist a class that's derived from the ButtonColumn class. Such a class would be indirectly derived from the DataGridColumn class, because it directly inherits the DataGridColumn class, but does so indirectly, because it inherits the ButtonColumn class, which inherits the DataGridColumn class.

When creating a DataGrid column class, we must use a .NET programming language, such as Visual Basic .NET or C#. After the code for the class has been written, to use it in an ASP.NET Web page, we need to compile in into an assembly (a DLL) and copy the assembly to the Web application's /bin directory. After these steps have been performed, the custom DataGrid column class can be used via a DataGrid in an ASP.NET Web page. Before we examine how to use a compiled DataGrid column class in an ASP.NET Web page, though, we must first examine the ins and outs of the code required for such a class.

To create a custom DataGrid class, then, we need to create a class that inherits, directly or indirectly, the DataGridColumn class. If it inherits this class directly, we'll need to provide, at a minimum, the code for the InitializeCell() method. If, on the other hand, we derive from the DataGridColumn class indirectly, by perhaps deriving our custom class from the BoundColumn class, we might be able to reuse the BoundColumn class's implementation of the InitializeCell() method, meaning we do not have to write our own method.

Let's start by creating a very simple custom DataGrid column class, derived directly from the DataGridColumn class. This DataGrid column class, when used in a DataGrid, will add a column to the DataGrid that displays the message "Hello, World!" To create our first DataGrid column class, follow these steps:

1. Fire up Visual Studio .NET and opt to create a New Project.

2. From the New Project dialog box, select the Visual Basic Projects option from the list of Project Types, and then choose to create a Class Library from the Templates list.

3. In the Name textbox, enter **SimpleColumn**.

4. Click the OK button.

NOTE

If you do not own a copy of Visual Studio .NET, you can create this class using your favorite text editor, such as the ASP.NET Web Matrix Project, or even Notepad. Name the file you create SimpleColumn.vb.

Listing 12.1 contains the source code for the custom DataGrid column class, MyFirstDataGridColumn.

LISTING 12.1   The Class MyFirstDataGridColumn Is Directly Derived from the DataGridColumn Class

```
1: Imports System
2: Imports System.Web
3: Imports System.Web.UI
```

LISTING 12.1 Continued

```
4: Imports System.Web.UI.WebControls
5:
6: Public Class MyFirstDataGridColumn
7:     Inherits DataGridColumn
8:
9:     Public Overrides Sub InitializeCell(ByVal cell As TableCell, _
10:            ByVal columnIndex As Integer, ByVal itemType As ListItemType)
11:         MyBase.InitializeCell(cell, columnIndex, itemType)
12:
13:         If itemType = ListItemType.AlternatingItem Or _
14:            itemType = ListItemType.Item Or _
15:            itemType = ListItemType.SelectedItem Then
16:             cell.Text = "Hello, World!"
17:         End If
18:     End Sub
19: End Class
```

The first thing to take note of in Listing 12.1 is that the MyFirstDataGridColumn class is directly derived from the DataGridColumn class (line 7). This means that the MyFirstDataGridColumn class has the same properties and methods that are included in the DataGridColumn class. As designers of this new class, it is our responsibility to add any necessary additional properties and methods, and to override methods from the DataGridColumn class that we need to customize for our own purposes. Because the MyFirstDataGridColumn class's purpose is to simply emit a "Hello, World!" message for each row in the DataGrid, we don't need to provide any properties other than those already included by the DataGridColumn class (refer back to Table 12.1 for a listing of those properties). Furthermore, we don't need to provide any additional methods to achieve our limited functionality.

Instead, the only code we need to provide is the code for the InitializeCell() method. Specifically, we must override the DataGridColumn class's version of this method and replace it with our own functionality. To override a base class's method, we must use the Overrides keyword, as shown on line 9. When overriding a function, we should call the base class's version of the method first. In Visual Basic .NET, this can be accomplished by referencing the MyBase object and calling the appropriate function, as shown on line 11. By calling the base class's version of this method, the base class will perform whatever work it usually does for this method. After it has completed this work, you can add whatever functionality you need to add in the remainder of the method. The benefit to this approach is that if there is a method whose functionality you want to augment, you can override the method, call the base class's version of the file, and then provide the augmented functionality in the remainder of the overridden method.

TIP

If you are creating your custom DataGrid column classes using C#, note that instead of using `MyBase` to refer to the derived classes base class (as done on line 11 in Listing 12.1), you should use `base`.

After we call the base class's version of the `InitializeCell()` method, we are ready to set the contents of the `TableCell` cell to the string "Hello, World!" This can be accomplished by simply setting the `TableCell`'s `Text` property to the string we want to emit. Alternatively, we could add a LiteralControl to the `TableCell`'s `Controls` collection, which would change line 16 in Listing 12.1 to

```
cell.Controls.Add(New LiteralControl("Hello, World!"))
```

Before we add the "Hello, World!" message to the `TableCell`, we first check to ensure that the item being added is an item, alternating item, or selected item, and not a header, footer, or edit item. This check occurs on lines 13–15, where we check to see that the passed-in `itemType` property is one of the proper types. The `InitializeCell()` method is called for every row that is created in the DataGrid. This includes header and footer rows, or when the row is marked as editable. (Recall from Chapter 9, "Editing the DataGrid Web Control," that the row whose index equals the DataGrid's `EditItemIndex` is considered to be in "edit mode.") If we omit the checks on lines 13–15, the message "Hello, World!" appears, regardless of the type of item being added. This means that the header and footer cells for this column would have that message.

Compiling Your Custom DataGrid Column Class

To use your custom DataGrid column class in an ASP.NET Web page, you will need to compile the class into an assembly (a DLL file) and deploy it to the Web application's /bin directory. Compiling the class is simple enough if you are using Visual Studio .NET—simply go to the Build menu and select the Build Solution option. Assuming you named your project SimpleColumn, this will create a DLL named `SimpleColumn.dll`. The location of this file is in the /bin subdirectory of the folder where you opted to save the Visual Studio .NET project. Before you can use this assembly in an ASP.NET Web page, you will need to copy the DLL file from its current location to the /bin directory of your Web application.

TIP

If you are developing your Web application using Visual Studio .NET as well, you can avoid having to move this DLL file yourself by adding both the Web application and SimpleColumn projects to the same solution, and then specifying the `SimpleColumn.dll` file as a reference for the Web application.

If you did not use Visual Studio .NET to create this class, you will need to compile it into an assembly from the command line. However, before you do this, a small change needs to be made to the code presented in Listing 12.1. Specifically, before line 6, you need to add `Namespace SimpleColumn`, and after line 16, you need to add `End Namespace`. This is not necessary when using Visual Studio .NET, because it automatically performs this step for you when compiling your project. After you have made this small change, drop to the command line and navigate to the directory where the `SimpleColumn.vb` file is located and enter

```
vbc /t:library /r:System.dll,System.Web.dll SimpleColumn.vb
```

This will create a file named `SimpleColumn.dll`, which you will then need to copy to the Web application's `/bin` directory.

Using Your Custom DataGrid Column Class in an ASP.NET Web Page

After you have created a custom DataGrid column class using Visual Studio .NET or your favorite text editor, compiled it into an assembly, and moved the assembly to your Web application's `/bin` directory, you are ready to use the custom column in a DataGrid Web control in an ASP.NET Web page! To accomplish this, you need to provide the following directive at the top of your ASP.NET Web page:

```
<%@ Register TagPrefix="prefixName" Namespace="Namespace" Assembly="Assembly" %>
```

Here, `Assembly` is the name of the assembly that contains the custom DataGrid class; `Namespace` is the namespace where the custom column class is found within the assembly, and `prefixName` is the prefix name you want to give to your control.

NOTE

The prefix of a Web control is what appears before the colon in the Web control declaration tag. All built-in ASP.NET Web controls have the prefix asp; for example, to declare a TextBox Web control, you use the prefix and then the class name:

```
<asp:TextBox ... />.
```

For our example, let's choose a `prefixName` of custCols. The `Assembly` value will be SimpleColumn, the name of our assembly, and the `Namespace` value will also be SimpleColumn, because that is the namespace in which MyFirstDataGridColumn class resides. After we provide a `Register` directive at the top of our ASP.NET Web page, we can use our custom DataGrid column just like we use any of the built-in DataGrid columns. Listing 12.2 illustrates how to create a simple DataGrid that uses our custom column control.

LISTING 12.2   A Custom DataGrid Column Is Used Just Like Any of the Provided DataGrid Columns

```
 1: <%@ Register TagPrefix="custCols" Namespace="SimpleColumn"
➥Assembly="SimpleColumn" %>
 2: <%@ import Namespace="System.Data" %>
 3: <%@ import Namespace="System.Data.SqlClient" %>
 4: <script runat="server" language="VB">
 5:     Sub Page_Load(sender as Object, e as EventArgs)
 6:        BindData()
 7:     End Sub
 8:
 9:
10:     Sub BindData()
11:        '1. Create a connection
12:         Const strConnString as String = "server=localhost;uid=sa;
➥pwd=;database=pubs"
13:        Dim objConn as New SqlConnection(strConnString)
14:
15:        '2. Create a command object for the query
16:        Const strSQL as String = "SELECT * FROM titles"
17:        Dim objCmd as New SqlCommand(strSQL, objConn)
18:
19:        objConn.Open()    'Open the connection
20:
21:        'Finally, specify the DataSource and call DataBind()
22:        dgTitles.DataSource = objCmd.ExecuteReader(CommandBehavior.
➥CloseConnection)
23:        dgTitles.DataBind()
24:
25:        objConn.Close()    'Close the connection
26:     End Sub
27: </script>
28:
29: <asp:DataGrid runat="server" id="dgTitles"
30:        AutoGenerateColumns="False"
31:        Font-Name="Verdana"  Font-Size="9pt"
32:        HeaderStyle-HorizontalAlign="Center"
33:        HeaderStyle-Font-Bold="True"
34:        AlternatingItemStyle-BackColor="#eeeeee">
35:    <Columns>
36:      <custCols:MyFirstDataGridColumn HeaderText="Welcome Message"
37:           ItemStyle-HorizontalAlign="Center" />
```

LISTING 12.2   Continued

```
38:        <asp:BoundColumn DataField="title" HeaderText="Title" />
39:    </Columns>
40: </asp:DataGrid>
```

If you ignore line 1 and the seemingly funny syntax for the DataGrid column control on line 36, the code in Listing 12.2 looks just like many of the examples we've seen throughout the last eleven chapters. That's the beauty of using custom DataGrid column controls—they serve as a means to encapsulate code and functional complexity. That is, when using the MyFirstDataGridColumn DataGrid column control, we don't need to worry how exactly the message "Hello, World!" is produced. We can use it without concerning ourselves with the implementation details. Similarly, when we use any of the built-in DataGrid column types, we don't worry about how they work behind the scenes. We just know that if we use a BoundColumn control, we'll see the value of a specified field in the DataSource; if we use a ButtonColumn control, we know that each row will have a command button associated with it.

The lines worth noting in Listing 12.2 are line 1, which includes the Register directive, and lines 36 and 37, which contain the custom DataGrid column control. We use the normal Web control syntax to display this column control, but instead of using asp as the prefix, we use the prefix specified in the Register directive. We put the name of the class we want to display after the prefix and preceding colon. After that, we can specify any properties.

Recall that the code for the MyFirstDataGridColumn class did not contain any properties (refer back to Listing 12.1 if needed). Rather, it only contained the overridden version of the InitializeCell() method. However, on lines 36 and 37, we specify properties for this column control. What gives? Remember that the MyFirstDataGridColumn class is derived from the DataGridColumn class, which means the MyFirstDataGridColumn class inherits the public and protected properties of the DataGridColumn class. It is the DataGridColumn class that contains the HeaderText and ItemStyle properties used in lines 36 and 37. This illustrates one of the benefits of inheritance—the MyFirstDataGridColumn class contains, for free, the functionality of the DataGridColumn class. That is, our MyFirstDataGridColumn class can utilize the properties listed in Table 12.1 without us having to write a single line of code!

Figure 12.1 contains a screenshot of Listing 12.2 when viewed through a browser. Note that the first column in the DataGrid has a "Hello, World!" message displayed for each row. The text "Welcome Message" is found in the header, which is the value of the HeaderText property (line 36). Finally, each "Hello, World" message in the DataGrid column is centered, as specified by the ItemStyle-HorizontalAlign property (line 37).

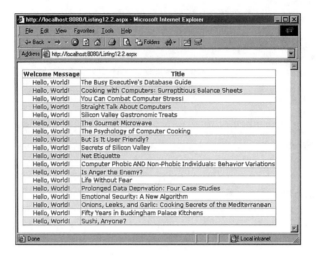

FIGURE 12.1   The first column in the DataGrid is a custom column control.

Creating Custom DataGrid Column Controls Derived from Existing DataGrid Column Controls

When creating a custom DataGrid column control, it is imperative that it is derived from the DataGridColumn class. For example, the custom column control created in Listing 12.1 inherits the DataGridColumn class using the Inherits keyword (line 7). However, your custom column class need not inherit the DataGridColumn class directly; rather, it can inherit a class that itself inherits the DataGridColumn class.

This is good news, because it means we can create a custom DataGrid column class by inheriting one of the pre-existing DataGrid column classes. This can provide useful if we want to extend the functionality of an existing DataGrid column class, because by inheriting the class, we obtain its functionality free of cost, and then can add our own customized code. For example, say that we want to create a column type that displays a text field from a DataSource, but rather than display the entire text field, we want to limit the display to a developer-specified number of characters. Let's create a custom DataGrid column class named LimitColumn that achieves this aim.

You can limit the amount of data displayed from a DataSource field by using a TemplateColumn that calls a custom function limiting the length of data, or by writing an event handler for the DataGrid's ItemDataBound event. (We examined these two approaches to modifying data before it is displayed in the previous chapter.) One benefit to using a custom DataGrid column class to achieve this functionality is that the column class hides the implementation details, leaving your ASP.NET page free from the excess code needed to provide this functionality with either a custom function or an event handler for the ItemDataBound event. Less code means fewer bugs and more maintainable code!

Because the LimitColumn class limits the number of characters of a particular field from the DataGrid's DataSource, it makes sense to have it derived from the BoundColumn class. After all, the BoundColumn was designed to render a particular field from the DataGrid's DataSource. By having our LimitColumn class inherit from the BoundColumn class, the LimitColumn class will have all the properties of the BoundColumn class, such as DataField and DataFormatString, in addition to the properties listed in Table 12.1. However, to implement our class, we'll need to add an additional property that specifies how many characters to limit the output of the column to. Let's call this property CharacterLimit, and make it of type Integer. Furthermore, let's apply the following semantics to the CharacterLimit property: If it's negative, no truncation occurs; if it's a positive value, each DataSource value displays only its first CharacterLimit number of characters, followed by an ellipsis (...).

In addition to needing a custom property, we must have some way to alter the contents of the DataSource field for each row of our column, displaying only the first CharacterLimit characters. We can accomplish this by overriding the BoundColumn's FormatDataValue(dataValue) method. The FormatDataValue(dataValue) method is called to format the data for each row in the BoundColumn prior to it being rendered. For example, in previous examples, we've looked at using a BoundColumn to display the price field in the titles database table. By setting the BoundColumn's DataFormatString property to {0:c}, we could have the price formatted as a currency. This formatting occurs in the BoundColumn's FormatDataValue(dataValue) method. As the DataGrid is being rendered, the price BoundColumn for each row has its InitializeCell() method called. A series of steps then occurs in the InitializeCell() method (which we'll discuss later in this chapter), and eventually the FormatDataValue(dataValue) method is called with the value of the price field passed in as the dataValue parameter. The FormatDataValue(dataValue) method returns a formatted version of the price field, which is then added to the Controls collection of the TableCell object passed into the InitializeCell() method.

Certainly, this process is a bit complicated! Fortunately, we do not have to concern ourselves with the ins and outs of what's occurring in the BoundColumn's InitializeCell() method. Instead, we can simply override the FormatDataValue(dataValue) method and return a truncated version of the dataValue parameter.

NOTE

We will be examining the InitializeCell() method for more complex DataGrid column types later in this chapter.

Listing 12.3 contains the source code for the LimitColumn class.

LISTING 12.3   The `LimitColumn` Class Only Displays a Specified Number of Characters from a Specified `DataSource` Field

```
 1: Imports System
 2: Imports System.Web
 3: Imports System.Web.UI
 4: Imports System.Web.UI.WebControls
 5:
 6: Public Class LimitColumn
 7:     Inherits BoundColumn
 8:
 9:     Private m_charLimit As Integer = -1
10:
11:
12:     Public Property CharacterLimit() As Integer
13:        Get
14:            Return m_charLimit
15:        End Get
16:        Set(ByVal Value As Integer)
17:            If Value >= 0 Then
18:                m_charLimit = Value
19:            Else
20:                m_charLimit = -1
21:            End If
22:        End Set
23:     End Property
24:
25:
26:     Protected Overrides Function FormatDataValue(ByVal dataValue As
➥Object) As String
27:         Dim result As String = MyBase.FormatDataValue(dataValue)
28:
29:         If m_charLimit = -1 Then
30:             'No restrictions should be applied to the length
31:             Return result
32:         Else
33:             'Only show the first m_charLimit characters
34:             If result.Length < m_charLimit Then
35:                 Return result
36:             Else
37:                 Return result.Substring(0, m_charLimit) & "..."
38:             End If
39:         End If
40:     End Function
41: End Class
```

Because the LimitColumn class is derived from the BoundColumn class (see line 7), the LimitColumn class inherits the public and protected properties and methods of the BoundColumn class. Therefore, without writing a line of code, our LimitColumn class has properties like DataField, DataFormatString, and all the properties inherent in the DataGridColumn class as well (see Table 12.1). Unfortunately these properties are not enough; rather, we need an additional property for our LimitColumn class, one that will enable the user to specify a character limit for the column. Lines 12 through 23 use a public Property statement to create a read/write CharacterLimit property of type Integer, with the value of the property being stored to the private member variable m_charLimit (declared on line 9). Note that the Set portion of the Property statement checks to see whether the passed-in value is not negative (lines 17). If it is, m_charLimit is assigned to the value specified by the user (line 18); otherwise, m_charLimit is assigned the value –1 (line 20). Also note that the m_charLimit has a default value of –1 (line 9), meaning that if the developer using our custom DataGrid control does not specify a CharacterLimit property value, no truncation will occur.

On lines 26 through 40, the BoundColumn's protected FormatDataValue(dataValue) method is overridden. Recall from our earlier discussions that this method has the value of the DataSource field specified by the BoundColumn's DataField property passed in as an object; the FormatDataValue(dataValue) method then formats the data according to the DataFormatString property and returns a formatted string, which is what is displayed in the BoundColumn. We can perform the truncating of data to the specified CharacterLimit limit by overriding this function and returning a truncated version of the dataValue parameter.

On line 27, a string variable named result is set equal to the result of the DataFormatString(dataValue) method of the BoundColumn class. Then the value of m_charLimit is checked (line 29). If m_charLimit equals –1, no truncating should be performed, and the value of result is returned (line 31). However, if m_charLimit does not equal –1, we check whether the length of result is greater than the value specified by m_charLimit (line 34). If the length of result is less than the value of m_charLimit, no truncation need occur, and the value of result is returned (line 35). However, if result has more characters than specified by the m_charLimit member variable, the Substring method is used to return only the first m_charLimit characters, and this result is followed by an ellipsis (line 37).

CAUTION

When overriding a method it is important to call the base class's version of the method. For example, on line 27 of Listing 12.3, a string variable named result is set equal to the result of the DataFormatString(dataValue) method of the BoundColumn class. This call to the BoundColumn's version of the DataFormatString(dataValue) method applies any formatting specified by the DataFormatString property. If you omit this call, the output result will not be formatted as directed by the DataFormatString property.

To use the `LimitColumn` class in an ASP.NET Web page, we must compile the class into an assembly. Rather than create a new assembly, we can add it to the `SimpleColumn` assembly created in Listing 12.1. To accomplish this using Visual Studio .NET, open up the `SimpleColumn` project and choose to add a new class to the project. Then enter the code from Listing 12.3 into that new class. Finally, build the solution, which will produce the file `SimpleColumn.dll`, an assembly that contains both the `MyFirstDataGridColumn` class from Listing 12.1 and the `LimitColumn` class from Listing 12.3.

If you used the command-line compiler to compile the class in Listing 12.1, you will need to make a small change to the code in Listing 12.3; namely, add `Namespace SimpleColumn` before line 6 and add `End Namespace` after line 41. Assuming you named the file containing the code from Listing 12.3 `LimitColumn.vb`, drop to the command line, navigate to the directory where both the `LimitColumn.vb` and `SimpleColumn.vb` files exist, and issue the following command:

```
vbc /t:library /r:System.dll,System.Web.dll SimpleColumn.vb LimitColumn.vb
```

Recall that `SimpleColumn.vb` is the name of the file that contains the code for the `MyFirstDataGridColumn` class (Listing 12.1).

After the `LimitColumn` class has been compiled, copy the assembly to the Web application's `/bin` directory. To use the `LimitColumn` class in an ASP.NET Web page, the first step is to include the `Register` directive. Because we are using the same assembly, and because the `LimitColumn` class is found under the same namespace as the `MyFirstDataGridColumn` class, the `Register` directive from Listing 12.2 can be used verbatim.

Listing 12.4 contains the code for an ASP.NET Web page that utilizes the `LimitColumn` class. Specifically, the `LimitColumn` class is used to display the `title` field from the `title` table, limiting the number of characters to 15.

LISTING 12.4   The `LimitColumn` Column Control Can Be Used to Restrict the Number of Characters Displayed

```
1: <%@ Register TagPrefix="custCols" Namespace="SimpleColumn"
➥Assembly="SimpleColumn" %>
2: <%@ import Namespace="System.Data" %>
3: <%@ import Namespace="System.Data.SqlClient" %>
4: <script runat="server" language="VB">
5:    '... The Page_Load event handler and BindData() subroutines have been ...
6:    ' ... omitted for brevity.  Refer back to Listing 12.2 for details ...
7: </script>
8:
9: <asp:DataGrid runat="server" id="dgTitles"
```

LISTING 12.4   Continued

```
10:        AutoGenerateColumns="False"
11:        Font-Name="Verdana"  Font-Size="9pt"
12:        HeaderStyle-HorizontalAlign="Center"
13:        HeaderStyle-Font-Bold="True"
14:        AlternatingItemStyle-BackColor="#eeeeee">
15:     <Columns>
16:        <custCols:LimitColumn HeaderText="Title"
17:           CharacterLimit="15" DataField="title" />
18:        <asp:BoundColumn DataField="price" HeaderText="Price" />
19:     </Columns>
20:  </asp:DataGrid>
```

Note that the Register directive on line 1 in Listing 12.4 is identical to the same line
in Listing 12.2. This is because the custom DataGrid column classes that we wanted
to use in both Listings 12.2 and 12.4 were found in the same assembly under the
same namespace. With this Register directive in place, to use the LimitColumn class as
a DataGrid column control, we simply specify the chosen *prefixName* from the
Register directive (custCols) followed by a colon, followed by the name of the class
we want to use. After this tag name, the properties follow. On line 16, we set the
HeaderText property to "Title"; on line 17, the DataField property is set to title,
meaning that the LimitColumn column will display the title field from the
DataSource, and the CharacterLimit property is set to 15, meaning that at most 15
characters will be displayed from the title field. If the value of the title field is a
string whose character count is greater than 15, only the first 15 characters will be
displayed, followed by an ellipsis.

Figure 12.2 shows a screenshot of Listing 12.4. Note that titles such as *Net Etiquette*
and *Sushi, Anyone?*, with fewer than 15 characters, are displayed as is. However,
longer titles are truncated at 15 characters and have their truncated value followed
by ellipses.

NOTE

The idea of creating a custom DataGrid column limiting the length of a DataSource field
came from an article written by John Dyer titled "Creating a Custom DataGridColumn Class."
In his article, John employed a more intelligent algorithm to limit the length of a DataSource
field so that the break would not occur in the middle of a word. If you are interested in this
approach or want a more detailed view of creating a custom DataGrid column class that
derives from the BoundColumn class, I highly encourage you to read John's great article. A
reference to the article can be found in the "On the Web" section at the end of this chapter.

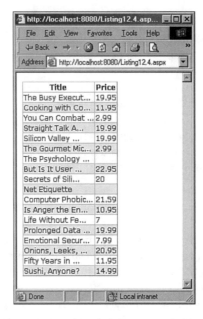

FIGURE 12.2   Only the first 15 characters of the `title` field are displayed.

Steps for Creating a Robust Custom DataGrid Column

In Listing 12.1, we saw a very simple custom DataGrid column class that displayed the message "Hello, World!" in each row. It accomplished this by overriding the `DataGridColumn` class's `InitializeCell()` method, setting the `Text` property of the passed-in `TableCell` to "Hello, World!" The code for Listing 12.1's `InitializeCell()` is overly simple, and such simple syntax, unfortunately, cannot be used for most custom DataGrid column classes.

To illustrate why the `InitializeCell()` syntax from Listing 12.1 can only be used in the simplest of cases, let's step through the creation of a custom DataGrid column class that censors profanity from the values it displays. For example, in previous chapters we examined displaying the contents of a `Comments` table that contains comments from an online guestbook. Clearly, these entries could contain offensive words. If we are using a DataGrid to display the contents of the online guestbook, we can display the database fields that might contain offensive material using a censor DataGrid column. That is, we can display our guestbook using the following DataGrid syntax:

```
<asp:DataGrid id="dgComments" runat="server" ...>
  <Columns>
    <asp:BoundColumn DataField="Name" HeaderText="Poster" />
```

```
    <custCols:CensorColumn DataField="Comment" HeaderText="Comment" />
  </Columns>
</asp:DataGrid>
```

The DataGrid specifies that two columns should be displayed: a standard BoundColumn column that displays the contents of the Name field, and a CensorColumn column that lists the contents of the Comment field, censoring the contents.

If your DataGrid column class needs to reference data from the DataGrid's DataSource, you can only access such information in the DataBinding event handler, not in the InitializeCell() method. Figure 12.3 shows a screenshot of the CensorColumn in action.

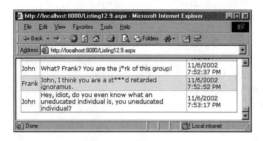

FIGURE 12.3   The CensorColumn displays the Comment field, censoring profane or offensive words.

Now that we understand the functionality of the CensorColumn column class, let's create this class.

Clearly, the CensorColumn class behaves a lot like the BoundColumn class—it displays contents from a database field and applies stylistic formatting to the results. Therefore, it would make sense to derive the CensorColumn class from the BoundColumn class, much like the LimitColumn class in Listing 12.3. However, let's take the nonsensical route and derive the CensorColumn class from the DataGridColumn class so that we can get a better understanding of what code needs to be provided in the InitializeCell() method to enable the contents of a DataGrid to be dependent upon the DataGrid's DataSource contents.

NOTE

Examining how to perform data binding from a class derived from the DataGridColumn class will also prove useful when examining more complex custom DataGrid column class examples. Additionally, it will give us insight as to how the BoundColumn class is implemented.

Displaying a DataSource **Field in a Custom DataGrid Column Class**

The BoundColumn class essentially accesses the DataSource field specified by its DataField property, and sets the TableCell's Text property to this DataSource field. Our CensorColumn class will essentially need to perform these same steps, but after it has the proper DataSource field, it needs to first censor the profane words from it (if any exist), and then have it displayed in the TableCell. To accomplish this, our CensorColumn class will need a DataField property just like the BoundColumn class.

Implementing the code to retrieve the proper field from the DataSource is a bit involved. Before we examine the code to accomplish this, let's first look at the shell of the CensorColumn class, as shown in Listing 12.5. The CensorColumn class is derived from the DataGridColumn class (line 7), and contains a DataField string property (lines 15–24). Beginning on line 9 is the overridden InitializeCell() method, which is called once for every row added to the column.

LISTING 12.5   The CensorColumn Class Is Derived from the DataGridColumn Class

```
 1: Imports System
 2: Imports System.Web.UI.WebControls
 3: Imports System.Web.UI
 4: Imports System.Web
 5:
 6: Public Class CensorColumn
 7:     Inherits DataGridColumn
 8:
 9:     Public Overrides Sub InitializeCell(ByVal cell As TableCell,
➥ByVal columnIndex As Integer, ByVal itemType As ListItemType)
10:         MyBase.InitializeCell(cell, columnIndex, itemType)
11:
12:          ' TODO: Bind the
13:     End Sub
14:
15:     Private m_dataField As String
16:
17:     Public Property DataField() As String
18:         Get
19:             Return Me.m_dataField
20:         End Get
21:         Set(ByVal Value As String)
22:             Me.m_dataField = Value
23:         End Set
24:     End Property
25: End Class
```

Now that we have the shell of the `CensorColumn` class in place, we can examine in detail the code needed to retrieve the proper `DataSource` field. Recall from Chapter 2, "Binding Data to the Data Controls," that the `DataGridItem` class has a `DataItem` property. When the DataGrid's `DataBind()` method is called, the `DataSource`'s contents are enumerated, and for each `DataSource` item, a new `DataGridItem` object is created and added to the DataGrid. At this time, the `DataSource`'s current item is assigned to the newly created `DataGridItem` object's `DataItem` property. So, if the `DataSource` contains the results of a SQL query, the `DataItem` will contain a particular row from the query results. Using data-binding syntax in a TemplateColumn, we can reference a particular field of the row using

```
DataBinder.Eval(Container.DataItem, "FieldName")
```

When such syntax appears within a TemplateColumn, we are dealing with a specific cell in the `DataGridItem`, so to reference the `DataGridItem`'s `DataItem` property, we have to use `Container.DataItem`.

To reference a particular field in the `DataSource` in our `CensorColumn`, we must use a similar approach, referencing the `DataGridItem`'s `DataItem` property. As with the data-binding syntax in the TemplateColumn, the `TableCell cell` in the `CensorColumn` class's `InitializeCell()` method is contained by the `DataGridItem`. Hence, we first have to reference the `DataGridItem` object that contains `cell` to get to the needed `DataItem` property.

After the last few paragraphs, I don't blame you if you're very confused! This is tricky subject matter. Let's look at some code that should help clarify things. The following snippet of code illustrates how the `DataItem` property can be referenced by examining the container of the `TableCell cell`.

```
'Get the DataGridItem that contains the TableCell cell
Dim gridItem as DataGridItem = cell.NamingContainer

'Get the DataItem property from gridItem
Dim DataItem as Object = gridItem.DataItem

'Display a particular DataItem field in the contents of cell
cell.Text = DataBinder.Eval(dataItem, "FieldName")
```

These three, short lines of code accomplish quite a bit. The first line accesses the object that contains the `TableCell cell`. This is accomplished by referencing `cell`'s `NamingContainer` property. (The `NamingContainer` property is defined in the `Control` class, meaning *all* Web controls, including `TableCell`, have this property.) Next, the `DataItem` property of the `DataGridItem gridItem` is referenced and stored in the local variable `dataItem`. Finally, the `DataBinder.Eval` method is used to retrieve a particular field from the `dataItem` object and assigns the value to `cell`'s `Text` property.

Unfortunately, the code just examined cannot be placed in the InitializeCell() method because when the InitializeCell() method is executed, the DataGridItem's DataItem property has yet to be set to the particular DataSource item. Rather, the code must be placed in the DataBinding event handler for the TableCell cell. Listing 12.6 provides the code for the CensorColumn class that correctly displays a DataSource field in the DataGrid column.

LISTING 12.6   The TableCell's Text Property Is Set in the TableCell's DataBinding Event Handler

```
 1: Imports System
 2: Imports System.Web.UI.WebControls
 3: Imports System.Web.UI
 4: Imports System.Web
 5:
 6: Public Class CensorColumn
 7:     Inherits DataGridColumn
 8:
 9:     Public Overrides Sub InitializeCell(ByVal cell As TableCell,
➥ByVal columnIndex As Integer, ByVal itemType As ListItemType)
10:         MyBase.InitializeCell(cell, columnIndex, itemType)
11:
12:         Select Case itemType
13:             Case ListItemType.AlternatingItem, ListItemType.Item,
➥ListItemType.SelectedItem
14:                 AddHandler cell.DataBinding, AddressOf Me.PerformDataBinding
15:         End Select
16:     End Sub
17:
18:     Private Sub PerformDataBinding(ByVal sender As Object,
➥ByVal e As EventArgs)
19:         Dim cell As TableCell = sender
20:         Dim gridItem As DataGridItem = cell.NamingContainer
21:         Dim dataItem As Object = gridItem.DataItem
22:
23:         If Me.DataField <> String.Empty Then
24:             cell.Text = DataBinder.Eval(dataItem, Me.DataField)
25:         End If
26:     End Sub
27:
28:
29:     Private m_dataField As String
30:
```

LISTING 12.6 Continued

```
31:     Public Property DataField() As String
32:         Get
33:             Return Me.m_dataField
34:         End Get
35:         Set(ByVal Value As String)
36:             Me.m_dataField = Value
37:         End Set
38:     End Property
39: End Class
```

The InitializeCell() method in Listing 12.6 (lines 9–16) checks to determine what type of cell is being added. In the event that an Item, AlternatingItem, or SelectedItem cell is being added, an event handler, PerformDataBinding, is added to the DataBinding event of the TableCell cell (line 14). After the DataGridItem that contains the TableCell cell has its DataItem property set, it will fire the DataBinding event, which will cause the PerformDataBinding event handler to execute. The PerformDataBinding event handler (lines 18–26), when executed, receives as its first input parameter the TableCell whose DataBinding event was wired up to the event handler. This input parameter, sender, is set to a local variable cell (line 19). Next, a DataGridItem local variable is created and used to reference the DataGridItem object that contains the TableCell whose DataBinding event has fired (line 20). Following that, the DataGridItem's DataItem property is referenced by the local variable dataItem (line 21). Finally, the Text property of the TableCell is set to the value of the DataField field in the dataItem object, assuming that the DataField property has been specified (lines 23–25) .

NOTE

When the added cell is an EditItem, Header, Footer, Pager, or SelectedItem, the event handler is not called. Instead, the cell's rendering is handled entirely by the DataGridColumn class's InitializeCell() method via the MyBase.InitializeCell method call on line 10.

Censoring Offensive Words in the CensorColumn Class

At this point, our CensorColumn mimics the functionality of the BoundColumn. To have the contents of the specified DataSource field censored, we need to provide a means for the contents of the cell's Text property to get rid of profanity. To accomplish this, we can use regular expressions to search for offensive words, replacing them with nonoffensive equivalents.

Given a string, we can replace all instances of a substring with another substring using the following code:

```
Dim strToCensor as String = "Hello, do you like my butt?"
Dim strDirtyWord as String = "butt"
Dim strCensoredWord as String = "behind"

'Replace all instances of "butt" with "behind"
Dim re as New Regex("\b" & strDirtyWord & "\b", RegexOptions.IgnoreCase)
Dim strCensoredString as String = re.Replace(strToCensor, strCensoredWord)
```

This code uses the `Regex.Replace` method to search the string `strToCensor`, replacing all instances of `strDirtyWord` with `strCensoredWord`, returning the updated string.

To censor the contents of the `TableCell`, we can simply iterate through each possibly offensive word and use `Regex.Replace` to replace it with a less offensive one. But what words should be considered offensive, and what should their replacements be? It would be ideal to let the developer using the `CensorColumn` class to determine this. One option would be to add a `Hashtable` property to the `CensorColumn` class, which would enable the user to specify those words that should be censored, and what their replacements should be. Another approach would be to let the developer create an XML file whose contents specified what words should be censored. Let's implement the latter approach, although you're encouraged to experiment with the former approach as well.

For our example, the XML file used must have the following structure: a root tag called `censors`, followed by zero to many `censor` tags, each of which contain a `find` and `replace` tag whose text contents are the words to censor and the words to replace the censored words, respectively. For example, if you want to censor the words *butt*, *ugly,* and *stupid* with *behind, unattractive,* and *unintelligent,* your XML file would look like this:

```
<censors>
    <censor>
        <find>butt</find>
        <replace>behind</replace>
    </censor>
    <censor>
        <find>ugly</find>
        <replace>unattractive</replace>
    </censor>
    <censor>
        <find>stupid</find>
        <replace>unintelligent</replace>
    </censor>
</censors>
```

To use an XML file for censored words, the CensorColumn class will need another string property called CensorFile, which specifies the filename of the XML file to use. Listing 12.7 contains the code for the PerformCensorship function, which takes as input a string to censor and censors it based on the contents of the XML file specified by the CensorFile property.

LISTING 12.7   The PerformCensorship Function Censors the Words Specified in an XML File

```
 1:    Private Function PerformCensorship(ByVal censorMe As String) As String
 2:        'If no CensorFile has been specified, return censorMe string
 3:        If Me.CensorFile = String.Empty Then
 4:            Return censorMe
 5:        End If
 6:
 7:        'Convert the CensorFile path into a physical path
 8:        Dim filepath As String = HttpContext.Current.Server.MapPath(Me.
➥CensorFile)
 9:
10:        'Make sure the file exists
11:        If Not File.Exists(filepath) Then
12:            Throw New Exception("File " & filepath & " does not exist!")
13:            Return censorMe
14:        End If
15:
```

LISTING 12.7   Continued

```
16:         'Read the XML file's contents
17:         Dim censorDoc As New XmlDocument()
18:         censorDoc.PreserveWhitespace = True
19:         censorDoc.Load(filepath)
20:
21:         Dim root As XmlNode = censorDoc.FirstChild
22:
23:         Dim findNodes As XmlNodeList = root.SelectNodes("/censors/censor/find")
24:         Dim replaceNodes As XmlNodeList = root.SelectNodes
➥("/censors/censor/replace")
25:
26:         Dim re As Regex
27:         Dim results As String = censorMe
28:         Dim i As Integer
29:         For i = 0 To findNodes.Count - 1
30:             re = New Regex("\b" & findNodes.Item(i).InnerText & "\b",
➥RegexOptions.IgnoreCase)
31:             results = re.Replace(results, replaceNodes.Item(i).InnerText)
32:         Next
33:
34:         Return results
35:     End Function
```

The PerformCensorship function takes as input a string, censorMe, and returns a
censored version of this input string. Before applying the censorship, though, a few
quick checks are made. On line 3, a check is made to ensure that the CensorFile
property has been specified. If it hasn't, the censorMe string is returned as is (line 4).
Next, a check is made to see whether the file specified by the CensorFile property
actually exists. First, on line 8, the CensorFile property is mapped to its physical file
path. Next, on line 11, the File.Exists method is used to check whether the file
exists. If the file does not exist, an Exception is thrown.

> **NOTE**
>
> The physical path of a file is given as DRIVELETTER:\DIRECTORY\...\FILENAME, like
> C:\Inetpub\wwwroot\profane.xml. To ease using the CensorColumn class in a DataGrid, the
> developer need only provide a CensorFile value that contains just the name of the XML file,
> like CensorFile="profane.xml". Assuming that the file profane.xml exists in the same direc-
> tory as the ASP.NET Web page using the file, the CensorColumn class's PerformCensorship
> function will automatically compute the physical path of the file using the Server.MapPath
> method (line 11).

If the control reaches line 16, then we know that a `CensorFile` property has been provided, and that it maps to the physical path specified by `filepath`. Therefore, we can load the contents of the XML file into an `XmlDocument` object (lines 17–19). Next, on line 21, the root node of the `XmlDocument` is retrieved. Then, two `XmlNodeList` instances are created—`findNodes` and `replaceNodes` (lines 23 and 24). The `findNodes` `XmlNodeList` contains a list of all XML nodes whose path expression matches `/censors/censor/find`, whereas the `replaceNodes` `XmlNodeList` contains a list of all XML nodes whose path expression matches `/censors/censor/replace`. Additionally, a regular expression variable is created (line 26), and a string variable `results` is created and assigned the value of the `censorMe` input string parameter (line 27) .

The nodes in the `findNodes` list are then enumerated (lines 29–32). For each `XmlNode` in the `findNodes` list, a new regular expression instance is created whose pattern is the `InnerText` of the particular `findNode` `XmlNode` (line 30). The contents of the local string variable `results` are then censored using the `Replace` method on line 31. Specifically, the contents of `results` are searched, and all instances of the `InnerText` of the current `findNode` are replaced with the `InnerText` of the current `replaceNode`. After this loop completes, the `PerformCensorship` function returns the value of `results`.

CAUTION

The code in the `PerformCensorship` function assumes that the XML file specified is in the proper format as described earlier. If the XML file has an invalid format—for example, having a censor tag that is missing a `replace` tag—an error will likely occur when iterating through the loop spanning lines 29 to 32.

Use of the `PerformCensorship` function requires some changes to the `CensorColumn` code that was last presented in Listing 12.6. Specifically, a `CensorFile` property must be added, and the `PerformDataBinding` event handler must be updated to call the `PerformCensorship` function. Also, additional `Imports` statements need to be added for the XML, IO, and regular expression functionality used in the `PerformCensorship` function. These changes are reflected in Listing 12.8, which contains the complete `CensorColumn` code to this point.

LISTING 12.8   The Complete Code for the `CensorColumn` Class

```
1: Imports System
2: Imports System.Text.RegularExpressions
3: Imports System.Web.UI.WebControls
4: Imports System.Web.UI
5: Imports System.Web
6: Imports System.Xml
7: Imports System.IO
8:
```

LISTING 12.8   Continued

```
 9: Public Class CensorColumn
10:     Inherits DataGridColumn
11:
12:     Public Overrides Sub InitializeCell(ByVal cell As TableCell,
➥ByVal columnIndex As Integer, ByVal itemType As ListItemType)
13:         MyBase.InitializeCell(cell, columnIndex, itemType)
14:
15:         Select Case itemType
16:             Case ListItemType.AlternatingItem, ListItemType.Item,
➥ListItemType.SelectedItem
17:                 AddHandler cell.DataBinding, AddressOf Me.PerformDataBinding
18:         End Select
19:     End Sub
20:
21:     Private Sub PerformDataBinding(ByVal sender As Object,
➥ByVal e As EventArgs)
22:         Dim cell As TableCell = sender
23:         Dim gridItem As DataGridItem = cell.NamingContainer
24:         Dim dataItem As Object = gridItem.DataItem
25:
26:         If Me.DataField <> String.Empty Then
27:             cell.Text = PerformCensorship(DataBinder.Eval
➥(dataItem, Me.DataField))
28:         End If
29:     End Sub
30:
31:
32:     Private Function PerformCensorship(ByVal censorMe As String) As String
33:         'If no CensorFile has been specified, return censorMe string
34:         If Me.CensorFile = String.Empty Then
35:             Return censorMe
36:         End If
37:
38:         'Convert the CensorFile path into a physical path
39:         Dim filepath As String = HttpContext.Current.Server.
➥MapPath(Me.CensorFile)
40:
41:         'Make sure the file exists
42:         If Not File.Exists(filepath) Then
43:             Throw New Exception("File " & filepath & " does not exist!")
44:             Return censorMe
```

LISTING 12.8   Continued

```
45:         End If
46:
47:         'Read the XML file's contents
48:         Dim censorDoc As New XmlDocument()
49:         censorDoc.PreserveWhitespace = True
50:         censorDoc.Load(filepath)
51:
52:         Dim root As XmlNode = censorDoc.FirstChild
53:
54:         Dim findNodes As XmlNodeList = root.SelectNodes
➥("/censors/censor/find")
55:         Dim replaceNodes As XmlNodeList = root.SelectNodes
➥("/censors/censor/replace")
56:
57:         Dim re As Regex
58:         Dim results As String = censorMe
59:         Dim i As Integer
60:         For i = 0 To findNodes.Count - 1
61:             re = New Regex("\b" & findNodes.Item(i).InnerText & "\b",
➥RegexOptions.IgnoreCase)
62:             results = re.Replace(results, replaceNodes.Item(i).InnerText)
63:         Next
64:
65:         Return results
66:     End Function
67:
68:
69:
70:     Private m_dataField As String
71:     Private m_censorFile As String
72:
73:     Public Property CensorFile() As String
74:         Get
75:             Return Me.m_censorFile
76:         End Get
77:         Set(ByVal Value As String)
78:             Me.m_censorFile = Value
79:         End Set
80:     End Property
81:
82:     Public Property DataField() As String
```

LISTING 12.8   Continued

```
83:        Get
84:            Return Me.m_dataField
85:        End Get
86:        Set(ByVal Value As String)
87:            Me.m_dataField = Value
88:        End Set
89:    End Property
90: End Class
```

The new CensorFile property can be found on lines 73 through 80. The added Imports statements can be found on lines 2, 6, and 7. Finally, note that the PerformDataBinding event handler has been updated. On line 27, the cell.Text property is set to the string returned by the PerformCensorship function with the value of the DataSource field passed in as input.

At this point, we can use the CensorColumn class as a DataGrid column in an ASP.NET Web page. Of course, before we can do so, we must compile the class into an assembly. As was done with the LimitColumn class examined in Listing 12.3, if you are using Visual Studio .NET, simply opt to add a new class to the SimpleColumn project. After you do this, rebuild the project and redeploy the SimpleColumn.dll to your Web application's /bin directory. If you are not using Visual Studio .NET, recompile the assembly using the command-line compiler, as was shown earlier.

TIP

If you are using the command-line compiler, be certain to add the Namespace SimpleColumn ... End Namespace statements to lines 8 and 91 in Listing 12.8, as discussed earlier.

LISTING 12.9   The CensorColumn Keeps the Online Guestbook Discussion Free from Profanity

```
1: <%@ Register TagPrefix="custCols" Namespace="SimpleColumn"
➥Assembly="SimpleColumn" %>
2: <%@ import Namespace="System.Data" %>
3: <%@ import Namespace="System.Data.SqlClient" %>
4: <script runat="server" language="VB">
5:    '... The Page_Load event handler and BindData() subroutine have
6:    '... been omitted for brevity.  They are strikingly similar to the
7:    '... Page_Load event handler and BindData() subroutine from Listing 12.2,
8:    '... with the exception that BindData() retrieves the records from the
9:            '... Comments table instead of the title table ...
```

LISTING 12.9 Continued

```
10: </script>
11:
12: <asp:DataGrid runat="server" id="dgComments"
13:       AutoGenerateColumns="False"
14:       Font-Name="Verdana"  Font-Size="9pt"
15:       HeaderStyle-HorizontalAlign="Center"
16:       HeaderStyle-Font-Bold="True"
17:       HeaderStyle-BackColor="Navy" HeaderStyle-ForeColor="White"
18:       AlternatingItemStyle-BackColor="#eeeeee">
19:   <Columns>
20:     <asp:BoundColumn HeaderText="Name" DataField="Name" />
21:     <custCols:CensorColumn HeaderText="Comment" DataField="Comment"
22:             CensorFile="profane.xml" />
23:     <asp:BoundColumn DataField="DateAdded" HeaderText="Date" />
24:   </Columns>
25: </asp:DataGrid>
```

The ASP.NET code in Listing 12.9 contains a DataGrid that displays the rows of the Comments table. A CensorColumn class is used to display the actual comment made by the user (lines 21 and 22). An XML file, profane.xml, located in the same folder as the ASP.NET Web page, contains the following content:

```
<censors>
  <censor>
    <find>jerk</find>
    <replace>j*rk</replace>
  </censor>
  <censor>
    <find>stupid</find>
    <replace>st***d</replace>
  </censor>
  <censor>
    <find>ignoramus</find>
    <replace>uneducated individual</replace>
  </censor>
</censors>
```

As you can see, it censors the words *jerk*, *stupid*, and *ignoramus*, replacing them with j*rk, st***d, and uneducated individual. Figure 12.4 shows a screenshot of the DataGrid using the CensorColumn class. Note that the word *jerk* has been replaced by j*rk in John's first comment. Also, *stupid* is replaced by st***d in Frank's comment, and both John and Frank have instances of *ignoramus* replaced by uneducated individual.

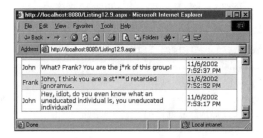

FIGURE 12.4   Offensive comments have been censored in the DataGrid's Comments column through the use of the custom `CensorColumn` class.

Providing a Default Editing Interface for a Custom DataGrid Column Class

In the `InitializeCell()` method in Listing 12.8, we check to see whether the cell being added is of type `Item`, `AlternatingItem`, or `SelectedItem` (see line 16, Listing 12.8). If it is one of these types, we assign the `TableCell`'s `DataBinding` event handler to the `PerformDataBinding` event handler. What if, though, the cell being rendered is of type `EditItem`?

NOTE

Recall from Chapter 9 that when a DataGrid row is selected for editing, the row is said to be in "edit mode," meaning that the `DataGridItem` representing the row in edit mode has its `ItemType` property set to `ListItemType.EditItem`.

One option would be to not provide an editing interface, instead just displaying the text of the `DataSource` field specified by the `DataField` property and censoring the contents. To accomplish this, we would need to simply adjust line 16 of Listing 12.8 to include `ListItemType.EditItem` in the `Case` statement:

```
Select Case itemType
   Case ListItemType.AlternatingItem, ListItemType.Item, ListItemType.
➥SelectedItem, ListItemType.EditItem
      AddHandler cell.DataBinding, AddressOf Me.PerformDataBinding
End Select
```

However, it would be more useful to provide our `CensorColumn` with the same editing functionality as the BoundColumn control. That is, when a row enters "edit mode," the `CensorColumns` should display the content in a standard TextBox Web control. In this editing interface, however, we don't want to display the text of the message as censored, because the administrator might want to remove the offensive words from the post. (In addition, keep in mind that the uncensored version of the message is what is actually stored in the database.)

To provide a default editing interface for our `CensorColumn`, we'll need to check to see whether the `itemType` property is equal to `ListItemType.EditItem`. If it is, we want to add a TextBox Web control to the `TableCell` in the `InitializeCell()` method. We can then create a new event handler for the TextBox's `DataBinding` event or simply reuse the `TableCell`'s `DataBinding` event handler. The code in Listing 12.10 uses the latter approach. The challenge involved with having the same `DataBinding` event handler being used for both edit mode and non-edit mode is that in the event handler, we must be able to determine whether the row being added is in edit mode. If it is in edit mode, we want to assign the `DataSource` field value to the TextBox's `Text` property; if it is not in edit mode, we want to set the `TableCell`'s `Text` property to the censored version of the `DataSource` field, as we did in Listing 12.8. There are a number of ways to accomplish this—one way is to add an `IsBeingEdited` private member variable to the `CensorColumn` class. This variable is set to `True` when a cell with `itemType` `EditItem` is being rendered, and is set to `False` otherwise. Then, in the `PerformDataBinding` event handler, the value of `IsBeingEdited` is checked to determine whether to set the `TableCell`'s `Text` property to the censored results of the `DataSource` field specified by `DataField`, or if the TextBox's `Text` property should be set to the results of the `DataSource` field instead.

Listing 12.10 contains updated code for the `CensorColumn`'s `InitializeCell()` method and `PerformDataBinding` event handler. With the following changes, the `CensorColumn` provides a default editing interface of a TextBox.

LISTING 12.10   The Updated `InitializeCell` Method and `PerformDataBinding` Event Handler Provides a Default Editing Interface for the `CensorColumn` Control

```
 1: Private IsBeingEdited As Boolean = False
 2:
 3: Public Overrides Sub InitializeCell(ByVal cell As TableCell, ByVal
➥columnIndex As Integer, ByVal itemType As ListItemType)
 4:     MyBase.InitializeCell(cell, columnIndex, itemType)
 5:
 6:     Select Case itemType
 7:         Case ListItemType.EditItem
 8:             'Add a TextBox
 9:             Dim txtProfane As New TextBox()
10:             txtProfane.ID = "txtProfane"
11:             cell.Controls.Add(txtProfane)
```

LISTING 12.10   Continued

```
12:             IsBeingEdited = True
13:
14:             AddHandler cell.DataBinding, AddressOf Me.PerformDataBinding
15:
16:         Case ListItemType.AlternatingItem, ListItemType.Item, ListItemType.
➥SelectedItem
17:             IsBeingEdited = False
18:             AddHandler cell.DataBinding, AddressOf Me.PerformDataBinding
19:     End Select
20: End Sub
21:
22:
23: Private Sub PerformDataBinding(ByVal sender As Object, ByVal e As EventArgs)
24:     Dim cell As TableCell = sender
25:     Dim gridItem As DataGridItem = cell.NamingContainer
26:     Dim dataItem As Object = gridItem.DataItem
27:
28:     If Me.DataField <> String.Empty Then
29:         If Not IsBeingEdited Then
30:             cell.Text = PerformCensorship(DataBinder.Eval(dataItem,
➥Me.DataField))
31:         Else
32:             Dim txtProfane As TextBox = cell.FindControl("txtProfane")
33:             txtProfane.Text = DataBinder.Eval(dataItem, Me.DataField)
34:         End If
35:     End If
36: End Sub
```

The code in Listing 12.10 belongs in the CensorColumn class provided in Listing 12.8. Note that with these changes, we've added a private member variable, IsBeingEdited, which is of type Boolean (line 1). In the InitializeCell() method, an additional Case statement was added to the Select Case starting on line 6. Specifically, the new Case statement checks to see whether the itemType property is set to ListItemType.EditItem (line 7)—if it is, a TextBox is added to the TableCell cell's Controls collection (lines 9–11). In addition, the IsBeingEdited member variable is set to True. Finally, the TableCell cell's DataBinding event is wired up to the PerformDataBinding event handler (line 14).

If the cell being rendered is of type Item, AlternatingItem, or SelectedItem, the IsBeingEdited member variable is set to False (line 17) before the TableCell cell's DataBinding event is wired up to the PerformDataBinding event handler (line 18).

On line 29 in the `PerformDataBinding` event handler, the `IsBeingEdited` property is checked. If it is `False`, then cell's `Text` property is assigned the censored value of the appropriate `DataSource` field, just as it was in Listing 12.8. However, if the `IsBeingEdited` property is `True`, the cell's `TextBox` is referenced (line 32) and its `Text` property is set to the value of the appropriate `DataSource` field (line 33).

Listing 12.11 illustrates the `CensorColumn` in use in an ASP.NET Web page with an editable DataGrid. Note that when a particular row is to be edited, the `CensorColumn` is rendered as a standard TextBox control.

LISTING 12.11   The `CensorColumn`'s Default Editing Interface Is a TextBox Web Control

```
 1: <%@ Register TagPrefix="custCols" Namespace="SimpleColumn"
➥Assembly="SimpleColumn" %>
 2: <%@ import Namespace="System.Data" %>
 3: <%@ import Namespace="System.Data.SqlClient" %>
 4: <script runat="server" language="VB">
 5:     '... The Page_Load event handler and BindData() subroutine have
 6:     '... been omitted for brevity.  They are strikingly similar to the
 7:     '... Page_Load event handler and BindData() subroutine from Listing 12.2,
 8:     '... with the exception that BindData() retrieves the records from the
 9:             '... Comments table instead of the title table ...
10:
11:     Sub dgComments_EditRow(sender as Object, e as DataGridCommandEventArgs)
12:         dgComments.EditItemIndex = e.Item.ItemIndex
13:     End Sub
14: </script>
15:
16: <form runat="server">
17:     <asp:DataGrid runat="server" id="dgComments"
18:         AutoGenerateColumns="False"
19:         Font-Name="Verdana"  Font-Size="9pt"
20:         HeaderStyle-HorizontalAlign="Center"
21:         HeaderStyle-Font-Bold="True"
22:         HeaderStyle-BackColor="Navy" HeaderStyle-ForeColor="White"
23:         AlternatingItemStyle-BackColor="#eeeeee"
24:
25:         OnEditCommand="dgComments_EditRow">
26:     <Columns>
27:         <asp:EditCommandColumn EditText="Edit" UpdateText="Update"
28:                 CancelText="Cancel" />
29:         <asp:BoundColumn HeaderText="Name" DataField="Name" />
30:         <custCols:CensorColumn HeaderText="Comment" DataField="Comment"
```

LISTING 12.11   Continued

```
31:                 CensorFile="profane.xml" />
32:         <asp:BoundColumn DataField="DateAdded" HeaderText="Date" />
33:     </Columns>
34:   </asp:DataGrid>
35: </form>
```

The code in Listing 12.11 should look familiar, as it's quite similar to code we examined in Chapter 9. Specifically, the DataGrid is placed inside a server-side form (see
lines 16 and 35) and is configured to be edited. This includes adding the
OnEditCommand on line 25 and providing an EditCommandColumn (lines 27 and 28).
The dgComments_EditRow event handler (lines 11–13) simply sets the EditItemIndex
property of the dgComments DataGrid to the index of the row whose Edit button was
clicked.

> **NOTE**
>
> A full, working example of an editable DataGrid would, of course, also include event handlers
> for when the user clicks the Update and Cancel buttons. These event handlers have been
> omitted in Listing 12.11 for brevity.

Figure 12.5 contains a screenshot of Listing 12.11 when viewed through a browser.
Note that the row being edited has its CensorColumn rendered as a standard TextBox,
and that the contents of the TextBox contain censoring.

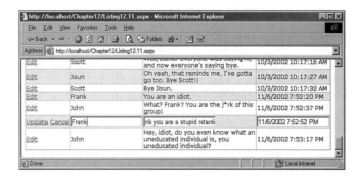

FIGURE 12.5   The CensorColumn's default editing interface is a TextBox.

Adding a ReadOnly Property to the CensorColumn Class

Recall that the BoundColumn control contains a ReadOnly property that, when set to
True, marks the column as read-only, meaning that for a row in edit mode, the

column will be rendered as a textual label instead of a TextBox. This would be a nice feature to add to the CensorColumn control, and can be added with only a few lines of code. Specifically, all we need to do is add a ReadOnly property to our class, and then in the InitializeCell() method, check the value of this property before creating and adding a TextBox to the TableCell cell.

The code in Listing 12.12 contains the complete code for the CensorColumn class, including the addition of the ReadOnly property. The pieces added to handle the ReadOnly feature are located on lines 94 through 103, where the ReadOnly property is added, and on lines 19 to 27, where the ReadOnly property is checked to determine whether a TextBox should be added to the TableCell cell. In the InitializeCell() method, if the cell being rendered is for a row in edit mode, the itemType will be set to ListItemType.EditItem, meaning that the Case statement starting on line 18 will execute. If the ReadOnly property is True, the IsBeingEdited member variable is set to False (line 20). It is vital that we set the IsBeingEdited member variable to False here, because it will ensure that the TableCell's Text property is set to the censored value of the specified DataSource field in the PerformCensorship event handler.

In the case that ReadOnly is False, the code from line 22 to line 26 is executed. This code, which we examined in Listing 12.10, adds a TextBox to the TableCell cell, and sets the IsBeingEdited member variable to True, causing the TextBox's Text property to be assigned the uncensored version of the specified DataSource field in the PerformCensorship event handler.

CAUTION

Notice on line 96 that the ReadOnly property has brackets around the word ReadOnly. This is because ReadOnly is a keyword in Visual Basic .NET. If you forget to place these brackets around ReadOnly, a compile-time error will result, so be certain to include them. (Another option would be to just use a property name that isn't a reserved keyword in the language, such as IsReadOnly or CannotWrite.)

LISTING 12.12   The Complete Code for the CensorColumn Class

```
 1: Imports System
 2: Imports System.Text.RegularExpressions
 3: Imports System.Web.UI.WebControls
 4: Imports System.Web.UI
 5: Imports System.Web
 6: Imports System.Xml
 7: Imports System.IO
 8:
 9: Public Class CensorColumn
10:     Inherits DataGridColumn
11:
```

LISTING 12.12   Continued

```
12:      Private IsBeingEdited As Boolean = False
13:
14:      Public Overrides Sub InitializeCell(ByVal cell As TableCell,
➥ByVal columnIndex As Integer, ByVal itemType As ListItemType)
15:         MyBase.InitializeCell(cell, columnIndex, itemType)
16:
17:         Select Case itemType
18:            Case ListItemType.EditItem
19:               If Me.ReadOnly Then
20:                  IsBeingEdited = False
21:               Else
22:                  'Add a TextBox
23:                  Dim txtProfane As New TextBox()
24:                  txtProfane.ID = "txtProfane"
25:                  cell.Controls.Add(txtProfane)
26:                  IsBeingEdited = True
27:               End If
28:
29:               AddHandler cell.DataBinding, AddressOf Me.PerformDataBinding
30:
31:            Case ListItemType.AlternatingItem, ListItemType.Item,
➥ListItemType.SelectedItem
32:               IsBeingEdited = False
33:               AddHandler cell.DataBinding, AddressOf Me.PerformDataBinding
34:         End Select
35:      End Sub
36:
37:
38:      Private Sub PerformDataBinding(ByVal sender As Object,
➥ByVal e As EventArgs)
39:         Dim cell As TableCell = sender
40:         Dim gridItem As DataGridItem = cell.NamingContainer
41:         Dim dataItem As Object = gridItem.DataItem
42:
43:         If Me.DataField <> String.Empty Then
44:            If Not IsBeingEdited Then
45:               cell.Text = PerformCensorship(DataBinder.
➥Eval(dataItem, Me.DataField))
46:            Else
47:               Dim txtProfane As TextBox = cell.FindControl("txtProfane")
48:               txtProfane.Text = DataBinder.Eval(dataItem, Me.DataField)
```

LISTING 12.12   Continued

```
49:                End If
50:            End If
51:        End Sub
52:
53:
54:        Private Function PerformCensorship(ByVal censorMe As String) As String
55:            'If no CensorFile has been specified, return censorMe string
56:            If Me.CensorFile = String.Empty Then
57:                Return censorMe
58:            End If
59:
60:            'Convert the CensorFile path into a physical path
61:            Dim filepath As String = HttpContext.Current.Server.
➥MapPath(Me.CensorFile)
62:
63:            'Make sure the file exists
64:            If Not File.Exists(filepath) Then
65:                Throw New Exception("File " & filepath & " does not exist!" )
66:                Return censorMe
67:            End If
68:
69:            'Read the XML file's contents
70:            Dim censorDoc As New XmlDocument()
71:            censorDoc.PreserveWhitespace = True
72:            censorDoc.Load(filepath)
73:
74:            Dim root As XmlNode = censorDoc.FirstChild
75:
76:            Dim findNodes As XmlNodeList = root.SelectNodes("/censors/
➥censor/find")
77:            Dim replaceNodes As XmlNodeList = root.SelectNodes("/censors/
➥censor/replace")
78:
79:            Dim re As Regex
80:            Dim results As String = censorMe
81:            Dim i As Integer
82:            For i = 0 To findNodes.Count - 1
83:                re = New Regex("\b" & findNodes.Item(i).InnerText & "\b",
➥RegexOptions.IgnoreCase)
84:                results = re.Replace(results, replaceNodes.Item(i).InnerText)
```

LISTING 12.12   Continued

```
85:          Next
86:
87:          Return results
88:     End Function
89:
90:
91:
92:     Private m_dataField As String
93:     Private m_censorFile As String
94:     Private m_readOnly As Boolean
95:
96:     Public Property [ReadOnly]() As String
97:         Get
98:             Return Me.m_censorFile
99:         End Get
100:        Set(ByVal Value As String)
101:            Me.m_censorFile = Value
102:        End Set
103:    End Property
104:
105:
106:    Public Property CensorFile() As String
107:        Get
108:            Return Me.m_censorFile
109:        End Get
110:        Set(ByVal Value As String)
111:            Me.m_censorFile = Value
112:        End Set
113:    End Property
114:
115:    Public Property DataField() As String
116:        Get
117:            Return Me.m_dataField
118:        End Get
119:        Set(ByVal Value As String)
120:            Me.m_dataField = Value
121:        End Set
122:    End Property
123: End Class
```

Using Custom DataGrid Columns to Extend the Functionality of the DataGrid

At this point you might be thinking, "Yes, creating custom DataGrid control classes sure looks neat, and they have the advantage of code reuse, encapsulation of complexity, and so on, but they don't provide any functionality I couldn't accomplish using a TemplateColumn." Although this might be true for the examples examined thus far through this chapter, there are certain tasks that can only be accomplished by rolling your own custom DataGrid column class.

One good example involves the use of radio buttons with a DataGrid. Imagine that you want to create a DataGrid control that has a column listing only a radio button, with the idea being that the user can select a particular row from the DataGrid by clicking on the row's appropriate radio button. You might think that this is an easy feature to add. After all, you might reason, you could just add a TemplateColumn whose ItemTemplate contains the following code:

```
<asp:TemplateColumn>
  <ItemTemplate>
    <asp:RadioButton runat="server" id="myRadioButton" GroupName="someName" />
  </ItemTemplate>
</asp:TemplateColumn>
```

The GroupName property of the RadioButton Web control specifies how radio buttons should be grouped. That is, if you have a set of RadioButton Web controls, all with the same GroupName, the user can only select one radio button from that group. Unfortunately, the preceding code would not work as expected. Rather than allowing the user to choose only one radio button from the DataGrid column, the user could select one or any of the radio buttons. Figure 12.6 illustrates this by showing a DataGrid that has multiple radio buttons selected.

This is because when the DataGrid is rendered, each Web control in the DataGrid is provided with a unique ClientID based on its control hierarchy. That is, if you create a Web control in a TemplateColumn and give it an ID of, say, MyControl, the ID of the corresponding rendered HTML control will be along the lines of DataGridID_DataGridItemID_MyControl. Because MyControl's parent is its DataGridItem control, the ID of its DataGridItem control will appear before it in the ID sent to the client. In addition, because the DataGridItem's parent is the DataGrid itself, the DataGrid's ID will also appear.

FIGURE 12.6   When creating a radio button in a TemplateColumn, all the radio buttons in the DataGrid cannot be grouped.

A quick code example should clear up any confusion. Assume that we are trying to provide a radio button for each row in the DataGrid by using the following DataGrid declaration:

```
<asp:DataGrid runat="server" id="dgTitles" ...>
<Columns>
    <asp:TemplateColumn>
        <ItemTemplate>
        <asp:RadioButton runat="server" ID="myRadioButton"
                GroupName="titleChoice" />
        </ItemTemplate>
    </asp:TemplateColumn>
    <asp:BoundColumn HeaderText="Title" DataField="title" />
    <asp:BoundColumn DataField="price" HeaderText="Price"
            DataFormatString="{0:c}" />
</Columns>
</asp:DataGrid>
```

The HTML produced by this DataGrid will be as follows:

```
<table cellspacing="0" ...>
<tr align="Center" style="...">
    <td> </td><td>Title</td><td>Price</td>
</tr><tr>
<td>
```

```
      <input id="dgTitles__ctl2_myRadioButton" type="radio" name="
➥dgTitles:_ctl2:titleChoice" value="myRadioButton" />
</td><td>The Busy Executive's Database Guide</td><td>$19.95</td>
</tr><tr style="background-color:#EEEEEE;">
<td>
      <input id="dgTitles__ctl3_myRadioButton" type="radio" name="
➥dgTitles:_ctl3:titleChoice" value="myRadioButton" />
</td><td>Cooking with Computers: Surreptitious Balance Sheets</td><td>$11.95</td>
</tr><tr>

      ...
```

Note the id and name attributes of the radio button input tags: dgTitles__ctl2_myRadioButton for the id, and dgTitles:_ctl2:titleChoice for the name. Essentially, the id is rendered as the server-side ID of the Web control concatenated with the IDs of the Web control's ancestors, with an underscore between each ID; the name applies the same algorithm for naming, except it delimits each ID by a colon (:).

The reason each radio button in the radio button column can be selected as in Figure 12.6 is because the browser determines whether radio buttons are grouped by the name attribute. That is, radio buttons that share the same name are considered to be grouped, and therefore the browser only allows one of the grouped radio buttons to be selected. However, because the name for each radio button that is sent to the client is unique, the browser allows all the radio buttons to be selected.

Is there a solution to this? I am not aware of any way this can be solved without using a custom DataGrid column class. This functionality can be included in a custom DataGrid column class by first writing a class that inherits the HtmlInputRadioButton class and overrides the HtmlInputRadioButton's RenderAttributes method. In overriding this method, this custom class can specify its own name and id attributes that are sent to the client. Hence, it can give all radio buttons in a particular DataGrid column the same name. In addition to this custom radio button class, you'll also need to provide a class for the actual DataGrid column control that then adds the custom radio button control to the TableCell in the InitializeCell() method.

If this sounds like a complex process, don't worry! Fortunately, this code has already been written, and is freely available from http://www.metabuilders.com. MetaBuilders.com is a site maintained by Andy Smith, and contains a number of helpful Web controls and custom DataGrid column classes. You can download the complete code for the radio button column class (called RowSelectorColumn) at http://metabuilders.com/Tools/RowSelectorColumn.aspx. Andy also has a number of other custom DataGrid column controls that you can download, including a BoundLookupColumn control and a BoundBooleanControl.

TIP

You can frequently find Andy Smith over at the ASP.NET Forums at `http://asp.net/forums/`. If you have a question about the source code for one of his controls, you can ask at the ASP.NET Forums or contact him directly from his Web site.

Summary

In this chapter, we examined how to create our own custom DataGrid column classes. These classes need to be derived, either directly or indirectly, from the `DataGridColumn` class, and need to override the `InitializeCell()` method. After these simple criteria have been met, you can add whatever functionality necessary to the class. To use the custom DataGrid column class in an ASP.NET Web application, the class needs to be compiled into an assembly (a DLL file) and then copied to the Web application's `/bin` directory. Additionally, the `@Register` directive needs to be included at the top of all ASP.NET Web pages that use the control.

If you want to create a custom DataGrid column that has a lot in common with an existing DataGrid column, such as a BoundColumn or ButtonColumn, you can have the custom column derived directly from the class whose functionality it closely resembles. By deriving from such a class, you get at your disposal all the properties and methods from the DataGrid column class being inherited. As we saw in Listing 12.3, a `LimitColumn` class can be implemented with a short amount of code by being derived from the BoundColumn class.

Custom DataGrid column classes can also be used to provide functionality that is not otherwise possible in the DataGrid Web control. A classic example is the use of a `RowSelectorColumn`, which presents a series of radio buttons in each row of a particular column, with the caveat that only one such radio button may be selected. This functionality is, to my knowledge, impossible to provide in a DataGrid without using a custom DataGrid column, such as Andy Smith's `RowSelectorColumn`.

On the Web

For more information on the topics discussed in this chapter, consider perusing the following online resources:

- "Creating a Custom DataGridColumn Class"—
  `http://aspnet.4guysfromrolla.com/articles/100202-1.aspx`

- "Using Object-Orientation in ASP.NET"—`http://www.4guysfromrolla.com/webtech/091800-1.shtml`

- "MetaBuilders Web Tools"—`http://metabuilders.com/`

Index

Symbols

A

How can we make this index more useful? Email us at indexes@samspublishing.com

D

How can we make this index more useful? Email us at indexes@samspublishing.com

How can we make this index more useful? Email us at indexes@samspublishing.com

E

R

How can we make this index more useful? Email us at indexes@samspublishing.com

U - V

W - Z

Your Guide to Computer Technology

www.informit.com